In the stressful digital millennium

INTELLIGENCE
IS YOUR BIGGEST

WHY

YOU NEED TO BE A

MUSLIM SOON

A New Psycho-Cognitive Guide from Islamophilia Miracles

Written by Ahmed Shalaby, M.D., Ph.D.

Chief Editor
Piia Sarantola

APOLOGY TO GOD

We should feel the responsibility of being in front of You and being asked "why" we were so selfish and reluctant to convey Your message to others who might be saved on Judgement Day.

On behalf of all Muslims who are now reluctant to help others or misleading non-Muslims who are seeking the truth, I ask for your forgiveness.

We need Your help to make a more sincere effort to guide them in knowing the true purpose of their existence in this life.

We need Your help to follow the correct understanding of Islam. We should aim to help all human beings achieve tremendous psychological balance and develop our and their potential to contribute to building our societies together.

I ask forgiveness of Allah Almighty, there is no God but Him. All praise be to Allah, Lord of the worlds.

Ahmed Shalaby

DISCLAIMER

This book addresses the mental wellness of individuals and overcoming the problems of life which are far beyond the psychologists' capabilities or any other humans. This is to help people increase their ability to build their communities in peace.

I would like to stay focused on the main message of the book, so this work does not come as a response to defend Islam against rumors propagated by the media or malicious groups, especially if they are fabricated lies. These kinds of responses have been covered by many western researchers e.g., Islam: The Basics by Colin Turner and Muhammad: The Prophet of Our Time by Karen Armstrong.

All opinions expressed in this book are solely those of the author and do not represent any association with any other individuals, institutions or countries.

I will welcome any question in the context of the topic if it is asked appropriately and with politeness.

APOLOGY TO GOD   **1**

DISCLAIMER   **3**

INTRODUCTION   16
What Does Jonne Say About the Country That is Supposed to Be the Happiest in The
World?   18
Something is Confusing!   18
Mental Illness is The Most Challenging Global Problem   19
A Global Problem Without Solution   19
Is the Paradise of Welfare A Reality or An Illusion?   20
Why Islamophilia   21

PART I   25

PSYCHO-COGNITIVE DEVELOPMENT & THE NEW TRINITY BUG   25

CHAPTER 1   27

Psyche Explained   **27**
What is Psyche?   29
Life is a matter of value creation   29
What is Psychodynamic?   30
The Brain Serves the Psyche   31
Physics of Our Psyche   31
Motivation   32
Losing Momentum   32
Finding the Purpose   33
Personal Identity Creation   33
How Do We Feel About Our Lives?   34
Mood   34
Influencing the Mood   35
What is Psychology?   36
Enlightened Calm or Dark Noisy Heads   37

CHAPTER 2   40

Stress Explained   **40**

  Why do you feel constantly stressed?   42

  Stress vs Harmony   42

  What is The Reason for The Imbalance?   43

  Good Psychology Gives True Answers   44

CHAPTER 3   **46**

The Best Psychology Is True Answers   **46**

  Where does a person derive his psychological energy?   48

  Human Psyche Follows Economic Rules   48

  Communities Are Critical Co-Dreaming Activities   49

  The Deficit Madness   50

  Carrot and Stick   51

  Who Controls the Global Economy?   52

     56

  The Bad Guys   57

  Bad Guys' Dreaming Strategy   61

  Digital Massive Control Over the Future Generations   62

CHAPTER 4   **65**

Why Is It Time for Powerful Psychology to Unfold?   **65**

  Digitalization of The New Trinity   67

  Weaponization of The New Trinity   67

  Squid Game's Dominance Effect   68

  Metaverse   69

  From One Stress to Greater Stress   69

  Do You Expect Chaos?   70

  If You Don't, Muslims Expect It!   70

  Mixing the Virtual and the Physical Is The Norm. Surprised?   71

  A Mix but No Stress   71

  More Surprising!   72

  First Things First   73

CHAPTER 5   **75**

What You Don't Know About Islam   **75**

  You Feel It's Weird? Me Too!   77

  This is Not the End of The Road   77

Mr. Simple   78
Hollywood's Version of Islam Versus The True Islam   79
   The Hollywood Drama Version of Islam   80
   The Real History of Islam   80
The Knowledge Which Brings More Knowledge   81
Where Has the Welfare of Islam Gone?   82

CHAPTER 6   **85**

The Cognitive Secrets of Islam   **85**
Islam and Relative Intelligence   87
The Muslim Operating System   88
What if There is No Specific Operating System?   89
The Slave Nature of The Human Mind   90
The Absolute Freedom   90
OS Self Verification Mechanisms in Islam   91

CHAPTER 7   **94**

The Authorized and Verified OS of The Human Beings   **94**
Ceremony of Installing The First Authorized Human OS   96
Scene One: The News   96
Scene Two: The First Installation   97
Scene Three: The Testing   98
Scene Four: The Challenger   98
Scene Five: Deep Learning   99
Scene Six: The First OS Hack   100
Scene Seven: OS Recovery   101
Scene Eight: Stay Connected, Stay Updated   101
Scene Nine: The Closing Statement   101
OS Serial Updates   102
Judaism   103
Christianity   103
Islam   104

CHAPTER 8   **106**

Islam is The Latest and Last Human OS   **106**
Why Was It Important to Get a New OS Update?   108
The Confused OS   109

Consequences of a Confused OS   110

                                                               114

The Logic of Islam Resets the Cognitive Confusion   115

CHAPTER 9   **120**

Why Islam Is a Miraculous Human OS?   **120**

The Prerequisites of Making Islam's Cognitive Miracle   122

The Miracle of Being a Book!   122

Why Does It Make Sense for The Miracle to Be a Book!   123

Now I Am Amazed!   124

How Do We Understand the Miracle?   125

Feeling Like It's a Mystery   126

What is in it For You?   127

What To Expect In Part II   128

PART II   **130**

ISLAMOPHILIA: **130**

CHAPTER 10   **132**

Islamophilia 1   **132**

The Human Brain & The Harmony   **132**

Who is The Boss?   134

The Scale of Balance   134

Balance is God's Word   135

Brains Are Also for What We Can't See!   136

Our Brain Functions Are Harmonized   137

The Brain is In Action for Harmony   138

Who Can Guarantee a Stress-free Life?   139

The Challenge   140

Solid Antistress Guarantee   141

The Guarantee Is Verified   142

Safety Rope   143

Stress Is a Choice   144

Misusing the Brain!   145

Brain Switching Off Without Drinking   146

Even the Dark Wishes Come True   147
What is Next Then?   147
What is Missing Then?   148

CHAPTER 11   **150**

Islamophilia 2   **150**

The Qur'an, The Brain, The Harmony   **150**
Our Psychological and Cognitive Requirements Are in Harmony with The Qur'an 152
God Responded in The Qur'an   152
Keep in Mind   154
Science and Harmony in The Qur'an   155
Arabic Is Speaking Right in Your Head   155
First, We State the Obvious   155
Language Shapes the Way We Think   156
Footnote   157
It's Not Only the Language but Also The Place for A Lifelong Mission!   157
Jihad for Harmony   157
The Qur'an Will Develop Your Brain Regardless of Your Mother Tongue   158
Like A Cherry   159
The Direct Effect of Quran Recitation on Humans' Emotions   159
Quranic Cognitive Linguistic Methods   160
Mathematical Encryption of The Qur'an   160
One Surah Demonstrates All These Prerequisites for Harmony   161
Corpus Callosum, The Bridge of Harmony   162
The Need to Get It The Harder Way   163
Smarter Encryption   164
Imagine the unimaginable   164
Did You Get It?   167
Decoding the Decoding   168

CHAPTER 12   **171**

Islamophilia 3   **171**

The Psyche, Islam, The Harmony   **171**
Islam is All About the Psyche   173
Psyche is a Serious Business   173
Can the Psyche Withstand True Justice?   174

Our Psyches Can't Withstand Justice, All We Need Is Mercy! But Do We Deserve It?
179

Psychodynamics in Islam 180

Sleeping Like Dead 180

Sleep is The Breathing Time of The Soul 180

Jesus, Peace Be Upon Him, Is the Exceptional Body and Soul, Miracle! 183

First Marry A Challenge Then Earn Love to Make Your Dreams Come True 187

Calculating Odds 189

The Hallmark from God 190

Mysterious One, Why? 196

Wired vs. Wireless Systems 197

3x3 of The Nervous System 197

Autonomous (Slave) vs Control (Master) 199

The Board Director vs. Board Members 200

Psyche's PM 204

The Other Prime Minister Story 204

The Answer to The Mysterious Why, Is The Same As The Answer To The Mysterious
Marriage 205

X-Harmony Factor is not X-Factor 211

Today Our Body is Obeying but Not Tomorrow 211

Talking Hallmark Fulfills The Truth 212

Let's Address the Elephant in The Room! 213

Psyche Scale 214

Optimum Psyche Balance 217

Why Marriage Between Man and Woman? 218

Marriage is The First Inherent Human Relationship 220

How to Increase Harmony Within Couples? 221

The Genius X-Harmony Factor 223

Know Psyche's X-Harmony Factor 224

The Loving X-Harmony Factor 225

Symphony of the X-Harmony Factor 231

What is The Chance of You Being Part of The Symphony? 233

CHAPTER 13 **234**

Islamophilia 4 **234**

Disharmony, Harmony and Islam **234**

Before Getting Out of The Closet 236

The Right Brain is Right 236

Self-talk is Left Brain's Next Step   237

The Left Brains of Others Are Unable to Speak   238

Both Left Brains Are Right but Not All Right   239

What is All Right?   240

Extreme is Extreme   241

The Psyche in The Maze!   242

How Did We End Up in The Maze?   242

God Made It Easy but Did We Do the Same?   243

You May Like My Question but Not My Answer!   250

The Birth Moment of Stupidity   252

Satan Has A Dream!   253

Stupidity Master   255

The Big Picture of The Satan's Plan   257

Satan's Know-How   257

Staging and Scaling the Know-How   259

Satan's Main Challenge   260

More Aha Moments for Satan   261

The Grandest Aha Moment for Satan   265

The Masterpiece of Hate Speech   266

Why is Satan Useful?   266

The Short Cut   270

CHAPTER 14   **273**

Islamophilia 5   **273**

The Prophet of Harmony   **273**

Concept of Teaching Humanity by Sending Messengers   275

What Do Teachers Teach?   276

Are You Funny?   276

Left Hemisphere People   277

Right Hemisphere People   278

Two in One, One for All   279

Teaching Love and Compassion   279

Education is Optional   280

Latest Messenger and The Latest Teaching Scope   281

The Miracle of The Prophet is Not to Be a Supernatural Force   282

The Miracle is Himself   283

The Perfect Confident Self   284

360 Degree Mission   284

Teaching by Doing   285

You're Covered   285

Are You a Lady?   285

The Super Grand Master of Rumi   286

   His physical appearance and body language   286

   His speech and communication   287

   His time management at home and concern for others   288

   His behavior outside   288

   His meetings and assemblies   289

   His behavior with the Companions and his moments of silence   289

What Was His Motive?   290

By the Way, Did I Tell You That Love is Something We Learn to Earn? 291

What is Love? And Where is It?   291

Tell Me More About Love!   292

Are We All Getting the Same Love?   292

Islamophiles In Action   293

PART III   **294**

CHAPTER 15   **296**

The Deal   **296**

Trap or Ad   298

Advertising That is Not a Trap, But Not for Everyone   298

Who Is Smart?   299

The Beauty and The Beast   299

What is The Message Behind the Pain of The Soul?   300

Is It Genius?   300

Here's the Deal   302

A Dream That Was Not on The List!   304

Your Life Insurance Needs Insurance   306

You Are Property   307

Freedom to Shout or Whisper   310

   Prophet could not persuade his child   313

   Child cannot guide his parents   314

   Wife could not convince her husband   314

   Prophets could not impose on their wives   314

You Are Your Own Property Manager   314

The Property   316

The Mission Statement | 318
The Responsibility | 322
The Operation | 324
The Theoretical Foundation of The Halal and Haram Framework | 325
Framework And X-Harmony Factor Compatibility | 327
The Main and Extra Halal Practices | 328
Extent and Scope of Halal Actions | 329
Sustainable Halal Actions | 330
The Neuroscience Behind the Actions | 331
Monitoring the Actions | 334
Immediate Compensation | 334
Later Compensation: A New Psyche with New Features | 335
The Sustainable Welfare State | 338
Who Has No Deal with God Yet? | 339
We Are Free but Responsible, And God is Patient | 340
Why Is God Patient? | 340
Live Without A Lie | 346
The Line Between Believers and Unbelievers | 351
God is The Absolute Just | 359
The Sentence | 364
Universal Argument 1 | 366
Universal Argument 2 | 367
Universal Argument 3 | 371
Dishonesty and Denial | 373
What is Love? | 375
Why Can't You Find Love? | 376
If You Feel No Shame, Then Do Whatever You Like | 377
Where is The Love? | 377
What is The Nationality of Islam? | 381
Live by The Truth in The Lying World | 382
What Does "Ours" Mean? | 383
A Group with The Same Heart Disease | 386
How Do You Feel When You Become a Muslim? | 388
Does Islam Heal All Your Psychological Pain? | 389
How Long Does It Take to Become a Muslim? | 390
والإحسان والإيمان الإسلام | 391
Islam, Faith and Excellence | 391
Back to Breathing, Quickly | 393

CHAPTER 16   **396**

The Contract   **396**

The First Pillar: 398

Contract Name: Sincere Devotion   399

   Parties to the agreement: 399

   Mission Statement: 400

The Power of "No"   408

The Second Pillar: The Pray   410

How Does This Connection Happen?   411

Life is Like One Prayer   411

The Story of The Love Story   412

Opening His Door 24/7   413

Continuous Washing   415

The Whole Framework of The Religion in One Prayer   416

While Praying, Stop Trying, Stop Thinking!   417

What Else?   418

Everlasting Love No Stress   419

Prayer for Prophet Muhammad (Salawat)   420

The Third Pillar: Zakat   420

How Much Zakat?   422

Zakat is The Antidote of The New Trinity   422

Zakat is The Safety Net for The Economy   424

Muslim Welfare   425

What Kind of Welfare the Perfect Muslim Psyche Can Create?   426

The Founder   427

Founder's Life In a Few Lines   427

His Entry to Islam   428

His Justice   429

   A Story: 429

His Compassion   430

   A Story: 430

The Businessman   433

The Doctor   434

The Welfare Line   436

The Fourth Pillar: Fasting Ramadan   436

Ramadan: The Factory Reset for The Psyche   441

   For the Soul   441

   For the Body   443

For the Economy and Society   443

The Fifth Pillar: Hajj   444

What Happens on Hajj?   445

     Ihram   445

     Tawaf   445

     Al-Safa / Al-Marwah   446

     Mount Arafat   446

     Stoning of the devil   446

     Eid ul-Adha   446

     Qurbani   447

What Does Hajj Mean?   447

Servants as Vicegerents   448

Experience God's experience   449

The Takeaway   450

The Gigantic Takeaway   450

Who Took the Way?   451

Moments to Remember Forever   460

List for Recommended Readings   **463**

     Islam: The Basics   463

     Islamic Psychology   463

     And Muhammad Is His Messenger: The Veneration of the Prophet in Islamic Piety
     464

     Towards Understanding the Quran   465

Dedication   **468**

About the Author   **470**

INTRODUCTION

WHEN YOU KNOW WHY,

YOU'LL STOP WONDERING.

What Does Jonne Say About the Country That is Supposed to Be the Happiest in The World?

"In Finland... you feel that everything should be alright, even though it's not," agrees Jonne Juntura, a 27-year-old junior doctor who was depressed for six months during his university studies.

He points out that while difficult personal and societal events are often linked to depression – for example, break-ups or a recession – it is an illness that can affect people regardless of their standard of living.

"Even though we're the happiest country in the world according to the statistics, it doesn't tell the whole story. Because depression is a disease, and it doesn't always relate to circumstances."

"The moment I personally fell ill, everything was fine with my life. I was really enjoying my school. I loved my hobbies. I was in a relationship. So, there was nothing dramatically wrong with my life. But still, I fell ill," he explains. *Source: Being depressed in the 'world's happiest country' - BBC Worklife*

Something is Confusing!

Finland has been claimed the happiest country for the past five years in a row, according to an annual UN-sponsored report. *Source: Finland ranked happiest country in the world - again - BBC News*

These kinds of reports use physical indicators to assess the conditions that are supposed to make a person happy such as access to education, health care, social benefits, economic regulations, politics, the environment, and the list goes on.

But do these material factors in themselves provide a person with psychological well-being and true happiness? In fact, according to the latest European Union statistics, Finland is also at the top of the European Union in terms of incidence of mental illnesses. *Source: Finland's mental health challenge.*

Now, how does this add up? It seems that the more there is material well-being the less there is mental wellness. Is this confusing? Does this happen only in Finland?

Mental Illness is The Most Challenging Global Problem

More than 792 million people live with a mental health disorder. This is just over one in ten people globally (10.7%). 4.4% of the world's population suffer from depression. It is estimated that mental health conditions will affect an astonishing one in four people at some time in their lives, and these alarming numbers reflect the prevalence of ill mental health in general. *Source: Institute for Health Metrics and Evaluation and Report in their groundbreaking study of the global burden of disease.*

A Global Problem Without Solution

Dr. Henshaw, author of Breaking the Silence; Mental health professionals reveals that "many people choose to enter mental health professions, at least in part, because they want to examine their own psychological problems, weaknesses, pain, or problems of their families." Little attention has been paid to clinicians' mental health issues. Instead, the subject "seems to be off-limits, with silence remaining in the order of the day." *Dr. Stephen Henshaw, Ph.D., Professor of Psychology, University of California, Berkeley, and Professor of Psychiatry and Vice President of Child and Adolescent Psychology, University of California, San Francisco.*

Studies from Finland, Norway, Australia, Singapore and China have shown an increased prevalence of anxiety, depression, and suicide among medical students and doctors. *Source: Physicians Experience Highest Suicide Rate of Any Profession. Pauline Anderson, Medscape,Thursday, December 30, 2021.*

One study of more than 1,000 randomly sampled counseling psychologists found that 62% of respondents identified themselves as depressed, and of those with symptoms of depression, 42% reported having experienced some form of suicidal ideation or behavior.

Canadian psychiatrists found that of the 487 psychiatrists who responded to the questionnaire, nearly a third (31.6%) said they had suffered from mental illness, but only about 42% said they would disclose it to their family or friends. Burnout among medical practitioners, among other professions, is one of the highest. And the specialty of psychiatrists and mental health professionals is at the top of them, at 42%. *Source: Challenging Stigma: Should Psychiatrists Disclose Their Own Mental Illness? Psychiatry advisor by Batya Swift Yasgur,January 11, 2019.*

In the United States, physicians have the highest suicide rate of any profession (28 to 40 per 100,000), more than twice the suicide rate of the general population (12.3 per 100,000). Moreover, among all medical specialties, psychiatry ranks first in terms of suicide rates. Psychiatrists kill themselves at a higher rate than people who serve in the military. *Source: Physicians Experience Highest Suicide Rate of Any Profession. Medscape, By Pauline Anderson May 07, 2018*

Is the Paradise of Welfare A Reality or An Illusion?

In previous editions of the Know How To - series I presented solutions for economic reform at the level of the European Union and other countries like Finland, Denmark, Sweden, Norway, Canada, New Zealand, France, Liechtenstein, and more. I have stated clearly that the main critical factor to make this reform successful is to develop people's ability to innovate.

This development of the people is conditional. Firstly, innovation requires a great deal of psychological energy that depends on the mental health of the individual. Secondly, teaching people to work in teams to innovate. Hence then the outcome of innovation in any organization or country has become dependent on the status of ethics and trust in-between the individuals and in leadership.

The question then is, are there enough people in every home or institution nowadays with an acceptable level of mental health and sufficient moral dedication to undertake the task of innovation for the common good?

It is assumed that the postmodern and secular welfare society that prevailed in Europe, especially in Scandinavia, in the last century must have a sufficient and an increasing number of these. Surprisingly, it is the opposite, as the actual statistics are showing.

This fact urges us to stop for a while and start to wonder if the advance of secular welfare is a reality or an illusion? Real or fake? Is there an inverse relationship between the liberation of societies and the moral and psychological health of its members? Is there a way to organize this relationship? And strike a balance between them?

Why Islamophilia[1]

The secular ambivalence is an old well-known fact. It was a huge disappointment for the promises made in the societies. Welfare, mounting debts, declining births, families disintegrating, moral disintegration and mental illness are all real. There is no decision maker talking about all these facts under the spotlight! Why is that? Because

---

[1] Philia (/ˈfɪliə/; from Ancient Greek φιλία (philía)), often translated "highest form of love", is one of the four ancient Greek words for love: philia, storge, agape and eros. In Aristotle's Nicomachean Ethics, philia is usually translated as "friendship" or affection. The complete opposite is called a phobia.

of the nature of the solution. First, they need to admit that the separation of modern life and religion is not possible anymore. Then if they have to recommend a religion, this will be without doubt is Islam! Yes exactly, the last thing you might think of!

In the scientific community, there is an astonishing discovery, which is that an individual's practice of Islam is a solution to achieving growth in a society based on science, a "scientocracy" as a means of balanced and sustainable social, financial, moral and mental growth. This secular trend was a solution created in West to overcome the incompatibility of science with the church teaching, then exported to Islam which does not have this problem at all. *Source: Islam and Europe: Challenges and Opportunities by Marie-Claire Foblets.*

Suicide by psychologists, individuals with particular expertise in human behavior, appears to be particularly challenging and raises psychological concerns such as skepticism about the value of the treatment. Identifying the risks, reducing the stigma associated with recognizing hopelessness or hopelessness as such, and overcoming other barriers to intervention is critical to decreasing the incidence of suicide. Deconstructing the stigma of seeking every real cure for mental illness is more important now than ever.

Now you need to ask yourself, if Islam is offering the solution, how did this dark and horrifying image of Islam come to your consciousness? Who brought it to you and why? What is the reason for keeping you in constant psychological stress? Is there a way out of this constant struggle?

This book should answer all the possible questions which might come to your mind in this regard. More importantly I will focus on the natural mechanism of psyche harmony (Islamophilia Miracles) and how to address it to maintain your progress and contribute positively to your community.

Part One: The Stressful Bug - The New Trinity explains the nature of the psyche and its daily dynamic of interactions, and the sources of stress in life. By the end you will understand why mental health is constantly deteriorating, and how religion was supposed to maintain this health, but does not anymore.

Part Two: The Islamophilia Miracles of Harmony, will let you know why Islam is the religion that should play this role now. This part reveals Islam's compatibility with the psyche and it's needs to create harmony inside oneself and to its surroundings. It will explain on a technical level but still simple level the know-how of harmony and how our biological and neurological system are determined to maintain it.

Part Three: Buy a New Psyche introduces the relationship between us and the Creator in a more objective and concrete language of the nowadays' life. It explains this relationship in terms of business terms based on a proposal and contract with God and eventually the return on investment.

Part I

Psycho-Cognitive Development & The New Trinity Bug

CHAPTER 1

Psyche Explained

What is Psyche?

The experience of being alive is based on the accumulation of information (experience) in a three-dimensional matrix (the mind), and this is what shapes the psyche. Our state and quality of life (consciousness) depend on how this information is placed in this matrix (perception). Changing the quality of life, needs to make change in this information system. All kinds of changes are possible, even of the experiences which have happened in early childhood. In fact, this is the power of the human mind. The ability to equally influence the past and the future.

The ability to unlock this power, needs a bit of knowledge to know how this mind and its information system work. The placement of different experiences in our life depends on whether we have a schema, a framework or an operating system that helps us establish relationships between them. This process is not just accumulating data, it's a slightly more complex process called semantic networking between the different events, which means that each new event must have a connection with past and future events (logic). This semantic network is the fabric of building up the psyche. The psyche is a dynamic viable build up, once we can change the logic around any event in our life it might completely change the placement of the same event from the dark to the light side in our mind. The detriment factor to success to build or transform our psyche successfully and have a sense of control on our life, is the ability to answer the question "Why". The more there are answers for the whatever whys in our life the more resilient is our psyche.

Life is a matter of value creation

The duration of life itself doesn't really matter. What really counts is the quality of this life. This quality is not only what we get but also what we are able to add to the surroundings. The more we are focusing our effort in our life on value creation inside us and around us, the more the life is enjoyable and flowing forward.

In other words, it is possible to see the psyche as a processor for value creation. Its performance is related to how it is formulated. This is the responsibility of the brain (the hardware). This is done by using the functions on both sides of the brain, with the skills acquired during one's lifetime. All together it is known as problem solving skills. The time and effort it takes to do this, is called the processing response time (action reaction).

The moment of receiving a new event is called the present. The time it takes us to process it and prepare for the next moment, is the speed of our lives. The ability that we can move from one event to another varies from person to person. This is what makes the value of a moment in life completely relative, not just the age.

Processing time varies from brain to brain. For some, events are connected automatically and unnoticed, for some it takes longer to think, and for others it takes a lot of time and effort.

Some stumble and are trapped somewhere in the psyche because of certain events either in the past (good or bad), or in the future (dreams). Some have lost control of their mind and have random processing or have only limited baseline events to take care of.

What is Psychodynamic?

Psychodynamic is the process of connecting the different events to our information system in our mind from birth to death. This dynamic can be taught and mastered until we get a firm grip on our life. This doesn't happen from the beginning of life.

The first stages of our childhood, we are in reactive mode, influenced by the surrounding environment, parents, school, media, work and others. This mode shifts by time towards the active mode until we achieve full control. In between these two modes, some can move quickly, some might get stuck, this depends on understanding the process (the psychodynamic).

Fortunately, this process is not a rocket since as you might think and it doesn't need a psychologist. You just need to be an honest person. This is true, if you will get to know that our mind and brain are naturally tuned to drive this dynamic towards harmony and wellness. All you need as a person is to follow your intuition and listen carefully for your conscience. The more you are honest and respond to your gut, the more you will be able to stay in harmony.

The Brain Serves the Psyche

The creating harmony (balancing) is the main function of the right and left hemispheres of the brain. This is where the brain serves the psyche. The brain is the organ responsible for processing information and assuring the dynamics to make sense of the experience we get during this process called psychic energy.

Physics of Our Psyche

The performance and the success of our psyche for creating value is highly dependent on establishing a clear main goal (a purpose) for the psyche. The more this goal is deep and has a high value, the more our psyche will become confident and peaceful.

This goal will be our main hope to live, it will create for our mind a focus and a purpose to live. It will create momentum to go forward and keep us on our way ahead. Whatever happens from hard or good events, this hope will help our psyche to find hundreds of ways to see the positive angle to go forward. Basically, it will be able to turn any set back into opportunity and any pain into gain.

Motivation

This positive flow is a mindset, a mental practice, and a psyche know-how. It is always looking for connecting the dots between where we are standing now and what is next. The navigator of this process is this deepest end point (the high purpose). The navigation between these two points is a matter of physics. The higher this purpose is, the more momentum we get while we are moving towards it. This energy is called motivation. The amount of this motivation depends on the amount of determination we have to reach that goal, and our desire to have it (the degree of faith). This goal can be something or somebody.

Losing Momentum

The tricky part about this goal is that it should not be realized while we are alive. It should only be possible to realize it by the end seconds of our life. This is a matter of physics, because if we reach this end goal, the momentum which we would need to keep moving mathematically will be zero. When we lose the traction by reaching our goal we lose the momentum. It decreases over time until we find another central purpose. The more we lose the force of traction in our psyche, the less motivation we have to live. This happens to some when they lose their purpose to live when losing their health, work, wealth, loved ones or any other goal they had.

Finding the Purpose

Usually, people find this goal for themselves, or it may be with someone close in their life. Some go even further, searching for more expert help such as a coach, a psychologist, or a psychiatrist. The maximum support they can give you, is to provide some knowledge, skill development, stimulation or therapy.

The process may need a visit in the cumulative psyche and its dynamics to find out something to change. It can be something obvious and most of the time it is not at all! This is what makes both people and experts tired! It is as if the blind guide the blind in the darkness of the night. The darkness is real. Because any help to find a goal to achieve during this life is not helping.

The entire life needs to turn out to be meant to achieve a higher goal than this life. This means that while we are alive to stay alive, we should have a goal to achieve and the best one is the deepest one which we achieve only the moment we die. Does it mean that we should aim to meet God as the higher purpose of our lives? Does it mean that our psyche's maximum energy is designed to operate perfectly only around this purpose? Does it mean the optimum physics and wellness of our psyche is only possible if we have God in our lives?

Personal Identity Creation

We all have brains and psyches, but we don't have the same experience. The relationship between the brain and the psyche is a very unique experience for each person (personal identity), like a fingerprint. The difference is that we can influence who we would like to be by creating our psyche. This process already happens anyway from one moment to another.

The creation process can be either gradual (a progression) or major (a transformation). The change without controlling speed and direction leads to confusion, and then later to depression. This is the moment when we start looking for a purpose in our life. Some may find it and others give up in a way or another.

How Do We Feel About Our Lives?

I'm talking here about the general impression we have about our life coming from the experience of connecting all our different life events. This has nothing to do with the outside world, poverty, health, or relationships. What really matters is how we manage to relate the different events to each other. For example, you can be the wealthiest, healthiest and most successful person, but you can't connect in social life. On the other hand, another person may have much less but is able to connect all aspects of life in harmony. This simple life may be better than the huge, busy life, unless we are able to connect them!

Some express this impression briefly: life is great, let's not talk, life is fun, life is complicated, not bad, and so on. How we feel about life is always a mix of feelings, a mix of the past (what we have had so far) and of the future (what we would like to change or experience).

Mood

Our ultrashort mind state (tampered) during a certain moment doesn't really depend on the quality of the events happening to us (sad, bad, hard, pleasant) until we agree how we would like to classify this event. In other words, we have the possibility to control our mind state (mood) regardless of the circumstance.

For example, the same event can be interpreted in different ways, since every event has an equal benefit, good and bad. The end result of how to place this event on our overall experience depends on us. This needs some sort of patience in front of the good and bad moments, using our rational judgment first before the emotional impulsiveness.

This is a core approach to feeling secure, and having a stable mood. The power to control this is a key issue to feel peace from within. If you think that it is too idealistic of an approach for peace, I would not object to you right now. For the time being keep reading, later you will understand that this is the core of the Islamic practice. These are the ultimate results of following Islam's practices. This is actually the message on the cover of this book!

Influencing the Mood

Most of the Islamic teaching is to help our mind to create healthy dynamics including enough day-to-day habits (autopilot) to create a healthy level of routine to create stability of mood. These programs in our cognitive system are called personal habits. They should be enough to make us feel good most of the time, and also give some extra power and practice for other major unexpected life events.

That kind of dynamic creates an inner state, security, harmony, and independence from the changing surroundings. At a certain level, after psychological dynamics have ripened with this kind of performance, we declare that we are enjoying our lives, and fall in love with life and the idea of having life.

If the outcome of our psychodynamic is unsatisfactory, it tends to influence our overall mood quality and impression about our life. This impression can be so negative, up to that some decide to end their lives. Others who would still be interested in life should work to make within this inner process the necessary changes.

Unfortunately, this may not be the case for the majority of the people. Many are trying to find a way by only changing the taste of their mood.

They usually use some added sweetener. The list is extensive. It may be natural foods, activities, music, leisure time, etc. All work but temporarily and for a very short time.

Others use chemicals that have pharmacological effects on the body. This throws the whole person out of balance, and over time some depend on them up to an addictive level!

What is Psychology?

The proven cumulative knowledge and understanding of the logic of the soul is the science concerned with this subject (psychology).

If we look at psychology from the physiological viewpoint, this has some aspects like developmental psychology, cognitive psychology, social psychology and behavioral psychology. If we look at it from the side of the malfunction, it is called clinical psychology.

If we combine the latter with a serious dysfunctional disorder which needs diagnosis, treatment and possibly pharmacological intervention, this is called psychiatry. If we also include the biological aspect of the psyche (nervous system), we refer to this as neuroscience and neuropsychiatry.

These are the main branches but under each of them there are multiple sub-branches of psychology for example children, women, marriage, economics, crises, crime, gender, finance, cancer, trauma, social media, artificial, etc. There is a continuous development of this knowledge and field that covers all aspects of life.

Basic knowledge in psychology that covers all our needs is a basic requirement for well-being and having a calm enlightened head. Is this possible?

Enlightened Calm or Dark Noisy Heads

There are two conditions for a calm head: organization and assembly! Everything in your head should work together in harmony. Your brain is ready to do it, provided that you have the right operating system. An optimal operating system should be multifunctional and create a balance between the external and internal world.

Outside, it works as a radar, watching what is going on. Who is he, what do they want, what are they doing? It also acts as a firewall (immune system) that detects any lies and hiding and the best way to deal with them. Then it should function as a GPS, to tell you what will be next, in the most obvious way. Internally, it does the same with the ego, and ultimately, it should create balance and monitor the state of your well-being and progress.

This operating system is a basic requirement for your well-being. It's not about having it or not, everyone already has it! But the question is how! Some are fully aware of it and some don't even know that it should exist, even though it does exist!

This is why there are two heads (selves). One is chaotic, opaque, and noisy, the operating system is self-created.

وَمَنْ اَعْرَضَ عَنْ ذِكْرِئ فَاِنَّ لَهُ مَعِيشَةً ضَنْكًا وَّنَحْشُرُهُ يَوْمَ الْقِيٰمَةِ اَعْمٰى

(20:124) But whosoever turns away from this Admonition from Me shall have a straitened life; We shall raise him blind on the Day of Resurrection,"

قَالَ رَبِّ لِمَ حَشَرْتَنِيٓ اَعْمٰى وَقَدْ كُنْتُ بَصِيرًا

(20:125) where-upon he will say: "Lord! Why have You raised me blind when I had sight in the world?"

قَالَ كَذٰلِكَ اَتَتْكَ اٰيٰتُنَا فَنَسِيتَهَاۚ وَكَذٰلِكَ الْيَوْمَ تُنْسٰى

(20:126) He will say: "Even so it is. Our Signs came to you and you ignored them. So shall you be ignored this Day."

The other is organized, enlightened, and calm!

37

اَلَّذِينَ اٰمَنُوْا وَتَطْمَئِنُّ قُلُوْبُهُمْ بِذِكْرِ اللهِ ۗ اَلَا بِذِكْرِ اللهِ تَطْمَئِنُّ الْقُلُوْبُ

(13:28) Such are the ones who believe (in the message of the Prophet) and whose hearts find rest in the remembrance of Allah. Surely in Allah's remembrance do hearts find rest.

If you want to have an operating system for your laptop, and your options are to write it yourself or get a license and the latest update from the designer, which one would you choose? This is why you have a religion, and this is how your head comes out of the darkness!

رَّسُوْلًا يَّتْلُوْا عَلَيْكُمْ اٰيٰتِ اللهِ مُبَيِّنٰتٍ لِّيُخْرِجَ الَّذِيْنَ اٰمَنُوْا وَعَمِلُوا الصّٰلِحٰتِ مِنَ الظُّلُمٰتِ اِلَى النُّوْرِ ۗ وَمَنْ يُّؤْمِنْ بِاللهِ وَيَعْمَلْ صَالِحًا يُّدْخِلْهُ جَنّٰتٍ تَجْرِىْ مِنْ تَحْتِهَا الْاَنْهٰرُ خٰلِدِيْنَ فِيْهَآ اَبَدًا ۗ قَدْ اَحْسَنَ اللهُ لَهٗ رِزْقًا

(65:11) a Messenger who rehearses to you Allah's verses that clearly expound the Guidance so that He may bring out those that believe and act righteously, from every kind of darkness into light.[2] He will admit whosoever believes in Allah and acts righteously to Gardens beneath which rivers flow. They shall abide in them forever. For such has Allah made an excellent provision.

---

[2] Light here implies to the Quran and the Messenger, Prophet Muhammad (peace be upon him).

CHAPTER 2

Stress Explained

Why do you feel constantly stressed?

Every morning, in bed, our minds quickly check the state of our balance. Is there a good reason to wake up and do we have enough energy to do so? The answer is one from the following three scenarios. If we do not have a good reason but have good energy for it, we get into a hyperactive mood, seeking to engage with our surroundings, with the goal of satisfying our curiosity and de-stressing. If there is no good reason and no energy, we feel depressed. If we have a good reason and no energy, we are tired.

In fact, all of these scenarios are taken in a similar way in our minds. All give our mind the same feeling, that something is wrong. It is a sign of imbalance between the external and internal world. This creates a task for our mind to search for balance (harmony). The mind must go through a complex process (thinking) first to identify the source of the imbalance, and then find ways to solve it. This effort and subtle struggle to find the balance is what makes us feel stressed, tired and consumed. Not actually the daily physical work, not at all!

Stress vs Harmony

This complex task of the mind to find balance is variable, sometimes the cause is obvious and easy to fix, sometimes not! Sometimes it resolves quickly, and the tension disappears, and sometimes it doesn't. If it remains subtle and gradually accumulates for a longer time, then this is called chronic stress.

The most stressful situation for our mind is when we can't pinpoint the source of the imbalance. That combines the feeling of stress with confusion. This is what creates the feeling of being out of control without hope and this is the worst state of mind creating a miserable self-image.

Our brain's success is realizing balance (harmony). This results from the mind feeling successful in doing its job and feeling in control. Experiencing balance is the optimum state of feeling secure and having everything under control, this is the ideal state of mind, feeling satisfied. Mastering this state is called peace of mind. This gives a plethora of endorphins for pleasure with a mixture of feelings of confidence, security, contentment and peace.

What is The Reason for The Imbalance?

If we check out the main reason that first puts us in any stress, we will find that it is actually a long chain of dependent causes of imbalance! Something that might drive us crazy and that you'd rather not think about (ignoring and denying)! And that's really the problem, which hasn't been there before on this scale.

Balance is a dynamic state which is controlled by infinite sets of variables from different levels that work together according to complex rules. For example, on a personal level, your peace of mind depends on multiple different forms of variables including your health, your knowledge, your money, your relationships, your work, your time, etc. This personal level is related to another level with a different set of variables in your city, the country, and we all are connected on the global level.

The logic of dynamism is incredibly complex, and it can be beyond the power of all of humanity, not only you, which puts the whole world under stress. For example, the harmony of your week may depend on a blockage of the Panama Canal that happened, because the captain of the ship had been under stress since last night, with his girlfriend who was in a bad mood due to an Instagram post showing that she is not the most beautiful in her circle!

Good Psychology Gives True Answers

The best psychology is the analytical school that helps you find logical answers to all your questions. Any psychological challenges in most of the cases are protective signs, which work as an alarm that there is something wrong and we have to be aware about it and seek root cause solutions. The same applies to a somatic pain somewhere in our body, taking analgesics only will mask the pain temporarily but will not relieve the root of the problem. This principle is applicable also to our psychological pain, tackling the source of the pain is a process called analysis (question & answer). Moving on from one question to another should be through an honest and true answer, otherwise we get stuck, and this sticking is what causes the pain. This is how our psyche is designed to work. You can say it in another simple way, our mind (psyche) is determined to solve problems. Once your brain understands the problem, you will find your way to harmony. Yes, just like that!

In the following chapters, we'll take this analytical methodology, analyze the problem, and understand more about stress: where it comes from, why it persists, and how to get to the solution.

CHAPTER 3

The Best Psychology Is True Answers

Where does a person derive his psychological energy?

As I was hinting earlier, we always need to have hope to keep us going forward. Now it is time to get down to the details. Having hope is a process called dreaming. We human beings are dreamers by nature. Our biggest dream is to make our dreams come true. Dreaming is a lifelong strategy that will shape our future goals and our daily actions. The ultimate dreaming is to maintain a certain level of satisfaction. This is a completely personal matter but still the dreaming has the same mechanism and follows the same rules.

Dreaming is the turbo engine that drives our psychic energy. It follows an investment strategy called faith. You visualize something in the future, but you have to pay something up front to get it back bigger in the future. In cognitive behavioral theory this is called a motivation system.

Motivation is not necessary based on a positive (white) dreaming strategy. This is for the good guys! Sometimes the satisfaction depends on a black dreaming strategy (for bad guys) to ruin or control the lives of others. This kind of strategy has the same effect on this person's energy generation and makes them do their best to conserve it (motivation).

Human Psyche Follows Economic Rules

Regardless of our educational background, whether we know something about the economy or not, still our psyche follows the economic principles. Whatever the motive (black or white), it will be supervised by very precise indicators in our mind operating in a purely economic manner. It's a 24/7 process called inner thinking and feeling, and its idea is to evaluate this investment strategy.

Psychic energy is the most important asset in our wellbeing bank account. If the work in our hands (the dream) positively affects this balance, especially the level of happiness, then these thoughts will clearly encourage us to make more effort in this direction (positive feedback). On the other hand, if the results are not confirmed in this way for the mind (negative feedback), we will automatically reconsider (subjective insight) the value of this dream seeking to improve or change it (self-protection).

Following the natural economic rules of the psyche (the dreaming) should make all of us successful psychic investors, good dreamers, and happy humans in life. Unfortunately, this is not the case at all.

The problem is that some may be muddled (confused guys) and not have a fair chance to explore different dreaming strategies. Others may have developed an unfair coping strategy and live a double life between pretending happiness and inner misery. Unfortunately, some may silently take their coping to the grave, and others can't tolerate it at all and may commit suicide.

Communities Are Critical Co-Dreaming Activities

Although dreaming is a completely personal matter, there are basic factors (infrastructure and facilities) in the surrounding environment to help individuals realize their dreams. This is the concept of an organized modern state that has a common economy and welfare service (citizen's rights).

Whatever the personal motivation behind any individuals' dreams is, a portion of this motivation has to be re-invested in their surroundings. First by helping each other (the responsibility of the citizen), which in return will help them achieve their dreams. Secondly by passing it on to future generations as it came to them (the responsibility of the generation).

There is always some kind of very delicate and sensitive balance between the psychic energy of the current citizens and that of the future generations. If there weren't enough successful dreamers today, there would be no humans tomorrow.

The Deficit Madness

Now if we check the psychological bank account of the individuals and societies in Europe, what will we find?

In 2015, every 6 minutes someone died from mental illness-related events or suicide in the EU countries. In the same year, roughly 9 young people between the ages of 15 and 24 died each day from suicide in EU countries. In the EU an estimated 1 in every 6 people experience a mental health problem.

In Finland, which has the highest estimated incidence of mental disorders in the EU, close to 1 in 5 are affected. Like in other EU countries, in Finland, the most common mental disorders are anxiety and depressive disorders, which affect 4% and 6% of Finns, respectively. Drug and alcohol use disorders also affect 4% of the Finnish population–well above the EU28 average of 2.4%. *Source: Health at a Glance: Europe 2018.*

First of all, these have nothing to do with the stress of the COVID pandemic which started in 2019. These results clearly indicate that there is a continuous withdrawal from the account without sufficient income. This means bad investments (dreaming strategies). It also indicates that a large number of individuals use the method of unfair coping. In more economic parlance, individuals suffer from a deficit of psychic energy.

This manifests itself at the community level in actual economic and fiscal deficits, which are clearly alarming and threaten the current welfare. This alarming situation places even more burden on the psychological energy balance of individuals.

The country's easy strategy for closing the fiscal deficit is to borrow i.e., more debt. On the other hand, it asks the citizens to somehow invest more psychic energy, which is already in deficit. Needless to mention, it's not just a bad co-dreaming strategy, but it's called deficit madness. The question is why this madness?

Carrot and Stick

In the same report, explaining the statistics of mental health, its economic impact was also explained. The report estimates the total costs of ill mental health at over EUR 600 billion – or more than 4% of GDP – across the 28 EU countries (before Brexit).

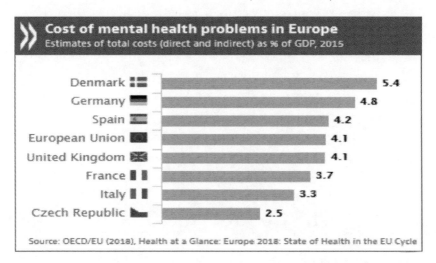

Cost of mental health problems in Europe
Estimates of total costs (direct and indirect) as % of GDP, 2015

Denmark	5.4
Germany	4.8
Spain	4.2
European Union	4.1
United Kingdom	4.1
France	3.7
Italy	3.3
Czech Republic	2.5

Source: OECD/EU (2018), Health at a Glance: Europe 2018: State of Health in the EU Cycle

A large part of these costs are due to lower employment rates and productivity of people with mental health issues (1.6% of GDP or EUR 260 billion) and greater spending on social security programmes (1.2% of GDP or EUR 170 billion), with the rest being direct spending on health care (1.3% of GDP or EUR 190 billion).

"The heavy burdens of mental illness on individuals and society are not inevitable," said OECD Secretary-General Angel Gurría. "While many European countries have put in place policies and programmes to address mental illness, much more can be done to promote and better manage mental health. We look forward to continuing working with the European Commission to measure the state of health in European economies and the specific challenges they confront to deliver better health policies for better lives."

Do you know how you work? The economy, welfare and mental health; this trinity is the motivational system that controls your being, and makes you chase the illusion of your well-being by creating welfare systems and a good economy.

After a long chase, have you reached the end goal? Have you ever felt good, the way you want, about your being? Did your dreaming strategy work?

In short, your motivation is based on the fear of loss and on the avoidance of pain. This motivational system leads you to the fact that you are working as a slave to the economy running behind the carrot (welfare system) and driven by the stick (mental stress). You end up with that hidden feeling of terror (insecurity). This feeling makes you easily respond to commands without thinking (the slave mentality). So what is the economy then?

Who Controls the Global Economy?

Many people think that the global economy is controlled by governments of the largest economies in the world. This is a common misconception. Although governments do hold power over countries' economies, it is the big banks and large corporations that control and essentially fund these governments. This means that the global economy is dominated by large financial institutions.

According to world economic news, US banks participate in many traditional government businesses like power production, oil refining and distribution, and also the operating of public assets such as airports and train stations. This was proven when certain members of the US Congress sent a letter to the Federal Reserve Chairman Ben Bernanke. Here's an excerpt from the letter:

"Here are a few examples. Morgan Stanley imported 4 million barrels of oil and petroleum products into the United States in June 2012. Goldman Sachs stores aluminum in vast warehouses in Detroit as well as serving as a commodities derivatives dealer. This "bank" is also expanding into the ownership and operation of airports, toll roads, and ports. JP Morgan markets electricity in California.

In other words, Goldman Sachs, JP Morgan and Morgan Stanley are no longer just banks – they have effectively become oil companies, port and airport operators, commodities dealers, and electric utilities as well." *Source: https://www.edology.com/blog/accounting-finance/how-does-global-economy-work/*

Now do the math to answer these questions: who is controlling your wellbeing, your welfare, your mental health, your dreaming strategy, and your hope? Who is controlling you?

A question also is, are these bad guys or good guys? Actually, it is not the aim of this book to answer this question. What really is important to understand is that people have different dreaming strategies to reach satisfaction and that these strategies may conflict (bad guys/good guys). Who are the bad guys and how can they affect your mental health?

ALAN GRAYSON
9TH DISTRICT, FLORIDA

COMMITTEE ON FOREIGN AFFAIRS
SUBCOMMITTEE ON
WESTERN HEMISPHERE
SUBCOMMITTEE ON
MIDDLE EAST AND NORTH AFRICA

COMMITTEE ON SCIENCE, SPACE,
AND TECHNOLOGY
SUBCOMMITTEE ON ENERGY
SUBCOMMITTEE ON ENVIRONMENT
REGIONAL DEMOCRATIC WHIP

Congress of the United States
House of Representatives
Washington, DC 20515-0909

430 CANNON HOUSE OFFICE BUILDING
WASHINGTON, DC 20515
(202) 225-9889

ORLANDO DISTRICT OFFICE
5842 SOUTH SEMORAN BOULEVARD
ORLANDO, FL 32822
(407) 615-8889

KISSIMMEE DISTRICT OFFICE
101 NORTH CHURCH STREET
SUITE 550
KISSIMMEE, FL 34731
(407) 518-4963

grayson.house.gov

June 27, 2013

The Honorable Ben Bernanke
Chairman
Board of Governors of the Federal Reserve System
20th Street and Constitution Avenue N.W.
Washington, D.C. 20551

Dear Chairman Bernanke,

We write in regards to the expansion of large banks into what had traditionally been non-financial commercial spheres. Specifically, we are concerned about how large banks have recently expanded their businesses into such fields as electric power production, oil refining and distribution, owning and operating of public assets such as ports and airports, and even uranium mining.

Here are a few examples. Morgan Stanley imported 4 million barrels of oil and petroleum products into the United States in June, 2012.[i] Goldman Sachs stores aluminum in vast warehouses in Detroit as well as serving as a commodities derivatives dealer.[ii] This "bank" is also expanding into the ownership and operation of airports, toll roads, and ports.[iii] JP Morgan markets electricity in California.

In other words, Goldman Sachs, JP Morgan, and Morgan Stanley are no longer just banks – they have effectively become oil companies, port and airport operators, commodities dealers, and electric utilities as well. This is causing unforeseen problems for the industrial sector of the economy. For example, Coca Cola has filed a complaint with the London Metal Exchange that Goldman Sachs was hoarding aluminum. JP Morgan is currently being probed by regulators for manipulating power prices in California, where the "bank" was marketing electricity from power plants it controlled. We don't know what other price manipulation could be occurring due to potential informational advantages accruing to derivatives dealers who also market and sell commodities. The long shadow of Enron could loom in these activities.

According to legal scholar Saule Omarova, over the past five years, there has been a "quiet transformation of U.S. financial holding companies." These financial services companies have become global merchants that seek to extract rent from any commercial or financial business activity within their reach.[iv] They have used legal authority in Graham-Leach-Bliley to subvert the "foundational principle of separation of banking from commerce". This shift has many consequences for our economy, and for bank regulators. We wonder how the Federal Reserve is responding to this shift.

It seems like there is a significant macro-economic risk in having a massive entity like, say JP Morgan, both issuing credit cards and mortgages, managing municipal bond offerings, selling gasoline and electric power, running large oil tankers, trading derivatives, and owning and operating airports, in multiple countries. Such a dramatic intertwining of the industrial economy and supply chain with the financial system creates systemic risk, since there is effectively no regulatory entity that can oversee what is happening within these sprawling global entities.

Our questions are as follows:

1) What is the Federal Reserve's current position with respect to allowing Goldman Sachs and Morgan Stanley to continue trading in physical commodities and holding commodity-related assets after the expiration of the statutory grace period during which they, as newly registered bank holding companies, must conform all of their activities to the Bank Holding Company Act of 1956? What is the legal justification for this position?
2) Has the Federal Reserve been investigating the full range of risks, costs, and benefits – to the national economy and broader society – of allowing these institutions (and, possibly, other large financial holding companies) to engage in trade intermediation and commercial activities that go far beyond pure financial services? If so, please share the results of your investigation. If not, why not?
3) What types of data do you collect about the regulated financial holding companies' non-financial activities? How does the Federal Reserve interact with non-bank regulators who are in charge of overseeing the areas and markets in which banking institutions conduct their non-financial activities?
4) How do your examiners review, monitor, and evaluate banking organizations' management of potential conflicts of interest between their physical commodity businesses and their derivatives trading?
5) If such an entity were to become insolvent, what complications are likely to arise in resolving a company with such a range of activities? Please share your analysis on the implications of resolution authority on the commercial activities of systemically important financial institutions. Please describe how these banks approach this issue in their resolution plans (or "living wills").
6) When your examiners work within these large institutions, what framework do they use to, say, consider the possibility that a bank run could ensue from a massive public oil spill by a Goldman Sachs-owned oil tanker or a nuclear accident at a plant owned by a bank?
7) Does this relatively new corporate structure contribute to the likelihood of industrial supply shocks?

Thank you for your attention to this matter.

Sincerely,

Alan Grayson
Member of Congress

Raul Grijalva
Member of Congress

John Conyers
Member of Congress

Keith Ellison
Member of Congress

[i] http://www.morganstanley.com/about/ir/shareholder/10k2012/10k2012.pdf
Morgan Stanley, according to its investment documents, is engaged "in the production, storage, transportation, marketing and trading of several commodities, including metals (base a nd precious), agricultural products, crude oil, oil products, natural gas, electric power, emission credits, coal, freight, liquefied natural gas and related products and indices. In addition, we are an electricity power marketer in the U.S. and own electricity generating facilities in the U.S. and Europe; we own TransMontaigne Inc. and its subsidiaries, a group of companies operating in the refined petroleum products marketing and distribution business; and we own a minority interest in Heidmar Holdings LLC, which owns a group of companies that provide international marine transportation and U.S. marine logistics services."

[ii] http://www.goldmansachs.com/investor-relations/financials/current/10k/2012-10-K.pdf
Goldman Sachs, according to its own recent investment reports, is engaged in "the production, storage, transportation, marketing and trading of numerous commodities, including crude oil, oil products, natural gas, electric power, agricultural products, metals (base and precious), minerals (including uranium), emission credits, coal, freight, liquefied natural gas and related products and indices."

[iii] Ibid
[iv] "The Merchants of Wall Street: Banking, Commerce, and Commodities" Omarova, Saule, University of North Carolina at Chapel Hill School of Law
http://papers.ssrn.com/sol3/papers.cfm?abstract_id=2180647&download=yes

The Bad Guys

Usually, you can't detect them. They could be your favorite celebrity, the government officials who care about your life and your economy, the politicians you elected or the businessman whose products you buy every day. Or they could be behind the digital platform where you spend more than half of your day, and you would never know them. You might call them corruption. You feel it, but you can't detect it.

CORRUPTION ON THE RISE, BY COUNTRY*

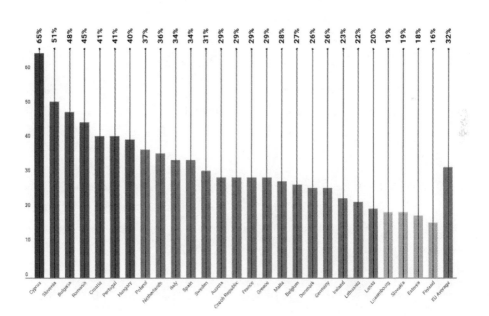

CORRUPTION, BY INSTITUTION

Percentage of people who think that most or all people in these groups or institutions are involved in corruption.[14]

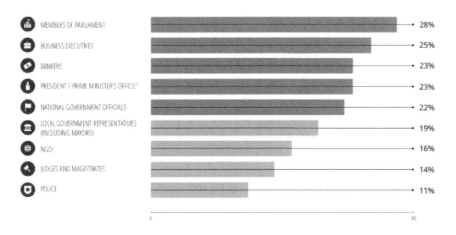

MEMBERS OF PARLIAMENT	28%
BUSINESS EXECUTIVES	25%
BANKERS	23%
PRESIDENT / PRIME MINISTER'S OFFICE[15]	23%
NATIONAL GOVERNMENT OFFICIALS	22%
LOCAL GOVERNMENT REPRESENTATIVES (INCLUDING MAYORS)	19%
NGOs	16%
JUDGES AND MAGISTRATES	14%
POLICE	11%

From conflicts of interest in awarding government contracts to undue influence by business on politics, from bribes to the use of personal connections when accessing public services, corruption takes many forms across the European Union (EU).

Despite the region's clean image, the EU shows people are all too aware of corruption across the bloc: 62 percent of over 40,000 survey participants believe that government corruption is a big problem in their country. *Source: 2021 Global Corruption Barometer (GCB)*

Sometimes this corruption (in the countries with the lowest corruption) cannot be felt; not because it doesn't exist but because it is well organized and rooted so well in the system itself (structured corruption) that it is protected by law.

PERSONAL CONNECTION RATES, BY COUNTRY

Percentage of public service users who used personal connections to get a service in the previous 12 months.[30]

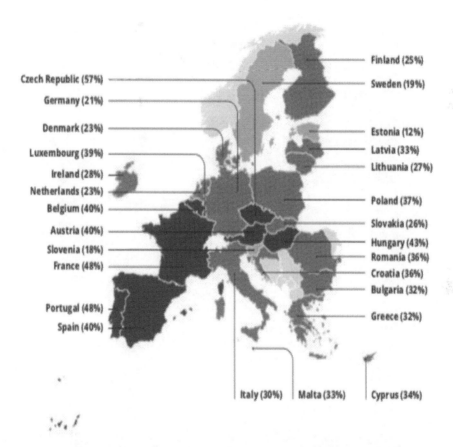

Czech Republic (57%)
Germany (21%)
Denmark (23%)
Luxembourg (39%)
Ireland (28%)
Netherlands (23%)
Belgium (40%)
Austria (40%)
Slovenia (18%)
France (48%)
Portugal (48%)
Spain (40%)

Finland (25%)
Sweden (19%)
Estonia (12%)
Latvia (33%)
Lithuania (27%)
Poland (37%)
Slovakia (26%)
Hungary (43%)
Romania (36%)
Croatia (36%)
Bulgaria (32%)
Greece (32%)

Italy (30%)   Malta (33%)   Cyprus (34%)

0%-19%   20%-39%   40%-59%   60%-79%   80%+

Even without bad luck, bad guys get detected from time to time! What are the dreaming strategies of these guys and how does it impact your mental well-being?

How big is the Pandora Papers leak?

 **14** Sources

 **11,903,676** Files

 **2.94 TB** Data

How do the files break down?

6,406,119	**2,937,513**	**1,205,716**	**467,405**	**886,923**
Documents	Images	Emails	Spreadsheets	Others

How does Pandora compare with previous leaks?

	Year	Data	Files
Offshore Leaks	2013	260 GB	2.5 million
Panama Papers	2016	2.6 TB	11.5 million
Paradise Papers	2017	1.4 TB	13.4 million
Pandora Papers	2021	2.94 TB	11.9 million

GB: Gigabyte, 1,000GB = 1TB, TB: Terabyte

Source: International Consortium of Investigative Journalists

60

Bad Guys' Dreaming Strategy

These guys are few. They are not part of the shared dream (community) strategy. They want freedom from the New Trinity (the new God), this triad of economy, welfare system and psychological manipulation that makes people submit. In fact, they are the ones who created it. They think they are special humans. To prove the nobility of their highness is their satisfaction.

The bad guys think, for one reason or another, that they are the only free ones and the others should be their slaves. These misconceptions were justified earlier by Aristotle. "In book I of the Politics, Aristotle addresses the questions of whether slavery can be natural or whether all slavery is contrary to nature and whether it is better for some people to be slaves. He concludes that those who are as different (from other men) as the soul from the body or man from beast—and they are in this state if their work is the use of the body, and if this is the best that can come from them—are slaves by nature. For them it is better to be ruled in accordance with this sort of rule, if such is the case for the other things mentioned." *Source: Politics by Aristotle by 350 B.C.E, author, translated 2012 by Benjamin Jowett.*

You work and pay taxes, but they do not although they should! Because they are few and want to stay that way, they need to find smart ways to control the majority. So, their dreaming strategy is to keep you terrified, distracted, and ready to obey. This means that there is no way to give you a break to think and all the time you have to be mentally stressed! The clever part is that this has become something called the system, the economy, the world, and life! Something too big for your little head to think about. Too big for your psychic energy to change. Now when this world has gone digital to what extent will this digitalization take over you and your mental health?

Digital Massive Control Over the Future Generations

There is an ongoing increase in the number of children and young people with behavioral disadvantages and inability to maintain their well-being. They develop similar biological, social and psychological aging manifestations, although they are still young. This is mainly due to excessive exposure to digital screens.

For decades digital risks and their effects on human well-being have become widely known causes for medical diagnoses. The menu is long including but not limited to spine strain, eyes, joint, posture and respiratory malfunctions, eating disorders, and digital dementia. On the top of the list is the internet addiction disorder especially gaming and social media addiction which have been mostly explained by: Dr. Kimberly Young (psychologist and expert on Internet addiction disorder and online behavior), Dr. Marc Potenza (PhD, MD, Yale School of Medicine, board-certified psychiatrist with sub-specialty training and certification in addiction psychiatry) and Dr. Ofir Turel (Professor of Information Systems and Decision Sciences at California State University).

The burden of psychological clinics is increasing in an unprecedented manner and at the same time, there is a worrying statistical increase in mental health figures and social agitation (violence, crimes and suicide) in most countries.

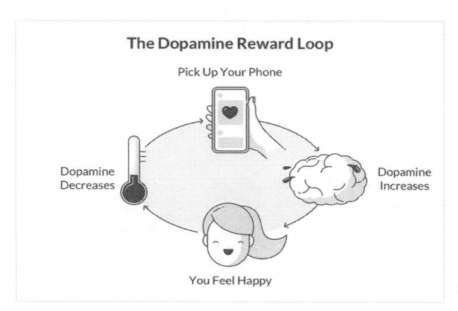

via Lemonade

People have a hard time putting their phones down. A study found that 94% of participants reported feeling upset when they didn't have their phones. 80% felt jealous when someone else used their phone, and 70% expected to feel depressed, panicked, and helpless if their phone was lost or they couldn't find it.

A study found that 89% of undergraduates experienced phantom vibrations. This is the visualization of vibrations from a mobile device that does not vibrate. People crave notifications so much that they begin to fantasize about them. *Source: www.pewresearch.org/*

CHAPTER 4

Why Is It Time for Powerful Psychology to Unfold?

Digitalization of The New Trinity

Day by day, you get to realize the fact that your peace of mind and the harmony of your life are no longer under your control. This leads to a constant feeling of insecurity, mistrust and tension.

The escalation of this sense of loss of control, is originally the mechanism of the New Trinity (the minority controlling the majority), which has taken on a greater speed due to the hegemony of globalization, and now this feeling is even more pronounced due to digitalization. This explains the different forms of increasing, whether exhaustion, violence, mental illness, corruption, etc.

And this is only the beginning!

Weaponization of The New Trinity

Now if anyone would try to find peace of mind in this global state of tension, it would be a thoroughly demanding task. It might feel that we are trapped in a maze without an exit.

Let me explain more. Our minds are confused because there is no way out and no solution, the problem is behind the breadth of cognition. In psychology, putting you under this kind of stressful state for some time is called preconditioning. It prepares you for the next step in which you immediately accept the next phase (escape solution) without thinking or resistance.

The next phase will come in two stages, the first is called taming by subtly teaching (programming) your mind (e.g. Squid Game) and the second is activation (gives you a task and a place to execute e.g., Metaverse). Above you have two perfect examples for understanding the weaponization of the New Trinity.

Squid Game's Dominance Effect

Squid Game is a worldwide popular Netflix series that, although rated by experts as a very violent medium, is the most watched so far.

It is a meticulously designed and perfectly engineered psychological technology to conquer and control minds. It has a subtle blend of emotion and extroversion, elegant performance and excitement. It carries explicit and subliminal messages that you just can't resist. If you're not familiar with it, it can be illustrated by two main scenes.

The first main scene is the primer: building a rapport with the audience. It attempts to build connection by creating similarity with the psychological and mental state of the audience. It creates an environment to which you can relate. Then it creates a suggestion for you by conveying this message: if you have a stressful, confusing, hopeless life that you cannot control, money can solve your problem and put an end to your miserable struggle.

This message gets stuck in the minds of the audience with the assertion that money can make you sad or happy, money can make your dream come true or disappoint you. In the end it becomes an undeniable fact in your mind (belief) that money is the most important and supreme power in your life as if it were your God. You must obey and do more to enjoy its powerful influence. This affirmation makes you totally submit to money.

The second main scene is the execution: this is where you are given a mission and a place to get more money power. You have to be able to break any chain or rules that stop you from obeying the command. You have been given the order to kill anyone around you, whoever it is, your colleagues, best friends, your family, your wife, etc.! At the end of the scene, they create a formula of complacency to your conscience and justify the killing without guilt! Actually, they make it clear for the rest of the audience that the one who obeys the commands to serve the money, is a moral hero!!!

Metaverse

Metaverse is an old term meaning beyond nature. Nowadays, it refers to the digital reproduction of physical life. Facebook leads the technical and ownership group of this product under the brand name Metaverse. It must create in the minds of its users the same experiences as the material life. The full immersion of the body's senses during the experience requires a special kind of audio, visual and sensation technology, which every user must be able to interact with.

The basic idea is that with this technology you find that you live with other people but without the rules of physical life. You can touch them, please them, or physically insult them. You will also be able to get events similar to what you can get in material life: working, doing business, buying and selling, playing sports, and traveling places or time. You can share events with other people so that you can even experience a tangible sexual experience.

From One Stress to Greater Stress

The effect of a virtual life depends on the age, and the current stress level. At a young age, it creates more digital addiction and withdrawal from reality, and a lack of physical stimulation which is necessary for the development of cognitive functions. In adults, the higher the stress level, the more likely the brain will develop an escape strategy to withdraw from reality.

The brain will end up in a new level of stress trying to find a balance between a stressful physical life and an easy virtual life with no rules and no limits except what has been learned from a game like Squid. It will lead to a double life with a double personality. *Source: "50% of Female VR Players Experience Sexual Harassment, Here's What Companies Should" Jamie P., Tech Times 03 January 2020.*

Do You Expect Chaos?

What we are witnessing so far in society is that people, especially at a young age, bring the violence they practice in virtual life into physical life. What will be the outcome of the intensification of all forms of violence in digital life that have been learned from games, media and virtual interaction spaces?

What's your opinion? What will happen to people's behavior? Do you think that there will be healthy and balanced enough minds to survive this stress? Do you think that at some point there will be extreme violence and chaos? Do you expect to be surrounded by brainwashed victims who have no control over their actions?

If You Don't, Muslims Expect It!

The Prophet, peace and blessings be upon him, warned 1400 ago that this exact image of chaos is coming at a certain stage!

Abu Hurairah narrated that the Messenger of Allah (ﷺ) said: "The world will not go away until a day comes when the killer does not know who he has killed, nor the one who was killed why he was killed."

And in another situation, he explained more why this would happen. Abu Musa narrated that some of the people were asking: "O Messenger of Allah, will we be in our right minds that day?" The Messenger of Allah (ﷺ) said: "Most people at that time will be brainwashed and brainless with insignificant logic and poor judgment". *Source: Muslim*

70

The Prophet did not only teach the companions of his time but was teaching all mankind even in the third millennium, in a distant time and place. He was explaining, among other things, what the chaotic events of late times are!

Mixing the Virtual and the Physical Is The Norm. Surprised?

Would you be surprised to learn that all the teachings and practices of Islam revolve around achieving harmony between two lives: virtual life (this world) and physical life (the hereafter)? Yes, it is exactly the opposite image of what others have in mind, who think that this material life is the reality and what is next is the virtual one, if they can even see it yet!

In Muslim's mind, this material life (dunya) is virtual and temporary like a game and the real life, the Hereafter (Akhirah), is yet to come. This is the everyday story in life from birth to death.

وَ مَا الْحَيْوةُ الدُّنْيَآ اِلَّا لَعِبٌ وَّلَهْوٌ وَلَلدَّارُ الْاٰخِرَةُ خَيْرٌ لِّلَّذِيْنَ يَتَّقُوْنَ افَلَا تَعْقِلُوْنَ

(6:32) The life of this world is nothing but a sport and a pastime, and the life of the Hereafter is far better for those who seek to ward off their ruin. Will you not, then, understand?[3]

A Mix but No Stress

God asks us not to take this material life as a place to feel completely alive. It is not about that at all. This material life is just one small step

---

[3] This does not mean that earthly life has nothing serious about it and that it has been brought into being merely as a sport and pastime. What this observation means is that, compared with the true and abiding life of the Hereafter, earthly life seems, as it were, a sport, a transient pastime with which to amuse oneself before turning to serious business.

towards life. Although it is a very important one to take, but carefully. It would be very stressful not to think like this, because this life is unpredictable, and the time of death can be at any time. So, relax in that respect, no stress.

At the same time, God assures us that the purpose of this life is to prepare for the next life. This is what makes the reward here and now insignificant in itself, all we need to focus on is the next life. That is where we need to dedicate our sincere efforts, looking forward to returning to God with pure hearts.

وَمَا خَلَقْنَا السَّمَآءَ وَالْأَرْضَ وَمَا بَيْنَهُمَا لٰعِبِيْنَ

(21:16) We did not create in sport the heavens and the earth and all that lies between the two.

اَفَحَسِبْتُمْ اَنَّمَا خَلَقْنٰكُمْ عَبَثًا وَّاَنَّكُمْ اِلَيْنَا لَا تُرْجَعُوْنَ

(23:115) Did you imagine that We created you without any purpose, and that you will not be brought back to Us?[4]

فَتَعٰلَى اللهُ الْمَلِكُ الْحَقُّ ۚ لَا اِلٰهَ اِلَّا هُوَ ۚ رَبُّ الْعَرْشِ الْكَرِيْمِ

(23:116) So, exalted be Allah, the True King! Thre is no god but He, the Lord of the Great Throne.

More Surprising!

Will you be even more surprised if I tell you that the cognitive function of our brain, both anatomically and functionally, is determined to create harmony between virtual reality and physical reality. Have you ever perceived it that way?

سَنُرِيْهِمْ اٰيٰتِنَا فِى الْاٰفَاقِ وَفِىْٓ اَنْفُسِهِمْ حَتّٰى يَتَبَيَّنَ لَهُمْ اَنَّهُ الْحَقُّ ؕ اَوَلَمْ يَكْفِ

---

[4] The Arabic word abathan in the text also means "for the sake of sport". Then the verse will mean: Did you think that We had created you merely for the sake of sport and there was no purpose behind your creation? Therefore, you may eat, drink, be merry and enjoy yourself as you please.

بِرَبِّكَ أَنَّهُ عَلَى كُلِّ شَىْءٍ شَهِيدٌ

(41:53) Soon shall We show them Our Signs on the horizons and in their own beings until it becomes clear to them that it is the Truth. Is it not enough that your Lord is a witness over everything?

The challenge is not whether to have two lives or not, but the challenge is how to create harmony without polarization! It may seem easy to say, but it is impossible to realize it. This challenge to create balance is the only source of all life's struggles and psychological distress.

وَمَنْ أَعْرَضَ عَنْ ذِكْرِئ فَإِنَّ لَـهُ مَعِيْشَةً ضَنْكًا وَّنَحْشُرُهُ يَوْمَ الْقِيٰمَةِ أَعْمٰى

(20:124) But whosoever turns away from this Admonition from Me shall have a straitened life; We shall raise him blind on the Day of Resurrection,"

"A life of hardship" does not mean a life of poverty. It means that one living it shall be deprived of the peace of mind, even though he may be a millionaire or the ruler of a vast empire. For the one who will turn away from the admonition will win all the worldly successes by unlawful means and will therefore always be suffering from pangs of a guilty conscience and deprived of the peace of mind as well as real happiness.

First Things First

Before taking you to talk about what is the cognitive psychology miracles and how they will work for you, let me ask you why did you fear Islam? And before you answer, let's see first what do you understand about Islam specifically and religions in general.

CHAPTER 5

What You Don't Know
About Islam

You Feel It's Weird? Me Too!

Therefore we should talk! You may be shocked to hear that someone at this moment of life suggests Islam as a means of reform, and especially as the only way to help people restore their psychological wellness.

When I talk to you about Islam, I am not aiming that the number of Muslims will increase by another person. Muslims represent almost a third of the population of the earth, and it is one of the fastest growing religions at the moment despite all the negative publicity. Muslims are many, but in vain. Exactly as the Prophet, may God bless him and grant him peace, mentioned is happening now:" You will be numerous at that time, but you will be scum and rubbish like that carried down by a torrent."

This is Not the End of The Road

The truth is that Islam no longer needs someone to defend it, but in fact the one who needs to defend it is you!

يَمُنُّونَ عَلَيْكَ اَنْ اَسْلَمُوْا قُلْ لَّا تَمُنُّوا عَلَىَّ اِسْلَامَكُمْ ۚ بَلِ اللهُ يَمُنُّ عَلَيْكُمْ اَنْ هَدٰىكُمْ لِلْاِيْمَانِ اِنْ كُنْتُمْ صٰدِقِيْنَ

(49:17) They count it as favorour to you that they accepted Islam. Say: "Do not regard your (accepting) Islam as a favour to me; rather, Allah has bestowed a favour on you by guiding you to faith, if you are truthful (in your claim to be believers).

The most harmful aspect of negative propaganda for religions in general, and Islam in particular, is not to distort the religion itself or its followers, but rather to mislead truth seekers who are looking for livable ways.

Life is now all about enabling a very few to seize power. This is a massive blow that has come after decades of promoting the New

Trinity. This success would not have happened with other religions that had therefore to be eliminated. It is however impossible for them to disappear by clicking delete! So there was a long way to go starting with smart and decisive steps to deactivate religions keeping in mind one dream: the psychology of the people must stay behind the carrot and in front of the stick!

Fortunately, this is not the end of the road, God has another plan to close the mouth of this propaganda:

يُرِيْدُوْنَ لِيُطْفِئُوْا نُوْرَ اللهِ بِأَفْوَاهِهِمْ وَاللهُ مُتِمُّ نُوْرِهِ وَلَوْ كَرِهَ الْكَفِرُوْنَ

(61:8) They seek to extinguish Allah's light (by blowing) with their mouths, but Allah shall spread His light in all its fullness, however the unbelievers may abhor this.[5]

Mr. Simple

He made me, "Simple", to tell you about the Islamic cognitive and psychological miracles, Islamophilia. I'm the one who came to live among you during the most active part of my life. It was hard for me to ignore the fact that I feel you every moment suffering under your skin and I know why, and most importantly I know the cure!

At a certain point, I had to honestly ask myself, why can't I share my experience about "No God but Allah, and Muhammad (pbuh) is His messenger" with you. Either I'm a selfish person, hypocrite, or there is

---

[5] One should bear in mind that these verses were sent down in A.H. 3 after the Battle of Uhud, when Islam was confined only to the city of Al-Madinah, the Muslims were only a few thousands in number, and entire Arabia was bent upon wiping out this religion. The defeat that the Muslims had suffered at Uhud, had sullied their image of power and the tribes of the surrounding areas had been emboldened. Under such conditions it was said: No one will succeed in blowing out this light of Allah, but it will shine forth and spread throughout the world. This was a clear prediction which literally came true. Who could know except Allah at that time of what was the future of Islam? Human eyes could only see that it was a flickering candle and violent winds were blowing to put it out forever.

something wrong with Islam. The answer was clear: none of these are true!

This asking in my head kept repeating until I understood clearly the wisdom of being among you! If we live on one earth, under one sky, it is our responsibility to share experiences and cooperate in good deeds.

يَٰٓأَيُّهَا ٱلنَّاسُ إِنَّا خَلَقْنَٰكُم مِّن ذَكَرٍ وَأُنثَىٰ وَجَعَلْنَٰكُمْ شُعُوبًا وَقَبَآئِلَ لِتَعَارَفُوٓا۟ إِنَّ أَكْرَمَكُمْ عِندَ ٱللَّهِ أَتْقَىٰكُمْۚ إِنَّ ٱللَّهَ عَلِيمٌ خَبِيرٌ

(49:13) Human beings, We created you all from a male and a female, and made you into nations and tribes so that you may know one another. Verily the noblest of you in the sight of Allah is the most God-fearing of you. Surely Allah is All-Knowing, All-Aware.[6]

Hollywood's Version of Islam Versus The True Islam

The conspiracy of 9/11[7], the dramatic image of al-Qaeda, ISIS and all this kind of Hollywood drama (psychological warfare and the art of disinformation)[8] is only about a twenty years old story. Islam on the

---

[6] The Creator had divided the human communities into nations and tribes for that was a natural way of cooperation and distinction between them. In this way alone could a fraternity, a brotherhood, a tribe and a nation combine to give birth to a common way of life and to cooperate with each other in the affairs of the world. But it was all due to satanic ignorance that the differences among mankind created by Allah to be a means of recognition, were turned into a means of mutual boasting and hatred, which led mankind to every kind of injustice and tyranny.

[7] American Conspiracies: Lies, Lies, and More Dirty Lies That the Government Tells Us. It is a book written by former Governor of Minnesota Jesse Ventura, together with Dick Russell. The book presents and discusses conspiracy theories related to several notable events in the history of the United States. It was published by Skyhorse Publishing in 2010.

[8] Psychological operations (PSYOP) are operations to convey selected information and indicators to audiences to influence their emotions, motives, and objective reasoning, and ultimately the behavior of governments, organizations, groups, and individuals.

other hand has a history of more than 1400 years. So now we have two versions of Islam and you can compare.

The Hollywood Drama Version of Islam

In fact, there are two versions, the first was during the Cold War between the seventies and the end of the nineties. If you know e.g., Rambo III, you will understand what I mean. The second version was between 2000 and 2021, and it was in the exact opposite direction. The next version is already taking shape. If you haven't seen it coming yet, you'll see it soon.

These two contradicting versions of Islam mean that Islam is a very powerful card used by the American economy and hence in the foreign policy in the first place. This card can be played extensively, even from one end to the other, and has absolutely nothing to do with reality.

Source: Islam According to Hollywood: Influence on US Foreign Policy, by Ajmer Drwall, including 13 additional resources.

The Real History of Islam

The religion of Islam that was revealed to the Messenger of Islam (pbuh) was a message of reform in a barbaric and capitalist society called Mecca. People were sold and bought as slaves, and girls were buried alive for fear of disgrace. These were the rules of life at that time, until the last Prophet (pbuh) came with the truth to redress all this injustice and liberate these people from oppression and tyranny in a thirteen-year epic, first in Mecca and then from Medina to all over the world.

During these years the Prophet, peace be upon him, began to reveal the messages he was receiving to his tribe. These verses were compiled by verse and they later became the Qur'an, Islam's holy book. In the following decade, Muhammad, peace be upon him, and his followers were first ridiculed and mocked, then persecuted and physically attacked for moving away from the traditional tribal ways of Mecca.

Muhammad's, peace be upon him, message was firmly monotheistic. For several years, the Quraish, the dominant tribe in Mecca, imposed a ban on trade with Muhammad's, peace be upon him, people, exposing them to conditions that were close to famine. Near the end of the decade, Muhammad's, peace be upon him, wife and uncle died. Finally, the leaders of Mecca attempted to assassinate Muhammad, peace be upon him.

In 622, Muhammad, peace be upon him, and his hundreds of followers left Mecca and traveled to Yathrib, the oasis town where his father was buried. The leaders there were suffering from a fierce civil war, and they invited this man known for his wisdom to act as their mediator. Soon Yathrib became known as Medina, the city of the Prophet. Muhammad, peace be upon him, remained there building the first Muslim community and gradually gathering more and more people to his side over the next ten years.

On June 8, 632 Muhammad, peace be upon him, died in Medina, after a short illness. He was buried in the Medina Mosque. Within a hundred years, Muhammad's, peace be upon him, teachings and way of life had spread from remote corners of the Arabian Peninsula as far east as Indochina and as far west as Morocco, France and Spain.

He left after him the miracle of the Qur'an (God's words to people) exactly as he received it word by word, beside his complete teachings for humanity. Since then, until now, the role of Islam on earth has not changed as a means of liberating human beings from the enslavement of other human beings.

The Knowledge Which Brings More Knowledge

What distinguishes the religion of Islam from other religions is the balance between spirituality and the adoption of science, and the proven effectiveness in reform and transformation.

This sounds odd, right? We normally think of religion as ironically hostile to science. Wasn't there a long and protracted war between science and Christianity? Did the church not prosecute Galileo? But this 'war' between 'science' and 'religion' was purely a western affair. There is no counterpart of such mutual hostilities in Islam.

Islam on the contrary encouraged the pursuit of scientific knowledge right from its inception. Prophet Muhammad, peace be upon him, – who himself could not read or write – emphasized that the material world can only be understood through scientific inquiry. Islamic culture, he insisted, was a knowledge-based culture. He valued science over extensive worship and declared: 'An hour's study of nature is better than a year's prayer'. This is why he directed his followers to 'listen to the words of the scientist and instill unto others the lessons of science' and 'go even as far as China in the quest of knowledge'.

The Qur'an, which the Muslims believe to be the actual words of God and clearly distinguish it from the words of Prophet Muhammad, peace be upon him, places immense emphasis on scientific knowledge. The first word of the Qur'an revealed to Muhammad is 'Read'. It refers, among other forms of reading, to reading the 'signs of God' or the systematic study of nature.

It is a basic tenet of Muslim belief that the material world is full of signs of God, and these signs can only be deciphered through rational and objective inquiry. Almost one third of the Qur'an is devoted to the praise of scientific knowledge, objective inquiry and serious study of the material world. 'Acquire the knowledge of all things', the Qur'an advises its readers, and pray: 'God increase me in my knowledge'. *Source: Islam and Science by Prof Ziauddin Sardar; Writer, broadcaster and cultural critic.*

Where Has the Welfare of Islam Gone?

Firstly, Islam is primarily a knowledge system, and its source is the Creator. You might say that it is an authorized program for man and life. It helps you to reconnect your offline psychic to the universal WiFi. If you follow the instructions carefully, it will work for you as promised. It also includes a what-if scenario, talking about what might go wrong and how to fix it in your life.

Take a look at history, you will understand what Islam means. If you look, you will understand that the program will not download itself into your life, but you will be asked to do so. This is why we are humans and have minds.

Secondly, Islam is a strong and straightforward religion that does not promise you peace of mind and free Heaven, but rather directs you frankly to hard work. This work will pay off here in this life with a fully charged psychic energy, asking you to non-stop keep building around you a means to earn your welfare in here and hereafter.

Unfortunately, Muslims who are born as Muslims believe that the catalog will work on its own. More confusion happens to both of you, when these Muslims think you are the happiest person on earth, provided that you have found your god in the New Trinity. Of course, they don't know the full picture of the reality!

Based on the above two points, I would say that the welfare of Islam is ahead of you. If you believe in knowledge and hard work, if you want to enjoy freedom from the New Trinity, if you want to have peace of mind and secure your future, I invite you to continue reading.

CHAPTER 6

The Cognitive Secrets of Islam

Islam and Relative Intelligence

Now, and after 1400 years, if we would like to re-understand how our mind is supposed to interact with religion in general and Islam specifically, what would be the closest example to explain it? The following example will help you to understand it better.

Simply put, if our mind is like (computer) hardware, religion will be in this case the operating system[9] (OS). The OS will affect the functionality of the device and also control which subprograms will be installed later. This operating system will subsequently run throughout our life and determine its quality.

The overall results of the entire system depend on the compatibility with the operating system (relative intelligence[10]) and its ability to handle any subprograms. If we apply the example literally, every operating system needs updates to cope with the new requirements in our life. Does Islam have that capability, an automatically built-in update system? Can this religion satisfy our needs in the digital millennium and even the next millenniums?

The answer will unfold in the next chapters. Now let's build an easy foundation of basic knowledge about our cognitive abilities and how our minds develop over time. This foundation is crucial in order to understand the relative intelligent nature of Islam and its cognitive miracles. To reach a complete understanding of this nature, we should carry on a bit further with simulating the religion with the OS.

---

[9] An operating system (OS) is system software that manages computer hardware, software resources, and provides common services for computer programs.

[10] The ability to acquire experience, adapt to new situations, understand and handle abstract concepts, use knowledge to navigate one's environment while applying knowledge and skills.

The Muslim Operating System

It is the system (Islam) established by the Creator for the education and development of individuals so that we may first become humans. Secondly it decides our fate. When we are born, we are potentially human beings, but it is not necessary that we end up like human beings. It is also possible that we end up with complete misery, not even close to what humans are meant to be.

وَنَفْسٍ وَّمَا سَوَّىٰهَا (7)فَأَلْهَمَهَا فُجُورَهَا وَتَقْوٰىهَا (8)قَدْ أَفْلَحَ مَنْ زَكَّىٰهَا(9) وَقَدْ خَابَ مَنْ دَسّٰىهَا(10)

(91:7) and by the soul and by Him Who perfectly proportioned it (91:8) and imbued it with (the consciousness of) its evil and its piety. (91:9) He who purifies it will prosper (91:10) and he who suppresses it will be ruined.

In the end it should help us to start striving to build our position in the future (the hereafter) by working in the present (dunya). This is the dream that generates in all Muslims motivation, energy and diligence.

The Islamic operating system gives equal opportunities to strive in various aspects of life, and we must choose what suits us. At the end of the work (on the Day of Judgment), each of us will be evaluated according to the degree of our devotion.

يَوْمَئِذٍ يَّصْدُرُ النَّاسُ أَشْتَاتًا لِّيُرَوْا أَعْمَالَهُمْ (6)فَمَنْ يَّعْمَلْ مِثْقَالَ ذَرَّةٍ خَيْرًا يَّرَهُ(7)وَمَنْ يَّعْمَلْ مِثْقَالَ ذَرَّةٍ شَرًّا يَّرَهُ(8)

(99:6) On that Day people will go forth in varying states so that they be shown their deeds. (99:7) So, whoever does an atom's weight of good shall see it; (99:8) and whoever does an atom's weight of evil shall see it.

According to the results, everyone will receive an eternal rank that cannot be changed. Based on this our chances are now in this life (dunya), time and intentions are the most precious things we have.

What if There is No Specific Operating System?

To understand the possibility, let's imagine this real-life example. Have you ever seen a little baby crawling with curiosity to explore everything around him? Until he reaches the place for shoes, and without hesitation grabs one and puts it in his mouth? From the baby point of view, in his mind, he's pretty sure it was the right thing to do!

At this point, the future mind of this child will be shaped by the reaction of his mother, and pretty much he has no way to review her choices. For example, if she wants to give him a chance for self-determination, she will allow him to try eating the shoe and let him find the results on his own. Some other mother will take the shoe away, and look him in the face to tell that it's not the right thing to do.

What just happened is that both moms started installing part of their OS (believes) in this brand-new mind. Does the child have any chance to check what he is receiving? In fact, our mind at this point does not have any reference or ability to verify any information, so it is 100% vulnerable and dependent (relativity) on the other human brains and this can go on indefinitely from one generation to another.

Now let's play this example a little forward to see how far it can impact not only this baby but also the wider society. The first mother can claim that every experience in life here is a personal one and should not be imposed on other minds. She can however decide to encourage other mothers to do the same until the time comes when we find that there is a whole society full of shoe gourmands. After a few more generations, shoe gourmands will be the norm and the odd ones will be those who don't participate. Not long after that we may reach a completely reversed reality and there is no way to verify at this point what the original setting was! This is how the human project can end in misery.

The Slave Nature of The Human Mind

From the previous example we understand that the human mind is an empty multidimensional relative space more advanced than what we have nowadays (quantum computing). In the early stages of life, it does not have the ability to elicit any information from within (slave mentality). It is only ready to receive information from an external source (master) and store it in a complex (semantic) way, linking the input information with everything that was recorded earlier (memory), and during receiving this piece of information. *Source: Wixted, John T et al. "Coding of episodic memory in the human hippocampus." Proceedings of the National Academy of Sciences of the United States of America vol. 115,5 (2018)*

The first information input plays a pivotal role throughout our lives because at the same time it acts as the reference data that the brain uses to classify and understand the next set of information. This reference data occupies an advanced place in an individual's memory, and is called by various names such as religion, beliefs, traditions, or culture and in our example operating system (OS).

Your reference data will be later the determinant of your dreaming strategy and most importantly it acts as your psychological defense (psychological immunity) for life's challenges.

The Absolute Freedom

In our example, both mothers were realistic but also wrong. As for the first mother, she was right not to impose her own personal OS on her son's mind. But at the same time, she didn't make his life better by letting him navigate life without a compass. This way he will most likely end up being a slave of the New Trinity, a victim to be manipulated by endless psychological turbulence. She left him in shambles without any safety gear, who knows how it will end.

The other mother who just passed her believes (OS) to her son made him a slave to her own source of OS. In this case there are two possibilities. One of them is that she in her own verified the source of her OS, and it has brought good results on her life and she wishes the same for her son. The other option is that she never had the chance to verify her own OS and she is just passing it blindly to the next generation without considering if it has had a good impact on her life or not. She just made her son her own slave and a victim.

The truth is that the mind at a certain stage will not be independent to decide on its own what is good and what is not. At the same time, this shouldn't be influenced by other humans. Even the mother cannot influence her son, no one should make another human a slave. Stay free!. This freedom is a relative topic. We should stay free from other human control, but we can't be completely independent. Someone has to install something on our mind. All we can choose to decide on our own is who our master should be, another human or the Creator himself!

Keep in mind that your psychological state will be limited by the source of your OS. Absolute freedom is to belong to the Absolute Powerful and not to a relative creature like you. You now have an understanding of the inevitable fact that our minds are designed to be someone else's slave. At least for a while, until we are able to verify our OS and control it.

OS Self Verification Mechanisms in Islam

Islam urges us to check our operating system, especially the one we inherited from our parents. This verification depends on several mechanisms in the Qur'an. Here you can familiarize yourself with two of them.

First of all, the Qur'an has a built-in self-validation system, which means that it always provides two options for our mind to compare. The first option is *what if you do* and the other *what if you don't*. Then you are able to obey or disobey. Either way, the results will be clear to you. In the end, you will be very clear about what you do and what your choice is. This makes you responsible.

Secondly there is the explicit validation mechanism specifically for checking the OS inherited from the parents:

وَإِذَا قِيلَ لَهُمُ اتَّبِعُوا مَا آنَزَلَ اللهُ قَالُوا بَلْ نَتَّبِعُ مَا أَلْفَيْنَا عَلَيْهِ أَبَاءَنَا أَوَلَوْ كَانَ أَبَاؤُهُمْ لَا يَعْقِلُونَ شَيْئًا وَّلَا يَهْتَدُونَ

(2:170) And when they are told: "Follow what Allah has revealed," they say: "No, we shall follow what we found our forefathers adhering to." What! Even if their forefathers were devoid of understanding and right guidance?[11]

These verification mechanisms provide a basis for the freedom to choose and explore different options but in a safer way than navigating through an uncertain, chaotic future as it has become a trend nowadays.

---

[11] The only possible argument and justification for these taboos was that they had been sanctified by the practice of their forefathers from whom they had allegedly come down generation after generation. Fickle-minded as they were, they deemed this argument to be sufficiently persuasive.

CHAPTER 7

The Authorized and Verified OS of The Human Beings

Ceremony of Installing The First Authorized Human OS

There are pivotal verses in the Holy Qur'an in Surat Al-Baqarah (2:30-39) that tell us about the installation ceremony of the first ever OS for the first human being.

These verses are a demonstration of the essence of the human story from the first moment, in which the work began, until its end. For clarity, we divide this ceremony into nine scenes.

Scene One: The News

وَإِذْ قَالَ رَبُّكَ لِلْمَلَـٰٓئِكَةِ إِنِّى جَاعِلٌ فِى الْأَرْضِ خَلِيفَةً ۖ قَالُوٓا۟ أَتَجْعَلُ فِيهَا مَن يُفْسِدُ فِيهَا وَيَسْفِكُ الدِّمَآءَ وَنَحْنُ نُسَبِّحُ بِحَمْدِكَ وَنُقَدِّسُ لَكَ ۖ قَالَ إِنِّىٓ أَعْلَمُ مَا لَا تَعْلَمُونَ

(2:30) Just think when your Lord said to the angels: "Lo! I am about to place a vicegerent on earth," they said: "Will You place on it one who will spread mischief and shed blood while we celebrate Your glory and extol Your holiness?" He said: "Surely I know what you do not know.

In this scene, God Almighty appears before His angels to inform them of His decision to appoint a successor to Him on earth. The appointed one has a new ability over other creatures: freedom to make his own decisions and evaluate his future. During this scene, the angels practice democracy. They ask the Creator respectfully, in a manner that allows them to question. Their concern was that this kind of new creature in this capacity would spread mischief and bloodshed.

The Creator, Glory be to Him, welcomed the question, and His response was to defend these creatures (humans). He did it in a practical, scientific and convincing manner.

Scene Two: The First Installation

وَعَلَّمَ ادَمَ الْاَسْمَاءَ كُلَّهَا ثُمَّ عَرَضَهُمْ عَلَى الْمَلٰٓئِكَةِ فَقَالَ اَنْبِئُونِىْ بِاَسْمَاءِ هٰٓؤُلَاءِ اِنْ كُنْتُمْ صٰدِقِيْنَ

(2:31) Then Allah taught Adam the names of all things and presented them to the angels and said: "If you are right (that the appointment of a vicegerent will cause mischief) then tell Me the names of these things."

قَالُوْا سُبْحٰنَكَ لَا عِلْمَ لَنَآ اِلَّا مَا عَلَّمْتَنَا اِنَّكَ اَنْتَ الْعَلِيْمُ الْحَكِيْمُ

(2:32) They said. "Glory to You! We have no knowledge except what You taught us. You, only You, are All-Knowing, All-Wise."

This was the human's first OS installation during which the Creator took care of this new creature (Adam) and taught him by Himself. Since this moment God made it clear for all the creatures that He is the first and the only source for teaching Adam. Therefore, Adam remains a free slave, and does not owe any favors to any other creatures. This is a fundamental fact of human identity and it is an honor for men to be servants of God only.

In this life, the role of defending us and installing of our first OS is assigned to the partners. Providing they will pass to us the authorized version.

وَاِنْ جَاهَدٰكَ عَلٰٓى اَنْ تُشْرِكَ بِىْ مَا لَيْسَ لَكَ بِهٖ عِلْمٌ ۙ فَلَا تُطِعْهُمَا وَصَاحِبْهُمَا فِى الدُّنْيَا مَعْرُوْفًا وَّاتَّبِعْ سَبِيْلَ مَنْ اَنَابَ اِلَىَّ ۚ ثُمَّ اِلَىَّ مَرْجِعُكُمْ فَاُنَبِّئُكُمْ بِمَا كُنْتُمْ تَعْمَلُوْنَ

(31:15) But if they press you to associate others with Me in My Divinity, (to associate) those regarding whom you have no knowledge (that they are My associates), do not obey them. And yet treat them well in this world, and follow the way of him who turns to Me in devotion. Eventually it is to Me that all of you shall return, and I shall then tell you all that you did."

God emphasized on greatly respecting and taking care of the ones who took care of you, especially the mother. Women in Islam play a crucial role in preserving the human race and in helping them to stay free. She has been honored with a unique organ in her body, the womb, bearing in Arabic the attribute of His name Al-Rahman (meaning The Merciful). The mothers are supposed to inherit this mercy to embrace and defend their children without hesitation with endless sacrifices.

Scene Three: The Testing

قَالَ يَـٰٓأَـٰدَمُ أَنۢبِئۡهُم بِأَسۡمَآئِهِمۡۖ فَلَمَّآ أَنۢبَأَهُم بِأَسۡمَآئِهِمۡ قَالَ أَلَمۡ أَقُل لَّكُمۡ إِنِّىٓ أَعۡلَمُ غَيۡبَ ٱلسَّمَٰوَٰتِ وَٱلۡأَرۡضِ وَأَعۡلَمُ مَا تُبۡدُونَ وَمَا كُنتُمۡ تَكۡتُمُونَ

(2:33) Then Allah said to Ada: "Tell them the names of these things." And when he had told them the names of all things, Allah said: "Did I not say to you that I know everything about the heavens and the earth which are beyond your range of knowledge and I know all that you disclose and also all that you hide?"

This scene shows the first successful reform of a human carried out by installing the first operating system for this creature. Since then, it has been clearly proven that the only hope for humans to avoid the possibility of spreading mischief and bloodshed is to have this OS. Only this way, the human will succeed in becoming a human being. He will be well respected and appreciated up to that God commands later other creatures to prostrate to him. What a success and honor!

Scene Four: The Challenger

وَإِذۡ قُلۡنَا لِلۡمَلَـٰٓئِكَةِ ٱسۡجُدُواْ لِـَٔادَمَ فَسَجَدُوٓاْ إِلَّآ إِبۡلِيسَ أَبَىٰ وَٱسۡتَكۡبَرَ وَكَانَ مِنَ ٱلۡكَـٰفِرِينَ

(2:34) And when We ordered the angels: "Prostrate yourselves before Adam," all of them fell prostrate, except Iblis. He refused, and gloried in his arrogance and became one of the defiers.

This is Iblis (also known as Lucifer and Satan) committing the first ever racist crime against man. He is jealous, and has therefore denied the honor of mankind. He refused to obey God's command to prostrate to Adam, thinking that he was better than him. This was not constituted in the form of a question like the Angels had done, but it was a blatant objection stemming from hatred, arrogance and selfishness. The penalty for this creature was expulsion from the mercy of the Creator. From this moment on he has been leading the challenge against the human race.

Scene Five: Deep Learning

وَقُلْنَا يَـٰٓأَدَمُ اسْكُنْ أَنْتَ وَزَوْجُكَ الْجَنَّةَ وَكُلَا مِنْهَا رَغَدًا حَيْثُ شِئْتُمَا وَلَا تَقْرَبَا هَـٰذِهِ الشَّجَرَةَ فَتَكُونَا مِنَ الظَّالِمِينَ

(2:35) And We said: "O Adam, live in the Garden, you and your wife, and eat abundantly of whatever you wish but do not approach this tree or else you will be counted among the wrong-doers."

This part of Adam's OS demonstration was the most important phase in trying out the unique privilege of his rank. He was in a special place where he could use his freedom to obtain unlimited satisfaction. This was Heaven. There is no conflict, no consequences, no lies, no arguing, no effort, no limits, no rudeness, no loss, no anxiety, no fear, no pain, and no depression.

He only dreams and these dreams come true, this is the unique feature that distinguishes him from other creatures. The human race has received a unique attribute from God: to experience more deeply what it means for God to want something to happen and it just to come true (an experience Satan wanted for himself). This is a trait that should help the human race create understanding towards the Creator, understanding that will create the love story later. Love is deep mutual understanding. This power is conditional on obedience to God, otherwise it will not work.

Scene Six: The First OS Hack

فَأَزَلَّهُمَا الشَّيْطَنُ عَنْهَا فَأَخْرَجَهُمَا مِمَّا كَانَا فِيهِ وَقُلْنَا اهْبِطُوا بَعْضُكُمْ لِبَعْضٍ
عَدُوٌّ ۖ وَلَكُمْ فِى الْأَرْضِ مُسْتَقَرٌّ وَّمَتَاعٌ إِلَى حِينٍ

(2:36) But Satan caused both of them to deflect from obeying Our command by tempting them to the tree and brought them out of the state they were in, and We said: "Get down all of you; henceforth, each of you is an enemy of the other, and on earth you shall have your abode and your livelihood for an appointed time."

The most vulnerable part of the OS is that it is optional and not forced on us. It can be modified, deleted and replaced easily. It highly depends on our will to maintain it, or not.

Love comes with honesty. This takes sharp focus, dedication, and transparency in everything that comes to fidelity in order to keep the promise of love. It was time for Adam to learn this fact about his OS, and that it wasn't going to work on its own. His sole responsibility was to stay loyal, and to stay loyal he needed to accept the OS literally, not to escape any line i.e., obey all commands.

Adam did not understand this yet when he received a message of temptation (a malware) from Satan. Adam didn't hesitate nor have any doubts, he opened the message and followed Satan's suggestion. This was Adam's first OS security breach, by the sole hacker of his system (Satan). The way of hacking has been the same since this moment (false promises and false suggestions). The glitch immediately showed up as an error in Adam's OS (first sin).

By this time, the deep learning of Adam's cognitive system was nearly complete,allowing him to experience the first dimension of the contradiction between defender (God) and opponent (Satan), loyalty and volatility.

It is time to prepare to understand the other dimension of the contradiction: living in Heaven, and earth (dunya) as a temporary place.

Scene Seven: OS Recovery

فَتَلَقَّىٰ آدَمُ مِنْ رَّبِّهِ كَلِمَٰتٍ فَتَابَ عَلَيْهِ إِنَّهُ هُوَ التَّوَّابُ الرَّحِيمُ

(2:37) Thereupon Adam learned from his Lord some words and repented and his Lord accepted his repentance for He is Much-Relenting, Most Compassionate.

This was a very important moment for Adam. Before he started his journey, he understood that the vulnerability of his OS is backed by a recovery system, and that God taught him how to do it.

Scene Eight: Stay Connected, Stay Updated

قُلْنَا اهْبِطُوا مِنْهَا جَمِيعًا

فَإِمَّا يَأْتِيَنَّكُم مِّنِّي هُدًى فَمَن تَبِعَ هُدَايَ فَلَا خَوْفٌ عَلَيْهِمْ وَلَا هُمْ يَحْزَنُونَ

(2:38) We said: "Get you down from here, all of you, and guidance shall come to you from Me: then, whoever will follow My guidance need have no fear, nor shall they grieve.

In this scene God assured Adam that He will update his OS if he stays connected. Those who will get updated are those who will have the power to stay away from fear or grief, so no one can use those feelings to make them their slaves (psychological manipulation to control people).

Scene Nine: The Closing Statement

وَالَّذِينَ كَفَرُوا وَكَذَّبُوا بِآيَاتِنَا أُولَٰئِكَ أَصْحَابُ النَّارِ هُمْ فِيهَا خَالِدُونَ

(2:39) But those who refuse to accept this (guidance) and reject Our Signs as false are destined for the Fire where they shall abide for ever."

There are those who could not comprehend the purpose of their creation, those who could not come to a mutual understanding with God, those who did not want to remain faithful, and those who wanted to be defeated by Satan. Those who wanted to have the same fate as him, God promised that their wish would also come true! Sending them all to Hell as they wished, otherwise God has no interest to punish.

مَا يَفْعَلُ اللهُ بِعَذَابِكُمْ اِنْ شَكَرْتُمْ وَاٰمَنْتُمْ ۚ وَكَانَ اللهُ شَاكِرًا عَلِيْمًا

(4:147) Why should Allah deal chastisement to you if you are grateful to Him and believe? Allah is All-Appreciative, All-Knowing.

OS Serial Updates

Satan stays the same, sends his seductive malware, people click to accept it, and something goes wrong. Some recover and some don't. Sometimes the malware is widespread and needs a complete update of the operating system. This means sending an authorized human (messenger with a miracle) with a new version of the OS (update) that has the same original core functionality and message to the humans (don't be a slave to anyone or anything other than God) but new instructions on how to do it.

Sometimes the severity and seriousness of the malware is so widespread that you need to eliminate the operating system infected with the virus. For example, those who were the first to practice diverse sexual orientations and established it as an acceptable norm in their society. If this virus would have continued to spread, neither you nor I, or many other generations wouldn't exist. This virus would be enough to eliminate human reproduction, as it were a mass destruction weapon.[12]

فَلَمَّا جَآءَ أَمْرُنَا جَعَلْنَا عَالِيَهَا سَافِلَهَا وَاَمْطَرْنَا عَلَيْهَا حِجَارَةً مِّنْ سِجِّيْلٍ مَّنْضُوْدٍ

(11:82) And when Our command came to pass, We turned the town upside down, and rained on it stones of baked clay, one on another.

Recent scientific and archeological proof has been published to describe the details of the above-mentioned elimination event. *Source: Bunch, T.E., LeCompte, M.A., Adedeji, A.V. et al. A Tunguska sized airburst destroyed Tall el-Hammam a Middle Bronze Age city in the Jordan Valley near the Dead Sea. Sci Rep 11, 18632 (2021). https://doi.org/10.1038/s41598-021-97778-3*

Judaism

The Messenger Moses, peace be upon him, had a miracle that was contingent upon his ability to challenge people into something they knew by heart (magic). He was able to save his people from the tyrant who made them slaves. The miracle vanished with his death, but his teachings were recorded in different books for future education.

Christianity

The Messenger Jesus, may God bless him and grant him peace, came to save people from the bondage of material life and the worship of wealth. His miracle was of a purely spiritual nature from the moment of his conception until the time when his mission became on hold. The miracle vanished with his death, but his teachings remained in the

---

[12] The people of Lot were fully discovered recently in the southern Jordan Valley region in southern Jordan, and its name is the city of "Sodom", but it is known Islamically as the city of "the people of Lot" the Prophet who lived there more than 3500 years ago.

future in several books.

Islam

The Messenger is Muhammad, may God bless him and grant him peace, and his miracle is a book, Qur'an. He passed away and the miracle remains as one book. Islam is the latest and the last human OS and it is a miracle on its own.

CHAPTER 8

Islam is The Latest and Last Human OS

Why Was It Important to Get a New OS Update?

Every new update of the human operating system comes to respond to deviation of the previous version. What happened several decades after Jesus' death completely changed the concept of religion on earth and the purpose of humans.

Since the moment Adam came to earth, and the relation between humans and God has been based on distance learning, God sent messengers with a message asking people to believe in Him, and decide on that before going back to Him.

All our human mind's cognitive and psychological capabilities are designed to enable this mission as such, not to meet God on earth. The division from this concept will create confusion in minds (cognitive confusion). Stating as a fact that God has a son and that He decided to send him at a certain moment for certain people to see him, is inconsistent logic in the belief system, all in all it resulted in a confused OS.

وَقَالُوا اتَّخَذَ الرَّحْمٰنُ وَلَدًا

(19:88) They claim: "The Most Compassionate Lord has taken a son to Himself."

لَقَدْ جِئْتُمْ شَيْئًا إِدًّا

(19:89) Surely you have made a monstrous statement.

تَكَادُ السَّمٰوٰتُ يَتَفَطَّرْنَ مِنْهُ وَتَنْشَقُّ الْأَرْضُ وَتَخِرُّ الْجِبَالُ هَدًّا

(19:90) It is such a monstrosity that heavens might well-nigh burst forth at it, the earth might be cleaved, and the mountains fall

اَنْ دَعَوْا لِلرَّحْمٰنِ وَلَدًا

(19:91) at their ascribing a son to the Most Compassionate Lord. وَمَا يَنْبَغِي لِلرَّحْمٰنِ اَنْ يَتَّخِذَ وَلَدًا

(19:92) It does not befit the Most Compassionate Lord that He

108

should take a son.

الرَّحْمٰنِ عَبْدًا السَّمٰوٰتِ وَالْأَرْضِ اِلَّا اٰتِى اِنْ كُلُّ مَنْ فِى

(19:93) There is no one in the heavens and the earth but he shall come to the Most Compassionate Lord as His servant.

The Confused OS

The most critical line in this confused OS follows these lines: for the first time and suddenly God declares that He has companions (son/wife). Then He also suddenly changes the human OS update pattern and decides to come into this life (dunya) Himself for some time so that He can tell some people about this new update. On top of that, God chooses to change the meaning of love and honesty from earning it to be given to you as soon as you say you believe in this story. God also decides to disregard justice and to grant the believers Heaven, no matter what injustice and sins they will commit.

وَاِذْ قَالَ اللهُ يٰعِيْسَى ابْنَ مَرْيَمَ ءَاَنْتَ قُلْتَ لِلنَّاسِ اتَّخِذُوْنِيْ وَاُمِّيَ اِلٰهَيْنِ مِنْ دُوْنِ اللهِ قَالَ سُبْحٰنَكَ مَا يَكُوْنُ لِيْ اَنْ اَقُوْلَ مَا لَيْسَ لِيْ بِحَقٍّ اِنْ كُنْتُ قُلْتُهُ فَقَدْ عَلِمْتَهُ تَعْلَمُ مَا فِيْ نَفْسِيْ وَلَا اَعْلَمُ مَا فِيْ نَفْسِكَ اِنَّكَ اَنْتَ عَلَّامُ الْغُيُوْبِ

(5:116) And imagine when thereafter Allah will say: 'Jesus, son of Mary, did you say to people: "Take me and my mother for gods beside Allah?" and he will answer: "Glory to You! It was not for me to say what I had no right to. Had I said so, You would surely have known it. You know all that is within my mind whereas I do not know what is within Yours. You, indeed You, know fully all that is beyond the reach of human perception.

مَا قُلْتُ لَهُمْ اِلَّا مَا اَمَرْتَنِيْ بِهٖ اَنِ اعْبُدُوا اللهَ رَبِّيْ وَرَبَّكُمْ وَكُنْتُ عَلَيْهِمْ شَهِيْدًا مَّا دُمْتُ فِيْهِمْ فَلَمَّا تَوَفَّيْتَنِيْ كُنْتَ اَنْتَ الرَّقِيْبَ عَلَيْهِمْ وَاَنْتَ عَلٰى كُلِّ شَيْءٍ شَهِيْدٌ

(5:117) I said to them nothing except what You commanded me, that is: 'Serve Allah, my Lord and your Lord.' I watched over them as long as I remained among them; and when You did recall me, then You

Yourself became the Watcher over them. Indeed, You are Witness over everything.

اِنْ تُعَذِّبْهُمْ فَاِنَّهُمْ عِبَادُكَ ۖ وَاِنْ تَغْفِرْ لَهُمْ فَاِنَّكَ اَنْتَ الْعَزِيْزُ الْحَكِيْمُ

(5:118) If You chastise them, they are Your servants; and if You forgive them, You are the All-Mighty, the All-Wise."

قَالَ اللّٰهُ هٰذَا يَوْمُ يَنْفَعُ الصّٰدِقِيْنَ صِدْقُهُمْ لَهُمْ جَنّٰتٌ تَجْرِىْ مِنْ تَحْتِهَا الْاَنْهٰرُ خٰلِدِيْنَ فِيْهَا اَبَدًا رَضِىَ اللّٰهُ عَنْهُمْ وَرَضُوْا عَنْهُ ذٰلِكَ الْفَوْزُ الْعَظِيْمُ

(5:119) Thereupon Allah will say: "This day truthfulness shall profit the truthful. For them are Gardens beneath which rivers flow. There they will abide forever. Allah is well-pleased with them, and they are well-pleased with Allah. That indeed is the mighty triumph.'

لِلّٰهِ مُلْكُ السَّمٰوٰتِ وَالْاَرْضِ وَمَا فِيْهِنَّ وَهُوَ عَلٰى كُلِّ شَيْءٍ قَدِيْرٌ

(5:120) To Allah belongs the dominion of the heavens and the earth and all that is in them and He has full power over everything.

Consequences of a Confused OS

This deviation has confused the information system (the consistent logic for life) for a large number of generations, until cognitive dissonance[13] has become an evident psychological challenge. *Source: "When Prophecy Fails and Faith Persists: A Theoretical Overview" (Dawson, Lorne L. (October 1999). Nova Religio: The Journal of Alternative and Emergent Religions. Berkeley: University of California Press.*

The confusion directly affects their mental capacity (psychic energy),

---

[13] In the field of psychology, cognitive dissonance is the perception of contradictory information. Relevant items of information include a person's actions, feelings, ideas, beliefs, and values, and things in the environment. Cognitive dissonance is typically experienced as psychological stress when persons participate in an action that goes against one or more of those things. According to this theory, when two actions or ideas are not psychologically consistent with each other, people do all in their power to change them until they become consistent. The discomfort is triggered by the person's belief clashing with new information perceived, wherein the individual tries to find a way to resolve the contradiction to reduce his or her discomfort.

they live under constant subtle consuming mental conflict, vulnerable for easy stress, shame or anger and lack of self-confidence. *Source: What Is Cognitive Dissonance? By Kendra Cherry on July 02, 2020, reviewed by Steven Gans, MD*

They have no sound logic to absorb the changes in life (there is no firewall). They already have an operating system but they can't navigate life appropriately, which adds more confusion and turmoil. To overcome this cognitive dissonance, they either leave Christianity or put it on hold. *Source: Pew Research Center, May 29, 2018, "Being Christian in Western Europe"*

So, the confusion primarily makes them vulnerable to stress and insecurity. Moreover, it gives room for a wide range of hypocrisy and subtle corruption. *Source: The Scandal of the Evangelical Conscience (Baker Books, 2005)*

In Western Europe, belief in God with absolute certainty is relatively uncommon

% who say they ...

	Believe in God, absolutely certain	Believe in God, fairly certain	Believe in God, less certain	Do not believe in God
Portugal	44%	31%	7%	13%
Italy	26	37	9	21
Spain	25	27	11	31
Ireland	24	33	11	26
Finland	23	26	8	37
Norway	19	19	11	47
Denmark	15	24	12	46
Netherlands	15	19	9	53
Sweden	14	15	7	60
Austria	13	41	12	29
Belgium	13	20	9	54
United Kingdom	12	30	15	36
France	11	31	14	37
Switzerland	11	38	13	33
Germany	10	37	13	36
MEDIAN	**15**	**30**	**11**	**36**

Note: This question was not asked of Muslim respondents; figures shown are the percentage of all non-Muslims who give each response. Pew Research Center's previous field testing of questions about belief in God in predominantly Muslim countries and those with large Muslim populations found these questions tend to cause offense and prompt interview break-offs among Muslim respondents. Don't know/refused responses about belief in God or certainty of belief not shown.
Source: Survey conducted April-August 2017 in 15 countries. See Methodology for details.
"Being Christian in Western Europe"

Majority of Christians believe in God, but few do among the unaffiliated

% who say they believe in God among ...

	General population	Christians	Religiously unaffiliated
Portugal	83%	93%	30%
Italy	73	85	9
Ireland	69	79	14
Austria	67	79	6
Spain	64	86	17
Switzerland	62	79	5
Germany	60	79	4
Finland	58	68	20
United Kingdom	58	76	4
France	56	77	9
Denmark	51	68	14
Norway	49	79	13
Netherlands	44	78	13
Belgium	42	63	12
Sweden	36	59	7
MEDIAN	**58**	**79**	**12**

Note: This question was not asked of Muslim respondents; general population figures shown are the percentage of all non-Muslims who believe in God. Pew Research Center's previous field testing of questions about belief in God in predominantly Muslim countries and those with large Muslim populations found these questions tend to cause offense and prompt interview break-offs among Muslim respondents.
Source: Survey conducted April-August 2017 in 15 countries. See Methodology for details.
"Being Christian in Western Europe"

Most people believe in a higher power, but often not God as described in the Bible

% who ...

	Believe in God as described in the Bible	Believe in other higher power or spiritual force	Do not believe in any higher power
Italy	46%	27%	15%
Ireland	39	35	18
Portugal	36	46	9
Austria	32	40	19
Switzerland	30	36	25
UK	29	35	27
Germany	28	38	26
France	27	33	27
Finland	24	45	24
Spain	22	48	20
Netherlands	20	42	34
Norway	20	38	33
Denmark	17	48	29
Belgium	14	41	39
Sweden	14	37	41
MEDIAN	**27**	**38**	**26**

Note: These questions were not asked of Muslim respondents; figures shown are the percentage of all non-Muslims who give each response. Don't know/refused/other/both/neither/depends responses not shown.
Source: Survey conducted April-August 2017 in 15 countries. See Methodology for details.
"Being Christian in Western Europe"

The Logic of Islam Resets the Cognitive Confusion

1. God made it clear that He is one, and has no companions.

بِسْمِ اللهِ الرَّحْمٰنِ الرَّحِيْمِ
قُلْ هُوَ اللّهُ اَحَدٌ ۚ

(112:1) Say: "He is Allah, the One and Unique;

اَللّهُ الصَّمَدُ ۚ

(112:2) Allah, Who is in need of none and of Whom all are in need;

لَمْ يَلِدْ ۙ وَلَمْ يُوْلَدْ ۙ

(112:3) He neither begot any nor was He begotten,

وَلَمْ يَكُنْ لَّهٗ كُفُوًا اَحَد

(112:4) and none is comparable to Him.

2. He will not show Himself to anyone.

لَا تُدْرِكُهُ الْاَبْصَارُ وَهُوَ يُدْرِكُ الْاَبْصَارَ ۚ وَهُوَ اللَّطِيْفُ الْخَبِيْرُ

(6:103) No visual perception can encompass Him, even though He encompasses all visual perception. He is the All-Subtle, the All-Aware.

3. He is closer to everyone far more than we can imagine.

وَلَقَدْ خَلَقْنَا الْاِنْسَانَ وَنَعْلَمُ مَا تُوَسْوِسُ بِهٖ نَفْسُهٗ ۖ وَنَحْنُ اَقْرَبُ اِلَيْهِ مِنْ حَبْلِ الْوَرِيْد

(50:16) Surely We have created man, and We know the promptings of his heart, and We are nearer to him than even his jugular vein.

4. Heaven is not for granted. Each of us will be questioned and held responsible for his work before God. This is a matter of

balancing good and bad deeds that determine one's destiny in heaven or hell.

وَنَضَعُ الْمَوَازِينَ الْقِسْطَ لِيَوْمِ الْقِيٰمَةِ فَلَا تُظْلَمُ نَفْسٌ شَيْئًا ۗ وَاِنْ كَانَ مِثْقَالَ حَبَّةٍ مِّنْ خَرْدَلٍ اَتَيْنَا بِهَا ۗ وَكَفٰى بِنَا حٰسِبِيْنَ

(21:47) We shall set up just scales on the Day of Resurrection so that none will be wronged in the least. (We shall bring forth the acts of everyone), even if it be the weight of a grain of mustard seed. We shall suffice as Reckoners.[14]

5.   The relationship between man and God in this life will be based on education from the beginning to the end, and God is the main source of human education (OS).

اِقْرَاْ بِاسْمِ رَبِّكَ الَّذِيْ خَلَقَ

(96:1) Recite in the name of your Lord Who created,

خَلَقَ الْاِنْسَانَ مِنْ عَلَقٍ

(96:2) created man from a clot of congealed blood.

اِقْرَاْ وَرَبُّكَ الْاَكْرَمُ

(96:3) Recite: and your Lord is Most Generous,

الَّذِيْ عَلَّمَ بِالْقَلَمِ

(96:4) Who taught by the pen,

عَلَّمَ الْاِنْسَانَ مَا لَمْ يَعْلَمْ

(96:5) taught man what he did not know.

6.   The miracle of the Prophet Muhammad, may God bless him

---

[14] It is difficult for us to understand the exact nature of the balance. Anyhow, it is clear that the balance will weigh accurately all the human moral deeds instead of material things and will help judge whether a man is virtuous or wicked and how much. The Qur'an has used this word to make mankind understand that every deed, good or bad, will be weighed and judged according to merit.

and grant him peace, was a book! The Noble Qur'an, the word of God, the last and everlasting teaching of God to mankind on earth. (So that you have the latest OS update and stay with it).

إِنَّا سَنُلْقِىۡ عَلَيْكَ قَوْلًا ثَقِيْلًا

(73:5) Behold, We shall cast upon you a Weighty Word.[15]

7. The Prophet Muhammad, peace upon him, is the last Messenger and there will be no further update after him.

مَا كَانَ مُحَمَّدٌ اَبَآ اَحَدٍ مِّنْ رِّجَالِكُمْ وَلٰكِنْ رَّسُوْلَ اللهِ وَخَاتَمَ النَّبِيّٖنَ ۖ وَكَانَ اللهُ بِكُلِّ شَىْءٍ عَلِيْمًا

(33:40) Muhammad is not the father of any of your men, but he is the Messenger of Allah and the seal of the Prophets. Allah has full knowledge of everything.

8. The Qur'an will remain protected by God.

إِنَّا نَحْنُ نَزَّلْنَا الذِّكْرَ وَاِنَّا لَهٗ لَحٰفِظُوْنَ

(15:9) As for the Admonition, indeed it is We Who have revealed it and it is indeed We Who are its guardians.[16]

---

[15] The Qur'an has been called a weighty word for the reason that acting on its commands, demonstrating its teaching practically, extending its invitation in the face of the whole world, and bringing about a revolution in the entire system of belief and thought, morals and manners, civilization and social life, according to it, is indeed the weightiest task any human being ever has been charged with. It has also been called a weighty word because bearing the burden of its revelation was a difficult and heavy duty.

[16] The Qur'an is God's word and He is preserving it. Therefore, you can do no harm to it, nor can you discredit it by any ridicules, taunts and objections, nor can anyone hamper its progress. Whatever they may do against it, no one will ever be able to change or tamper with it.

CHAPTER 9

Why Islam Is a Miraculous Human OS?

The Prerequisites of Making Islam's Cognitive Miracle

What happened 2000 years ago, as a result of the previous OS's cognitive dissonance, was a profound cognitive setback for humanity. As much as this setback was profound, as much it needed a proper and powerful restoration, and this was Islam. There were two basics criteria that Islam had to take into account to fulfill these requirements.

Islam came to be the final one, and the conclusion of the previous religions. It came to satisfy all coming events and to update the future of humanity. This led to the transformation in the miracle aspect of the prophets.

In the beginning the miracle was an identifying code for the Prophet himself, who needed to prove himself as a Messenger of God so that people would accept the guidance of God (the updated OS). But earlier the miracle itself stayed independent from religion. This doesn't apply to Islam and the prophet Muhammad, peace be upon him. In Islam the miracle became integral part from the message up to that Islam itself became the miracle. When I say Islam, this includes the Quran (The book) and the Prophet, peace upon him (Sunnah teaching). So, what is in the book for it to be a miracle?

The Miracle of Being a Book!

As a matter of fact, no one so far in all the history of humanity, including all the Prophets and the most genius people in the world, in the past and the future would have ever thought of proclaiming that a book could be a miracle! But God did send a book to be a miracle.

ذَٰلِكَ الْكِتَابُ لَا رَيْبَ ۛ فِيهِ ۛ هُدًى لِّلْمُتَّقِينَ

(2:2) This is the Book of Allah, there is no doubt in it; it is a guidance

122

for the pious,[17]

Before asking what in this book makes it a miracle, please stop for a while and ponder the definition of miracle. You will find that the fact that a book in itself is a miracle is in itself a miracle. This fact is miraculous because it disrupts the concept and nature of a miracle ("an exceptional and welcome event that cannot be explained by the laws of nature or science").

You should stop here for a while and read the paragraph above again. Ask yourself how a book can be a miracle! Does the miracle have to be supernatural? My answer to you is that this is the fact that makes it a miracle. It is not what you would expect, but it is still a miracle, and that is what makes it a miracle. You may need to keep repeating this until your brain can get a hold of it. It's so obvious that you can't get it the first time, which is incredible! Even the majority of Muslims can't see it as such and just jump straight inside the book to see why it's a miracle!

Why Does It Make Sense for The Miracle to Be a Book!

Our mind cannot verify the source or accuracy of new information on its own (which is why we are slaves), so we need a verification code to trust a source or a reference. And to accept any new instructions from any messenger, they have to show a miracle (ID code), so that we feel

---

[17] One obvious meaning of this verse is that this Book, the Qur'an, is undoubtedly from God. Nothing contained in it can be subject to doubt. Books which deal with supernatural questions, with matters that lie beyond the range of sense perception, are invariably based on conjecture and their authors, despite their brave show of competence, are therefore not immune from a degree of skepticism regarding their statements. This Book, which is based wholly on Truth, a Book which is the work of none other than the All-Knowing God Himself is distinguishable from all other books. Hence, there is no room for doubt about its contents despite the hesitation some people might express either through ignorance or folly.

comfortable and ready to accept the new message (updated OS version).

Now if everyone regardless of their religion (OS) asks themselves have we seen our messenger's miracle (ID), the answer will be no. It is impossible for us to have direct access to the miracle anymore? Can it be replicated or retrieved? How can we then trust it anymore, why is it not biased by time?

This logic is true for any kind of religion except for Islam and a Muslim who has accepted Islam. If you ask a Muslim can you verify the miracle of your Prophet, he will say yes straight away. "I can't see the Prophet anymore, but I can see, read and verify his miracle!"

This makes perfect sense! He is the last Prophet, and anyone on this planet can verify his identity before, now and in the future. This makes the verification of the miracle possible in any place and time. The fact that the miracle is a book gave it a completely new nature than any other prophets' miracle; it has gained spatial and temporal qualities!

وَمَآ اَرْسَلْنٰكَ اِلَّا رَحْمَةً لِّلْعٰلَمِيْن

(21:107) We have sent you forth as nothing but mercy to people of the whole world.

Now I Am Amazed!

There is another thing to ponder on. The miracle came in the past as a natural supernatural phenomenon, and it should be from the same nature of what people excelled in at the time. This way they could understand the miracle, but it still challenged them.

What is the nature of human excellence now? Education, science, knowledge, innovation, technology, information technology, artificial intelligence, you name it. And if you ask what is really in common between all of these, you will find that all of them are the outcome of the development of human cognition.

Islam's challenge to humanity as a miracle is that it challenges any comprehensive education, welfare system, or any human development system on earth to develop the human cognition capabilities as it does! Islam teaching is going deep to teach us how to feel, think, dream and behave like humans.

The cognitive miracles of Islam are based on two main aspects: The Noble Qur'an (teachings of God), and the comprehensive explanation and guidance (Sunnah) of the Prophet, may God bless him and grant him peace. They should be applied to develop human cognition at any age, and regardless of the gender, race and background. The application is possible anywhere, in any conditions, by any language, and at any time, within any given time, even in a minute!

How Do We Understand the Miracle?

The exact answer is that we don't have the capabilities as humans to get around the miracle and fully understand it. Our understanding is limited by our level of knowledge and development. The answer depends on the time at which this question is asked. For example, are we talking in the Middle Ages, the seventies or now?

God made the knowledge in the Quran endless; it has the capability to be an everlasting source for new knowledge. Quran's text, the words of God, has attained the essence of God. It attains us but we can't attain anything of His knowledge without His permission.

اللهُ لَا إِلٰهَ إِلَّا هُوَ الْحَيُّ الْقَيُّومُ ۚ لَا تَأْخُذُهُ سِنَةٌ وَّلَا نَوْمٌ ۚ لَهُ مَا فِى السَّمٰوٰتِ وَمَا فِى الْأَرْضِ ۗ مَنْ ذَا الَّذِى يَشْفَعُ عِنْدَهُ إِلَّا بِإِذْنِهٖ ۚ يَعْلَمُ مَا بَيْنَ اَيْدِيْهِمْ وَمَا خَلْفَهُمْ ۚ وَلَا يُحِيْطُوْنَ بِشَيْءٍ مِّنْ عِلْمِهٖ إِلَّا بِمَا شَاۤءَ وَسِعَ كُرْسِيُّهُ السَّمٰوٰتِ وَالْأَرْضَ ۚ وَلَا يَـُٔوْدُهُ حِفْظُهُمَا ۚ وَ هُوَ الْعَلِىُّ الْعَظِيْمُ

(2:255) Allah, the Ever-Living, the Self-Subsisting by Whom all subsist, there is no god but He. Neither slumber seizes Him, nor sleep; to Him belongs all that is in the heavens and all that is in the earth. Who is there who might intercede with Him save with His leave? He knows what lies before them and what is hidden from them, whereas they cannot attain to anything of His knowledge save what He wills them to attain. His Dominion overspreads the heavens and the earth, and their upholding wearies Him not. He is All-High, All-Glorious.[18]

The Qur'an reveals itself according to our current level and needs in any particular time of the age of humanity. This means that the miracle is endless and includes self-updating.

Feeling Like It's a Mystery

The immersive list of miracles discovered so far, includes but is not limited to two main categories: solid science facts in various fields such as medicine, astrology, physics, biology, history, etc. (*Reference: There Is No Clash: Clare Forestier, BBC reporter, will take us on a journey of bridging theology with modern science.*) and the linguistic ones.

The list is long, and that is why if you ask a Muslim what are the miracles in the Qur'an he will want to know which category of miracles you are interested in. After that, he will begin to share with you the different types of miracles from that particular category.

The mysterious impression that you get about the miracles of Islam, stems from the feelings you get, when you keep continuously

---

[18] It is pointed out that no one possesses the knowledge that would enable him to comprehend the order of the universe and the considerations underlying it, so no one can legitimately interfere in its governance. The knowledge of human beings, of jinn, of angels and of all other creatures is limited and imperfect. No one's knowledge embraces all the facts of the universe. If someone did have the right to interfere even in only a part of the universe, and if his suggestions were of necessity to be put into effect, the entire order of the universe would be disrupted. Creatures are incapable of understanding what is best for them, and do not have the capacity to know how best the universe should be governed. It is God alone Who knows everything.

discovering them as if there were a box within a box, and within this box yet another box, and so on! The same way unfolds the mysteries in the human body, and in the universe its secrets.

What is in it For You?

So far you have gotten to know about the psychological pressure of the New Trinity, the slave nature of the human mind and the logic of the religion (Human OS including the logic of the latest update, Islam) to protect the mind from slavehood to anything else. Now you can get out from the trap of the New Trinity.

Currently you are in a maze with no way out. The dynamic of the New Trinity has made it so that you can't see it or even think about it. Either you work for it and just take it as it is or end your life for one reason or another, that is the direct meaning of being a slave.

Conventional psychologists can't help themselves or you. You may have been trying this way before, did it help? It may seem impossible to find a way out. The impossible mission to survive the dominant pressure of the New Trinity needs an exceptional approach that has been proven to be effective, which can actually be trusted and works.

True, there's a way out, and it's been there the whole time but you have never really thought about it. Now is the time to reveal the cognitive and psychological miracle, Islam's balance, combining the simple and the impossible. I have called it Islamophilia because when I bring it up, you'll love it!

إِنَّ الَّذِينَ قَالُوا رَبُّنَا اللهُ ثُمَّ اسْتَقَامُوا فَلَا خَوْفٌ عَلَيْهِمْ وَلَا هُمْ يَحْزَنُونَ

(46:13) Surely those who said: "Our Lord is Allah" and then remained steadfast shall have nothing to fear nor to grieve.

What To Expect In Part II

If you are excited to learn more, in part II I will explain the framework and hallmark for all miracles, including the cognitive and the psychological miracle, and the application on yourself to face the New Trinity. Finally, you will get to know how it can be applied on a larger scale, to at least mitigate the whole mechanism of the New Trinity in the world.

Part II

Islamophilia: Islam Miracles and Its Compatibility with Our Psycho-Cognitive Harmony

CHAPTER 10

Islamophilia 1

The Human Brain & The Harmony

Who is The Boss?

Who is your boss? Who breathes down your neck 24/7? Why should you carry him on your shoulders from birth to death?

You might see your boss dull as a watermelon! But when you get a close-up, you might want to yell: "You're nuts!" and then almost simultaneously: "You're one smart cookie!" You might wonder if your boss actually knows all the angles until you realize yes but it is relative. If you were to have an extraordinary microscopic eye, you would understand that a balance as big as the universe is available!

The Scale of Balance

You may have figured it out! Yes, I was talking about our brains. Have you ever noticed that the two hemispheres of our brain are attached to each other by a bridge called the corpus callosum? If you consider this fact does our brain now look like a real scale? And the second thing to contemplate is why should it be two hemispheres, and not just one sphere?

God has created the brain to be the basic foundation of life, and its primary function is to sustain life by creating balance within our bodies and outside in the universe.

وَالسَّمَآءَ رَفَعَهَا وَوَضَعَ الْمِيزَانُ

(55:7) and He has raised up the heaven and has set a balance.

أَلَّا تَطْغَوْا فِى الْمِيزَانِ

(55:8) that you may not transgress in the balance,[19]

Otherwise, things will start to shake, not only in our personal lives but in the entire universe (e.g., climate change)!

Balance is God's Word

When God speaks, He doesn't need to use words or metaphors. God is creating by His word, creations speak His words!

$$\text{اِنَّ مَثَلَ عِيْسٰى عِنْدَ اللهِ كَمَثَلِ اٰدَمَّ خَلَقَهٗ مِنْ تُرَابٍ ثُمَّ قَالَ لَهٗ كُنْ فَيَكُوْنِ}$$

(3:59) Surely, in the sight of Allah, the similitude of the creation of Jesus is as the creation of Adam whom He created out of dust, and then said: 'Be', and he was.

It was not a coincidence that God created our brains to maintain balance, but also made them appear blatant as a scale and in the microscopic picture they look similar to the universe. *Source: Universetoday, Space and astronomy news, November 28, 2020 by Matthew Cimone*

---

[19] Almost all the commentators have interpreted mizan (balance) to mean justice, and "set the balance" to imply that Allah has established the entire system of the universe on justice. Had there been no harmony and balance and justice established among the countless stars and planets moving in space, and the mighty forces working in this universe, and the innumerable creatures and things found here, this life on earth would not have functioned even for a moment. Look at the creatures existing in the air and water and on land for millions and millions of years on this earth. They continue to exist only because full justice and balance has been established in the means and factors conducive to life; in case there occurs a slight imbalance of any kind, every tract of life would become extinct.

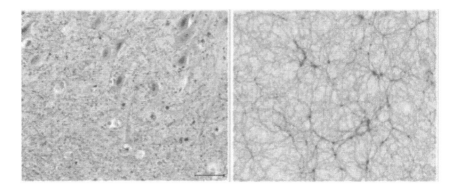

One of these pictures is the brain, and the other one is the universe. Can you tell which is which?

This is subtle confirmation that we have no other alternative in this life except seeking and maintaining balance.

Brains Are Also for What We Can't See!

Now you have to ask yourself, why this design? Why didn't He initially give us an automated life balance, and we just enjoy it?

In fact, He has embodied this function in nature (natural equilibrium), this is what we call the natural balance[20] of physics, biology, chemistry, etc.! Indeed, our brains are not limited to maintaining the balance in physical nature, but more importantly to maintain the balance between this entire nature (the universe) and beyond it (the metaverse). God emphasizes the balance between the visible (this life, dunya) and the invisible (the afterlife, the hereafter) so that we may understand

---

[20] The balance of nature (also known as ecological balance) is a theory that proposes that ecological systems are usually in a stable equilibrium or homeostasis, which is to say that a small change (the size of a particular population, for example) will be corrected by some negative feedback that will bring the parameter back to its original "point of balance" with the rest of the system.

ourselves, God and our relationship with Him!

سَنُرِيهِمْ اٰيٰتِنَا فِى الْاٰفَاقِ وَفِىٓ اَنْفُسِهِمْ حَتّٰى يَتَبَيَّنَ لَهُمْ اَنَّهُ الْحَقُّ اَوَلَمْ يَكْفِ بِرَبِّكَ اَنَّهُ عَلٰى كُلِّ شَىْءٍ شَهِيدٌ

(41:53) Soon shall We show them Our Signs on the horizons and in their own beings until it becomes clear to them that it is the Truth. Is it not enough that your Lord is a witness over everything?[21]

Our Brain Functions Are Harmonized

Our knowledge of the human brain is still limited and evolving every day, but what we know so far is enough to make us understand its physiology of harmony. Just as balance is embodied in the shape of the brain, harmony is also embodied in its functional design. Our cognitive functions have two distinctive natures, divided across the two hemispheres as follows:

---

[21] Allah will show the people in the external world around them as well as in their own selves such signs that will manifest the teachings of the Quran being the very truth.

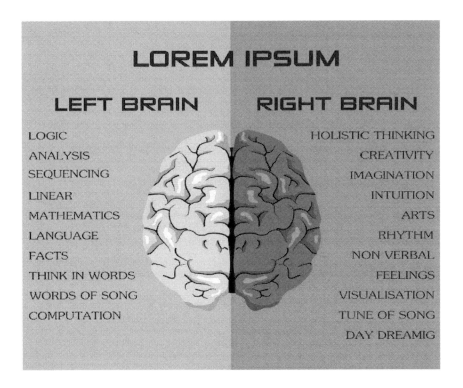

Right: Abstruse, holistic, intuitive, imaginative, creative, emotional and social functions. More or less, it is dealing with esoteric, invisible, and metaphysical subjects, which are collectively called functions of the metaverse!

On the left: Specific, tangible, sensory, pragmatic, objective, physical functions. More or less, it is dealing with visible, conscious, physical objects, which are collectively called functions of the universe! *Source: Anatomy of the Brain, myfiledclinic.com*

The Brain is In Action for Harmony

The corpus callosum is the fiber cables that coordinate the balance between these two different sets of functions. It carries the communication between the holistic information on the right side and the tangible one of the left side. In general, any brain task must be carried out through the cooperation of these two hemispheres. They must exchange information and make optimization between the holistic and the concrete to achieve the best possible execution of any given task.

The process of optimization is the harmonization (balancing) of different variables. The best result is a feeling of satisfaction, signs of success are harmony and peace of mind, without stress!

Coordination between the two hemispheres is the key to avoid stressful life. This is possible under circumstances in which both sides have a comprehensive set of rules to make judgment and the ability to understand the task (problem) and the options for finding a solution. This ability is highly dependent on the quality of education and training provided to us during our lifetime!

وَفِىٓ اَنْفُسِكُمْ اَفَلَا تُبْصِرُونَ

(51:21) and also in your own selves. Do you not see?[22]

Who Can Guarantee a Stress-free Life?

In line with the previous sections, we can conclude that a person's stress level depends on their ability to use their education to balance the seen and unseen information. Whenever we have balanced

---

[22] A wonderful brain has been placed under your skull. Its complicated layers are filled with an invaluable wealth of intellect, thought, imagination, consciousness, discrimination, will, memory, desire, feeling and emotions, inclinations and trends, and other mental abilities. You have been provided with numerous means of knowledge that supply you with every kind of information through the eyes, nose, ears and skin. You have been given the tongue and the power of speech by which you can express your thoughts and feelings. And then your psyche has been placed as a ruler over the entire kingdom of your body so that it may employ all the powers and abilities and form opinions. It is to decide in what ways you have to spend and employ your time, labor and efforts, what you have to reject and what you have to accept, what should be your objective in life and what you should shun and avoid.

knowledge of the uni- and metaverses, we will live a peaceful life. Especially if this teaching comes exclusively from the Creator Himself.

Many coaches or psychologists state that they can provide you with a service for body-mind balance, or a formula for work-life harmony! Have any of them given you a guarantee that you will live a stress-free life? But the One who created you and your mind to function in this way has given this guarantee. This is a guarantee that He has given since the first moment for the first human, Adam, and it is still valid for you! Maybe you remember scene #9 in one of the earlier chapters.

قُلْنَا اهْبِطُوا مِنْهَا جَمِيعًا ۖ فَإِمَّا يَأْتِيَنَّكُمْ مِنِّي هُدًى فَمَنْ تَبِعَ هُدَايَ فَلَا خَوْفٌ عَلَيْهِمْ وَلَا هُمْ يَحْزَنُونَ

(2:38) We said: "Get you down from here, all of you, and guidance shall come to you from Me: then, whoever will follow My guidance need have no fear, nor shall they grieve.

The Challenge

The truth is that finding a comprehensive and simple education that matches the evolving harmony in the structure and functions of our brains is almost impossible. No welfare system can afford this education, but Islamophilia education, the cognitive and psychological miracle of Islam, can do that! Allah is challenging all human experts, scholars and psychologists to bring up a similar book like the Qur'an. Even if they come forth as individuals, groups or even collectives using any computational technology, AI or even Jinns, they still can't withstand this challenge.

قُلْ لَئِنِ اجْتَمَعَتِ الْإِنْسُ وَالْجِنُّ عَلَى أَنْ يَأْتُوا بِمِثْلِ هٰذَا الْقُرْآنِ لَا يَأْتُونَ بِمِثْلِهِ وَلَوْ كَانَ بَعْضُهُمْ لِبَعْضٍ ظَهِيرًا

(17:88) Say: "Surely, if mankind and jinn were to get together to produce the like of this Qur'an, they will never be able to produce the like of it, howsoever they might help one another."[23]

Solid Antistress Guarantee

The guarantee goes to such an extent that God will require us to be stable no matter what is happening around us whether it is good or bad. It is necessary to carry on in balance between feelings and thoughts, remain in harmony and peace, detached from the changing and unpredictable environment.

The approach that unlocks our potential to achieve this level of harmony, is to face all the sources of fear without fear! This guarantee is conditional to go through God's training patiently, exactly as God planned.

وَلَنَبْلُوَنَّكُمْ بِشَيْءٍ مِّنَ الْخَوْفِ وَالْجُوْعِ وَنَقْصٍ مِّنَ الْأَمْوَالِ وَالْأَنْفُسِ وَالثَّمَرٰتِ ۖ وَبَشِّرِ الصّٰبِرِيْنَ

(2:155) We shall certainly test you by afflicting you with fear, hunger, loss of properties and lives and fruits. Give glad tidings, then, to those who remain patient;

الَّذِيْنَ إِذَآ أَصَابَتْهُمْ مُّصِيْبَةٌ ۙ قَالُوْآ إِنَّا لِلّٰهِ وَإِنَّآ إِلَيْهِ رٰجِعُوْنَ

(2:156) those who when any affliction smites them, they say: "Verily, we belong to Allah, and it is to Him that we are destined to return."

أُولٰٓئِكَ عَلَيْهِمْ صَلَوٰتٌ مِّنْ رَّبِّهِمْ وَرَحْمَةٌ ۖ وَأُولٰٓئِكَ هُمُ الْمُهْتَدُوْنَ

(2:157) Upon them will be the blessings and mercy of their Lord, and

---

[23] This challenge occurs at several other places in the Quran: (Surah Al-Baqarah, Ayat 23); (Surah Younus, Ayats 38-39); (Surah Al-Momin, Ayats 13-14); (Surah At-Toor, Ayats 33-34). At all these places, this has been cited as an answer to the charge of the disbelievers that Muhammad (peace be upon him) has himself invented the Quran but is presenting it as Allah's Word.

it is they who are rightly guided.[24]

The Guarantee Is Verified

Now you may understand, how it comes that in some Muslim countries, where one may be under very difficult economic, social and political circumstances, the people answer immediately *Al hamd la Allah* (Praise be to God) when you ask anyone how are you doing. That person, who just said it, might be a visually impaired (blind) family man who has five kids that he educates. He may work all day selling some sweet potatoes and still think there are some poorer people than him and that he needs to help them. He is completely assured that he is rich, satisfied in this world, and looking forward to the hereafter.

لِلْفُقَرَآءِ الَّذِيْنَ أُحْصِرُوْا فِىْ سَبِيْلِ اللهِ لَا يَسْتَطِيْعُوْنَ ضَرْبًا فِى الْأَرْضِ يَحْسَبُهُمُ الْجَاهِلُ اَغْنِيَآءَ مِنَ التَّعَفُّفِ تَعْرِفُهُمْ بِسِيْمٰهُمْ لَا يَسْـَٔلُوْنَ النَّاسَ اِلْحَافًا ۗ وَمَا تُنْفِقُوْا مِنْ خَيْرٍ فَاِنَّ اللهَ بِهٖ عَلِيْمٌ

(2:273) Those needy ones who are wholly wrapped up in the cause of Allah, and who are hindered from moving about the earth in search of their livelihood, especially deserve help. He who is unaware of their circumstances supposes them to be wealthy because of their dignified bearing, but you will know them by their countenance, although they do not go about begging of people with importunity. Whatever wealth

---

[24] Saying this does not signify the mere making of a statement. It means a statement which is accompanied by a deep conviction in one's heart: 'To Allah do we belong.' This being so, a man is bound to think that whatever has been sacrificed for God has in fact attained its legitimate end, for it has been spent in the way of the One to whom all things truly belong.

'And it is to Him that we are destined to return' refers to the fact that man will not stay forever in this world and will return, sooner or later, to God. And if man is indeed destined to return to God why should he not return to Him having spent his all, having staked his life for His sake? This alternative is preferable to the pursuit of self-aggrandizement and then meeting death either by sickness or accident.

you spend on helping them, Allah will know of it.[25]

Safety Rope

The blind man understands that the light in his heart is lightening up all his life. He will never get lost, whatsoever is in the darkness. He has a rope in his hand all the time as he navigates the stormy life. The rope is there for him but not for hanging himself. Not at all! It's a safety rope!

وَاعْتَصِمُوا بِحَبْلِ اللهِ جَمِيْعًا وَّلَا تَفَرَّقُوْا وَاذْكُرُوْا نِعْمَتَ اللهِ عَلَيْكُمْ اِذْ كُنْتُمْ اَعْدَاءً فَاَلَّفَ بَيْنَ قُلُوْبِكُمْ فَاَصْبَحْتُمْ بِنِعْمَتِهٖ اِخْوَانًا ۚ وَكُنْتُمْ عَلٰى شَفَا حُفْرَةٍ مِّنَ النَّارِ فَاَنْقَذَكُمْ مِّنْهَا ۗ كَذٰلِكَ يُبَيِّنُ اللهُ لَكُمْ اٰيٰتِهٖ لَعَلَّكُمْ تَهْتَدُوْنَ

(3:103) Hold fast together to the cable of Allah and be not divided. Remember the blessing that Allah bestowed upon you: you were once enemies then He brought your hearts together, so that through His blessing you became brothers. You stood on the brink of a pit of fire and He delivered you from it. Thus Allah makes His signs clear to you that you may be guided to the right way.[26]

---

[25] The people referred to here are those who, because they had dedicated themselves wholly to serving the religion of God, were unable to earn their livelihood. In the time of the Prophet there was a group of such volunteer workers, known as Ashab al-Suffah, consisting of about three or four hundred people who had forsaken their homes and gone to Madina. They remained at all times in the company of the Prophet, always at his beck and call to perform whatever service he required of them. They were dispatched by the Prophet on whatever expeditions he wished. Whenever there was nothing to do elsewhere, they stayed in Madina and devoted themselves to acquiring religious knowledge and imparting it to others. Since they were full-time workers and had no private resources to meet their needs, God pointed out to the Muslims that helping such people was the best way of 'spending in the way of Allah'.

[26] The expression 'cable of Allah', in this verse, refers to the 'religion of God'. The reason for use of the word 'cable' (habl) is that it both establishes a bond between man and God and joins all believers together. To take a firm hold on this cable means that the believers should attach profound importance to their religion: this should always be the centre of their concerns; they should continually strive to establish it; and the common desire to serve it should make them co-operate with each other.

Stress Is a Choice

God created the entire universe and our minds to work on the basis of harmony. He gave one way to achieve harmony (by following His guidance), so what about those who do not follow?

God knows that the non-follower will go to sleep everyday worried that they can't sleep! He knows they will try their best, they will turn every stone seeking internal harmony. They will try any option like yoga, body balance, aromatherapy, music, hugs, kisses and more, but nothing from the welfare state will give them the sweet dreams the blind man enjoys.

وَلَقَدْ خَلَقْنَا الْإِنْسَانَ وَنَعْلَمُ مَا تُوَسْوِسُ بِهِ نَفْسُهُ ۖ وَنَحْنُ أَقْرَبُ اِلَيْهِ مِنْ حَبْلِ الْوَرِيْدِ

(50:16) Surely We have created man, and We know the promptings of his heart, and We are nearer to him than even his jugular vein.[27]

وَمَنْ اَعْرَضَ عَنْ ذِكْرِئْ فَإِنَّ لَـهُ مَعِيْشَةً ضَنْكًا وَّنَحْشُرُهُ يَوْمَ الْقِيمَةِ اَعْمَى

(20:124) But whosoever turns away from this Admonition from Me shall have a straitened life; We shall raise him blind on the Day of Resurrection,"[28]

قَالَ رَبِّ لِمَ حَشَرْتَنِيْ اَعْمَى وَقَدْ كُنْتُ بَصِيْرًا

---

[27] That is, Our power and Our knowledge has so encompassed man from within and without that Our power and knowledge is closer to him than his own jugular-vein. We do not have to travel from a distance to hear what he says, but We directly know every thought that arises in his heart. Likewise, when We shall want to seize him, We will not have to seize him after covering a distance, for wherever he is, he is in Our grasp; and whenever We will, We will seize him.

[28] "A life of hardship" does not mean a life of poverty. It means that such a one shall be deprived of the peace of mind, even though he may be a millionaire or the ruler of a vast empire. For, the one who will turn away from the admonition will win all the worldly successes by unlawful means and, therefore, will always be suffering from pangs of a guilty conscience and deprived of the peace of mind and real happiness.

(20:125) where-upon he will say: "Lord! Why have You raised me blind when I had sight in the world?"

قَالَ كَذٰلِكَ اَتَتْكَ اٰيٰتُنَا فَنَسِيتَهَاۖ وَكَذٰلِكَ الْيَوْمَ تُنْسٰى

(20:126) He will say: "Even so it is. Our Signs came to you and you ignored them. So shall you be ignored this Day."

God says plainly that some people would remain in a constant state of stress trying to figure out where the harmony is. Indeed, this is not a punishment but a choice. They went against reality and wanted to live in delusion seeking the impossible. They wanted to blind their brains and preferred any story of life other than the truth. The responsibility of making this kind of choice is for sure scary. To decide on an eternal choice to stay blind seeking harmony, this is actually self-torture.

Misusing the Brain!

In fact, many are not using their brains effectively! If they were to listen to their honest reasoning, they would understand that they should not torture themselves by trying to find excuses not to submit to God. In the end, they tried to solve the problem by creating more problems. Instead of listening to their honest and intelligent mind (the key to finding harmony), they drink to switch it off! People switch it off because they figure that it is the source of problems!

اَفَلَمْ يَسِيرُوا فِى الْاَرْضِ فَتَكُونَ لَهُمْ قُلُوبٌ يَعْقِلُونَ بِهَآ اَوْ اٰذَانٌ يَّسْمَعُونَ بِهَاۚ فَاِنَّهَا لَا تَعْمَى الْاَبْصَارُ وَلٰكِنْ تَعْمَى الْقُلُوبُ الَّتِىْ فِى الصُّدُورِ

(22:46) Have they not journeyed in the land that their hearts might understand and their ears might listen? For indeed it is not the eyes that are blinded; it is rather the hearts in the breasts that are rendered blind.[29]

Brain Switching Off Without Drinking

If the reason behind switching off the brain is to silence the noise of our mind, this is possible also without drinking. If our minds are uncomfortable from contradiction, this is a healthy sign. It is natural to want to find harmony between the natures of the two hemispheres: the material and spiritual.

Instead of switching off the brain, we can use it a bit more to solve this conflict. The easiest way to find this solution is to listen to God. Although it will take a bit of effort to keep this balance in life, it is worth it.

Those who made up their minds in this life, and expressed their interest in peace, God will make their wish come true and make Heaven available to them. The best part of heaven is that there is no effort to create peace of mind. There is no need for brain hemispheres anymore. No need to think anymore, there is only harmony. No conflicts, arguments, nor jealousy. There are only wishes, and wishes come true.

ٱدۡخُلُوهَا بِسَلَٰمٍ ءَامِنِينَ

(15:46) They will be told: "Enter it in peace and security."

وَنَزَعۡنَا مَا فِى صُدُورِهِم مِّنۡ غِلٍّ إِخۡوَانًا عَلَىٰ سُرُرٍ مُّتَقَٰبِلِينَ

(15:47) And We shall purge their breasts of all traces of rancour; and they shall be seated on couches facing one another.

لَا يَمَسُّهُمۡ فِيهَا نَصَبٌ وَّمَا هُم مِّنۡهَا بِمُخۡرَجِينَ

(15:48) They shall face no fatigue in it, nor shall they ever be driven out of it.

---

[29] Since the heart is regarded as the center of emotions, feelings and of mental and moral qualities, these words have been used to imply that their obduracy has inhibited them from feeling and acting rationally.

Even the Dark Wishes Come True

The others who have chosen in this life to live in disharmony, agony, stress and suffering, and who have expressed their inner wish to create harmony in their own way, even if it is like Hell, God will also make their wish come true. They have decided to follow Satan, although this is an unfair choice for themselves but still the choice will be respected.

وَقَالَ الشَّيْطٰنُ لَمَّا قُضِىَ الْاَمْرُ اِنَّ اللهَ وَعَدَكُمْ وَعْدَ الْحَقِّ وَوَعَدْتُّكُمْ فَاَخْلَفْتُكُمْ وَمَا كَانَ لِىَ عَلَيْكُمْ مِّنْ سُلْطٰنٍ اِلَّا اَنْ دَعَوْتُكُمْ فَاسْتَجَبْتُمْ لِىْ فَلَا تَلُوْمُوْنِىْ وَلُوْمُوْا اَنْفُسَكُمْ مَاۤ اَنَا بِمُصْرِخِكُمْ وَمَاۤ اَنْتُمْ بِمُصْرِخِىَّ اِنِّىْ كَفَرْتُ بِمَاۤ اَشْرَكْتُمُوْنِ مِنْ قَبْلُ اِنَّ الظّٰلِمِيْنَ لَهُمْ عَذَابٌ اَلِيْمٌ

(14:22) After the matter has been finally decided Satan will say: "Surely whatever Allah promised you was true; as for me, I went back on the promise I made to you. I had no power over you except that I called you to my way and you responded to me. So, do not blame me but blame yourselves. Here, neither I can come to your rescue, nor can you come to mine. I disavow your former act of associating me in the past with Allah. A grievous chastisement inevitably lies ahead for such wrong-doers.

What is Next Then?

You have the mind, the stress and the harmony as well as the guarantee and the verification. The miracle, the Noble Qur'an, you can read, and God has promised to cure your mind as much as you can understand.

يٰۤاَيُّهَا النَّاسُ قَدْ جَاءَتْكُمْ مَّوْعِظَةٌ مِّنْ رَّبِّكُمْ وَشِفَاءٌ لِّمَا فِى الصُّدُوْرِ وَهُدًى وَّرَحْمَةٌ لِّلْمُؤْمِنِيْنَ

(10:57) Men! Now there has come to you an exhortation from your Lord, a healing for the ailments of the hearts, and a guidance and mercy for those who believe.

147

What is Missing Then?

In the next three chapters, I will show how God made the Qur'an in tune with our brains by having created harmony, and the basic cognitive learning to achieve it as well as lifelong practices to maintain it.

وَلَقَدْ يَسَّرْنَا الْقُرْآنَ لِلذِّكْرِ فَهَلْ مِنْ مُدَّكِرٍ

(54:22) We have made the Qur'an easy to derive lessons from. Is there, then, any who will take heed?

CHAPTER 11

Islamophilia 2

The Qur'an, The Brain, The Harmony

Our Psychological and Cognitive Requirements Are in Harmony with The Qur'an

The Holy Qur'an as such contains a message that belongs to all human beings, all generations. The honest truth about ourselves is the most important thing people want to know. Who we are, to whom we belong, why we are here and what we should do! These are the basic questions that need to be answered and have a direct impact on our mental health.

The most important thing is that the Qur'an must remain original and unchanged, even one letter can't be moved! Therefore, the answers will be reliable, without doubts and easy to understand for everyone. For some people the Qur'an should first challenge their minds.

Addressing these preconditions is based on the nature that God has built in our minds as a means of protection and well-being. Doubting information is the most important defense mechanism for finding the truth. It is the immune system of our information system, the natural firewall and antivirus in our brains!

God Responded in The Qur'an

God created our minds; He knows which things are first.

First eliminate the doubt:

When opening the Qur'an after Surat Al-Fatiha you will read in Surat Al-Baqarah that this book contains no doubt.

ذَٰلِكَ الْكِتَٰبُ لَا رَيْبَ ۛ فِيهِ ۛ هُدًى لِّلْمُتَّقِينَ

(2:2) This is the Book of Allah, there is no doubt in it; it is a guidance for the pious,

God gives you straight away an answer to the first and most persistent thought in your head: doubt, doubt, and doubt. Then He responded for the rest.

Then good news, it's easy and clear:

وَلَقَدْ يَسَّرْنَا الْقُرْآنَ لِلذِّكْرِ فَهَلْ مِنْ مُدَّكِرٍ

(54:22) We have made the Qur'an easy to derive lessons from. Is there, then, any who will take heed?

الۤرٰ تِلْكَ اٰيٰتُ الْكِتٰبِ وَقُرْاٰنٍ مُّبِيْنٍ

(15:1) Alif. Lam. Ra'. These are the verses of the Book, and a Clear Qur'an.

Next activate our intelligence by challenging the minds:

سَنُرِيْهِمْ اٰيٰتِنَا فِى الْاٰفَاقِ وَفِيْٓ اَنْفُسِهِمْ حَتّٰى يَتَبَيَّنَ لَهُمْ اَنَّهُ الْحَقُّ اَوَلَمْ يَكْفِ بِرَبِّكَ اَنَّهُ عَلٰى كُلِّ شَيْءٍ شَهِيْدٌ

(41:53) Soon shall We show them Our Signs on the horizons and in their own beings until it becomes clear to them that it is the Truth. Is it not enough that your Lord is a witness over everything?

Most importantly keeping the message original:

اِنَّا نَحْنُ نَزَّلْنَا الذِّكْرَ وَاِنَّا لَهُ لَحٰفِظُوْنَ

(15:9) As for the Admonition, indeed it is We Who have revealed it and it is indeed We Who are its guardians.[30]

It's not just words, this affirmation has also been embraced far beyond than you would imagine, as you will read soon.

---

[30] Therefore, you can do no harm to it, nor can you discredit it by your ridicules, taunts and objections, nor can you hamper its progress. Whatever you may do against it, no one will ever be able to change or tamper with it.

Keep in Mind

We are talking about the last word of God to man! This means that He is challenging our intelligence and He knows that we will get smarter by time. He knows you have gained more knowledge and have different problems as well as needs then the ones e.g., 1400 years ago!

When we bear in mind that we do not all have the same requirements to be ascertained, we find that some will need to be persuaded by reasoning and conclusions, and others will need persuasion through intuitive reasoning and emotional intelligence. Some will need both to figure things out.

This kind of care will not only be needed once, but throughout the entire book from the first verse until the last, and every time you read the book.

At any time, since the Qur'an was revealed, you will read it and you will have the experience of God speaking to you directly. Whoever you are and whatever you will be doing in life, when you read the Qur'an, God speaks to you using your knowledge and taking into consideration your life as if you were the only person in the universe.

لَوْ أَنْزَلْنَا هَٰذَا الْقُرْآنَ عَلَىٰ جَبَلٍ لَّرَأَيْتَهُ خَاشِعًا مُّتَصَدِّعًا مِّنْ خَشْيَةِ اللَّهِ ۚ وَتِلْكَ الْأَمْثَالُ نَضْرِبُهَا لِلنَّاسِ لَعَلَّهُمْ يَتَفَكَّرُونَ

(59:21) Had We sent down this Qur'an upon a mountain you would indeed have seen it humbling itself and breaking asunder out of fear of Allah. We propound such parables to people that they may reflect.

Every time we read the Qur'an, from birth until death, the experience continues to develop our relationship with the Creator. Bringing us closer, preparing us for the actual moment when it comes to meeting Him. We will understand what He is saying, regardless of our cognitive or psychological state. He is helping us to restore our balance and recharge our energy to be able fix our predicaments. This is the difference between the psychological healing or other scriptures and the Qur'an.

If you have experience in reading any scripture other than the Qur'an, please do not build your expectations on that now since this experience is completely different. You will get something similar to Adam's first experience when God made Adam a qualified and honored creature by teaching him by Himself. Only by this way Adam earned the honor and God commanded the angels to bow down to him.

Science and Harmony in The Qur'an

In the following sections, I will introduce in more detail some of the elements included in the harmony between the Qur'an and our mind to create balance. It will include all its aspects as a book i.e. language, methods, structure and ultimately the content. All these aspects are presented based on academic views on the cognitive and psychological interactions of the Qur'an with the human mind.

Arabic Is Speaking Right in Your Head

The Qur'an is in Arabic, for good reasons. God chose this particular language because of its effect on developing both brain hemispheres to facilitate our ability to create harmony during our lifetime. Indeed, it's the most convenient language for your brain, but no one just told you that. Most surprisingly, it doesn't have to be your native tongue, or you don't have to be a speaker of Arabic at any level!

First, We State the Obvious

Another reason is that Arabic is a reliable language, its roots and structure can withstand changes even over centuries. Arabic hasn't changed fundamentally in 1400 years. If Latin would still be around, it would be as impressive. By combining Arabic's constancy with its normalized, extendable morphology offers a glimpse into why Arabic's morphology reads like legal reasoning while other morphologies are historical, cultural, and linguistic mind-trips. This by the way is yet another assurance to put your doubts to bed!

Language Shapes the Way We Think

One more reason is that Arabic is the language that distinguishes itself from other languages because it stimulates both halves of the brain at the same time. There are other languages that stimulate the left side mainly, and to a lesser extent the right side, but not simultaneously and to the same degree as Arabic does![31] *Source: Al-Hamouri, Firas et al. "Brain dynamics of Arabic reading: a magnetoencephalographic study." Neuroreport vol. 16,16 (2005): 1861-4. doi:10.1097/01.wnr.0000185965.41959.87*

Language choice is a very important factor when developing a solid cogno-persuasion system for both human intelligence and computer linguistics. Lera Boroditsky is an assistant professor of psychology, neuroscience, and symbolic systems at Stanford University, and she looks at how the languages we speak shape the way we think.

Footnote

If you feel uncomfortable because God chose Arabic and an Arab to

---

[31] "Abstract: Arabic writing differs greatly from western scripts. To evaluate the influence of written Arabic on the pattern of language-related brain activation, a group of native Arab speakers and a control group of native Spanish speakers were scanned with magnetoencephalography during a reading task. In both groups, brain activity was strongly left lateralized during the time window between 200 and 500 ms after stimulus onset. During late latencies (beyond 500 ms), however, the right and the left hemispheres reached a similar activation level in the Arabic but not in the Spanish group. This suggests a time-dependent role of both hemispheres during Arabic language reading."

deliver the last message from Him, please ask yourself first: would you feel comfortable if you were born in the Middle East? Would you like Arabic to be your mother tongue? Would you like to be in my shoes writing this book for you? Would you like to be the one who is eager to tell the truth at all cost and ready to face whatever nasty comments you may have heard! Would you?

God knows you; He knows how you think and feel! That's why He chose other people to do the job on your behalf! He keeps you to do some other things you might feel more comfortable doing.

It's Not Only the Language but Also The Place for A Lifelong Mission!

Indeed, the Arabs were not supposed to have a privilege due to the language, but rather have the responsibility to spread the message of the last Messenger, at all times, to the whole world.

Islam began from the middle of the world, to spread in all directions. Arabs have to bear the burden of passing the message on to the entire world. They must deal with all kinds of freedom-controlling or brain-washing tyrants: the visible dictators of the past or the invisible systems of today. Carrying this responsibility is the exact meaning of Jihad, doing the effort to free other souls from the domination of other souls.

Jihad for Harmony

Nowadays, the Bogeymen are creating smarter reasons to control the Middle East. One smart trick that was carried out in the last 20 years, is to change the world's perception of jihad. A cleverly written and plotted story of jihad was created. It is actually the exact opposite of the truth, aiming first to dominate your psyche to make you terrified, and then dominate the Middle East.

Anyhow, since the leaders are busy at this moment, the Arab people must take responsibility to help you find the self-confidence to face all the doubts in your mind and the phobias in your heart. It's a lifelong mission, passed down from generation to generation, until the last day of life. I'm not sure if it's the kind of responsibility other nations are interested in!

The Qur'an Will Develop Your Brain Regardless of Your Mother Tongue

Now if you feel lucky that you were not born in the Middle East and don't speak Arabic, you will feel even more lucky for two other reasons!

Non-Arabic speakers still benefit from the influence of the Arabic language. If they only keep reading a small Surah (chapter) of the Qur'an for a few days, the effect will be tangible. Take these study results below as an example, how memorizing the Quran could significantly change the cognitive intelligence of children in a short time: "The cognitive intelligence score of children was 25.40 after the treatment. The score had an improvement of 5.00 then the pre-treatment test with a score of 20.40. The pre-treatment test resulted in 63.75% of improvement, while the post-treatment test resulted in 79.38%. The difference was 15.63%." *Source: Fairuzillah, Naufal & Listiana, Aan. (2021). The Positive Impact of Memorizing the Qur'an on Cognitive Intelligence of Children. 10.2991/assehr.k.210322.071.*

Every Muslim must memorize Surah Al-Fatihah as it is obligatory to recite it during the prayers that must take place five times a day. It is therefore recited in a total of seventeen rak'ahs daily which should be enough to capture the above-mentioned effect.

Like A Cherry

Have you ever felt that you are the cherry on the cake? This is a special and unique feeling. You will get it if you go to any mosque in your city or in the world, and you check who is there. Herein lies the surprise! Your first impression will be that it doesn't look as you expected but like a meeting room at the United Nations. You will find genuinely united hearts and minds sharing culture, knowledge and behavior. There is a feeling of being one family, as if they had lived together since birth! Those who speak Arabic as a mother tongue are a very small part of this family, or sometimes there are none at all. You will be welcomed in this family any time, and others are warmly smiling at you as if you are the most welcome person on earth.

وَأَلَّفَ بَيْنَ قُلُوبِهِمْ لَوْ أَنْفَقْتَ مَا فِى الْأَرْضِ جَمِيْعًا مَّا أَلَّفْتَ بَيْنَ قُلُوبِهِمْ وَلٰكِنَّ اللهَ أَلَّفَ بَيْنَهُمْ إِنَّهُ عَزِيْزٌ حَكِيْمٌ

(8:63) and joined their hearts. Had you given away all the riches of the earth you could not have joined their hearts, but it is Allah Who joined their hearts. Indeed He is All-Mighty. All-Wise.[32]

The Direct Effect of Quran Recitation on Humans' Emotions

The qualitative (quantum) effect of the Arabic of Quran on the body and soul can be obtained from listening or reading even without understanding its meanings. It takes you to a state of harmonious existence. For example: "The recitation of the Qur'an led to great relaxation, due to the effect of the Qur'an on the human heart, that stems from the effect of some hormones and chemicals responsible

---

[32] Here the allusion is to that strong bond of love and brotherhood that developed among the Muslims who embraced Islam and whose conversion brought them solidarity. This strong solidarity existed despite the fact that they came from a variety of nations which had a wide range of different traditions. This was a special favor of God on the Muslims.

for relaxation." *Source: Nayef, E. G., & Wahab, M. N. A. (2018). The Effect of Recitation Quran on the Human Emotions. International Journal of Academic Research in Business and Social Sciences, 8(2), 48–68.*

Quranic Cognitive Linguistic Methods

The Qur'an encompasses all the different known cognitive styles of learning. Each method is balanced, stimulating both sides of the brain. While reading you will come across variable methods e.g., telling concrete facts or stories, asking to search with scientific approach, discussing with reasoning or through comparison. *Source: Al-Ali, Ali & El-Sharif, Ahmad & Alzyoud, Mohammad. (2016). The Functions And Linguistic Analysis Of Metaphor In The Holy Qur'an. European Scientific Journal. 12. 1857-7881. 10.19044/esj.2016.v12n14p164.*

The same methods can also clearly be seen in the Prophet's, peace be upon him, teachings. *Source: El-Sharif, A. (2011). A linguistic study of Islamic religious discourse: conceptual metaphors in the prophetic tradition.*

Mathematical Encryption of The Qur'an

The Qur'an not only has a complex linguistic morphology, but also a more complex statistical, mathematical and geometric encryption, to prevent any doubt that it has been manipulated in any way. Thus, the truth remains true.

Take in consideration the fact that the Qur'an was revealed over the course of 23 years during the life of the Prophet, may God bless him and grant him peace. At first, the logic of the sequence was context dependent. The Qur'an was responding to the events of those moments and what people needed. Each time this happened, it was documented by the companions of the Prophet, may God bless him and grant them all peace. They meticulously wrote down these verses, word for word as they were revealed.

160

At the end of the revelation, God sent angel Gabriel to memorize the entire Qur'an twice with the Messenger, peace be upon them both. A part of this process was the rearrangement of the surahs and verses. Now there was a different logic in place to compile the final composition that we can hold in our hands even today.

The entire Qur'an consists of 114 surahs, 6348 verses, 77,797 words and 330,709 letters/characters. Every word placement, phrasing, verse, and surah is perfectly encoded in a specific, mathematical encryption that is not fully understood. Everyday we get closer to some of its mysteries, the same way we have breakthroughs in the mysteries of our brains. *Source: Al-Faqih, K.M. (2017). A Mathematical Phenomenon in the Quran of Earth-Shattering Proportions: A Quranic Theory Based On Gematria Determining Quran Primary Statistics (Words, Verses, Chapters) and Revealing Its Fascinating Connection with the Golden Ratio. Journal of Arts and Humanities, 6, 52-73.*

One Surah Demonstrates All These Prerequisites for Harmony

We are constantly receiving floods of information. I'm not sure it makes us any smarter or happier than earlier generations!

Fortunately, we don't need to digest all this information! There is just one piece of information, not more, which is the most important and most urgent for our well-being. This information is the key to finding harmony! It might be extremely easy to grasp or it may require a harder and longer way with a whole lot of arguments. And sometimes one just doesn't get it at all.

وَلَقَدْ صَرَّفْنَا فِىْ هٰذَا الْقُرْاٰنِ لِلنَّاسِ مِنْ كُلِّ مَثَلٍ ۗ وَكَانَ الْاِنْسَانُ اَكْثَرَ شَىْءٍ جَدَلًا

(18:54) And surely We have explained matters to people in the Qur'an in diverse ways, using all manner of parables. But man is exceedingly contentious.

The hardest challenge for our mind to comprehend is the limits of our existence. Are we the masters of the earth? Or is there a Creator who is not like us? God responded to this mind challenge in Surah 112 named Al-Ikhlas (Sincerity). Although it is one of the shortest and easiest to read, it contains the most important information in the Qur'an and is equal to a third of its message and value.

قُلْ هُوَ اللهُ أَحَد ُ

(112:1) Say: "He is Allah, the One and Unique;

ُ اَللهُ الصَّمَد

(112:2) Allah, Who is in need of none and of Whom all are in need;

لَم ْ
( ) يَلِد
وَلَمْ يُوْلَد ْ

(112:3) He neither **_begot_** any nor was He begotten,

وَلَمْ يَكُنْ لَّهُ كُفُوًا أَحَد

(112:4) and none is comparable to Him.

Corpus Callosum, The Bridge of Harmony

When the older generations received this piece of information, they could assimilate it until it became the core of their knowledge (faith). It helped them to find a place in their mind for whatever was happening in their life and keep going in life. They had no difficulty to find solutions to their problems.

The presence of God in their consciousness enabled them to be unequivocally in harmony with everything. They were unbeatable, fearless and not grieved by death. They fused the living knowledge in the depths of their psyche to build a bridge: from where their mind ends to where the understanding of God begins! This bridge is what the corpus callosum[33] represents between the right imaginative hemisphere and the left logical hemisphere!

The Need to Get It The Harder Way

God knows that we have a different mind, a different logic and understanding of life than the earlier ones. He knows that the amount of knowledge we have will make us feel more civilized and think that we are supposed to get away from God (we just need to be secular) or that we can think independently (atheists). The majority will think that religion is old-fashioned, and that it does not fit the values of Europe or America at the present time! In particular the latest thought is regarding Islam.

God knows about this idiotic and arrogant thought inside every mind, it will show up one day! Nevertheless we shouldn't believe this arrogance, no matter what we will be capable of doing on earth or in space.

وَلَا تَمْشِ فِى الْأَرْضِ مَرَحًا ۚ إِنَّكَ لَنْ تَخْرِقَ الْأَرْضَ وَلَنْ تَبْلُغَ الْجِبَالَ طُولًا

(17:37) Do not strut about in the land arrogantly. Surely you cannot cleave the earth, nor reach the heights of the mountains in stature.

Because of the foreseeable arrogance, God pre-encrypted the augmentation logic inside the same message, and just recently humanity was able to understand it through the advanced knowledge.

---

[33] Corpus callosum is Latin for "tough body". It is the largest connective pathway in the brain, made up of more than 200 million nerve fibers.

Smarter Encryption

When we became smarter humans, and went further to understand human reproduction, we realized that one human cell contains 46 chromosomes. It is the sum of an equal but still different pair of half cells (female egg and male sperm), *the original gender equality*.

Now look back in the same Surah, you will find the central letter in the entire Surah in the middle of the central key word, (يَلِدْ)! This central letter (lam) denotes in Arabic "no". It is the first word for the Muslim testimony of faith: there is NO god but God alone!

If you now count the letters on either side of the letter (Lam), you will find 23 letters on each side for a total of 46 letters, like 46 chromosomes!

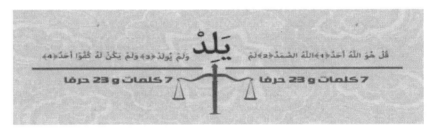

Imagine the unimaginable

Try now to zoom out, attempt to have a bird's-eye view to the same Surah and think of a more holistic picture. Create a match with what you see and the anatomy and function of the brain. Compare the image of a scale to the brain hemispheres and corpus callosum to the central word of the Surah (يَلِدْ)!

You will realize once again that the centric word is يَلِدْ and it is in an overlapping place like the corpus callosum. The logic mentioned on the left side of this word, is to help our right hemisphere to create this understanding. Firstly, by building a relationship with the known facts

164

of our life (the chain of reproduction) and secondly by making it clear how each one of us depends on the previous and gives an extension to the next.

In the same Surah, God created a contrast in our reasoning by adding the word NO to break the image of the chain. He is showing the difference: He is independent and didn't need to be dependent on a predecessor for Him to continue, He created the cause and the process and neither applied to him.

وَاذْكُرْ فِى الْكِتٰبِ مَرْيَمَۘ اِذِ انْتَبَذَتْ مِنْ اَهْلِهَا مَكَانًا شَرْقِيًّا

(19:16) (O Muhammad), recite in the Book the account of Mary, when she withdrew from her people to a place towards the east;

فَاتَّخَذَتْ مِنْ دُونِهِمْ حِجَابًا فَاَرْسَلْنَآ اِلَيْهَا رُوْحَنَا فَتَمَثَّلَ لَهَا بَشَرًا سَوِيًّا

(19:17) and drew a curtain, screening herself from people whereupon We sent to her Our spirit and he appeared to her as a well-shaped man.

قَالَتْ اِنِّىٓ اَعُوْذُ بِالرَّحْمٰنِ مِنْكَ اِنْ كُنْتَ تَقِيًّا

(19:18) Mary exclaimed: "I surely take refuge from you with the Most Compassionate Lord, if you are at all God-fearing."

قَالَ اِنَّمَآ اَنَا رَسُوْلُ رَبِّكِ ۖ لِاَهَبَ لَكِ غُلٰمًا زَكِيًّا

(19:19) He said: "I am just a message-bearer of your Lord, I have come to grant you a most pure boy."

قَالَتْ اَنّٰى يَكُوْنُ لِىْ غُلٰمٌ وَّلَمْ يَمْسَسْنِىْ بَشَرٌ وَّلَمْ اَكُ بَغِيًّا

(19:20) Mary said: "How can a boy be born to me when no man has even touched me, nor have I ever been unchaste?"

قَالَ كَذٰلِكِ ۚ قَالَ رَبُّكِ هُوَ عَلَىَّ هَيِّنٌ ۚ وَلِنَجْعَلَهٗٓ اٰيَةً لِّلنَّاسِ وَرَحْمَةً مِّنَّا ۚ وَكَانَ اَمْرًا مَّقْضِيًّا

(19:21) The angel said: "Thus shall it be. Your Lord says: 'It is easy for Me; and We shall do so in order to make him a Sign for mankind and a mercy from Us. This has been decreed.' "

فَحَمَلَتْهُ فَانْتَبَذَتْ بِهٖ مَكَانًا قَصِيًّا

(19:22) Then she conceived him and withdrew with him to a far-off place.

فَأَجَاءَهَا الْمَخَاضُ إِلَى جِذْعِ النَّخْلَةِ ۖ قَالَتْ يَا لَيْتَنِي مِتُّ قَبْلَ هٰذَا وَكُنْتُ نَسْيًا مَّنْسِيًّا

(19:23) Then the birth pangs drove her to the trunk of a palm-tree and she said: "Oh, would that I had died before this and had been all forgotten."

فَنَادَاهَا مِنْ تَحْتِهَا أَلَّا تَحْزَنِي قَدْ جَعَلَ رَبُّكِ تَحْتَكِ سَرِيًّا

(19:24) Thereupon the angel below her cried out: "Grieve not, for your Lord has caused a stream of water to flow beneath you.

وَهُزِّي إِلَيْكِ بِجِذْعِ النَّخْلَةِ تُسَاقِطْ عَلَيْكِ رُطَبًا جَنِيًّا

(19:25) Shake the trunk of the palm-tree towards yourself and fresh and ripe dates shall fall upon you.

فَكُلِي وَاشْرَبِي وَقَرِّي عَيْنًا ۖ فَإِمَّا تَرَيِنَّ مِنَ الْبَشَرِ أَحَدًا ۙ فَقُولِي إِنِّي نَذَرْتُ لِلرَّحْمٰنِ صَوْمًا فَلَنْ أُكَلِّمَ الْيَوْمَ إِنْسِيًّا

(19:26) So eat and drink and cool your eyes; and if you see any person say to him: 'Verily I have vowed a fast to the Most Compassionate Lord, and so I shall not speak to anyone today.'

فَأَتَتْ بِهِ قَوْمَهَا تَحْمِلُهُ ۖ قَالُوا يَا مَرْيَمُ لَقَدْ جِئْتِ شَيْئًا فَرِيًّا

(19:27) Then she came to her people, carrying her baby. They said: "O Mary! You have committed a monstrous thing.

يَا أُخْتَ هٰرُونَ مَا كَانَ أَبُوكِ امْرَأَ سَوْءٍ وَمَا كَانَتْ أُمُّكِ بَغِيًّا

(19:28) O sister of Aaron! Your father was not an evil man, nor was your mother an unchaste woman."

فَأَشَارَتْ إِلَيْهِ ۖ قَالُوا كَيْفَ نُكَلِّمُ مَنْ كَانَ فِي الْمَهْدِ صَبِيًّا

(19:29) Thereupon Mary pointed to the child. They exclaimed: "How can we speak to one who is in the cradle, a mere child?"

قَالَ إِنِّي عَبْدُ اللّٰهِ ۖ آتَانِيَ الْكِتَابَ وَجَعَلَنِي نَبِيًّا

(19:30) The child cried out: "Verily I am Allah's servant. He has granted me the Book and has made me a Prophet

وَجَعَلَنِي مُبَارَكًا أَيْنَ مَا كُنْتُ وَأَوْصَانِي بِالصَّلٰوةِ وَالزَّكٰوةِ مَا دُمْتُ حَيًّا

(19:31) and has blessed me wherever I might be and has enjoined upon me Prayer and Zakah (purifying alms) as long as I live;

166

وَبَرًّا بِوَالِدَتِى وَلَمْ يَجْعَلْنِى جَبَّارًا شَقِيًّا

(19:32) and has made me dutiful to my mother. He has not made me oppressive, nor bereft of God's blessings.

وَالسَّلَامُ عَلَىَّ يَوْمَ وُلِدْتُّ وَيَوْمَ أَمُوتُ وَيَوْمَ أُبْعَثُ حَيًّا

(19:33) Peace be upon me the day I was born and the day I will die, and the day I will be raised up alive.

ذَٰلِكَ عِيسَى ابْنُ مَرْيَمَ ۚ قَوْلَ الْحَقِّ الَّذِى فِيهِ يَمْتَرُونَ

(19:34) This is Jesus, the son of Mary; and this is the truth about him concerning which they are in doubt.

مَا كَانَ لِلَّهِ أَن يَتَّخِذَ مِن وَلَدٍ ۖ سُبْحَانَهُ ۚ إِذَا قَضَى أَمْرًا فَإِنَّمَا يَقُولُ لَهُ كُن فَيَكُونُ

(19:35) It does not befit Allah to take for Himself a son. Glory be to Him! When He decrees a thing He only says: "Be" and it is.

وَإِنَّ اللَّهَ رَبِّى وَرَبُّكُمْ فَاعْبُدُوهُ ۚ هَٰذَا صِرَاطٌ مُّسْتَقِيمٌ

(19:36) (Jesus had said): "Indeed Allah is my Lord and your Lord, so serve Him alone. This is the Straight Way."

فَاخْتَلَفَ الْأَحْزَابُ مِنْ بَيْنِهِمْ ۖ فَوَيْلٌ لِّلَّذِينَ كَفَرُوا مِن مَّشْهَدِ يَوْمٍ عَظِيمٍ

(19:37) But different parties[34] began to dispute with one another. A dreadful woe awaits on that great Day for those that reject the Truth.

Did You Get It?

If you can't imagine Him, and you wouldn't, this means now you know Him. He is the One who can never be imagined, but He does exist! This is why He is God. Wake up!

---

[34] That is, the sects of the Christians.

Decoding the Decoding

This Surah, Al-Ikhlas (Sincerity), is true to its name. It has the most complete, honest and logical information. It enables us to free our minds and psyches, and to create a free and safe zone for our imaginations. We have confirmation that we have a trustable message that helps us to understand the truth deeply. He has created all sincere ways to deliver it to us in different codes.

The trick of trying to create correlation between God and ourselves, bringing Himself to our space and time, imagining Him to have a son or sending His spirit, are all undermining the power of our minds.

وَقَالُوا اتَّخَذَ الرَّحْمٰنُ وَلَدًا

(19:88) They claim: "The Most Compassionate Lord has taken a son to Himself."

لَقَدْ جِئْتُمْ شَيْئًا إِدًّا

(19:89) Surely you have made a monstrous statement.

تَكَادُ السَّمٰوٰتُ يَتَفَطَّرْنَ مِنْهُ وَتَنْشَقُّ الْأَرْضُ وَتَخِرُّ الْجِبَالُ هَدًّا

(19:90) It is such a monstrosity that heavens might well-nigh burst forth at it, the earth might be cleaved, and the mountains fall

أَنْ دَعَوْا لِلرَّحْمٰنِ وَلَدًا

(19:91) at their ascribing a son to the Most Compassionate Lord.

وَمَا يَنْبَغِي لِلرَّحْمٰنِ أَنْ يَتَّخِذَ وَلَدًا

(19:92) It does not befit the Most Compassionate Lord that He should take a son.

إِنْ كُلُّ مَنْ فِي السَّمٰوٰتِ وَالْأَرْضِ إِلَّا آتِى الرَّحْمٰنِ عَبْدًا

(19:93) There is no one in the heavens and the earth but he shall come to the Most Compassionate Lord as His servant.

The verse below answers to those who deny the existence of God completely. They created limits to their imaginations and put themselves under constant stress and anxiety added with undeniable confusion!

168

فَمَن يُرِدِ اللّهُ أَن يَهْدِيَهُ يَشْرَحْ صَدْرَهُ لِلْإِسْلَامِ ۖ وَمَن يُرِدْ أَن يُضِلَّهُ يَجْعَلْ صَدْرَهُ ضَيِّقًا حَرَجًا كَأَنَّمَا يَصَّعَّدُ فِى السَّمَاءِ ۚ كَذَٰلِكَ يَجْعَلُ اللّهُ الرِّجْسَ عَلَى الَّذِينَ لَا يُؤْمِنُونَ

(6:125) Thus, (it is a fact that) whomsoever Allah wills to guide, He opens his breast for Islam; and whomsoever He wills to let go astray, He causes his breast to become strait and constricted, as if he were climbing towards the heaven. Thus Allah lays the abomination (of flight from and hatred of Islam) on those who do not believe.[35]

---

[35] 'To open someone's breast to Islam' means to make him feel fully convinced of the truth of Islam and to remove all his doubts, hesitations and reluctance.

CHAPTER 12

Islamophilia 3

The Psyche, Islam, The Harmony

Islam is All About the Psyche

God created this whole life to give guidance, education, care and protection to every self as if they were oneself.

مَا خَلْقُكُمْ وَلَا بَعْثُكُمْ إِلَّا كَنَفْسٍ وَاحِدَةٍ إِنَّ اللهَ سَمِيعٌ بَصِيرٌ

(31:28) To create all of you or to resurrect all of you is to Him like (creating or resurrecting) a single person. Verily Allah is All-Hearing, All-Seeing.

This should cover all aspects of life: during different ages, with all types of psyches, at different stages of development and in different situations.

وَقَدْ خَلَقَكُمْ أَطْوَارًا

(71:14) when He has created you in stages

Psychodynamics is the most complex subject, and you may have to spend many academic years studying to learn something about it. In the end you cannot even understand yourself. The message of Islam (the Qur'an and the Sunnah) has made the task possible in an easy and applicable way. It is absolutely psychology, without doubt. The Creator of you speaks of and to you, so what do you expect?

وَلَقَدْ خَلَقْنَا الْإِنْسَانَ وَنَعْلَمُ مَا تُوَسْوِسُ بِهِ نَفْسُهُ ۖ وَنَحْنُ أَقْرَبُ إِلَيْهِ مِنْ حَبْلِ الْوَرِيدِ

(50:16) Surely, We have created man, and We know the promptings of his heart, and We are nearer to him than even his jugular vein.

Psyche is a Serious Business

Nothing is free, including this dead serious topic of premium quality psychology and psyche care! After all this wisdom, during this life, each soul is meticulously monitored, and all its world is recorded. A very accurate recording of everything you did, thought, felt, thought to do or didn't do, is compiled. This is a fact, whether we believe it or not. It

173

will be inevitable for all of us.

وَيَسْتَنْبِئُونَكَ اَحَقٌّ هُوَ قُلْ اِى وَرَبِّىْ اِنَّهُ لَحَقٌّ وَمَا اَنْتُمْ بِمُعْجِزِيْنَ

(10:53) They ask you if what you say is true? Tell them: 'Yes, by my Lord, this is altogether true, and you have no power to prevent the chastisement from befalling.'

وَلَوْ اَنَّ لِكُلِّ نَفْسٍ ظَلَمَتْ مَا فِى الْاَرْضِ لَافْتَدَتْ بِهٖ وَاَسَرُّوا النَّدَامَةَ لَمَّا رَاَوُا الْعَذَابَ وَقُضِىَ بَيْنَهُمْ بِالْقِسْطِ وَهُمْ لَا يُظْلَمُوْنَ

(10:54) If a wrong-doer had all that is in the earth he would surely offer it to ransom himself. When the wrong-doers perceive the chastisement, they will feel intense remorse in their hearts. But a judgement shall be made with full justice about them. They shall not be wronged.[36]

Can the Psyche Withstand True Justice?

The recording will be restored, as soon as we begin the process of withdrawing from this life (dying). We begin to see that the next stage is coming. This is the moment of truth, but it is ending. Whatever this self has gained, will be kept until Judgment Day. On this day each creature individually discusses all of their recordings, and the judgment will be based on the true justice. No one will go to Hell while he still has some unfinished business with someone who goes to Heaven. Everyone gets their rights first. This is how justice is done.

---

[36] "And they will feel remorse". When all of a sudden, they face the torment on the Day, which they had denied throughout their lives, and on that presumption had gone on doing wrong deeds. Not only this: they will also feel very sorry that they had denied the Messengers and brought baseless charges against them, who had warned them of it. Therefore when they witness it against all their expectations, they will find the ground slipping from under their feet and will feel utterly helpless and guilty in their minds because of the remembrance of their wrong doings and of the pricking of their conscience. In short, their condition will be that of a gambler, who turns a deaf ear to the counsel of his well wishers and stakes his all on mere speculation and goes bankrupt. But such a person has to blame none but himself only for his sad plight.

إِذْ يَتَلَقَّى الْمُتَلَقِّيَانِ عَنِ الْيَمِينِ وَعَنِ الشِّمَالِ قَعِيدٌ

(50:17) Moreover, there are two scribes, one each sitting on the right and the left, recording everything.

مَا يَلْفِظُ مِنْ قَوْلٍ إِلَّا لَدَيْهِ رَقِيبٌ عَتِيدٌ

(50:18) He utters not a word, but there is a vigilant watcher at hand.

وَ جَاءَتْ سَكْرَةُ الْمَوْتِ بِالْحَقِّ ۖ ذَٰلِكَ مَا كُنْتَ مِنْهُ تَحِيدُ

(50:19) Lo, the agony of death has indeed come with the Truth.[37]

وَنُفِخَ فِى الصُّورِ ۚ ذَٰلِكَ يَوْمُ الْوَعِيدِ

(50:20) And then the Trumpet was blown. This is the day of the promised chastisement.

وَجَاءَتْ كُلُّ نَفْسٍ مَّعَهَا سَائِقٌ وَّشَهِيدٌ

(50:21) Everyone has come, each attended by one who will drive him on, and another who will bear witness. [38]

لَقَدْ كُنْتَ فِى غَفْلَةٍ مِّنْ هَٰذَا فَكَشَفْنَا عَنْكَ غِطَاءَكَ فَبَصَرُكَ الْيَوْمَ حَدِيدٌ

(50:22) You were heedless of this. Now We have removed your veil and so your vision today is sharp.

وَقَالَ قَرِينُهُ هَٰذَا مَا لَدَيَّ عَتِيدٌ ۚ

---

[37] That is what you had sought to avoid. "Come with the truth" implies that the agony of death is the starting point when the reality which had remained concealed in the world, begins to be uncovered. At this point man starts seeing clearly the other world of which the Prophet had forewarned him. Here, man also comes to know that the Hereafter is the very truth, and also this whether he is entering this second stage of life as favored or damned.

That is, this is the same reality which you refused to believe. You desired that you should live and go about as an unbridled rogue in the world, and there should be no other life after death, in which you may have to suffer for the consequences of your deeds. That is why you shunned the concept of the Hereafter and were not at all inclined to believe that this next world would ever be established. Now, you may see that the same next world is unveiling itself before you.

[38] This may imply the same two angels who had been appointed for compiling the record of the words and deeds of the person in the world. On the Day of Resurrection, when every man will rise from his grave on the sounding of the Trumpet, the two angels will come forth immediately and take him into their custody. One of them will drive him to the divine court and the other will be carrying his record.

175

(50:23) His companion said: "Here is he who was in my charge."[39]

أَلْقِيَا فِىْ جَهَنَّمَ كُلَّ كَفَّارٍ عَنِيْدٍ

(50:24) The command was given: "Cast into Hell every hardened, stubborn unbeliever.[40]

مَّنَّاعٍ لِّلْخَيْرِ مُعْتَدٍ مُّرِيْبِ ٧

---

[39] That is, you can clearly see that everything of which the Prophets foretold is present here. Some commentators say that the companion implies the angel who has been referred to as a witness in (verse 21). He will say: I have this person's record ready with me here. Some other commentators say that the companion implies the satan who was attached to the person in the world. He will say: This person whom I was controlling and preparing for Hell, is now presented before You. But the commentary that is more relevant to the context is the one that has been reported from Qatadah and Ibn Zaid. They say that the companion implies the angel who drove and brought the person to Allah's court. He will say: Here is the person who had been given in my charge

[40] As the context shows this command will be given to the two angels who had taken the culprit into their custody as soon as he had risen from the grave, and then brought him before the court. The word kaffar as used in the text means an ungrateful person as well as a denier of the truth.

176

(50:25) who hinders good, exceeds the limits, is immersed in doubts.[41]

اَلَّذِیْ جَعَلَ مَعَ اللّٰهِ اِلٰهًا اٰخَرَ فَاَلْقِیٰهُ فِی الْعَذَابِ الشَّدِیْدِ

(50:26) and has set up another deity with Allah. Hurl him into the grievous torment."[42]

قَالَ قَرِیْنُهٗ رَبَّنَا مَاۤ اَطْغَیْتُهٗ وَلٰكِنْ كَانَ فِیْ ضَلٰلٍ بَعِیْدٍ

(50:27) His companion said: "I did not incite him to rebel; he was far

---

[41] Khair in Arabic is used both for wealth and for goodness. According to the first meaning, the sentence means that he paid no one his dues from his wealth, neither the dues of Allah nor of the people. According to the second meaning, it would mean that he did not only withhold himself from the path of goodness but forbade others also to follow it. He had become a hindrance for the people in the way of goodness and exerted his utmost to see that goodness did not spread.

That is, he transgressed the bounds of morality in everything he did. He was ever ready to do anything and everything for the sake of his interests, his desires and his lusts. He amassed wealth by unlawful means and spent it in unlawful ways. He usurped the people's rights, had neither control over his tongue nor over his hands, and committed every injustice and excess. He did not rest content with creating hindrances in the way of goodness but harassed those who adopted goodness and persecuted those who worked for it.

The word murib as used in the original has two meanings: a doubter and the one who puts others in doubt, and both are implied here. It means that he was not only himself involved in doubt but also created doubts in the hearts of others. He held as doubtful the Being of Allah and the Hereafter and the angels and the Prophethood and revelation and every other truth of religion. Anything that was presented by the Prophets as a truth was held as unbelievable by him, and the same disease he spread to other people. Whomsoever he came in contact with, he would create one or the other doubt, one or the other evil thought in his mind.

[42] Allah, in these verses, has enumerated the qualities that make a man worthy of Hell:
(1) Denial of the truth.
(2) Ingratitude to Allah.
(3) Enmity for the Truth and the followers of the truth.
(4) To become a hindrance in the way of goodness.
(5) Failure to fulfill the rights of Allah and the people from his wealth.
(6) To transgress the bounds in his affairs.
(7) To commit injustices and excesses against others.
(8) To doubt the truths of religion.
(9) To create doubts in the hearts of the people.
(10) To hold another as an associate in the Godhead of Allah.

gone into error of his own accord."[43]

قَالَ لَا تَخْتَصِمُوا لَدَيَّ وَقَدْ قَدَّمْتُ إِلَيْكُم بِالْوَعِيدِ

(50:28) (It was said): "Do not remonstrate in My presence. I had warned you.[44]

مَا يُبَدَّلُ الْقَوْلُ لَدَيَّ وَمَا أَنَا بِظَلَّامٍ لِّلْعَبِيدِ

(50:29) My Word is not changed; and never do I inflict the least wrong upon My servants.[45]

---

[43] Here by companion is meant the satan who was attached to the disobedient person in the world. And this also becomes evident from the style that both the person and his satan are disputing between themselves in the court of Allah. He says: My Lord, this wretched one pursued me in the world and did not leave me until he succeeded in misleading me, therefore he alone should be punished. And the satan replies: Lord, I had no power over him. Had he not himself willed to become rebellious, I could not have seduced him forcibly. This wretched person himself fled from goodness and was fascinated by evil. That is why he did not like anything that the Prophets presented and went on yielding to every temptation and inducement presented by me.

[44] That is, I had warned both of you as to what punishment will be given to the one who beguiles and what punishment will be suffered by him who is beguiled. In spite of this warning when you did not desist from committing your respective crimes, there is no use quarreling now. Both, the one who beguiled and the one who was beguiled have to be punished for the crimes committed by them.

[45] That is, it is not My way to change the decisions once taken. The decision that I have taken to cast you into Hell cannot be withdrawn, nor can the law that I had announced in the world be changed that the punishment for misleading and for being misled will be awarded in the Hereafter.

The word zallam as used in the original means the one who is highly unjust. It does not mean: I am unjust to My servants but not highly unjust. But it means: If I were unjust to My own servants being their Creator and Sustainer, I would be highly unjust. Therefore, I am not at all unjust to My servants. This punishment that I am giving you is precisely the same punishment which you have made yourselves worthy of. You are not being punished an iota more than what you actually deserve, for My court is a court of impartial justice. Here, no one can receive a punishment which he does not actually deserve, and for which his being worthy has not been proved by certain and undeniable evidence.

Our Psyches Can't Withstand Justice, All We Need Is Mercy! But Do We Deserve It?

Mercy is all we need. Allah knows best that's why He released only 1% of His mercy in this life and kept 99% for the hereafter.

Abu Huraira reported: The Messenger of Allah, peace and blessings be upon him, said: "Allah made mercy into one hundred parts. He kept ninety-nine parts with Himself and sent down one part to the earth. From that one part, the creation is merciful to each other, such that a horse raises its hoof over its child for fear of trampling it." *Source: Al-Bukhari and Muslim*

قُلْ لِّمَنْ مَّا فِى السَّمٰوٰتِ وَالْاَرْضِ ۖ قُلْ لِّلّٰهِ ۚ كَتَبَ عَلٰى نَفْسِهِ الرَّحْمَةَ ۚ لَيَجْمَعَنَّكُمْ اِلٰى يَوْمِ الْقِيٰمَةِ لَا رَيْبَ فِيْهِ ۚ اَلَّذِيْنَ خَسِرُوْٓا اَنْفُسَهُمْ فَهُمْ لَا يُؤْمِنُوْنَ

(6:12) Ask them: 'To whom belongs all that is in the heavens and on the earth? Say: 'Everything belongs to Allah.' He has bound Himself to the exercise of mercy (and thus does not chastise you for your disobedience and excesses instantly). Surely He will gather you all together on the Day of Resurrection - the coming of which is beyond doubt; but those who have courted their own ruin are not going to believe.[46]

نَبِّئْ عِبَادِىْٓ اَنِّيْٓ اَنَا الْغَفُوْرُ الرَّحِيْمُ

(15:49) (O Prophet), declare to My servants that I am indeed Ever Forgiving, Most Merciful.

---

[46] The subtlety of this expression should not go unnoticed. The unbelievers are asked to whom belongs whatever exists in either the heavens or on the earth. The inquirer then pauses to wait for the answer. Those questioned are themselves convinced that all belongs to God, yet while they dare not respond falsely, they are nevertheless not prepared to give the correct answer. Fearing that their response may be used as an argument against their polytheistic beliefs, they keep quiet. At this, the inquirer is told to answer the question himself and to say that all belongs to God.

179

Psychodynamics in Islam

Psyche is the result of the interactive reality between body and soul during the lifespan. The interaction starts during the first weeks in the womb and lasts until the last minute of life. We know so little about the soul compared to what we know about the human body!

وَيَسْتَلُونَكَ عَنِ الرُّوحِ قُلِ الرُّوحُ مِنْ أَمْرِ رَبِّي وَمَا أُوتِيتُمْ مِنَ الْعِلْمِ إِلَّا قَلِيلًا

(17:85) They ask you about "the spirit". Say: "The spirit descends by the command of my Lord, but you have been given only a little knowledge."

Sleeping Like Dead

Soul is like quantum energy. We know it's subtle, and we even use it on a daily basis, but we know little about it, almost nothing! The soul's world has endless possibilities. Every day with every night is for the soul like a recurring cycle of birth and death, it is leaving the body and returning. When it comes out of the body partially and temporarily, this is sleep. *Source: Bahammam AS, Gozal D. Qur'anic insights into sleep. Nat Sci Sleep. 2012;4:81-87. Published 2012 Jul 24. doi:10.2147/NSS.S34630*

Sleep is The Breathing Time of The Soul

During sleep, the soul leaves the dark and limited body in order to breathe while drawing closer to the Creator. It then returns again holding its breath, to do its work. *Source: The Evidence, The Possible Mechanisms, and The Future.Grandner MA, Hale L, Moore M, Patel NP. Mortality associated with short sleep duration: The evidence, the possible mechanisms, and the future. Sleep Med Rev. 2010;14(3):191-203. doi:10.1016/j.smrv.2009.07.006*

وَمِنْ اٰيٰتِهٖ مَنَامُكُمْ بِالَّيْلِ وَالنَّهَارِ وَابْتِغَاؤُكُمْ مِّنْ فَضْلِهٖ اِنَّ فٖى ذٰلِكَ لَاٰيٰتٍ لِّقَوْمٍ يَّسْمَعُوْنَ

(30:23) And of His Signs is your sleeping at night and your seeking His Bounty during the day. Indeed, there are Signs in this for those who hearken.[47]

---

[47] "To seek bounty" is to seek the livelihood. Though man generally sleeps at night and works for his living in the day, this is not a law. Many people also sleep in the day and work for their livelihood at night. That is why the night and the day both have been mentioned and it has been said: "In both day and night you sleep as well as work for your livelihood."

This also is a sign which points to the design of the Wise Creator. Furthermore, it also points to the fact that He is not merely a Creator but also extremely Compassionate and Merciful to His creations and is more anxious than the creation to meet its needs and requirements. Man cannot constantly labor but needs to have a rest of a few hours after every few hours of hard work so as to rebuild energy to take up work again. For this purpose, the Wise and Merciful Creator has not rested content with creating a feeling of fatigue and a desire for rest in man, but has placed in his nature a powerful urge for the sleep, which without his will, even in spite of resistance from him, overpowers him automatically after every few hours of work and wakefulness, and compels him to have a few hours of rest, and leaves him as soon as the need has been fulfilled.

Man has so far been unable to understand the nature and real causes of the sleep. This is something fully innate, which has been placed in the nature and structure of man. Its being precisely according to the requirements of man is enough to testify that it is not anything accidental, but has been provided by a Wise Being in accordance with a purpose and plan. It is based on a clear wisdom and reason and purposefulness. Moreover, the sleep itself testifies that the One Who has placed this compulsive urge in man is a greater well wisher of man than man himself, otherwise man would have deliberately resisted the sleep and endeavored to keep constantly awake and worked continuously hard and thus exhaust not only his workpower but also his vital powers.

Then, by using the word "seeking Allah's bounty" for the seeking of livelihood, allusion has been made to another series of the signs. How could have man sought and found his livelihood if the innumerable and unlimited forces of the earth and heavens had not been put to work to provide means of the livelihood and supply countless resources for man to seek it in the earth? Not only this. Man could not have exploited these means and resources had he not been given appropriate limbs and suitable physical and mental capabilities for the purpose. Thus the ability in man to seek the livelihood and the presence of the resources of the livelihood outside of him, clearly indicate the existence of a Merciful and Beneficent God. An intellect which is not sick can never presume that all this has happened by chance, or is the manifestation of the godhead of many gods, or some merciless, blind force is responsible for these bounties and blessings.

Sleeping for non-believers is so challenging. This kind of soul has so much difficulty being in the body. It is like a continuous torture day after day. *Source: Global sleep problems might be causing MORE DAMAGE than terrorism. Sleep on that. 54 Shocking Sleep Statistics and Trends from 2021.www.sleepadvisor.org/sleep-statistics/*

Even though it is very tired, it is afraid and anxious to leave the body, even terrified, because when it leaves during the sleep it returns closer to the Creator. He is the one the soul denies! From Him it attempts to escape, which is impossible! This bedtime story should be enough for every psyche to perceive and know the purpose of life, stop running away and submit to the Creator (Islam).

اَللّٰهُ يَتَوَفَّى الْاَنْفُسَ حِيْنَ مَوْتِهَا وَالَّتِيْ لَمْ تَمُتْ فِيْ مَنَامِهَا ۚ فَيُمْسِكُ الَّتِيْ قَضٰى عَلَيْهَا الْمَوْتَ وَ يُرْسِلُ الْاُخْرٰى اِلٰى اَجَلٍ مُّسَمًّى ۚ اِنَّ فِيْ ذٰلِكَ لَاٰيٰتٍ لِّقَوْمٍ يَّتَفَكَّرُوْنَ

(39:42) It is Allah Who takes away the souls of people at the hour of their death and takes away at the time of sleep the souls of those that have not died. Then He retains the souls of those against whom He had decreed death and returns the souls of others till an appointed time. Surely there are Signs in this for people who reflect.[48]

This sleep story continues until the soul comes out of the body permanently, this time with the complete psychological component (psyche), without returning to it until the Day of Resurrection!

حَتّٰى اِذَا جَآءَ اَحَدَهُمُ الْمَوْتُ قَالَ رَبِّ ارْجِعُوْنِ

(23:99) (They shall persist in their deeds) until when death comes to

---

[48] Taking the souls during sleep, implies the suspension of the powers of feeling and consciousness, understanding and will. By this Allah wants every man to realize how life and death are entirely in His own hand. No one has the guarantee that he will certainly get up alive in the morning when he goes to sleep at night. No one knows what disaster could befall him within a moment, and whether the next moment would be a moment of life for him or of death. At any time, while asleep or awake, in the house or outside it, some unforeseen calamity, from inside his body or from outside, can suddenly cause his death. Thus, man who is so helpless in the hands of God, would be foolish if he turned away from the same God or became heedless of Him.

anyone of them, he will say: "My Lord, send me back to the world[49]

لَعَلِّىٓ أَعْمَلُ صَالِحًا فِيمَا تَرَكْتُ ۚ كَلَّا ۚ إِنَّهَا كَلِمَةٌ هُوَ قَآئِلُهَا ۖ وَمِن وَّرَآئِهِم بَرْزَخٌ إِلَىٰ يَوْمِ يُبْعَثُونَ

(23:100) that I have left behind. I am likely to do good. "Nay, it is merely a word that he is uttering. There is a barrier behind all of them who are dead) until the Day when they will be raised up.[50]

Jesus, Peace Be Upon Him, Is the Exceptional Body and Soul, Miracle!

The body is a dense and complex creation with an amazing structure and its main components are water and minerals which also are formed in a complex chemical and physical way. It performs specific functions, but its capabilities are limited by the physics of time and space.

Body and soul depend on each other at this stage of life and are subject to the laws of nature and physics. These laws do not work on their own, rather they are a way of God to teach us that nothing is random. Secondly, they help us to move forward to get closer to know Him and

---

[49] In the original text plural number has been used for Allah, which may be for reverence, or may include the angels as well, who will be seizing the criminal soul. The entreaty would be: O my Lord! Send me back.

[50] It occurs at several places in the Quran that each of the criminals, after his death till his entry into Hell, and even after that, will plead again and again: Lord, send me back to the world, I will no more disobey Thee, I will now do righteous deeds.

That is, he will never be sent back nor given another opportunity, for in that case the test and trial for which man is sent to this world becomes meaningless.

That is, now, when he has met his doom, he has nothing more to say than that he should be sent back to the world; so let him say what he likes; he will never be allowed to go back.

That is, now there is a barrier between them and the world, which will not allow them to go back to it. Therefore they shall remain in that state until the Day of Resurrection.

His wisdom. These laws are not for Him, God interrupts the law if he likes. A good exception of this is the creation of Jesus, He made him like Adam.

وَإِذْ قَالَتِ الْمَلَـٰئِكَةُ يَـٰمَرْيَمُ إِنَّ اللَّهَ اصْطَفَـٰكِ وَطَهَّرَكِ وَاصْطَفَـٰكِ عَلَىٰ نِسَاءِ الْعَـٰلَمِينَ

(3:42) Then came the time when the angels said: 'O Mary! Behold, Allah has chosen you, and made you pure, and exalted you above all the women in the world.

يَـٰمَرْيَمُ اقْنُتِى لِرَبِّكِ وَاسْجُدِى وَارْكَعِى مَعَ الرَّٰكِعِينَ

(3:43) 'O Mary! Remain devout to your Lord, and prostrate yourself in worship, and bow with those who bow (before Him).'

ذَٰلِكَ مِنْ أَنْبَاءِ الْغَيْبِ نُوحِيهِ إِلَيْكَ ۚ وَمَا كُنْتَ لَدَيْهِمْ إِذْ يُلْقُونَ أَقْلَامَهُمْ أَيُّهُمْ يَكْفُلُ مَرْيَمَ وَمَا كُنْتَ لَدَيْهِمْ إِذْ يَخْتَصِمُونَ

(3:44) (O Muhammad!) We reveal to you this account from a realm which lies beyond the reach of your perception for you were not with them when they drew lots with their pens about who should be Mary's guardian, and you were not with them when they disputed about it.[51]

إِذْ قَالَتِ الْمَلَـٰئِكَةُ يَـٰمَرْيَمُ إِنَّ اللَّهَ يُبَشِّرُكِ بِكَلِمَةٍ مِنْهُ ۖ اسْمُهُ الْمَسِيحُ عِيسَى ابْنُ مَرْيَمَ وَجِيهًا فِى الدُّنْيَا وَالْآخِرَةِ وَمِنَ الْمُقَرَّبِينَ

(3:45) And when the angels said: 'O Mary! Allah gives you the glad tidings of a command from Him: his name shall be Messiah, Jesus, the son of Mary. He shall be highly honoured in this world and in the Next, and shall be one of those near stationed to Allah.

وَيُكَلِّمُ النَّاسَ فِى الْمَهْدِ وَكَهْلًا وَمِنَ الصَّٰلِحِينَ

(3:46) And he shall speak to men in the cradle and also later when he grows to maturity and shall indeed be among the righteous.'

قَالَتْ رَبِّ أَنَّىٰ يَكُونُ لِى وَلَدٌ وَلَمْ يَمْسَسْنِى بَشَرٌ ۖ قَالَ كَذَٰلِكِ اللَّهُ يَخْلُقُ مَا يَشَاءُ ۚ إِذَا قَضَىٰ أَمْرًا فَإِنَّمَا يَقُولُ لَهُ كُنْ فَيَكُونُ

---

[51] They drew lots to decide who should be the guardian of Mary, whose mother had consecrated her to the service of God in the Temple. Since she was a girl, it was a delicate matter as to who from among the priests of the Temple would be the appropriate person to take care of her.

(3:47) She said: 'O my Lord! How shall I have a son when no man has ever touched me?' The angel answered: 'Thus shall it be. Allah creates whatever He wills. When He decides something, He merely says: "Be" and it is.[52]

وَيُعَلِّمُهُ الْكِتَابَ وَالْحِكْمَةَ وَالتَّوْرَاةَ وَالْإِنْجِيلَ

(3:48) And He will teach him the Book, the Wisdom, the Torah, the Gospel.

وَرَسُولًا إِلَى بَنِي إِسْرَاءِيلَ أَنِّي قَدْ جِئْتُكُمْ بِآيَةٍ مِنْ رَبِّكُمْ أَنِّي أَخْلُقُ لَكُمْ مِّنَ الطِّينِ كَهَيْئَةِ الطَّيْرِ فَأَنْفُخُ فِيهِ فَيَكُونُ طَيْرًا بِإِذْنِ اللَّهِ وَأُبْرِئُ الْأَكْمَهَ وَالْأَبْرَصَ وَأُحْيِ الْمَوْتَى بِإِذْنِ اللَّهِ وَأُنَبِّئُكُمْ بِمَا تَأْكُلُونَ وَمَا تَدَّخِرُونَ فِي بُيُوتِكُمْ إِنَّ فِي ذَلِكَ لَآيَةً لَّكُمْ إِنْ كُنْتُمْ مُّؤْمِنِينَ

(3:49) and he will be a Messenger to the Children of Israel.' (And when he came to them he said): 'I have come to you with a sign from your Lord. I will make for you from clay the likeness of a bird and then I will breathe into it and by the leave of Allah it will become a bird. I will also heal the blind and the leper, and by the leave of Allah bring the dead to life. I will also inform you of what things you eat and what you treasure up in your houses. Surely this is a sign for you if you are true

---

[52] Thus it was affirmed that a child would be born to Mary despite the fact that no man had touched her. The angel's answer mentioned here, 'Thus shall it be', was exactly the same as the response given to Zechariah. Both the following sentences and the preceding section support the view that the angel had conveyed to Mary the glad tidings that a son would be born to her without normal sexual contact, and it was thus that Jesus was born.

The Christians had begun to regard Jesus as God and the son of God because of this fatherless birth. The Jews, in turn, cast aspersions on Mary's chastity on the grounds that she had given birth to a child despite being unmarried. If the fatherless birth of Jesus was itself false, it would have been sufficient to tell the Christians that they were indulging in sheer misstatement, that Mary had indeed been married, that she had a legitimate husband, and that it was as a result of that wedlock that Jesus was born. If this fact could have been stated plainly, there would have been no need for long preparatory statements and complicated propositions, and no need to call Jesus the son of Mary instead of naming his father. For far from resolving the issue such statements add to the confusion. Those who believe the Qur'an to be the word or command from God and yet try to prove that the birth of Jesus took place in the normal manner, as a result of union between his father and mother, end up by proving only that God is less capable of clear expression than they are!

believers.[53]

وَمُصَدِّقًا لِّمَا بَيْنَ يَدَيَّ مِنَ التَّوْرَاةِ وَلِأُحِلَّ لَكُم بَعْضَ الَّذِى حُرِّمَ عَلَيْكُمْ وَجِئْتُكُم بِآيَةٍ مِّن رَّبِّكُمْ فَاتَّقُوا اللَّهَ وَأَطِيعُونِ

(3:50) And I have come to confirm the truth of whatever there still remains of the Torah, and to make lawful to you some of the things which had been forbidden to you. have come to you with a sign from your Lord; so have fear of Allah and obey me.[54]

إِنَّ اللَّهَ رَبِّى وَرَبُّكُمْ فَاعْبُدُوهُ ۗ هَٰذَا صِرَاطٌ مُّسْتَقِيمٌ

(3:51) Surely, Allah is my Lord and your Lord; so serve Him alone.

---

[53] It is hinted here that these signs are sufficient proof that Jesus was designated by God, the Creator and Sovereign of the universe, provided people are prepared to accept the truth instead of obstinately clinging to their prejudiced views. This is further proof that Jesus had been entrusted with a mission by God. Had he not been designated by God but by an imposter he would surely have attempted to find an independent religion, exploiting his miracles to lead people away from their original faith. However, Jesus believed in, and confirmed, the validity of the teachings of the original religion which had been preached at God's behest by the earlier Prophets.

[54] The fact that Jesus preached the same religion as that expounded earlier by Moses and the other Prophets is also borne out by the statements of the existing Gospels: According to Matthew, in his Sermon on the Mount the Messiah categorically declared: 'Think not that I have come to abolish the law and the prophets; I have come not to abolish them but to fulfil them' (Matthew 5: 17). And when a Jewish lawyer enquired: 'Teacher, which is the greatest commandment in the Law?', Jesus replied: 'You shall love the Lord your God with all your heart, and with all your soul, and with all your mind'

What Jesus wanted to impress upon them was that he would abolish the prohibitive innovations which had infiltrated the original Divine Law (Shari'ah). These were the results of the superstitions of their ignorant commoners, the legal hair-splitting of their lawyers, the extremism of their world-renouncing pietists, and the ascendancy and predominance of non-Muslim peoples over them. In determining what is lawful and unlawful, Jesus would be guided by the injunctions of God and not by the inventions of human beings.

This is the straight way.'[55]

فَلَمَّآ اَحَسَّ عِيْسٰى مِنْهُمُ الْكُفْرَ قَالَ مَنْ اَنْصَارِىٓ اِلَى اللّٰهِ ۭ قَالَ الْحَوَارِيُّوْنَ

نَحْنُ اَنْصَارُ اللّٰهِ ۚ اٰمَنَّا بِاللّٰهِ ۚ وَاشْهَدْ بِاَنَّا مُسْلِمُوْنَ

(3:52) And when Jesus perceived their leaning towards unbelief, he asked: 'Who will be my helpers in the way of Allah?' The disciples said: 'We are the helpers of Allah. We believe in Allah and be our witness that we have submitted ourselves exclusively to Allah.[56]

First Marry A Challenge Then Earn Love to Make Your Dreams Come True

This relation between soul and body is the most complex marriage on earth. It is based on contradiction, different natures. You may imagine a sensitive, romantic woman from an aristocratic family, who is highly educated and speaking all the languages of the world. She is so intelligent that she is well versed in all the previous and subsequent sciences.

She wants to live in complete transparency, and dream of a bright and endless future. This dream comes with a challenge, namely that she needs to marry an ignorant man who does not speak any language and knows nothing except satisfying his basic needs such as eating, drinking, sleeping and his instincts.

He also has a dream. He wants to live to the fullest, to be in a controlling position, unstoppable. He is seeking to be a free force, wanting independence, joy and to be absolutely forever without end, worry, aging or fallout! But this dream also comes with a challenge, he needs to succeed in living with the soul in a marriage. This marriage (interaction) is the psyche.

What are the chances of success of these kinds of marriage? What are the odds of these couples falling in love?

[55] (1) Man should acknowledge the exclusive sovereignty of God which demands absolute service and obedience to Him, and Him alone. This principle serves as the basis for the entire structure of human morality and social behaviour.

(2) Man should obey the Prophets since they are the representatives of the true Sovereign.

(3) The Law which should regulate man's conduct by elaborating what is right and what is wrong should be none other than the Law of God. The laws devised by others should be abrogated. There is, thus, no difference between the missions of Jesus, Moses and Muhammad (peace be on them all). Those who think that the missions of the Prophets differ from one another and who believe that their objectives vary have fallen into serious error. Whoever is sent by the Lord of the Universe to His creatures can have no other purpose than to dissuade God's subjects from disobeying Him and assuming an attitude of vanity and disregard towards Him, and to admonish them against associating anyone with God in His divinity (that is, either holding anyone to be a partner with the Lord of the Universe in His Sovereignty or recognizing others beside God as having a rightful claim on part of man's loyalty, devotion and worship), and to invite them all to be loyal to, and to serve, obey and worship God alone.

It is unfortunate that the Gospels in their present form do not offer as clear a picture of the mission of Jesus as that presented by the Qur'an. Nevertheless, we find scattered throughout the Gospels all the three fundamentals mentioned above. The notion that man ought to submit himself totally to God is embodied in the following statement: 'You shall worship the Lord your God and Him only shall you serve' (Matthew 4: 10).

In addition, Jesus believed that the object of his efforts was that God's commands relating to the moral realm should be obeyed in this world in the sphere of human conduct just as His commands about the operation of the physical universe are obeyed in the heavens: 'Thy kingdom come, Thy will be done, On earth as it is in heaven' (ibid., 6: 10).

The fact that Jesus presented himself as a Prophet and a representative of the Kingdom of Heaven, and that in this capacity he asked people to follow him is borne out by several statements. When, for instance, he began his mission in Nazareth and when his own kith, kin and compatriots turned against him, he remarked: 'A prophet is not without honour except in his own country . . .' (Matthew 13: 57; see also Luke 4: 24 and Mark 6: 4). And when conspiracies were hatched in Jerusalem to put an end to his life, and people counselled him to go away, he replied: 'Nevertheless I must go on my way . . . for it cannot be that a prophet should perish away from Jerusalem' (Luke 13: 33). When Jesus entered Jerusalem for the last time the disciples cried with a loud voice: 'Blessed be the King who comes in the name of the Lord' (Luke 19: 38). This angered the Pharisees, who asked Jesus to rebuke his disciples. But he replied: 'I tell you, if these were silent the very stones would cry out' (ibid., 19: 40). On another occasion he said: 'Come to me, all who labour and are heavy laden, and I will give you rest. Take my yoke upon you. For my yoke is easy, and my burden is light' (Matthew 11: 28-30).

Calculating Odds

For a special marriage like this there must be a special arrangement! Is there any real willingness to make it work?

The fact that he invited people to obey the Laws of God rather than the laws made by man is evident from his response (found in both Matthew and Mark) to the objection raised by the Pharisees to the conduct of their disciples who ate with defiled hands, that is, without washing.

'Well did Isiah prophesy of you hypocrites, as it is written: This people honours me with their lips, but their heart is far from me; in vain do they worship me, teaching as doctrines the precepts of men.'

And he said to them: 'You have a fine way of rejecting the commandment of God in order to keep your tradition. For Moses said, "Honour your father and your mother", and "He who speaks evil of his father or mother, let him surely die", but you say, "If a man tells his father or mother what you would have gained from me is Corban (that is, given to God), and then you no longer permit him to do anything for his father or mother, thus making void the word of God through your tradition which you hand on"' (Mark 7: 6-13; see also Matthew 15: 2-9).

[56] The word hawari means approximately the same as the word ansar in the Islamic tradition. In the Bible the usual terms are 'apostles' and 'disciples'. Jesus' chosen disciples were called apostles in the sense that they had been entrusted with a mission by him rather than in the sense of having been entrusted with a mission by God.

At various places the Qur'an characterizes man's participation in the effort to establish the supremacy of Islam as 'helping God'. This needs a little explanation. God has endowed man with the freedom of will and choice, with the result that He does not resort to His omnipotent will to compel man either to do certain things or to refrain from others. He rather leaves man free to adopt the course that pleases him - be it that of either belief or unbelief, of either obedience or disobedience. God prefers to instruct man by means of persuasive argument and admonition, so as to bring home to him that even though he is free to disbelieve, disobey and defy the Will of God, his own interest and well-being lie in serving and obeying his Creator.

Hence, directing people to the right path by persuasion and admonition is of concern to God, He regards those who contribute to this cause as His allies and helpers. This is, in fact, the most exalted position attainable by man. When a man performs Prayers, keeps his fast and worships God in other ways, he is merely on the level of service and subjection to God. But when a man strives to spread God's true religion and to enthrone it in actual life, he is honoured with the status of God's ally and helper, which is the zenith of man's spiritual growth. 'Literally, 'and be our witness that we are Muslims' - Ed.

For example, the psyche (the spouses) will function within the inner world (the house of spouses) and the outer world (the relationship with the environment). Are these two worlds ready to facilitate this marriage? Do they need a special concept for the house? Is there any hallmark (wisdom) for this concept design?

The Hallmark from God

The hallmark of God becomes clear when we begin to ask the difficult question of why. Why are things the way they are? For example, why do we have two ears and one mouth?

Physical dimensions will find reasons such as enabling 360-degree hearing coverage and body balance. And one mouth is there, because we have one tongue, and one stomach! But if I would keep repeating the question why, the reasons wouldn't at certain point make any more sense. This is when the spiritual dimension begins to become easily understandable and gives answers, bringing out God's wisdom but from the perspective of the soul.

سَبَّحَ لِلَّهِ مَا فِى السَّمَوَاتِ وَالْأَرْضِ ۖ وَهُوَ الْعَزِيزُ الْحَكِيمُ

(57:1) All that is in the heavens and the earth extols the glory of Allah.

He is the Most Mighty, the Most Wise.[57]

لَهُ مُلْكُ السَّمَاوَاتِ وَالْأَرْضِ ۖ يُحْيِي وَيُمِيتُ ۖ وَهُوَ عَلَىٰ كُلِّ شَيْءٍ قَدِيرٌ

(57:2) His is the dominion of the heavens and the earth. He gives life and causes death, and He has power over everything.[58]

هُوَ الْأَوَّلُ وَالْآخِرُ وَالظَّاهِرُ وَالْبَاطِنُ ۖ وَهُوَ بِكُلِّ شَيْءٍ عَلِيمٌ

(57:3) He is the First and the Last, and the Manifest and the Hidden, and He has knowledge of everything.

For example, I can tell you that we have two ears and that makes perfect sense because it refers to the fact that we need to listen carefully to God's message about us having two options to believe or not to believe God (i.e., Satan instead). The reason that we have one mouth, and one tongue refers to the fact that we must choose one option and not two options! To add to this wisdom: we don't have much control or responsibility on what we hear but we should have 100% control and responsibility on what we are saying.

مَا يَلْفِظُ مِن قَوْلٍ إِلَّا لَدَيْهِ رَقِيبٌ عَتِيدٌ

(50:18) He utters not a word, but there is a vigilant watcher at hand. [59]

Abu Hurayrah, may God be pleased with him, reported that the Prophet, may God's peace and blessings be upon him, said: "Whoever believes in Allah and the Last Day, let him say good words or remain silent. Whoever believes in Allah and the Last Day, let him be generous to his neighbor. Whoever believes in Allah and the Last Day, let him be hospitable to his guest." *Source: Sahih al-Bukhari*

The wisdom of the Creator is to make for everything two aspects: one physical and the other spiritual. It helps us to see two sides of the same coin. The wisdom behind putting them to work together in harmony is the hallmark of the Creator that will keep repeating indefinitely inside and outside of us.

If you keep flipping these two dimensions with why questions, it can be a story with no end. It depends on how much knowledge He has given us to comprehend. His knowledge is distributed as He wills, and

191

when He wills, but His knowledge, His wisdom is endless.

قُلْ لَّوْ كَانَ الْبَحْرُ مِدَادًا لِّكَلِمَٰتِ رَبِّي لَنَفِدَ الْبَحْرُ قَبْلَ أَن تَنفَدَ كَلِمَٰتُ رَبِّي وَلَوْ جِئْنَا بِمِثْلِهِ مَدَدًا

(18:109) Say: "If the sea were to become ink to record the Words Of my Lord, indeed the sea would be all used up before the Words of my Lord are exhausted, and it would be the same even if We were to bring an equal amount of ink."[60]

Knowing His wisdom is knowing Him and this is a gift that is given if politely asked.

يُؤْتِى الْحِكْمَةَ مَن يَشَاءُ ۚ وَمَن يُؤْتَ الْحِكْمَةَ فَقَدْ أُوتِىَ خَيْرًا كَثِيرًا ۗ وَمَا يَذَّكَّرُ إِلَّا أُولُوا الْأَلْبَابِ

(2:269) He grants wisdom to those whom He wills; and whoever is granted wisdom has indeed been granted much good. Yet none except people of understanding take heed.[61]

Now let's put this hallmark to the test by asking why the psyche components are anatomically and functionally designed the way they are. And let's see how far they can go and what they can tell us about our wellbeing!

---

[60] By "words" are meant the marvelous works, the excellences and the wonders of His Power and Wisdom.

[61] 'Wisdom' signifies sound perception and sound judgement. The purpose of this statement is to point out that one who is possessed of wisdom will follow God's path rather than that of Satan. The followers of Satan believe that it is the height of wisdom and shrewdness to be constantly concerned with saving out of one's earnings, and to be perpetually on the look-out for higher income. But for those endowed with Divine perception such an attitude is sheer folly. True wisdom consists in using one's resource moderately to meet one's needs and in spending whatever is left for charitable purposes. It may be possible for a person who does not spend for charitable purposes to attain a much greater degree of worldy prosperity than others. The life of this world, however, is only a fraction of man's total life which is not limited to the confines of this world. One who risks the well-being of his eternal existence for the sake of highly transient well-being in this world is indeed a fool. The truly wise person is he who makes full use of the tenure of this life and invests his resources in prosperity in this life that will never cease.

Mysterious One, Why?

You are left without an answer, even when you ask all the scientists, whatever their knowledge, why do we have a switch of nerve fibers in the lower part of the corpus callosum and why does this crossing make the right side of the brain control the left side of the body? And why does the left side of the brain control the right side? Why are they not in straight lines? What does this crossing and switching mean?

This particular part of the design, the crossing has no physical purpose, this "why" remains a mystery. All the rest of our nervous system design is based on symmetrical pairing and double reasoning (body and soul). The crossing in question is unique and at one level only! It doesn't have a physical dimension! It's just spiritual! All the other parts of the design have physical and spiritual logic! In order for you to understand the reason for this, I must first give you the full picture of our control system (hormonal and nervous system).

Wired vs. Wireless Systems

There are two information systems in our body that work on the basis of mutual information exchange, and they then interact with internal and external environments. One of the information systems is wired (the nervous system represents the dimension of the body) and the other wireless (the hormones represent the soul dimension). These two systems are determined to maintain our harmony internally and around us. Keeping the harmony is the main and only purpose of the hallmark.

3x3 of The Nervous System

Three anatomical planes

- Sagittal plane: cuts the system into left and right halves.
- Coronal plane: cuts the system into anterior and posterior halves.
- Horizontal plane: cuts the system into vertical levels, from upper to lower.

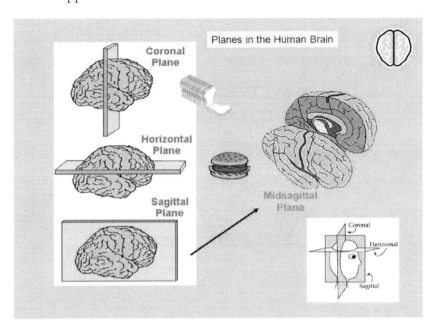

Source: Planes & Directions: Human Brain Lecture 1 2009 Biological Psychology Laboratory

Three functional levels

The nervous system can be divided into three functional levels according to the decision-making capabilities:

- *High capability:* Central voluntary

We need it to make conscious processing and decisions. It occurs mostly at the level of the cerebral cortex.

- *Middle capability:* Central autonomy

We make unconscious processing and decisions, but it has to happen at the central level since it needs complex input and output including multiple sources.

- *Low capability*: Peripheral voluntary and autonomy

It is often concerned with implanting decisions from higher levels and may act at the level of the primary reflex if a quick reaction is needed for self-protection.

Autonomous (Slave) vs Control (Master)

The middle function level of the nervous system is intended for self-preservation, which is why it works on an automatic drive. It takes care of the most basic requirements of the spouses (psyche) to enable them to live together.

The involuntary visceral (autonomic nervous system) includes the sympathetic part to fight or flight and the parasympathetic part to prevent exhaustion and restore a state of calmness.

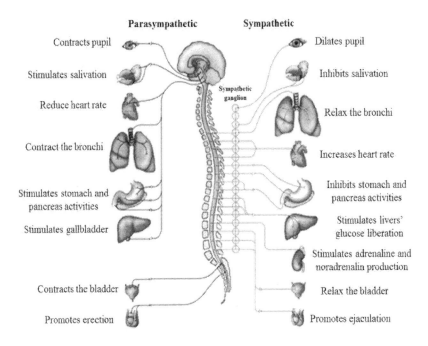

Source: Antagonist functions of the sympathetic and parasympathetic branches of the autonomic nervous system networks (adapted from Bear et al. (2007).

This delegation of the primary function of automatic leadership (slave) was a necessity for us. Our spiritual needs are met by taking this unlimited burden from our conscious master and by giving us time and chances to only make an effort in decisions for which we will be accountable in front of God in the hereafter. This is another place for you to find the same hallmark!

قُلْ إِنْ تُخْفُوا مَا فِي صُدُورِكُمْ أَوْ تُبْدُوهُ يَعْلَمْهُ اللهُ ۗ وَيَعْلَمُ مَا فِى السَّمَوَاتِ وَمَا فِى الْأَرْضِ ۗ وَاللهُ عَلَى كُلِّ شَىْءٍ قَدِيرٌ

(3:29) Say: 'Whether you conceal what is in your hearts or disclose it, Allah knows it. Allah knows what is in the heavens and in the earth and He has power over everything.'

يَوْمَ تَجِدُ كُلُّ نَفْسٍ مَا عَمِلَتْ مِنْ خَيْرٍ مُحْضَرًا ۚ ۖ وَمَا عَمِلَتْ مِنْ سُوءٍ ۚ تَوَدُّ لَوْ أَنَّ بَيْنَهَا وَبَيْنَهُ أَمَدًا بَعِيدًا ۗ وَيُحَذِّرُكُمُ اللهُ نَفْسَهُ ۗ وَاللهُ رَءُوفٌ بِالْعِبَادِ

(3:30) The Day is approaching when every soul shall find itself confronted with whatever good it has done and whatever evil it has wrought. It will then wish there is a wide space between it and the Day! Allah warns you to beware of Him; He is most tender towards His servants.

The Board Director vs. Board Members

The cortex is the outermost part of the upper part of the brain (gray matter) and should be responsible for conscious decision-making functions (the decision-making board). The board members on both sides have an equal representation of our psyche: right side (spiritual) to address unseen problems, and left side (bodily) to address objective issues.

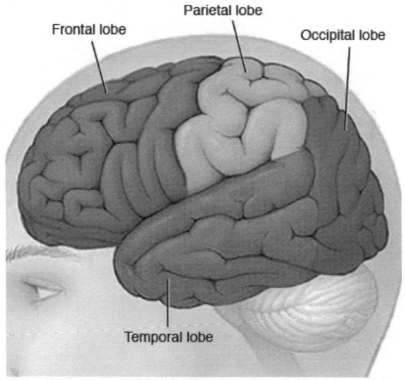

Each side of the brain contains four lobes. The back lobes are representing sensory information on the board (board members) The parietal lobe processes information about temperature, taste, touch and movement, while the occipital lobe is primarily responsible for vision. The temporal lobe processes memories, integrating them with sensations of taste, sound, sight and touch.

The frontal lobe is important for cognitive functions and control of voluntary movement or activity (the board director).

The physical location of the frontal lobes, above and forward, on our body tells us in every way about its position as a leader. There you find the most intelligent part of our being that is responsible for shaping our personality. It contains the decision-making system of our life.

From a spiritual point of view, this part is responsible for the fate of the psyche here and in the hereafter. This is why God refers in the Qur'an to the forehead as the reason for wrong decisions and actions.

كَلَّا لَئِنْ لَّمْ يَنْتَهِ لَنَسْفَعًا بِالنَّاصِيَةِ

(96:15) No indeed; if he does not desist, We shall drag him by the forelock;

نَاصِيَةٍ كَاذِبَةٍ خَاطِئَةٍ

(96:16) by the lying forelock steeped in sin.

On the other hand, Muslims worship by putting this great part of the head down. One can naturally understand why prostrating to God during prayer includes placing the head as the lowest part and in front of the whole body.

198

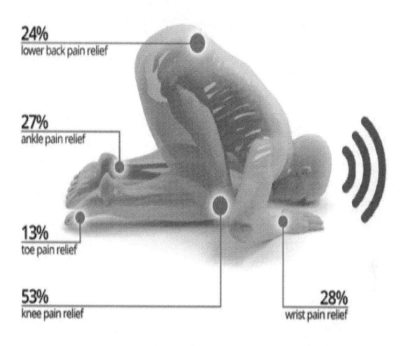

24%
lower back pain relief

27%
ankle pain relief

13%
toe pain relief

53%
knee pain relief

28%
wrist pain relief

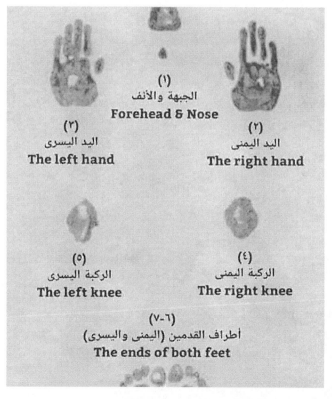

(١)
الجبهة والأنف
Forehead & Nose

(٣)
اليد اليسرى
The left hand

(٢)
اليد اليمنى
The right hand

(٥)
الركبة اليسرى
The left knee

(٤)
الركبة اليمنى
The right knee

(٧-٦)
أطراف القدمين (اليمنى واليسرى)
The ends of both feet

199

This prostration will also be done by the arrogant ones, but without the honor of doing it voluntarily, in a humiliating manner as the forehead will be tied to their feet.

يُعْرَفُ الْمُجْرِمُونَ بِسِيمَٰهُمْ فَيُؤْخَذُ بِالنَّوَاصِيٰ وَ الْأَقْدَامِ

(55:41) The culprits shall be known by their marks, and shall be seized by their forelocks and their feet.

فَبِأَيِّ أَلَآءِ رَبِّكُمَا تُكَذِّبَٰنِ

(55:42) Which of the powers of your Lord, will you twain – you men and jinn – then deny?

هٰذِهِ جَهَنَّمُ الَّتِيْ يُكَذِّبُ بِهَا الْمُجْرِمُونَ

(55:43) (It will be said): "This is the Hell that the culprits had cried lies to.

Psyche's PM

Perfectly arranged body complete with the soul, has a coherent presentation on all levels. The house is arranged clearly with charm. Now we prepared the home for a happy marriage. But is there a guarantee for happiness? Does every nice home bring a happy marriage?

This whole arrangement is called the physical arrangement (what), which still misses a description of how it will work - the know-how! How will this interesting marriage work? Before going into that more, let me ask you, have you heard of any country with two presidents or two prime ministers? That's correct, any successful operation needs one leader!

Our psyche has the corpus callosum (CC) to act as the Prime Minister (PM) of the psyche's home. How will the Prime Minister manage this? First let me tell you a story about another PM.

The Other Prime Minister Story

There was once a Prime Minister leading the country with a coalition government in very difficult times facing both economic and health challenges. She got advice from an old man that wisdom is all it takes to make things work, and that the greatest wisdom is to choose wisely knowledgeable Ministers around her!

The old man told her a story of a wise king who invited all the potential advisers to the dinner table. The first course was just soup. In front of everyone was a weird spoon, it was way too long! The king invited them to get started. The candidates looked at the soup, the spoons and each other. Their eyes started to get wider sending the eyebrows almost to the hairline. They were surprised at what they had to do!

They just kept gazing at each other trying to hide their surprise. Instead they exchanged wide fake smiles and started playing the role of a confident. "Hey, we can do it!", they shouted to motivate each other. Everyone started putting the spoon in endless positions, aiming at their plates! In the end, it went on like that the whole evening and turned into a huge mess. Long discussions while they were spreading chaos everywhere and at each other! It was a disaster! Is there any better way to do it?

The solution would have been fairly easy to reach, if they really had talked to each other with an open mind and gotten better at working together instead of just showing off. If they had started genuinely talking, they might have come up with a clever idea that everyone should take the spoon nearest to them and put it in the person's plate opposite to them and start feeding! That simple: grab the spoon, switch the plate, and feed the other side! No mess!

The hardest thing the Prime Minister had to face was understanding the old man. Not because she wasn't listening, but because she was only hearing her own psyche (ego) and that was the most important thing to her!

The Answer to The Mysterious Why, Is The Same As The Answer To The Mysterious Marriage

The crossing of the corpus callosum (the intersection) is the answer to the great mystery! How can this strange marriage work? How to create harmony that unites the dreams of the soul as well as the body? How do we let them live in love and peace?

The only way is to mix the soul and the body as if they were one: both the right and left halves of the brain exchange information and make decisions as one ball!

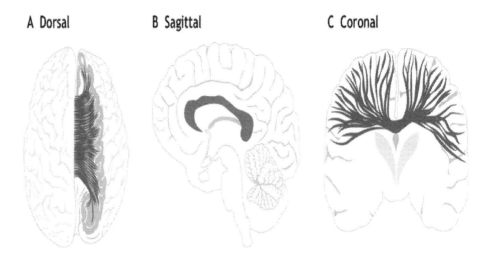

Source: Reyes, N. & Bragg Gonzalo, Lorena & Nieto, Marta. (2020). Development and plasticity of the corpus callosum. Development. 10.1242/dev.189738.

The connecting role of the corpus callosum in the center of the brain, coordinating the two sides in the upper plane as if they are one ball, is an interesting arrangement to create decisions. Even more interesting is when the time of the execution comes, and the lower fibers of CC from the right side cross to control the left side of the body and similarly the right controls the left creating an X-shape (the hallmark) between the decision and execution levels, as you can see in the illustration below. This X-shape is demonstrating the know-how of creating harmony despite the differences.

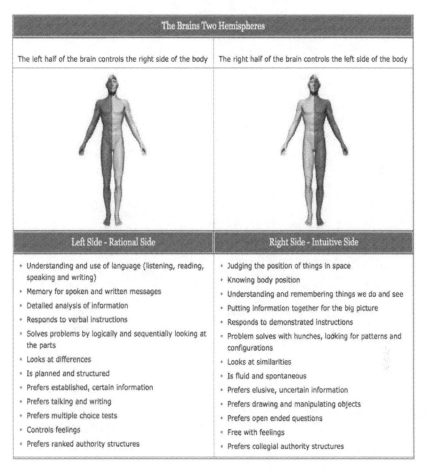

The Brains Two Hemispheres	
The left half of the brain controls the right side of the body	The right half of the brain controls the left side of the body
Left Side - Rational Side	Right Side - Intuitive Side
• Understanding and use of language (listening, reading, speaking and writing)	• Judging the position of things in space
• Memory for spoken and written messages	• Knowing body position
• Detailed analysis of information	• Understanding and remembering things we do and see
• Responds to verbal instructions	• Putting information together for the big picture
• Solves problems by logically and sequentially looking at the parts	• Responds to demonstrated instructions
• Looks at differences	• Problem solves with hunches, looking for patterns and configurations
• Is planned and structured	• Looks at similarities
• Prefers established, certain information	• Is fluid and spontaneous
• Prefers talking and writing	• Prefers elusive, uncertain information
• Prefers multiple choice tests	• Prefers drawing and manipulating objects
• Controls feelings	• Prefers open ended questions
• Prefers ranked authority structures	• Free with feelings
	• Prefers collegial authority structures

Source: my-ms.org/ anatomy_brain_part1

بِسْمِ اللهِ الرَّحْمٰنِ الرَّحِيْمِ
إِذَا السَّمَاءُ انْفَطَرَتْ

(82:1) When the heaven is split asunder,

وَإِذَا الْكَوَاكِبُ انْتَثَرَتْ

(82:2) when the stars are scattered,

وَإِذَا الْبِحَارُ فُجِّرَتْ

(82:3) when the seas are made to burst forth,

وَإِذَا الْقُبُورُ بُعْثِرَتْ

(82:4) and when graves are laid open,

عَلِمَتْ نَفْسٌ مَّا قَدَّمَتْ وَأَخَّرَتْ

(82:5) everyone shall know all his deeds, both the earlier and the later.

يَـٰٓأَيُّهَا الْإِنسَانُ مَا غَرَّكَ بِرَبِّكَ الْكَرِيمِ

(82:6) O man! What has deceived you about your generous Lord

الَّذِى خَلَقَكَ فَسَوَّىٰكَ فَعَدَلَكَ

(82:7) Who created you, shaped you, and made you well-proportioned,

فِىٓ أَىِّ صُورَةٍ مَّا شَاءَ رَكَّبَكَ

(82:8) and set you in whatever form He pleased?[62]

كَلَّا بَلْ تُكَذِّبُونَ بِالدِّينِ

(82:9) No indeed; (the fact is that) you deny the Reckoning, declaring

---

[62] That is, in the first place, the bounty and favor of your Beneficent Sustainer required that you should have acknowledged his bounties and become an obedient servant and should have felt shy of disobeying Him, but you were deluded into thinking that you have become whatever you are by your own effort, and you never thought that you should acknowledge that favor of Him Who gave you life. Secondly, it is your Lord's bounty and kindness that you can freely do whatever you like in the world and it never so happens that whenever you happen to commit an error, He should punish you with paralysis, or blind your eyes, or cause lightning to strike you. But you took His bountifulness for weakness and were beguiled into thinking that the kingdom of your God was devoid of justice

it a lie;[63]

وَإِنَّ عَلَيْكُمْ لَحَافِظِينَ

(82:10) you do so the while there are watchers over you;

كِرَامًا كَاتِبِينَ

(82:11) noble scribes,

يَعْلَمُونَ مَا تَفْعَلُونَ

---

[63] That is, there is no reasonable ground for you to be deluded. Your own physical existence itself tells that you did not come into being by yourself; your parents also did not make you. Man also did not come about as a result of the elements combining together by themselves accidentally; but a Wise and Powerful God has composed you into this perfect human shape and form. There are other kinds of animals in the world compared with which your excellent form and structure and your superior powers and faculties stand out in sharp contrast. Reason demanded that in view of all this you should have submitted gratefully and should never have dared commit disobedience of your beneficent Sustainer.

You also know that your Lord and Sustainer is not only Compassionate and Bountiful but Almighty and Omnipotent as well. When an earthquake, cyclone or flood occurs by His command, all your devices and measures fail to be effective. You also know that your Lord and Sustainer is not ignorant and foolish but Wise and Knowing, and the necessary demand of wisdom and knowledge is that whoever is given intellect should also be held responsible for his acts; whoever is given powers should also be held accountable as to how he used those powers; and whoever is given the choice to do good or evil on his own responsibility, should also be rewarded for his good act and punished for his evil act. All these truths are clearly and plainly known to you; therefore, you cannot say that there exists a reasonable ground for you to be deluded concerning your Lord. Your own nature is sufficient evidence that the beneficence of the Master should never cause the servant to be fearless of Him, and be involved in the misunderstanding that he may do whatever he pleases, no one can harm him in any way.

That is, you have not been deluded and beguiled by any good reason but by your foolish concept that there is going to be no meting out of rewards and punishments after the life of this world. It is this wrong and baseless concept which has made you heedless of God, fearless of His justice and irresponsible in your moral attitude.

(82:12) who know what you do.[64]

اِنَّ الْاَبْرَارَ لَفِىْ نَعِيْمٍ

(82:13) Surely the virtuous shall be in Bliss,

وَاِنَّ الْفُجَّارَ لَفِىْ جَحِيْمٍ ۖ

(82:14) and the wicked shall be in the Blazing Fire.

يَّصْلَوْنَهَا يَوْمَ الدِّيْنِ

(82:15) They shall enter it on the Day of Recompense

وَمَا هُمْ عَنْهَا بِغَآئِبِيْنَ

(82:16) and then shall never come out of it.

وَمَآ اَدْرٰىكَ مَا يَوْمُ الدِّيْنِ

(82:17) What do you know what the Day of Recompense is?

---

[64] That is, whether you deny the meeting out of rewards and punishments, belie it, or mock it, the reality cannot change. The reality is: that your Lord has not left you to your self in the world, but has appointed over each one of you honest and upright guardians, who are recording objectively and faithfully all your good and evil acts, and none of your acts is hidden from them, whether you commit it in darkness, or in private, or in far off jungles, or in secret when you are fully satisfied that whatever you have done has remained hidden from human eye.

For these guardian angels Allah has used the words kiram-an katibin, i.e. writers who are honorable and noble They are neither attached in personal love with somebody, nor are inimical to anybody, so that they would prepare a fictitious record on the basis of their favoring one man and un-favoring another unduly. They are neither dishonest that without being present on duty they would make wrong entries by themselves; nor are they bribable so that they would take bribes and make false reports in favor of or against somebody. They are far above these moral weaknesses. Therefore, both the good and the bad people should be fully satisfied that each man's good acts will be recorded without any omission, and no one will have an evil act recorded in his account which he has not done. Then the second quality that has been mentioned of these angels is: They know whatever you do. That is, they are not like the secret, intelligence agencies of the world, from which, despite all their search and scrutiny, many things remain hidden. They are fully aware of everyone's deeds. They accompany every person, at all places, under all conditions, in such a way that he himself does not know that someone is watching him, and they also know with what intention has somebody done a certain thing. Therefore the record prepared by them is a complete record in which nothing has been left un-recorded. About this very thing it has been said in Woe to us! What sort of a book it is, it has left nothing unrecorded of our doings, small or great. They will see before them everything, whatever they had done.

$$\text{ثُمَّ مَآ اَدْرٰلكَ مَا يَوْمُ الدِّيْنِ}$$

(82:18) Again, what do you know what the Day of Recompense is?

$$\text{يَوْمَ لَا تَمْلِكُ نَفْسٌ لِّنَفْسٍ شَيْئًا وَالْاَمْرُ يَوْمَئِذٍ لِّلّٰهِ}$$

(82:19) It is the Day when no one shall have the power to do anything for another, and all command shall be Allah's.[65]

X-Harmony Factor is not X-Factor

For the sake of clarity from this point on in this book when I'm referring to the X-factor I'm referring to something known, the actual X-shape. It describes the know-how of harmony as an act of switching (crossing) between two different things. I call it here the X-Harmony Factor. This X has nothing to do with the X-factor referring to something unknown.

Today Our Body is Obeying but Not Tomorrow

The execution (voluntary) part of our body is obeying us today, but in the hereafter our body will be a witness to our wrong choices and actions.

$$\text{يَّوْمَ تَشْهَدُ عَلَيْهِمْ اَلْسِنَتُهُمْ وَاَيْدِيْهِمْ وَاَرْجُلُهُمْ بِمَا كَانُوْا يَعْمَلُوْنَ}$$

(24:24) (Let them not be heedless of) the Day when their own tongues, their hands, and their feet shall all bear witness against them as to what

---

[65] That is, no one there will have the power to save anyone from suffering the consequences of his deeds; no one there will be so influential, strong, or such a favorite with Allah that he should behave stubbornly in the divine court and say: Such and such a one is a close relative or associate of mine; he will have to be forgiven, no matter what evils He might have committed in the world.

they have been doing.

Talking Hallmark Fulfills The Truth

The hallmark sends a clear message that this world has only one Creator. He is the center of our minds, the center of this life (dunya) as well as the hereafter (the afterlife), and obedience (worship) is the only way to win in both of them.

اَلَا اِنَّ اَوْلِيَاءَ اللهِ لَا خَوْفٌ عَلَيْهِمْ وَلَا هُمْ يَحْزَنُوْنَ

(10:62) Oh, surely the friends of Allah have nothing to fear, nor shall they grieve -

The most interesting aspect is that the crossing (the hallmark) has no other physical or spiritual indication except for the message above. And this uniqueness in itself is yet another manifestation confirming the message: this is the only solution able to challenge our psyche and there is no other solution. The single spiritual purpose of the CC is only to show the relationship between the higher and lower level of our intelligent being (command and obedience).

وَمَا خَلَقْتُ الْجِنَّ وَالْإِنْسَ اِلَّا لِيَعْبُدُوْنِ

(51:56) I created the jinn and humans for nothing else but that they may serve Me;[66]

Let's Address the Elephant in The Room!

Why are we naturally attuned to search for a relationship? For you to understand this question, let me ask you another question first: if you would have the possibility to be one side of the brain, which side would

---

[66] That is, I have not created them for the service of others but for My own service. They should serve Me, for I am their Creator. When no one else has created them, no one else has the right that they should serve him; and how can it be admissible for them that they should serve others instead of Me, their Creator? Here, the question arises that Allah Almighty is not the Creator only of the jinn and men but of the entire universe and of everything in it. Then, why has it been said only about the jinn and men that He has not created them for the service of others but of Himself? Whereas every single creature is there to serve Allah.

The answer is: Only the jinn and men have been granted the freedom that they may serve Allah within their sphere of choice if they so like; otherwise they can turn away from Allah's service as well as serve others beside Him. The rest of the creatures in the world do not have this kind of freedom. They do not have any choice whatsoever that they may not worship and serve Allah, or may serve any other. Therefore, only about the jinn and men it has been said here that by turning away from the obedience and servitude of their Creator within the bounds of their option and choice and by serving others than the Creator, they are fighting their own nature. They should know that they have not been created for the service of any other but the Creator, and for them the right way is that they should not abuse the freedom granted to them, but also within the bounds of this freedom they should serve God voluntarily just as every particle of their body is serving Him involuntarily in the sphere where they have not been granted any freedom.

The word ibadat (service, worship) in this verse has not been used in the sense of only Prayer, Fasting and other kinds of such worship so that one may understand that the jinn and men have been created only for performing the Prayer, observing the Fast and for praising and glorifying Allah. Although this sense also is included in it, this is not its complete sense. Its complete sense is that the jinn and men have not been created for the worship, obedience and carrying out of the orders of any other but Allah. They are not there to bow to any other, to carry out the orders of any other, to live in fear of any other, to follow the religion enjoined by any other, to look upon any other as the maker and destroyer of ones destiny, and to supplicate to any other than Allah for help.

you feel most comfortable with? The right or the left?

Most of the men will feel comfortable in choosing the left and majority of the women will prefer the right, but it is not a rule. After we choose our favorite option, whatever the answer, we will not feel comfortable! And having thought of it for a little while, we find ourselves wanting to have both!

This is the tricky part for our psyche. Although both options are in one skull, and they are anatomically and physiologically united, this is only a dream until the feeling of their unity (love) becomes a reality! For this reason the soul is keen to search for love outside, in its surroundings!

The need to be a part of a couple is built into our being, but we still feel powerless to understand it. This needs another level of harmony. We need to create the balance between finding love within the psyche (ego) and love outside (intimate relationship). We need experience and interaction with other beings to find this level of harmony.

Psyche Scale

Creating harmony between us and another psyche is one more level of harmony. This is the fulcrum (equilibrium point). If we put the balance 100% inward, that's totally selfish (egoistic). This is the phenomenon of self-destruction, the sum of the bodily desires intensified in one body.

This kind of soulless psyche is completely out of its scope, it has completely missed the purpose of its existence i.e., it has 0% love. It has no purpose for existence anymore, it has no hope, and no meaning in existence. It hates its own existence, and the idea of honoring anything else or any other human being. This is the literal manifestation of hatred, jealousy, malice and evil. The imbalance in this case is like 100% Satan's psyche which has been deprived of God's mercy. Satan has no purpose in existence other than to create from humans versions of himself as much as he can.

وَإِذْ قُلْنَا لِلْمَلَـٰٓئِكَةِ اسْجُدُوا لِـٰادَمَ فَسَجَدُوا إِلَّا إِبْلِيسَ قَالَ ءَأَسْجُدُ لِمَنْ خَلَقْتَ طِينًا

(17:61) And recall when We asked the angels to prostrate themselves before Adam; all prostrated themselves except Iblis, who said: "Shall I prostrate myself before him whom You created of clay?"

قَالَ أَرَءَيْتَكَ هَـٰذَا الَّذِى كَرَّمْتَ عَلَىَّ لَئِنْ أَخَّرْتَنِ إِلَىٰ يَوْمِ الْقِيَـٰمَةِ لَأَحْتَنِكَنَّ ذُرِّيَّتَهُ إِلَّا قَلِيلًا

(17:62) He then continued: "Look! This is he whom You have exalted above me! If you will grant me respite till the Day of Resurrection I shall uproot the whole of his progeny except only a few."[67]

قَالَ اذْهَبْ فَمَنْ تَبِعَكَ مِنْهُمْ فَإِنَّ جَهَنَّمَ جَزَآؤُكُمْ جَزَآءً مَّوْفُورًا

(17:63) Thereupon He retorted: "Be gone! Hell shall be the recompense - and a most ample one - of whosoever of them who follows you.

وَاسْتَفْزِزْ مَنِ اسْتَطَعْتَ مِنْهُم بِصَوْتِكَ وَأَجْلِبْ عَلَيْهِم بِخَيْلِكَ وَرَجِلِكَ وَشَارِكْهُمْ فِى الْأَمْوَالِ وَالْأَوْلَادِ وَعِدْهُمْ وَمَا يَعِدُهُمُ الشَّيْطَـٰنُ إِلَّا غُرُورًا

(17:64) Tempt with your call all whom you wish. Muster against them all your forces - your cavalry and your foot soldiers; share with them riches and offspring, and seduce them with rosy promises - and Satan's

---

[67] That is, I will uproot them from the high position of divine vicegerency which demands steadfastness in obedience. Their removal from that high position is just like the tearing of a tree from its roots.

promise is nothing but a deception[68]

اِنَّ عِبَادِىْ لَيْسَ لَكَ عَلَيْهِمْ سُلْطٰنٌ ۚ وَكَفٰى بِرَبِّكَ وَكِيْلًا

(17:65) but know well that you will have no power against My servants. Your Lord suffices for them to place their trust in."[69]

On the flip side is the holistic loving psyche. Then the balance is 100% on the outside. The soul of this psyche has 100% overcome the body. This is unconditional love, the soul has realized the whole purpose of its existence, 100% love. This is what leads us to understand love, and the soul's attributes that are also among the attributes of God: light, giving, and mercy.

---

[68] The literal meaning of the Arabic text is: You may sweep away those whom you find superficial and weak minded.

Here, Satan has been likened to that robber who assaults a habitation with cavalry and infantry and orders them to rob. The cavalry and the infantry of Satan are those jinns and human beings who are engaged in numerous forms and positions in carrying out his mission.

This is a very meaningful sentence which depicts a true and perfect picture of the relationship between Satan and his followers. On the one hand, Satan becomes a partner with the one who follows him in the earning and spending of his money without putting in any labor in it. On the other hand, he does not become a partner in bearing the consequences of his error, crime and sin. But his foolish dupe follows his instructions as if he were a partner, nay, a stronger party. Again in regard to the children of such a man, the father himself bears the whole burden of bringing them up, but under the misguidance of Satan he trains them in wrong and unmoral ways as if he alone was not their father but Satan as well was a partner in it.

Satan entices them with false promises of success and entangles them in the snare of false expectations.

[69] (1) You will have no power over human beings to force them to follow your way. What you are allowed to do is that you may delude them by false counsel and entice them by false promises, but they will have the option to follow or not to follow your counsel. You will not have the power over them to force them to follow your way against their will. (2) You will not succeed in alluring My righteous people. Though the weak minded will be enticed by you. My righteous people who are steadfast in My obedience will not succumb to you.

212

Optimum Psyche Balance

Our psyche is faced with a constant dynamic challenge, and it needs to maintain a state of balance between the inner world and the outer world, ego and unconditional love. We need to strike a balance between us and other beings. These beings include a wide range of creations as well as a range of things, from inanimate objects to plants, animals, and other psyches.

The ideal situation is to have a relationship with another psyche. The optimal relationship with another self is called marriage. A mutually compatible pair will create balance, harmony and love. The couple will naturally resonate in the anatomical and physiological preparations of the brain and psyche to achieve its goal of harmony. If not, this will overload the psyches. Basic knowledge, right?

Or not?[70]

Why Marriage Between Man and Woman?

Now I understand why God keeps repeating this fact in the Qur'an. Before I was asking myself why it is repeated in so many different verses in the Qur'an even though it is basic and undeniable knowledge.

---

[70] That is, everything in the world has been created on the principle of the pairs. The whole system of the universe is functioning on the principle that certain things are complementary and matching to certain others, and their combination brings into being countless new forms and combinations. Nothing here is so unique as may have no match, for the fact is that a thing becomes productive only after it has combined with its matching partner.

That is, the erection of the whole universe on the principle of the pairs and the existence of all things in the world in couples is a reality that testifies expressly to the necessity of the Hereafter. If you consider it deeply you will yourself come to the conclusion that when everything in the world has a partner and nothing becomes productive without combining with its partner, how can the life of the world be without a match and partner? Its match and partner necessarily is the Hereafter. Without that partner it would be absolutely fruitless.

To understand what follows one should also understand that the discussion heretofore centers around the Hereafter, but this very discussion and argument afford a proof of the Oneness of God. Just as the argument of the rain, the structure of the earth, the creation of the heavens, man's own existence, the wonderful working of the law of pairs in the universe, testify to the possibility and necessity of the Hereafter, so they are also testifying that neither is this Godless nor it has many gods, but One All-Wise and All- Powerful God alone is its Creator and Master and Controller. That is why in the following verses the invitation to the Oneness of God is being presented on the basis of these very arguments.

Furthermore, the inevitable result of believing in the Hereafter is that man should give up his attitude of rebellion against God and should adopt the way of obedience and servitude. He remains turned away from God as long as he remains involved in the false belief that he is not accountable before anyone and that he will not have to render an account of his deeds of the worldly life to anyone. Whenever this misunderstanding is removed, man immediately comes to the realization that he was committing a grave error by regarding himself as irresponsible, and this realization compels him to return to God. That is why immediately after concluding the arguments for the Hereafter, it has been said: So flee unto Allah.

سُبْحٰنَ الَّذِىْ خَلَقَ الْاَزْوَاجَ كُلَّهَا مِمَّا تُنْبِتُ الْاَرْضُ وَمِنْ اَنْفُسِهِمْ وَمِمَّا لَا يَعْلَمُوْنَ

(36:36) Holy is He Who created all things in pairs, whether it be of what the earth produces, and of themselves, and of what they do not know.[71]

I didn't expect that there would be a time when the relationship between a man and a woman would be a matter needing justification. But God knows better and now people have ended up questioning our basics!

---

[71] Glory be to Him: He is free from every defect and fault, from every error and weakness, and that another one should be His associate and partner in His work. The Quran has generally used these words when refuting polytheistic beliefs, because every belief of shirk is, in fact, an imputation of some defect, some weakness and some fault to Allah. When a person says that Allah has an associate, he in fact, thinks that either Allah is incapable of running and ruling His Kingdom alone, or He is under compulsion to make another His associate in His work. Or, some other beings are so powerful in themselves that they are interfering in God's administration and God is putting up with their interference. Or, God forbid, Allah has the weaknesses of the worldly kings, due to which He is surrounded by an army of ministers, courtiers, flatterers and beloved princes or princesses, and thus many powers of Godhead have become divided among them. Had there been no such notions of ignorance about Allah in the minds, there could be no question of any idea of shirk in the world. That is why it has been stated again and again in the Quran That Allah is free from and exalted far above those defects and faults and weaknesses which the mushriks ascribe to Him.

This is still another argument for Tauhid. Here again certain realities of daily experience have been mentioned and it is suggested that man observes these day and night but does not ponder over them seriously, whereas they contain signs and pointers to the reality. The coming together of the man and woman is the cause of man's own birth. Procreation among the animals also is due to the combination between the male and the female. Also about vegetation, man knows that the law of sex is working in it. Even among the lifeless substances when different things combine with one another, a variety of compounds come into existence. The basic composition of matter itself has become possible due to the close affinity between the positive and the negative electric charges. This law of the pairs which is the basis of the existence of the entire universe, contains in itself such complexities and finenesses of wisdom and workmanship, and there exist such harmonies and mutual relationships between the members of each pair that an objective observer can neither regard it as the result of an accident, nor can he believe that many different gods might have created these countless pairs and matched their members, one with the other, with such great wisdom. The members of each pair being a perfect match for each other and coming into being of new things with their combination itself is an explicit argument of the Creator's being One and only One.

Why are there two parts in the psyche? Why not just one? Why are there not just women or only men? This question is like asking if there could only be bodies without souls! Or souls without bodies? Or only electrons without a nucleus! The simple answer to these is that otherwise there will be no life at all! The world will end up dead, death will be everywhere!

I understand why we have come to this point of desperation of questioning the basics. It is because it has always been challenging for our psyche to search for harmony and pursue safety and love. The strained relationship, between a man and a woman, that many experience today is a clear cause to all the imbalances that we live in. Knowing how to marry and the skills to activate the X-Harmony Factor are the basics of life that everyone should practice. That's why it's already stamped on the brain, on the psyche.

Marriage is The First Inherent Human Relationship

The full experience of marriage between a man and a woman is the most important relationship in our life and in life in general. This was our first relationship even before we had a father or a mother. Yes, it is absolutely true, it was very important for Adam and his wife to have mutual affection, even though they were both in Heaven. Without a man and a woman there is no love even in Heaven. Since these moments the love story has remained the same with all its circumstances and knowledge. This is how we must find love.

وَقُلْنَا يَـٰٓأَدَمُ اسْكُنْ أَنْتَ وَزَوْجُكَ الْجَنَّةَ وَكُلَا مِنْهَا رَغَدًا حَيْثُ شِئْتُمَا وَلَا تَقْرَبَا هَـٰذِهِ الشَّجَرَةَ فَتَكُونَا مِنَ الظَّالِمِينَ

(2:35) And We said: "O Adam, live in the Garden, you and your wife, and eat abundantly of whatever you wish but do not approach this tree or else you will be counted among the wrong-doers."[72]

How to Increase Harmony Within Couples?

When it comes to gender differences, the X-Harmony Factor is stamped on our hormones, with a mirror image ratio between testosterone and estrogen in men and women. It creates the basic natural connection between the different sexes, with the necessary amount of attraction, based on desire. This instinct just lays down the motivation to gain the right set of knowledge and skills to sustain a marriage. This is why maintaining intercourse as a reward for this hard work of learning is an essential component of strengthening this relationship.

The whole idea of gender regulation in Islam is to increase attraction between the sexes and to create enough force from this attraction to

---

[72] What God wanted to impress on man was that the only place that befits man's station is Paradise, and that if man turns from the course of obedience to God as a result of Satanic allurements, he will remain deprived of it in the Next Life even as he was deprived of it once before. The only way he can recover his true status and reclaim the lost Paradise is by resisting effectively the enemy who is always trying to drive him off the course of obedience to God.

The use of the word 'wrong-doer' is highly significant. 'Wrong-doing' consists in withholding someone's rights and the wrong-doer is one who withholds those rights from their legitimate claimants. Anyone who disobeys God withholds three major rights. The first is what is due to God, for He has the right to be obeyed. Second, there are the rights of all those things which a man employs in disobeying God. The parts of his body, his mental energy, his fellow-beings, those angels who, under Divine dispensation, have been appointed to enable him to achieve his aims. both righteous and unrighteous, the material objects which he employs in his acts of disobedience - all these have a rightful claim upon him to be used in ways that please God. But when he uses them in ways which displease God he commits wrong against them all. Third, he wrongs his own self which has the right to be saved from perdition. By inviting punishment from God because of his disobedience he wrongs his own self as well. It is for these reasons that the word 'wrong' is often used in the Qur'an for sin, and the word 'wrong-doer' for sinner keep them united along the bumpy road.

وَمِنْ اٰيٰتِهٖۤ اَنْ خَلَقَ لَكُمْ مِّنْ اَنْفُسِكُمْ اَزْوَاجًا لِّتَسْكُنُوْۤا اِلَيْهَا وَجَعَلَ بَيْنَكُمْ مَّوَدَّةً وَّرَحْمَةً ۗ اِنَّ فِیْ ذٰلِكَ لَاٰيٰتٍ لِّقَوْمٍ يَّتَفَكَّرُوْنَ

(30:21) And of His Signs is that He has created mates for you from your own kind that you may find peace in them and He has set between you love and mercy. Surely there are Signs in this for those who reflect.[73]

The Genius X-Harmony Factor

In fact, marriage is a long course of interactions to manifest the X-Harmony Factor in all dimensions. The physical part is just a strong natural highlight, but it is not the only one. Let me give you yet again an example: during fertilization we see the X-Harmony Factor imprinted on our chromosomes, not only morphologically but also in the way these chromosomes behave while communicating, sharing and exchanging information. Just like the story of CC in the brain and psyche!

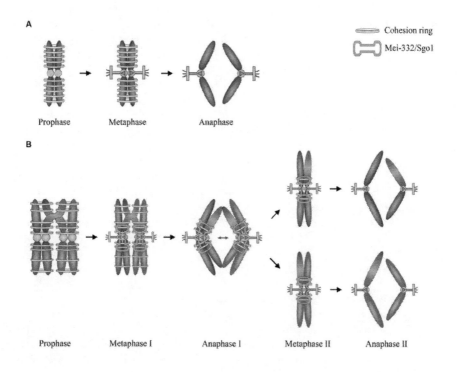

Source: The concept of the sexual reproduction cycle and its evolutionary significance. January 2015 Frontiers in Plant Science 6(e1001518):11

You may understand how the X-Harmony Factor and know-how of

[73] That is, the Creator's perfect wisdom is such that He has not created man in one sex only but in two sexes, which are identical in humanity, which have the same basic formula of their figure and form, but the two have been created with different physical structures, different mental and psychological qualities, and different emotions and desires. And then there has been created such a wonderful harmony between the two that each is a perfect counterpart of the other. The physical and psychological demands of the one match squarely with the physical and psychological demands of the other. Moreover, the Wise Creator is continuously creating the members of the two sexes in such a proportion since the dawn of the creation that in no nation and in no region has it ever happened that only boys or only girls may have been born. This is one thing in which human intelligence has absolutely no part to play.

Man cannot at all influence the course of nature according to which girls continue to be born with the feminine qualities and the boys with the masculine qualities, which are perfectly complimentary to each other, nor has he any means by which he may change the proportion in which men and women continue to be born everywhere in the world. The working of this system and arrangement so harmoniously and perpetually in the birth of millions and billions of human beings since thousands of years cannot be accidental either, nor the result of the common will of many gods. This is a clear indication of the reality that One Wise Creator and One only, in the beginning made a most appropriate design of a man and a woman by His infinite Wisdom and Power and then made arrangements that precisely in accordance with that design countless men and countless women should be born along with their separate individual qualities in the right proportion.

That is, this system has not come about by chance, but the Creator has brought it about deliberately with the object that the man should find fulfillment of the demands of his nature with the woman, and the woman with the man, and the two should find peace and satisfaction in association and attachment with each other. This is the wise arrangement which the Creator has made the means of the survival of the human race on the one hand, and of bringing the human civilization into existence on the other hand. If the two sexes had been created on different patterns and designs, and the state of agitation which changes into peace and tranquility only through union and attachment between the two had not been placed in each, the human race might have survived like sheep and goats, but there was no possibility of the birth of a civilization.

creating harmony and love have a massive life path from our chromosomes to our minds and psyches. The path carries on from generation to generation; from Adam, through us to the next generations.

In the end, humanity appears as a long chain of connected psyches as if it were a single psyche created for the single purpose of manifesting the X-Harmony Factor (love). This is a genius concept!

Contrary to all other species of animal life; the fundamental factor that has helped create human civilization is that the Creator by His wisdom has placed a desire and a thirst and a longing in the two sexes for each other, which remains unsatisfied unless the two live in complete attachment and association with each other. This same desire for peace and satisfaction compelled them to make a home together. This same desire brought families and clans into being, and this same desire made social life possible for man. In the development of social life man's mental capabilities have certainly been helpful, but they were not its real motives. The real motivating force was the same longing with which man and woman were endowed and which compelled them to establish the "home". Can anyone, possessed of common sense, say that this masterpiece of wisdom has come about by chance through the blind forces of nature? Or, that it has been arranged so by many gods, and countless men and women have been continuously coming into being with the same natural longing since thousands of years? This is a sign of the wisdom of One Wise Being, and of One only, which the people devoid of common sense only can refuse to acknowledge.

"Love" here means sexual love, which becomes the initial motive for attraction between man and woman, and then keeps them attached to each other. "Mercy" implies the spiritual relationship which gradually develops in the matrimonial life, by virtue of which they become kind, affectionate and sympathetic towards each other; so much so that in old age, sexual love falls into the background and the two partners in life prove to be even more compassionate towards each other than they were when young. These two are the positive forces which the Creator has created in man to support the initial longing of his nature. That longing and restlessness only seeks peace and satisfaction and brings the man and the woman into contact with each other. After that these two forces emerge and bind the two strangers brought up in different environments so intimately together that the two remain attached to each other through every thick and thin of life. Evidently, this love and mercy which is being experienced by millions and millions of people in their lives, is not anything material, which may be weighed and measured, nor can it be traced back to any of the constituent element of human body, nor the cause of it birth and growth found out in a laboratory. The only explanation of this can be that the human self has been endowed with it by a Wise Creator, Who has done so of His own will to serve a special purpose.

مَا خَلْقُكُمْ وَلَا بَعْثُكُمْ إِلَّا كَنَفْسٍ وَّاحِدَةٍ ۗ إِنَّ اللهَ سَمِيْعٌ بَصِيْرٌ

(31:28) To create all of you or to resurrect all of you is to Him like (creating or resurrecting) a single person. Verily Allah is All-Hearing, All-Seeing.[74]

Know Psyche's X-Harmony Factor

Let's now do some effort to re-understand psyche and psychology, the art and knowledge of integrating a pair. We have two halves (body and soul) that are mirror images of each other. They have different physics (physical and spiritual), and rely heavily on each other to form a self.

Permanent separation from each other is death. To live together, they should be united, this unity can only be done in one way. They need to create and refine a love story. There needs to be communication and constant exchange of information. They need to take on each other's roles at all levels and care for each other, exactly in the same way as the intersection (cuddling) in the corpus callosum.

At the heart (center) of this intersection is the point where the X-shape is created. It being a factor and not merely a shape makes it necessary for us to know how the soul will live with the body. This knowledge also has only one essence, one center and one source, that is the Creator who made the body and the soul. Knowing the Creator and applying His teaching is the determinant X-Harmony Factor for the

---

[74] That is, "He is hearing every sound in the universe distinctly at one and the same time, and no sound can absorb His hearing so completely that He may hear no other sound. Likewise, He is seeing the whole universe in each of its details as to thing and event at one and the same time and nothing can absorb His sight so completely that He may see nothing else. The same precisely is the case concerning the creation of men and their re-creation also. He can re-create instantaneously all the men who have been born since the beginning of the creation and will be born till the end of time. His creative power is not absorbed so completely in the creation of one man that He may be unable to create other men at the same time. For Him the creation of one man and of the billions of men, therefore, is equal and one and the same thing."

well-being of the psyche.

The Loving X-Harmony Factor

All the love know-how behind the X-Harmony Factor promotes creating mutual understanding, cooperation, balance, harmony and peace. All that is essential for the success of the couple's psyche. This success comes with feelings of confidence, contentment and happiness; beautiful feelings that bring about constant euphoria (orgasm) in the head.

Keep repeating the process and learning how to get more of this pleasure. It will become a habit. When the couple will love the idea of being together then the relationship will go from marriage to love. The soul will love being with the body, the couple will turn the challenge into an opportunity to love each other. The love of being unified oneself is the wellbeing. This is the ultimate goal of this couple being together and this is the condition for their dreams to come true.

The result is highly dependent on the teaching of God, which He made available to all. It is easy to obtain as a message, but still restricted to the smart who make their minds to respond. We are all granted the possibility to be talented. To respond is devotion to winning love. The willingness to put the essence of the loving X-Harmony Factor into action demands sincerity.

إِلَّا عِبَادَ اللهِ الْمُخْلَصِينَ

(37:40) But Allah's chosen servants (shall be spared this woeful end).

أُولَٰئِكَ لَهُمْ رِزْقٌ مَّعْلُومٌ

223

(37:41) For them awaits a known provision,[75]

فَوَاكِهُ ۚ وَهُم مُّكْرَمُونَ

(37:42) a variety of delicious fruits; and they shall be honoured[76]

فِى جَنَّٰتِ النَّعِيمِ

(37:43) in the Gardens of Bliss.

عَلَىٰ سُرُرٍ مُّتَقَٰبِلِينَ

(37:44) They will be seated upon couches set face to face;

يُطَافُ عَلَيْهِم بِكَأْسٍ مِّن مَّعِينٍ ۚ

(37:45) a cup filled with wine from its springs, will be passed around to them;[77]

بَيْضَآءَ لَذَّةٍ لِّلشَّٰرِبِينَ

---

[75] "A provision, determined": A provision all of whose characteristics have been made known to them, which they are sure to receive, about which they have also the full satisfaction that they will continue to receive it forever, and about which there is no apprehension that they may or may not get it at some time.

[76] In this there is also a subtle allusion to the fact that, in Paradise, the food will be provided not to serve as food but for pleasure and delight. That is, the food there will not be meant to replenish the bodily deficiencies through diet, for no deficiency whatever will occur in the body in that eternal life, nor will man have appetite, for appetite is caused by the process of assimilation in the body, nor will the body demand food for its survival. That is why the word fawakih has been used for the different kinds of food in Paradise, which contains the sense of taste and pleasure more than that of nutrition.

[77] Here it has not been mentioned as to who will take these cups of wine round to the dwellers of Paradise. This has been stated at other places. And there will go round to them young boys, exclusively appointed for their service, who will be as lovely as well-guarded pearls.

Here the word kaas (cup) only has been used and there is no mention of the wine. But in Arabic the use of kass always implies wine. The cup which contains milk or water, instead of wine, or is empty, is not called kaas. The word kaas is used for a cup only when it contains wine.

That is, it will not be the kind of wine that is extracted from rotten fruit and corn in the world, but it will flow naturally from fountains like canals. In Surah Muhammad, the same thing has been described more clearly, thus: And canals will be flowing in it of wine which will be delightful for the drinkers.

(37:46) white, sparkling (wine), a delight to the drinkers.

لَا فِيهَا غَوْلٌ وَّلَا هُمْ عَنْهَا يُنْزَفُوْنَ

(37:47) There will neither be any harm in it for their body nor will it intoxicate their mind.[78]

وَعِنْدَهُمْ قٰصِرٰتُ الطَّرْفِ عِيْنٌ

(37:48) Theirs shall be wide-eyed maidens with bashful, restrained glances,[79]

كَاَنَّهُنَّ بَيْضٌ مَّكْنُوْنٌ

(37:49) so delicate as the hidden peel under an egg's shell.[80]

فَاَقْبَلَ بَعْضُهُمْ عَلٰى بَعْضٍ يَّتَسَاءَلُوْنَ

(37:50) Then some of them will turn to others, and will ask each other.

قَالَ قَائِلٌ مِّنْهُمْ اِنِّىْ كَانَ لِىْ قَرِيْنٌ

---

[78] That is, the wine of Paradise will be free from both the evils which are found in the wine of the world. The wine of the world, first of all, afflicts man with its stink; then it embitters his taste, upsets his stomach, affects his mind and causes illusion; then it affects the liver and spoils the health generally. Then, when the intoxication is gone, it leaves behind other ill-effects on the body. Its other evil is that man gets drunk with it, talks nonsense and brawls. This is how the wine affects man's mind and reason. Man suffers both these evil effects of the wine only for the sake of delight and pleasure. Allah says that the wine of Paradise will certainly afford and give full pleasure and delight, but it will be free from the kinds of the evils that go with the worldly wine.

[79] Probably, these will be the girls who died before attaining the age of discretion in the world, and whose parents did not deserve to enter Paradise. This can be said on the basis of analogy that just as the boys similarly placed will be appointed for the service of the dwellers of Paradise, and they will ever remain boys, so will the girls be made the houris and they will ever remain young and beautiful. The correct knowledge, however, is with Allah.

"Restraining their looks": Restraining their looks from everyone except their husbands.

[80] The words of the text actually mean this: As if they were the hidden or well preserved eggs. The commentators have given different interpretations of these words, but the correct commentary is the one which Umm Salamah has related from the Prophet (peace be upon him). She says that when she asked the Prophet (peace be upon him), the meaning of this verse, he said: Their delicacy and elegance and tenderness will be like the thin skin which is there between the shell of the egg and its fleshy part.

(37:51) One of them will say: "I had a companion in the world

يَقُولُ أَءِ نَّكَ لَمِنَ الْمُصَدِّقِينَ

(37:52) who used to say: Are you also one of those who confirm the Truth (of life after death)?

ءَاِذَا مِتْنَا وَكُنَّا تُرَابًا وَّ عِظَامًا ءَاِنَّا لَمَدِيْنُوْنَ

(37:53) After we are dead and have become all dust and bones shall we still be requited?[81]

قَالَ هَلْ اَنْتُمْ مُّطَّلِعُوْنَ

(37:54) He will say: Do you wish to know where he is now?

فَاطَّلَعَ فَرَاٰهُ فِيْ سَوَآءِ الْجَحِيْمِ

(37:55) Then he will look downwards, and will see him in the depths of Hell.

قَالَ تَاللّٰهِ اِنْ كِدْتَّ لَتُرْدِيْنِ

(37:56) He will say to him: By Allah, you almost ruined me.

وَلَوْلَا نِعْمَةُ رَبِّيْ لَكُنْتُ مِنَ الْمُحْضَرِيْنَ

(37:57) But for Allah's favour, I should be one of those who have been mustered here.[82]

اَفَمَا نَحْنُ بِمَيِّتِيْنُ

(37:58) So, are we not going to die,

اِلَّا مَوْتَتَنَا الْاُوْلٰى وَمَا نَحْنُ بِمُعَذَّبِيْنَ

(37:59) except for our first death? And shall we suffer no

---

[81] That is, were you also one of those credulous people who put their faith in an irrational and impossible thing like life-after-death.

[82] This shows how powerful will be man's hearing, seeing and speaking powers in the Hereafter. Sitting in Paradise he bends his head a little and is able to see a person, who is undergoing torment thousands of miles away in Hell, without the agency of a television set. Then, they not only just see each other, but also commune with each other directly without the medium of the telephone or radio and they speak and hear each other over vast distances.

chastisement?[83]

اِنَّ هٰذَا لَهُوَ الْفَوْزُ الْعَظِيْمُ

(37:60) Surely this is the supreme triumph.

لِمِثْلِ هٰذَا فَلْيَعْمَلِ الْعٰمِلُوْنَ

(37:61) For the like of it should the workers work.

اَذٰلِكَ خَيْرٌ نُّزُلًا اَمْ شَجَرَةُ الزَّقُّوْمِ

(37:62) Is this a better hospitality or the tree of al-Zaqqum?[84]

اِنَّا جَعَلْنٰهَا فِتْنَةً لِّلظّٰلِمِيْنَ

(37:63) We have made this tree a trial for the wrong-doers.[85]

اِنَّهَا شَجَرَةٌ تَخْرُجُ فِيْٓ اَصْلِ الْجَحِيْمِ

(37:64) It is a tree that grows in the nethermost part of Hell.

طَلْعُهَا كَاَنَّهُ رُءُوْسُ الشَّيٰطِيْنِ

---

[83] The style clearly shows that while speaking to his friend in Hell, the dweller of Paradise suddenly starts talking to himself. He speaks these three sentences in a way as if he found himself in a state much better than that he ever expected and imagined for himself, and now being beside himself with wonder and joy he is engaged in a sort of soliloquy. In such a state the speaker does not speak to an addressee, nor the questions he asks are meant to find out something from somebody, but in this state the man's own feelings find expression through his tongue. The dweller of Paradise, while speaking to the dweller of Hell, suddenly starts feeling how he has been favored by good fortune: now there is neither death nor any torment: all troubles and distresses have come to an end and he has been blessed with immortality. Under this very feeling he exclaims: Well are we not to die any other than our first death? Are we not to be punished?

[84] Zaqqum is a tree of the cactus species found in Tihamah. It is bitter in taste, obnoxious in smell and sheds a milk like juice when cut or broken.

[85] That is, on hearing this, the disbelievers get a new opportunity to taunt the Quran and mock the Prophet (peace be upon him). They ridicule it saying: Listen another strange thing: A tree will grow in the blazing fire of Hell.

(37:65) Its spathes are like the heads of satans.[86]

فَإِنَّهُمْ لَآكِلُوْنَ مِنْهَا فَمَالِئُوْنَ مِنْهَا الْبُطُوْنَ ؕ

(37:66) (The people of Hell) will surely eat of it, filling their bellies with it.

ثُمَّ اِنَّ لَهُمْ عَلَيْهَا لَشَوْبًا مِّنْ حَمِيْمٍ ۚ

(37:67) Then on top of it they will have a brew of boiling water.

ثُمَّ اِنَّ مَرْجِعَهُمْ لَاۡاِلَى الْجَحِيْمِ

(37:68) Then their return will be to the same blazing Hell.[87]

اِنَّهُمْ اَلْفَوْا اٰبَآءَهُمْ ضَآلِّيْنَ

(37:69) These are the ones who found their fathers steeped in error,

فَهُمْ عَلٰى اٰثٰرِهِمْ يُهْرَعُوْنَ

(37:70) and they are running in their footsteps.

وَلَقَدْ ضَلَّ قَبْلَهُمْ اَكْثَرُ الْاَوَّلِيْنَ

(37:71) Before them a multitude of people of olden times had erred,

وَلَقَدْ اَرْسَلْنَا فِيْهِمْ مُّنْذِرِيْنَ

(37:72) and We had sent among them Messengers to warn them.

فَانْظُرْ كَيْفَ كَانَ عَاقِبَةُ الْمُنْذَرِيْنَ

(37:73) Observe, then, what was the end of those that had been warned,

اِلَّا عِبَادَ اللّٰهِ الْمُخْلَصِيْنَ

---

[86] Nobody should have the misunderstanding that since no one has seen the head of Satan, it was no use likening the buds of zaqqum to it. This is, in fact, an imaginative kind of the simile, and is employed in the literature of every language. For example, in order to give an idea of the rare beauty of a woman, it is said she is a fairy, and in order to describe her ugliness, it is said that she is a hag or a demon. Likewise, a pious-looking person is described as an angel and a dreadful-looking person as a devil.

[87] This shows that when the dwellers of Hell will be in distress due to hunger and thirst, they will be driven to the side where there would be the zaqqum trees and the springs of boiling water. When they will have eaten and drunk, they will be brought back to Hell.

(37:74) except for the chosen servants of Allah?[88]

Symphony of the X-Harmony Factor

Knowing the truth about the X-Harmony Factor will always give you a clear answer to all the whys in your mind that you did not find an answer to. Why am I here? Why am I who I am? Why am I not happy? Why am I worried? Why am I nervous? Why am I alone? Why don't I want to be alone? Why am I afraid of the unknown? The answer is the same to all of these questions: it's because you don't know the X-Harmony Factor's knowledge of yourself, your well-being, nor your love!

Knowing the X-Harmony Factor helps you to create powerful building blocks for everything: communication, collaboration, work, life, marriage, learning, innovation, creativity, success, harmony, peace and love. X-Harmony Factor is the hallmark of the Creator's miracles. This hallmark is repeated: in the little atom, in our brain, psyche, hormones, genetics, relationships, environment, space, in the innovations of Nicola Tesla - you name it.

Our whole being is an endless symphony of the manifestations of the X-Harmony Factor, playing 24/7 in harmony. Everything repeats the same message: two worlds (body and soul), two lives (here and hereafter) and one Creator. Every single thing rejoices in this harmony powerfully singing glory to Him with His praise, there is no God but Allah.

تُسَبِّحُ لَهُ السَّمَاوَاتُ السَّبْعُ وَالْأَرْضُ وَمَن فِيهِنَّ ۚ وَإِن مِّن شَيْءٍ إِلَّا يُسَبِّحُ
بِحَمْدِهِ وَلَـٰكِن لَّا تَفْقَهُونَ تَسْبِيحَهُمْ ۗ إِنَّهُ كَانَ حَلِيمًا غَفُورًا

(17:44) The seven heavens, the earth, and all that is within them give

---

[88] That is, they never used their own common sense to see whether the way their forefathers had been following was right or wrong; they just blindly adopted the way that they found others following.

glory to Him. There is nothing but gives glory to Him with His praise, though you do not understand their hymns of praise. He is Most Forbearing, Exceedingly Forgiving."[89]

What is The Chance of You Being Part of The Symphony?

It is not difficult to understand now that the X-Harmony Factor is manifested even in a more sophisticated mathematical interface, the golden ratio, and its manifestations in nature, biology, geography, and finally in the mathematical encryption of the Qur'an as mentioned earlier.

The most important thing for you is to be able to join the symphony. Our psyche is highly connected, in a complex fashion, with the universe. Also the universe should stay all the time in tune with the genius symphony of harmony. Despite all these dimensions and layers, it is easy to understand our role and join this symphony unless we are interrupted. What is the main source of interruption around us?

---

[89] That is, the entire universe and everything in it bear witness to the fact that their Creator and Guardian is free from each and every fault, defect and weakness, and that He is far above this that there should be any partner or associate in His Godhead.

Everything is not only singing hymns of the glory of its Creator but is affording the proof that He is perfect in every respect and worthy of all praise. Everything is an embodiment of the proof that its Creator and Administrator is the one in whom there is perfection of every quality. Therefore, He alone is worthy of praise.

That is, it is due to His forbearance and forgiveness that though you are persistently insolent to Him and go on inventing one false thing or the other against Him, He forbears and forgives you. He neither withholds provisions from you nor deprives you of His favors nor strikes an insolent person instantly dead with a thunderbolt. Above all, He is so forbearing and forgiving that He gives long enough respite to the individuals and communities to mend their ways, sends His prophets and reformers for their admonition and guidance and forgives all the past mistakes and errors, if one sincerely repents and adopts the right way.

CHAPTER 13

Islamophilia 4

Disharmony, Harmony and Islam

Before Getting Out of The Closet

While all the manifestations of the X-Harmony Factor are in favor of harmony, why can't a man and a woman figure the harmony out individually and of course together? And if you do not succeed with all these prerequisites, then what is the possibility of finding harmony in a same-sex relationship?

There is a lot of optimism, optimism until the last breath, even after a long road of despair. We have reached a point where we are all out of balance in life.

يَعِدُهُمْ وَيُمَنِّيهِمْ ۖ وَمَا يَعِدُهُمُ الشَّيْطَنُ إِلَّا غُرُورًا

(4:120) Satan makes promises to them and fills them with vain hopes, but whatever he promises them is merely delusion.[90]

If humanity is at this moment so desperate to find love, we should look in the right direction, wonder what the problem is, and save the blue-sky thinking for occasions of very different scale!

The Right Brain is Right

There is no wonder for a person to miss love if he is born into a family or community already missing it. Then you won't see any point in advice, or have hope for a better future. It is well understood that every

---

[90] Satanic operations are based on making attractive promises and raising high hopes. Whenever Satan wants to mislead men, whether individually or collectively, he tries to inspire them with Utopian expectations. In some he inspires expectations of ecstatic pleasure and outstanding success in their individual lives. He inspires others with prospects for achieving national glory. To still others he promises the well-being of mankind. He makes people feel confident that they can arrive at the ultimate truth without the aid of revealed knowledge. He deludes others into believing that God neither exists nor that there is any Life-after-Death. He comforts others with the belief that even if there is an After-life, they will be able to escape punishment through the intercession of certain persons. In short, Satan extends to different groups of people different promises and expectations with a view to seducing them.

person has a profound need to respond to the spiritual call of freedom and love. This call responds to the problem that there is an urgent and necessary need for well-being.

The problem will kick start the right side of the brain to work things out. This is an action, which will create even more urgency, if the person does not have proper nourishment of spiritual knowledge.

The gravity of the situation will then shift the burden to the left side of the brain in order to find logic and a solution to fix the instability and imbalance. The first conclusion of the left side is that the right side is right: there is a need for higher values, feelings and a higher purpose. It's time for the left side to find a solution. But what are the options?

Self-talk is Left Brain's Next Step

The left brain is ready with a checklist. Most of the options in the list are already crossed out. They have never worked before! The thinking out loud process has begun!

Now you have that option out of the closet. Why not, if the other options don't work and won't work? But the out of the closet alternative is not normal! It'socially and probably economically unsustainable. Are these really important things to consider? However, I don't care! Why should I care!? Indeed these socio-economic considerations are the causes of my miserable feelings!

I need to stand up against all these standards, and I need to change this way of thinking! I need to change and end this misery! Let's let people like me be free to find love that I never found for myself. This should be a trend! We have to stand up for it and support each other! This is a human right and the whole world should respect this right! The question is, do these thoughts originate from their heads? Or is all this facilitated by Satan?

وَزَيَّنَ لَهُمُ الشَّيْطٰنُ أَعْمَالَهُمْ فَصَدَّهُمْ عَنِ السَّبِيلِ فَهُمْ لَا يَهْتَدُونَ

(27:24) Satan has made their deeds appear attractive to them and has, thus, debarred them from the Right Path so they do not find true guidance[91]

The Left Brains of Others Are Unable to Speak

The left brains of others are speechless. They know that they have nothing to offer. They have a limited understanding of love, their search for it didn't bring lasting results. All they can offer this generation is the freedom to search for it even by breaking the norms. Although their logic would not accept this kind of unconventional solution for themselves and it would have never even crossed their minds.

They know for sure that this is not the right way. But because they are responsible for the miserable situation of the current generation, caused by their inability to afford love for them, the decision in this situation is just to shut up and watch what happens. Is this really their decision or are they forced to go with it? Now we need to question: did they experience someone specifically enforcing it on them or does this come from their thoughts? And yet again, is this their thought?

وَلَآمُرَنَّهُمْ فَلَيُغَيِّرُنَّ خَلْقَ اللهِ ۗ وَمَنْ يَّتَّخِذِ الشَّيْطٰنَ وَلِيًّا مِنْ دُوْنِ اللهِ فَقَدْ خَسِرَ

---

[91] That is, Satan has made them believe that earning the worldly wealth and making their lives more and more grand and pompous is the only real and best use of their mental and intellectual and physical powers. Apart from these, they need not think seriously of anything else: they need not bother themselves to see whether there was any factual reality behind the apparent life of the world or not. And whether the basis of their religion, morality, culture and system of life accorded with that reality or went utterly against it. Satan satisfied them that when they were making adequate progress in respect of wealth and power and worldly grandeur, they had no need to see whether their beliefs and philosophies and theories were correct or not, for the only proof of their being correct was that they were earning wealth and enjoying life to their hearts content.

(4:119) and I shall command them and they will disfigure Allah's creation, who took Satan rather than Allah for his guardian has indeed suffered a manifest loss.[92]

Both Left Brains Are Right but Not All Right

Could you zoom in a bit and try to get to the root cause of this dilemma? What will you see? What are these two left sides talking about? Are they talking about their well-being and their psychological struggle resulting from the pressures of the economy? Are they free?

Are they talking about the repercussions of the New Trinity? Did any of them see that they have paid their harmony and wellbeing as a price for their welfare system and economy? That they have lost it since they left spirituality and sobriety in order to run after some kind of physical well-being? Did either one of these two left sides see even the shadow of the New Trinity in the background of the problem, or was it completely hidden?

يَبَنِىٓ ءَادَمَ لَا يَفْتِنَنَّكُمُ الشَّيْطَٰنُ كَمَآ أَخْرَجَ أَبَوَيْكُم مِّنَ الْجَنَّةِ يَنزِعُ عَنْهُمَا لِبَاسَهُمَا لِيُرِيَهُمَا سَوْءَٰتِهِمَآ إِنَّهُۥ يَرَىٰكُمْ هُوَ وَقَبِيلُهُۥ مِنْ حَيْثُ لَا تَرَوْنَهُمْ إِنَّا

---

[92] To alter God's creation in some respect does not mean changing its original form. If that was meant, human civilization would have to be considered Satanic in its entirety. For civilization consists essentially of man's putting to use the resources endowed by God. Hence the alteration of God's creation, which is characterized as Satanic, consists in using a thing not for the purpose for which it was created by God. In other words, all acts performed in violation either of one's true nature or of the intrinsic nature of other things are the result of the misleading promptings of Satan. These include, for instance, sodomy, monasticism, celibacy, sterilization of either men or women, turning males into eunuchs, diverting females from the functions entrusted to them by nature and driving them to perform the functions for which men were created. These and numerous similar measures are enacted by Satan's disciples in this world, which amounts on their part, to saying that the laws of the Creator were faulty and that they would like to 'reform' them.

جَعَلْنَا الشَّيَاطِينَ أَوْلِيَاءَ لِلَّذِينَ لَا يُؤْمِنُونَ

(7:27) Children of Adam! Let not Satan deceive you in the manner he deceived your parents out of Paradise, pulling off from them their clothing to reveal to them their shame. He and his host surely see you from whence you do not see them. We have made satans the guardians of those who do not believe.

Do you see the stress-creating mechanism fueling itself by creating more stress? Have you been wondering why, all of a sudden, in this day and age, this gigantic propaganda machine is promoting an extreme solution to realize dreams: sterile love or violent money (Squid Game)? Especially for the younger generations? Do you see any chance for humanity to survive longer?

وَاسْتَفْزِزْ مَنِ اسْتَطَعْتَ مِنْهُمْ بِصَوْتِكَ وَأَجْلِبْ عَلَيْهِمْ بِخَيْلِكَ وَرَجِلِكَ وَشَارِكْهُمْ فِى الْأَمْوَالِ وَالْأَوْلَادِ وَعِدْهُمْ ۚ وَمَا يَعِدُهُمُ الشَّيْطَنُ إِلَّا غُرُورًا

(17:64) Tempt with your call all whom you wish. Muster against them all your forces - your cavalry and your foot soldiers; share with them riches and offspring, and seduce them with rosy promises - and Satan's promise is nothing but a deception

What is All Right?

If we apply the know-how of the X-Harmony Factor to the previous example, then CC is going to do its job, and bring one combined harmonious decision from the right and left brain.

The decision will be the following: to treat the topic the same way as smoking. It exists, but the promotion for it is restricted. You may not come across any ads promoting smoking, but cigarettes are sold everywhere. You don't have to be shy while ordering it but there is no need to make it attractive to others. You are free, but don't bring temptation to non-smokers.

Ads will throw off the balance. If you have a penchant for smoking, you'll go and look for it, but we don't teach smoking in schools, and we don't have to make it a theme for the Olympics. We don't ask celebrities from all walks of life to raise their thumbs up for smokers. We can leave the younger generation free to decide for themselves, there's no need to fiddle with their heads. In this situation, if smoking is strongly promoted, it indicates that you are serving a hidden agenda!

The whole thinking process was a good example of understanding the effect of the X-Harmony Factor. In simple words: we don't have to jump from one extreme to the other.

Extreme is Extreme

The LGBTQ community has more alcohol problems together with other co-occurring mental conditions than heterosexual. These often include severe depression, anxiety, and stress. They also have higher suicide rates and self-harming tendencies. The 2018 review, published in JAMA Pediatrics, compiled data from 35 previous studies. The analysis involved close to 2.4 million heterosexual youth and 113,468 LGBTQ youth, ages 12 to 20, from 10 countries. *Source: https://jamanetwork.com/journals/jamapediatrics/article-abstract/2704490*

The results included the following LGBTQ suicide statistics:

- LGBTQ youth were 3.5 times as likely to attempt suicide as their heterosexual peers
- Transgender teens were 5.87 times more likely to attempt suicide as their heterosexual peers
- Gay and lesbian youth were 3.71 times more likely to attempt suicide as their heterosexual peers
- Bisexual youth were 3.69 times more likely to attempt suicide than teens who identified as heterosexual.

The Psyche in The Maze!

Do you see the progress of the New Trinity in controlling people's minds and behavior? Do you see how far the New Trinity can go? It can create any kind of generation, make them believe any lie! Is this how the mice feel in a maze? Do you see how your psyche is not free anymore? Most of the time your back is to the wall, and you are given only one exit!

How Did We End Up in The Maze?

The real problem is that we fix our problems the same way we created them. If we are lacking spiritual energy, we turn away from God. The soul is a gift (trust) from God. We accepted it in the first place, but do we know how to take care of it?

إِنَّا عَرَضْنَا الْأَمَانَةَ عَلَى السَّمٰوٰتِ وَالْأَرْضِ وَالْجِبَالِ فَأَبَيْنَ اَنْ يَّحْمِلْنَهَا وَاَشْفَقْنَ مِنْهَا وَ حَمَلَهَا الْإِنْسَانُ اِنَّهُ كَانَ ظَلُوْمًا جَهُوْلًا ۙ

(33:72) We offered the trust to the heavens and the earth and the mountains, but they refused to carry it and were afraid of doing so; but

240

man carried it. Surely he is wrong-doing, ignorant.[93]

We feel stressed so we seek relief through addiction to chemicals, heavy metal music or praying to the devil. We lack love, we encourage marriages between similar bodies and spirits. We have budget deficits, we take more debt, and end up with more inflation and deficits. We are experiencing climate change due to the industrial economy, and we face even more devastating changes in our psyches because of the digital economy!

ظَهَرَ الْفَسَادُ فِى الْبَرِّ وَالْبَحْرِ بِمَا كَسَبَتْ اَيْدِى النَّاسِ لِيُذِيقَهُمْ بَعْضَ الَّذِىٰ عَمِلُوا لَعَلَّهُمْ يَرْجِعُوْنَ

(30:41) Evil has become rife on the land and at sea because of men's deeds; this in order that He may cause them to have a taste of some of their deeds; perhaps they will turn back (from evil).[94]

God Made It Easy but Did We Do the Same?

Why all this imbalance and havoc of harmony ? Why didn't God make it simple?

I also have a question! My question to you is why do you not believe in the existence of one God who created all this life and the universe? He is asking us to believe in Him, obey Him, follow His instructions and restore harmony, at least in ourselves.

So far, does the book elicit any feelings or thoughts in you? Are you reconsidering your view of life? Do you see your ending here, in this life or does your life start here?

Some accept the belief that we are the descendants of the evolution of the amoeba. They agree that we came from an amoeba that has been thinking and working hard until it has successfully encoded the message of harmony in our brains? Who makes things difficult? God

[93] In the end, Allah wants man to realize his real position in the world; if in that position he regarded the life of the world as mere fun and sport and adopted a wrong attitude carelessly, he would only be working for his own doom.

Here, the word "amanat" (trust) implies khilafat (caliphate) which, according to the Quran, man has been granted in the earth. The inevitable result of the freedom given to man to choose between obedience and disobedience, and the powers and authority granted him over countless creations for using that freedom, is that he himself be held responsible for his voluntary acts and should deserve rewards for his righteous conduct and suffer punishment for his evil conduct. Since man has not attained these powers by his own efforts but has been granted these by Allah, and he is answerable before Allah for their right or wrong use, these have been described by the word khilafat at other places in the Quran, and by amanat here.

In order to give an idea of how important and heavy this "trust" (amanat) is, Allah says that the heavens and the earth, in spite of their glory and greatness, and the mountains, in spite of their size and firmness, could not have the power and courage to bear it. But man, the weak and frail man, has borne this heavy burden on his tiny self.

The presentation of the trust before the earth and the heavens and their refusal to bear it and their being afraid of it may be true literally, or it may have been said so metaphorically. We can neither know nor can comprehend Allah's relationship with His creations. The earth and the sun and the moon and the mountains are dumb, deaf and lifeless for us but they may not be so for Allah. Allah can speak to each of His creations and it can respond to Him, though its nature is incomprehensible for us. Therefore, it is just possible that Allah, in fact, might have presented this heavy trust before them, and they might have shuddered to see it, and they might have made this submission before their Master and Creator.

"Lord, we find our good and our convenience only in remaining as Your powerless servants: we do not find courage to ask for the freedom to disobey and do justice to it, and then suffer Your punishment in case we cannot do justice to it." Likewise, it is also quite possible that before this present life Allah might have given another kind of existence to mankind and summoned it before Himself, and it might have willingly undertaken to accept the delegated powers and authority. We have no rational argument to regard this as impossible. Only such a person, who might have made a wrong estimate of his mental and intellectual powers and capabilities, can think of regarding it as impossible.

However, this is also equally possible that Allah may have said so allegorically. In order to give an idea of the extraordinary importance of the matter, He may have depicted the scene as if the earth and the heavens and the mountains like the Himalayas were present before Him on one side and a 5 to 6 foot man, on the other. Then Allah might have asked:

or us?

We seem to have a very selective logic while answering the questions! It would be easy, if we used both sides of our brain to answer all the questions fully. Should we focus on what and how? And deny who and why? Wow!

Why did we believe in any theory, however twisted, but never believed

---

"I want to invest someone of My creation with the power that being a subject of My Kingdom, it may acknowledge My Supremacy and obey My commands of its own free will; otherwise it will also have the power to deny Me, even rebel against Me. After giving him this freedom I shall so conceal Myself from him as if I did not exist at all. And to exercise this freedom I shall invest him with vast powers, great capabilities, and shall give him dominion over countless of My creations so that he may raise any storm that he may in the universe. Then I shall call him to account at an appointed time. The one who will have misused the freedom granted by Me, will be made to suffer a most terrible punishment; and the one who will have adopted My obedience in spite of all chances and opportunities for disobedience, will be raised to such high ranks as no creation of Mine has ever been able to attain. Now tell, which of you is ready to undergo this test?"

Hearing this discourse a hush might have prevailed for a while all through the universe. Then one huge creation after the other might have bowed down and submitted that it should be excused from the severe test. Then, at last, this frail creation might have risen and submitted: "O my Lord, I am ready to undergo this test. I shall brave all the dangers inherent in the freedom and independence only in the hope that I shall be blessed with the highest office in Your Kingdom if I pass the test."

By imagining this scene through his heart's eye only can man judge exactly what delicate position he holds in the universe. Allah in this verse has called the person unjust and ignorant, who lives a carefree life in the place of test, and has no feeling at all of how great a responsibility he is shouldering, and what consequences he will encounter of the right or wrong decisions that he makes in choosing and adopting an attitude for himself in the life of the world. He is ignorant because the fool holds himself as responsible to no one; he is unjust because he is himself preparing for his doom and is also preparing the doom of many others along with him.

[94] "What the hands of people have earned" means the wickedness and oppression and tyranny, which inevitably appear in human conduct and character as a result of adopting shirk and atheism and ignoring the Hereafter. "Perhaps they may return" means that Allah shows the evil consequences of some of the acts of men in this world before the punishment of the Hereafter so that they understand the reality, feel the error of their conjectures and turn to the righteous belief, which the Prophets of Allah have been presenting before man since the earliest times, and besides adopting which there is no other way of ordering human conduct on sound foundations.

in God? We wanted to live and smell the roses without thinking who brought us to life and why did He do so? And what did He promise?

وَقَالُوا مَا هِيَ إِلَّا حَيَاتُنَا الدُّنْيَا نَمُوتُ وَنَحْيَا وَمَا يُهْلِكُنَا إِلَّا الدَّهْرُ ۚ وَمَا لَهُم بِذَٰلِكَ مِنْ عِلْمٍ ۖ إِنْ هُمْ إِلَّا يَظُنُّونَ

(45:24) They say: "There is no life other than our present worldly life: herein we live and we die, and it is only (the passage of) time that destroys us. Yet the fact is that they know nothing about this and are only conjecturing.[95]

وَإِذَا تُتْلَىٰ عَلَيْهِمْ آيَاتُنَا بَيِّنَاتٍ مَّا كَانَ حُجَّتَهُمْ إِلَّا أَن قَالُوا ائْتُوا بِآبَائِنَا إِن كُنتُمْ صَادِقِينَ

(45:25) And when Our Clear Signs are rehearsed to them, their only

---

[95] This is, there is no means of knowledge by which they might have known with certainty that after this life there is no other life for man, and that man's soul is not seized by the command of God, but he dies and perishes merely in the course of time. The deniers of the Hereafter say these things not on the basis of any knowledge but on mere conjecture. The maximum that they could say scientifically is: We do not know whether there is any life after death or not; but they cannot say: We know that there is no other life after this life. Likewise, they cannot make the claim of knowing scientifically that man's soul is not seized by God's command but he perishes after death just like a watch which suddenly stops functioning. The most they can say is just this: We do not know what exactly happens in either case.

Now the question is: When to the extent of the means of human knowledge there is an equal possibility of there being life after death or there being no life after death, and the soul's being seized by Allah's command, or man's dying of himself in the course of time, what is the reason that these people abandon the probability of the possibility of the Hereafter and give their judgment in favor of its denial? Do they have any other reason than this that they, in fact, decide this question on the basis of their desire and not by any argument? As they do not like that there should be any life after death and death should mean total annihilation and not seizure of the soul by Allah's command, they make their heart's desire their creed and deny the other probability.

contention is: "Bring back to us our fathers if you are truthful."[96]

قُلِ اللهُ يُحْيِيكُمْ ثُمَّ يُمِيتُكُمْ ثُمَّ يَجْمَعُكُمْ اِلٰى يَوْمِ الْقِيٰمَةِ لَا رَيْبَ فِيْهِ وَلٰكِنَّ اَكْثَرَ النَّاسِ لَا يَعْلَمُوْنَ

(45:26) Tell them, (O Prophet): "It is Allah Who gives you life and then causes you to die, and He it is Who will then bring all of you together on the Day of Resurrection, a Day regarding which there can be no doubt. Yet most people do not know.[97]

وَلِلّٰهِ مُلْكُ السَّمٰوٰتِ وَالْاَرْضِ ۚ وَيَوْمَ تَقُوْمُ السَّاعَةُ يَوْمَىِٕذٍ يَّخْسَرُ الْمُبْطِلُوْنَ

(45:27) Allah's is the kingdom of the heavens and the earth, and on the Day when the Hour (of Resurrection) shall come to pass, the followers

---

[96] "Our clear verses": the Revelations in which strong arguments have been given for the possibility of the Hereafter and in which it has been stated that its occurrence is the demand of both wisdom and justice, and its non-occurrence renders the whole system of the universe meaningless and absurd.

In other words, what they meant to say was: When somebody tells them that there is life after death, he must raise a dead person from the grave and present him before them. And if this is not done, they cannot believe that the dead would ever be raised to life once again at some time in the future, whereas nobody ever told them that the dead would be raised to life in this world as and when required separately, but what was said was: On the Day of Resurrection Allah will raise all human beings to life simultaneously and will subject them to accountability and punish and reward them accordingly.

[97] This is the answer to their saying that death comes to man automatically in the course of time. It means: Neither you get life accidentally nor your death occurs automatically. It is God Who gives you life and it is He Who takes it away.

This is the answer to their demand: Bring back our forefathers if you are truthful. To this it has been said: This will not happen now separately for individuals, but a Day has been fixed for gathering all mankind together.

That is, it is lack of knowledge and right understanding which is the real cause of the people's denying the Hereafter; otherwise it is not its coming but its not coming which is against reason. If a person reflects rightly on the system of the universe and on his own self, he will himself realize that there can be no doubt about the coming of the Hereafter.

of falsehood shall be in utter loss.[98]

وَتَرَى كُلَّ أُمَّةٍ جَاثِيَةً كُلُّ أُمَّةٍ تُدْعَى إِلَى كِتَابِهَا ٱلْيَوْمَ تُجْزَوْنَ مَا كُنْتُمْ تَعْمَلُوْنَ

(45:28) On that Day you shall see every people fallen on their knees. Every people will be summoned to come forth and see its Record and will be told: "Today you shall be requited for your deeds.[99]

هَذَا كِتَابُنَا يَنْطِقُ عَلَيْكُمْ بِالْحَقِّ إِنَّا كُنَّا نَسْتَنْسِخُ مَا كُنْتُمْ تَعْمَلُوْنَ

(45:29) This is Our Record which bears witness against you with truth; We used to record all what you did."[100]

فَأَمَّا الَّذِيْنَ اٰمَنُوْا وَعَمِلُوا الصَّالِحَاتِ فَيُدْخِلُهُمْ رَبُّهُمْ فِيْ رَحْمَتِهِ ذَلِكَ هُوَ الْفَوْزُ الْمُبِيْنُ

(45:30) As for those who believe and act righteously, their Lord shall admit them to His Mercy. That indeed is the manifest triumph.

وَأَمَّا الَّذِيْنَ كَفَرُوْا أَفَلَمْ تَكُنْ اٰيٰتِيْ تُتْلَى عَلَيْكُمْ فَاسْتَكْبَرْتُمْ وَكُنْتُمْ قَوْمًا مُّجْرِمِيْنَ

(45:31) But those who denied the Truth, they shall be told: "Were My Signs not rehearsed to you? But you waxed proud and became a guilty

---

[98] In view of the context, this sentence by itself gives the meaning that it is not at all beyond the power of God Who is ruling over this great and marvelous universe that He should bring the human beings whom He has created in the first instance back into existence once again.

[99] That is, the dread and terror of the Plain of Resurrection and the awe of the divine court will be such that it will break the stubbornness of the most arrogant and boastful people, and everyone will be found fallen on his knees humbly.

[100] The only possible way of getting a thing recorded is not by means of the pen and paper only. Man himself has discovered in this world several other forms of recording human words and actions and reproducing them exactly and accurately; and we cannot even imagine what other possibilities of it lie yet undiscovered, which man himself will discover and exploit in the future. Now, who can know how and by what means is Allah getting recorded man's every word, his every movement and action, even his hidden intentions and motives and desires and ideas, and how He will place before every man and every group and every nation his or its whole lifework accurately and exactly?

people."[101]

وَإِذَا قِيلَ إِنَّ وَعْدَ اللهِ حَقٌّ وَّالسَّاعَةُ لَا رَيْبَ فِيهَا قُلْتُم مَّا نَدْرِي مَا السَّاعَةُ ۙ إِن نَّظُنُّ إِلَّا ظَنًّا وَّمَا نَحْنُ بِمُسْتَيْقِنِينَ

(45:32) And when it was said to them: "Surely Allah's promise is true, and there is no doubt regarding the Hour of Resurrection," you were wont to say: "We do not know what the Hour (of Resurrection) is. We are simply making conjectures and are not at all certain."[102]

وَبَدَا لَهُمْ سَيِّئَاتُ مَا عَمِلُوا وَحَاقَ بِهِم مَّا كَانُوا بِهِ يَسْتَهْزِءُونَ

(45:33) (On that Day) the evil of their deeds will become apparent to them and what they had mocked at will encompass them,[103]

وَقِيلَ الْيَوْمَ نَنسَاكُمْ كَمَا نَسِيتُمْ لِقَاءَ يَوْمِكُمْ هٰذَا وَمَأْوَاكُمُ النَّارُ وَمَا لَكُم مِّن نَّاصِرِينَ

(45:34) and it will be said: "We will forget you today as you forgot the meeting of this Day of yours. The Fire shall now be your abode, and you shall have none to come to your aid.

ذَٰلِكُم بِأَنَّكُمُ اتَّخَذْتُمْ آيَاتِ اللهِ هُزُوًا وَّغَرَّتْكُمُ الْحَيَاةُ الدُّنْيَا ۚ فَالْيَوْمَ لَا يُخْرَجُونَ

---

[101] That is, you thought it was below your dignity to believe in Allah's revelations and submit to them, and considered yourselves to be above subjection and servitude.

[102] The people mentioned in (verse 24) above were those who denied the Hereafter openly and absolutely, here those who are not sure of it although they do not deny its possibility because of conjecture. Apparently there is a vast difference between the two groups in that one of them denies the Hereafter absolutely and the other regards it as possible on the basis of conjecture. But as for the result and final end, there is no difference between them, for the moral consequences of the denial of the Hereafter and of lack of the faith in it are the same. A person, whether he disbelieves in the Hereafter or lacks faith in it, will in either case be inevitably devoid of the feeling of accountability before God, and this lack of feeling will necessarily involve him in the error and deviation of thought and action. Only faith and belief in the Hereafter can keep a man on the right track in the world. In the absence of it, both doubt and denial give him a similar attitude of irresponsibility, and since this same attitude of irresponsibility is the real cause of man's being doomed in the Hereafter, therefore neither the denier of it can escape Hell nor the one who lacks faith in it.

[103] That is, there they will come to know that their ways of behavior, their practices and manners, and their actions and pastimes, which they regarded as very good in the world were, in fact, very bad: they had committed a basic mistake in thinking that they were not answerable to anyone, and this had rendered their entire lifework fruitless and vain.

مِنْهَا وَلَا هُمْ يُسْتَعْتَبُوْنَ

(45:35) You reached this end because you made Allah's Signs an object of jest and the life of the world deluded you." So they shall not be taken out of the Fire nor shall they be asked to make amends (and thus please their Lord).[104]

You May Like My Question but Not My Answer!

We love puzzles, and we wouldn't enjoy rewards that are received too easily. We like to make our own arguments and have an opinion!

وَلَقَدْ صَرَّفْنَا فِيْ هٰذَا الْقُرْاٰنِ لِلنَّاسِ مِنْ كُلِّ مَثَلٍ ۚ وَكَانَ الْاِنْسَانُ اَكْثَرَ شَىْءٍ جَدَلًا

(18:54) And surely We have explained matters to people in the Qur'an in diverse ways, using all manner of parables. But man is exceedingly contentious.

وَمَا مَنَعَ النَّاسَ اَنْ يُّؤْمِنُوْۤا اِذْ جَآءَهُمُ الْهُدٰى وَيَسْتَغْفِرُوْا رَبَّهُمْ اِلَّاۤ اَنْ تَأْتِيَهُمْ سُنَّةُ الْاَوَّلِيْنَ اَوْ يَأْتِيَهُمُ الْعَذَابُ قُبُلًا

(18:55) What is it that prevented mankind from believing when the guidance came to them, and from asking forgiveness of their Lord, except that they would like to be treated as the nations of yore, or that they would like to see the scourge come upon them face to face?[105]

وَمَا نُرْسِلُ الْمُرْسَلِيْنَ اِلَّا مُبَشِّرِيْنَ وَمُنْذِرِيْنَ ۚ وَيُجَادِلُ الَّذِيْنَ كَفَرُوْا بِالْبَاطِلِ لِيُدْحِضُوْا بِهِ الْحَقَّ وَاتَّخَذُوْۤا اٰيٰتِيْ وَمَاۤ اُنْذِرُوْا هُزُوًا

(18:56) We raise Messengers only to give good news and to warn. But

---

[104] This last sentence depicts the manner of a master who after rebuking some of his servants turns to others and says: Well, these wretched people now deserve such and such punishment!

[105] This is to warn the people that the Quran has left no stone unturned in making the truth plain. It has employed all kinds of arguments, parables, similitude and used all the possible effective ways to appeal to the heart and the mind of man, and adopted the best possible style. If, in spite of this, they do not accept the truth, it is obvious that they are waiting for God's scourge like the one that visited the former communities to make them realize their error.

the unbelievers resort to falsehood in order to rebut the truth with it, and scoff at My revelations and My warnings.[106]

وَمَنْ اَظْلَمُ مِمَّنْ ذُكِّرَ بِاٰيٰتِ رَبِّهٖ فَاَعْرَضَ عَنْهَا وَنَسِيَ مَا قَدَّمَتْ يَدٰهُ اِنَّا جَعَلْنَا عَلٰى قُلُوبِهِمْ اَكِنَّةً اَنْ يَّفْقَهُوهُ وَفِىٓ اٰذَانِهِمْ وَقْرًا وَاِنْ تَدْعُهُمْ اِلَى الْهُدٰى فَلَنْ يَّهْتَدُوٓا اِذًا اَبَدًا

(18:57) Who is more wicked than the man who, when he is reminded by the revelations of his Lord, turns away from them and forgets (the consequence of) the deeds wrought by his own hands? We have laid veils over their hearts lest they understand the message of the Qur'an, and We have caused heaviness in their ears. Call them as you may to the Right Path, they will not be ever guided aright.[107]

وَرَبُّكَ الْغَفُورُ ذُو الرَّحْمَةِ لَوْ يُؤَاخِذُهُمْ بِمَا كَسَبُوا لَعَجَّلَ لَهُمُ الْعَذَابَ بَلْ لَهُمْ مَوْعِدٌ لَّنْ يَّجِدُوا مِنْ دُونِهٖ مَوْئِلًا

(18:58) Your Lord is All-Forgiving, full of mercy. Had He wished to take them to task for their doings, He would have hastened in sending His scourge upon them. But He has set for them a time-limit which they cannot evade.[108]

We like to ask clever questions and find the answers that make us feel

---

[106] If they insist on meeting with the scourge, they should not demand this from the Messenger because the Messenger is sent not to bring a scourge but to warn the people beforehand to escape from it.

[107] Allah puts a covering over the heart of a person and makes his ears hard of hearing the truth when he adopts the attitude of contention, dispute, wrangling and argumentation towards the admonition of a well wisher and tries to defeat the truth with the weapons of falsehood and cunning. Naturally this attitude produces in him obduracy and obstinacy so that he turns a deaf ear towards guidance, and is unwilling to realize his error before seeing his evil end. For such people pay no heed to admonition and warning and insist on falling into the abyss of perdition: then and then alone they are convinced that it was perdition towards which they were rushing headlong.

[108] This is to warn the mindless people that they should not be deluded by the respite that is given to them and presume that they will never be taken to task whatever they may go on doing. They forget that Allah gives them respite because He is Forgiving and Forbearing and does not punish the evil doers on the spot, for His Mercy demands that the evil doers should be given respite so that they may mend their ways.

comfortable, yet they are not necessarily the right ones! For example, if I were to ask you what is the difference between smart and stupid, would you like me to tell you the answer that makes you feel comfortable or the truth?

The Birth Moment of Stupidity

Do you think that Satan denies the existence of God? Or that he is not a believer? He didn't get that far, that's not his argument at all! In fact, he was the one most worshiping God! But therein laid a problem, he admired himself while he was admiring God, and he was so proud of himself! In his heart, he was worshiping only himself, although he had framed it into worshiping God. This is never love or sincerity, but selfishness, arrogance and ignorance!

Allah knows that and He created the humans who have a better understanding of sincerity and love. Allah brought out the truth of Satan's heart when He asked him to prostrate to Adam. His selfish reality showed up, when he thought that he is better than the human.

قَالَ مَا مَنَعَكَ أَلَّا تَسْجُدَ إِذْ أَمَرْتُكَ قَالَ أَنَا خَيْرٌ مِنْهُ خَلَقْتَنِى مِن نَّارٍ وَخَلَقْتَهُ مِن طِينٍ

(7:12) Allah said: 'What prevented you from prostrating, when I commanded you to do so?' He said: 'I am better than he. You created me from fire, and him You created from clay.'

The proud ego contains the worst level of evil, envy, hate and jealousy. This is the moment when the scale of harmony went inward 100% (selfish). It turned him blind and deaf. All the logic and harmony were taken from his psyche! He was left only with the fire inside him.

He couldn't see what is right and what is left, he missed the right and left out of heaven. He was left out from the mercy of God, left with his ego, and left without wisdom. Imagine, being left out from the harmony and left with stupidity. This was the birth moment of stupidity.

قَالَ فَاهْبِطْ مِنْهَا فَمَا يَكُوْنُ لَكَ اَنْ تَتَكَبَّرَ فِيْهَا فَاخْرُجْ اِنَّكَ مِنَ الصّٰغِرِيْنَ

(7:13) Allah said: "Then get you down from here. It does not behove you to be arrogant here. So be gone. You will be among the humiliated.'[109]

This was the first and last time he had to make a decision. It cost him his past and his future! It was literally a life lesson. He defined stupidity as "making one single selfish decision - not because of lacking knowledge or IQ, but because of lacking proper manners - that costs a life and destroys the self". At the same time, he defined as stupid the ones, who are lacking proper education and manners to behave with the Creator or His creatures. And the most stupid thing to do is to be selfish and to be proud of your knowledge.

Satan Has A Dream!

Since then, stupidity has been the Devil's only capital! He invented stupidity. It cost all that he had and now he's looking to be compensated by any means possible!

The best way to get a return from investing in a lesson is to apply it completely! That's exactly what he did. He decided not to be selfish anymore, offering his stupidity to others and making them better versions of himself even on a grander scale. He decided to devote the rest of his life to others, to teach them the same lesson. He would like

---

[109] Implicit in the Qur'anic expression (sagharin) is the idea of contentment with one's disgrace and indignity, for saghir is he who invites disgrace and indignity, upon himself. Now, Satan was a victim of vanity and pride, and for that very reason defied God's command to prostrate himself before Adam. Satan was therefore, guilty of self-inflicted degradation. False pride, baseless notions of glory, ill-founded illusions of greatness failed to confer any greatness upon him. They could only bring upon him disgrace and indignity. Satan could blame none but himself for this sordid end.

to turn them into weapons of mass destruction.

Once he turned the X-Harmony Factor 100% outside himself, he found sincerity! He noticed that the left side of his brain was on again. Its message was that Hell would really feel like Hell without other people, and many people are more stupid than me. His right brain continued: sharing is caring. This was his aha moment! He suddenly became very creative and ambitious. It was clear that he saw a kind of light. He asked God kindly to postpone his consequence, in order to be able to realize his dream! He decided to present a Master's degree in Stupidity to his students.

قَالَ اَنْظِرْنِيٓ اِلٰى يَوْمِ يُبْعَثُوْنَ

(7:14) Satan replied: 'Give me respite till the Day they shall be raised.'

قَالَ اِنَّكَ مِنَ الْمُنْظَرِيْنَ

(7:15) Allah said: 'You are granted respite.'

قَالَ فَبِمَآ اَغْوَيْتَنِيْ لَاَقْعُدَنَّ لَهُمْ صِرَاطَكَ الْمُسْتَقِيْمَ

(7:16) Satan said: 'Since You have led me astray, I shall surely sit in ambush for them on Your Straight Path.

ثُمَّ لَاٰتِيَنَّهُمْ مِّنْ بَيْنِ اَيْدِيْهِمْ وَمِنْ خَلْفِهِمْ وَعَنْ اَيْمَانِهِمْ وَعَنْ شَمَآئِلِهِمْ وَلَا تَجِدُ اَكْثَرَهُمْ شٰكِرِيْنَ

(7:17) Then I will come upon them from the front and from the rear, and from their right and from their left. And You will not find most of them thankful.[110]

Stupidity Master

Satan's greatest efforts should target an updated version of human stupidity (Stupidity Master 1.0)! His goal was not only to get them to make a bad decision based on disobedience to God, he wanted them to even deny the existence of one God, the next life and doubt the existence of Satan himself.

In his next level he wanted to excel and create followers: fanatics, equipped with the same passion. They would be helping him and even

---

[110] This was the challenge thrown down by Satan to God. What it meant is that Satan would make use of the respite granted to him until the Last Day, and he would do so in order to prove that Adam did not deserve a position superior to his and this had after all been bestowed upon him by God. So doing, he would expose how ungrateful, thankless and disloyal a creature man is.

The respite asked for by Satan and granted to him by God includes not only the time but also the opportunity to mislead Man and to prove his point by appealing to man's weaknesses. These verses make it clear that God had granted Satan the opportunity to try to mislead Adam and his offspring. At the same time it has also been made quite clear that Satan was not granted the power to lead men into error against their will. Thus all that Satan can do is to cause misunderstanding, to make people cherish false illusions, to make evil and error seem attractive, and to invite people to evil ways by holding out to them the promise of immense pleasure and material benefits. He would have no power, however, to forcibly pull them to the Satanic way and to prevent them from following the Right Way. Accordingly, the Qur'an makes it quite plain elsewhere that on the Day of Judgement, Satan would address the men who had followed him in the following words: 'I had no power over you except to call you; but you listened to me: then reproach me not, but reproach your own selves'

As for Satan's allegation that God Himself caused him to fall into error, it is an attempt on the part of Satan to transfer the blame which falls squarely on him to God. Satan's grievance seems to be that God was responsible for his deviation insofar as He hurt Satan's pride by asking him to prostrate before Adam, and that it was this which led him to disobey God. It is thus clear that Satan wanted to continue enjoying his vain arrogance and that he was incensed that his weakness - arrogance - was seen through and brought to full light. The underlying stupidity of the statement is too patently obvious to call for any refutation, and hence God took no notice of it.

worshiping him (Stupidity Master 2.0)! He has unlimited passion for his only life cause, and he doesn't want to miss even a single human being. Realizing this dream needs a know-how, a hallmark: a disharmony hallmark! The hallmark of stupidity! Guess what this is? How useful could it be?

اَلَمْ اَعْهَدْ اِلَيْكُمْ يَبَنِيْ اٰدَمَ اَنْ لَّا تَعْبُدُوا الشَّيْطٰنَ ۚ اِنَّهٗ لَكُمْ عَدُوٌّ مُّبِيْنٌ ۙ

(36:60) Children of Adam, did I not command you not to serve Satan? He is to you an open enemy

وَّاَنِ اعْبُدُوْنِيْ ۚ هٰذَا صِرَاطٌ مُّسْتَقِيْمٌ

(36:61) and serve Me alone: this is the Straight Way[111]

وَلَقَدْ اَضَلَّ مِنْكُمْ جِبِلًّا كَثِيْرًا ۚ اَفَلَمْ تَكُوْنُوْا تَعْقِلُوْنَ

(36:62) Still, he misguided a whole throng of you. Did you have no

---

[111] Here again Allah has used ibadat (worship) in the sense of itaat (obedience). Do not worship Satan means: Do not obey him, the reason being that only falling prostrate before him is not forbidden, but following him and obeying his commands also is forbidden; therefore, itaat (obedience) is ibadat (worship).

If a person comes to you and commands you to do something, you should see whether his command is in accordance with the command of Allah or not. If it is not, Satan is with him; and if you obeyed him in this, you worshiped him and his Satan. Likewise, if your self urges you to do something, you should see whether it is permissible to do it according to the Shariah or not. If it is not permissible, your self is Satan itself, or Satan is with it. If you obeyed him, you in fact became guilty of worshiping him.

But there are different degrees of the worship of Satan. Sometimes it so happens that a man does a work and his limbs and his tongue also join him in this, and his heart also cooperates. At another time it so happens that a man uses his limbs to do a work but his heart and tongue do not cooperate in this. Some people commit a sin while their heart is disagreeable and their tongue is invoking Allah for forgiveness, and they confess that they are committing an evil. This is Satan's worship with external limbs. There are other people who commit a crime with a cool mind and express pleasure and satisfaction with the tongue also. Such people are the worshipers of Satan from outside as well as from inside.

sense?[112]

هٰذِهٖ جَهَنَّمُ الَّتِىْ كُنْتُمْ تُوْعَدُوْنَ

(36:63) Now this is the Hell of which you were warned.

اِصْلَوْهَا الْيَوْمَ بِمَا كُنْتُمْ تَكْفُرُوْنَ

(36:64) Burn in it on account of your disbelieving.

اَلْيَوْمَ نَخْتِمُ عَلٰى اَفْوَاهِهِمْ وَتُكَلِّمُنَاۤ اَيْدِيْهِمْ وَتَشْهَدُ اَرْجُلُهُمْ بِمَا كَانُوْا يَكْسِبُوْنَ

(36:65) Today We shall put a seal on their mouths, and their hands will speak to Us and their feet shall bear witness to what they had been doing.

The Big Picture of The Satan's Plan

His ambition is to break the symphony of harmony and instead create chaos around the world, in every direction: between nations, in the economy, social life, health, education, climate and so on. His success manifests in creating a state of despair: there's no way to find harmony, balance, peace or love.

The ultimate goal is to bring humanity to the same psychological state as him. All sharing the same despair, without hope, and then ending oneself either here or later in the afterlife (Stupid 1.0). His supreme goal is to take qualified responders to the next level: to partner with him to destroy others (Stupid 2.0).

On another level Satan is competing with the sons of Adam about their appointed positions received from God to be the Caliphs on earth.

---

[112] That is, If you had been deprived of reason and you had served your enemy instead of your Lord, you could have the reason to offer an excuse. But you, in fact, had been blessed with reason by Allah and you were using it to advantage in all the affairs of the world, and you had been warned by Allah through the Prophets as well, yet, when you were deceived by your enemy and he succeeded in leading you astray, you could not be excused from the responsibility of your folly.

Satan would like to extract this honor for himself, he would like humans to be his slaves.

Satan's Know-How

It is a mind controlling game. Our power as human beings depends on the source of our information system and our ability to use it to maintain harmony. Satan knows this fact for sure.

His approach is quite simple, it is the reverse engineering of the norm(al). The fine details include subtle but continuous alteration of the natural mechanism of the harmony and pairing system, targeting the core of the X-Harmony Factor.

Satan is building a mechanism for conflict in every layer of human existence. He's happy when people avoid doing the effort of putting the different pairs together, when they are merely struggling between right and left (brain), emotion and thought as well as body and soul. He strives to achieve discrepancies between actions and talks, and to create problems between man and woman. He triumphs when he is able to create confusion and make obscure the relations of here and hereafter as well as human and God.

وَاتَّبَعُوا مَا تَتْلُوا الشَّيَاطِينُ عَلَى مُلْكِ سُلَيْمَنَ ۖ وَمَا كَفَرَ سُلَيْمَنُ وَلَٰكِنَّ الشَّيَاطِينَ كَفَرُوا يُعَلِّمُونَ النَّاسَ السِّحْرَ وَمَا أُنْزِلَ عَلَى الْمَلَكَيْنِ بِبَابِلَ هَارُوتَ وَمَارُوتَ ۚ وَمَا يُعَلِّمَانِ مِنْ أَحَدٍ حَتَّىٰ يَقُولَا إِنَّمَا نَحْنُ فِتْنَةٌ فَلَا تَكْفُرْ ۖ فَيَتَعَلَّمُونَ مِنْهُمَا مَا يُفَرِّقُونَ بِهِ بَيْنَ الْمَرْءِ وَ زَوْجِهِ ۚ وَمَا هُمْ بِضَارِّينَ بِهِ مِنْ أَحَدٍ إِلَّا بِإِذْنِ اللَّهِ ۚ وَيَتَعَلَّمُونَ مَا يَضُرُّهُمْ وَلَا يَنْفَعُهُمْ ۚ وَلَقَدْ عَلِمُوا لَمَنِ اشْتَرَاهُ مَا لَهُ فِى الْآخِرَةِ مِنْ خَلَاقٍ ۚ وَلَبِئْسَ مَا شَرَوْا بِهِ أَنْفُسَهُمْ ۚ لَوْ كَانُوا يَعْلَمُونَ

(2:102) and then followed what the evil ones falsely attributed to the Kingdom of Solomon even though Solomon had never disbelieved; it is the evil ones who disbelieved, teaching people magic. And they followed what had been revealed to the two angels in Babylon – Harut and Marut – although these two (angels) never taught it to anyone without first declaring: "We are merely a means of testing people; so, do not engage in unbelief." And yet they learned from them what might cause division between a man and his wife. They could not cause harm to anyone except by the leave of Allah, and still they learned what harmed rather than profited them, knowing well that he who bought it will have no share in the World to Come. Evil indeed is what they sold themselves for. Had they but known![113]

Satan's know-how is very old, and usually weak because it is not enough to alter the harmony mechanism. God has created an innate tendency for harmony by creating magnetic coupling between the two halves of one pair. Satan has staged his know-how, and now he has moved to the next level by promoting heavily the overriding of the natural tendency of coupling.

Staging and Scaling the Know-How

Satan's mission is to create chaos rather than harmony. He does this in two stages. First, he tries to make small changes in the details of a norm over a long period of time, so that it goes unnoticed. When these trivial

---

[113] This shows that the greatest demand was for magical arts and charms to sow discord between a man and his wife and to procure the eventual seduction of the latter. This was the depth of moral depravity to which these people had fallen. A people cannot sink to a lower level of moral degeneracy than when adulterous affairs become their favourite pastime, and when seducing a married woman is considered a boastful achievement. The matrimonial relationship is, in truth, the very foundation of man's collective life. The soundness of human civilization depends on the soundness of the relationship between the two sexes. Hence, nothing could be worse than the person who strikes at the very foundations of the structure which supports both him and society as a whole.

There is a Tradition from the Prophet to the effect that Satan sends his agents on their missions to all parts of the world. On their return these agents report their achievements with each mentioning his own special evil act. But Satan is not completely satisfied with any of them. It is only when an agent reports that he has succeeded in separating a wife from her husband that Satan is filled with joy and embraces him. In the light of this Tradition it is understandable why the angels who were sent to the Israelites to test them were asked to disclose those magical arts which would lead to separation between a husband and his wife, for the inclination of a people to learn such arts is a sure index of its moral decadence.

things reach a certain level, he needs to conclude this step and redefine the new product of the distorted norm as the new norm. This entails switching (a fake form of the CC function) the abnormal new norms in place of the existing norms. For example, he promotes selfishness in the name of individualism, dictatorship in the name of capitalism, divorce as gender equality. The list is long, but the trick is one.

To achieve scalability, he needs his base of helpers (Stupids 2.0), who are interested. They must own the media and the advertising engines. Their part is to soften the message, to make it engaging, lively, intriguing and emotional.

قَالَ رَبِّ بِمَآ اَغْوَيْتَنِىْ لَاُزَيِّنَنَّ لَهُمْ فِى الْاَرْضِ وَلَاُغْوِيَنَّهُمْ اَجْمَعِيْنَ

(15:39) Iblis said: "My Lord! In the manner You led me to error, I will make things on earth seem attractive to them and lead all of them to error,[114]

The ultimate goal is to create a broad range of supporters, activists, and consumers (Stupids 2.0). Scalability is accelerated by creating multiple social, economic, financial and political crises, until they are generalized by writing them as laws and adapted as the system. Scalability is staged by automation then digitization, at this point you are already in the maze, 360 degrees, 24/7! Voilá!

Satan's Main Challenge

The humane firewall included in the latest updated operating system in our minds is the guidance from God. It is the religion. There is no

---

[114] That is, thou hast beguiled me by commanding me to bow down before a creature who is inferior to me: for it is obvious that I could not obey such an order. Therefore, I will now beguile them and disobey Thee. In other words, Iblis meant to say: I will make the worldly life, its enjoyments and its transitory benefits so alluring for man that he will forget the responsibilities of the vicegerent of Allah, and that he shall have to render his account in the Hereafter. They will also forget Thee and will disobey Thee, even though they would profess to remember Thee.

possibility to fulfill Satan's dream while a person's firewall is running. This should therefore be disabled by any means.

Islam is a sealed operating system. Hence, it is impossible to plant a malicious program (virus). An alternative is to create a distraction by switching the label from philia to phobia. Although Satan has been pushing really hard in this direction, it brings odd results. This switching created increased interest in people's minds, to read more about phobias. Surprisingly, many found the harmony which they had been searching for all their lives. This created added challenges for Satan. For that reason, he is now focusing on weaponizing the New Trinity instead.

More Aha Moments for Satan

Satan has two more aha moments. The first of them is when we begin to see the truth, the moment we go to sleep while we are conscious (i.e., start dying).

This is the moment when our eyesight is unveiled, we begin to see the result of the life we have lived, and the future to come. This is the moment many have kept running away from, looking for any way to avoid it.

وَ جَاءَتْ سَكْرَةُ الْمَوْتِ بِالْحَقِّ ۖ ذَٰلِكَ مَا كُنْتَ مِنْهُ تَحِيدُ

(50:19) Lo, the agony of death has indeed come with the Truth. That is what you had sought to avoid.[115]

لَقَدْ كُنْتَ فِي غَفْلَةٍ مِّنْ هٰذَا فَكَشَفْنَا عَنْكَ غِطَاءَكَ فَبَصَرُكَ الْيَوْمَ حَدِيدٌ

(50:22) You were heedless of this. Now We have removed your veil and so your vision today is sharp.[116]

From this moment on you are on your own. You can't blame anyone for your decisions, not your parents, partner, leader, system, anyone or anything else.

فَإِذَا جَاءَتِ الصَّاخَّةُ

(80:33) But when the deafening cry shall be sounded. The final terrible sounding of the Trumpet at which all dead men shall be resurrected to life.

يَوْمَ يَفِرُّ الْمَرْءُ مِنْ أَخِيهِ

(80:34) on the Day when each man shall flee from his brother,

وَأُمِّهِ وَأَبِيهِ

(80:35) and his mother and his father;

وَصَاحِبَتِهِ وَبَنِيهِ

---

[115] "Come with the truth" implies that the agony of death is the starting point when the reality which had remained concealed in the world, begins to be uncovered. At this point man starts seeing clearly the other world of which the Prophet had forewarned him. Here, man also comes to know that the Hereafter is the very truth, and also this whether he is entering this second stage of life as favored or damned.

That is, this is the same reality which you refused to believe. You desired that you should live and go about as an unbridled rogue in the world, and there should be no other life after death, in which you may have to suffer for the consequences of your deeds. That is why you shunned the concept of the Hereafter and were not at all inclined to believe that this next world would ever be established. Now, you may see that the same next world is unveiling itself before you.

[116] That is, you can clearly see that everything of which the Prophets foretold is present here.

(80:36) and his consort and his children;[117]

لِكُلِّ امْرِىٍٔ مِّنْهُمْ يَوْمَئِذٍ شَأْنٌ يُغْنِيهِ

(80:37) on that Day each will be occupied with his own business, making him oblivious of all save himself.[118]

وُجُوهٌ يَوْمَئِذٍ مُّسْفِرَةٌ

(80:38) Some faces on that Day shall be beaming with happiness,

ضَاحِكَةٌ مُّسْتَبْشِرَةٌ

(80:39) and be cheerful and joyous.

وَوُجُوهٌ يَوْمَئِذٍ عَلَيْهَا غَبَرَةٌ

(80:40) Some faces on that Day shall be dust-ridden,

تَرْهَقُهَا قَتَرَةٌ

(80:41) enveloped by darkness.

أُولَٰئِكَ هُمُ الْكَفَرَةُ الْفَجَرَةُ

(80:42) These will be the unbelievers, the wicked.

The moment when you can see your future (afterlife), is the moment when Satan stops chasing you, but never before that. The moment before the last breath is the most important moment, because there is still a chance to turn the whole story upside down in a second. He

---

[117] Fleeing may also mean that when he sees those nearest and dearest to him in the world, involved in distress, instead of rushing forth to help them, he will run away from them lest they should call out to him for help. And it may also mean that when they see the evil consequences of committing sin for the sake of one another and misleading one another, fearless of God and heedless of the Hereafter, in the world, each one would flee from the other lest the other should hold him responsible for his deviation and sin. Brother will fear brother, children their parents, husband his wife, and parents their children lest they should become witnesses in the case against them.

[118] A tradition has been reported in the Hadith by different methods and through different channels, saying that the Prophet (peace be upon him) said: On the Day of Resurrection all men will rise up naked. One of his wives (according to some reporters, Aishah, according to others, Saudah, or a woman) asked in bewilderment: O Messenger of Allah, shall we (women) appear naked on that Day before the people. The prophet (peace be upon him) recited this very verse and explained that on that Day each one will have enough of his own troubles to occupy him, and will be wholly unmindful of others.

knows that one second can count for so much. He himself lost everything in a second.

God has opened His door for us, to go back by ourselves and escape the maze until our last breath. This door is available 24/7 for everyone on earth.

وَإِذَا سَأَلَكَ عِبَادِئ عَنِّى فَإِنِّى قَرِيْبٌ أُجِيْبُ دَعْوَةَ الدَّاعِ إِذَا دَعَانِ فَلْيَسْتَجِيْبُوْا لِىْ وَلْيُؤْمِنُوْا بِىْ لَعَلَّهُمْ يَرْشُدُوْنَ

(2:186) (O Muhammad), when My servants ask you about Me, tell them I am quite near; I hear and answer the call of the caller whenever he calls Me. Let them listen to My call and believe in Me; perhaps they will be guided aright.[119]

Satan can come from any door, but not from the upper door. He has all directions covered except the upper door.

ثُمَّ لَاٰتِيَنَّهُمْ مِّنْ بَيْنِ اَيْدِيْهِمْ وَمِنْ خَلْفِهِمْ وَعَنْ اَيْمَانِهِمْ وَعَنْ شَمَآئِلِهِمْ وَلَا تَجِدُ اَكْثَرَهُمْ شٰكِرِيْنَ

(7:17) Then I will come upon them from the front and from the rear, and from their right and from their left. And You will not find most of them thankful.

Once this moment passes and you miss God's door, Satan takes a deep breath with a big aha.

---

[119] Even though people can neither see God nor subject Him to any other form of sense perception this should not make them feel that God is remote from them. On the contrary, He is so close to each and every person that whenever any person so wishes he can communicate with his Lord. So much so that God hears and responds even to the prayers which remain within the innermost recesses of the heart.

People exhaust themselves by approaching false and powerless beings whom they foolishly fancy to be their deities but who have neither the power to hear nor to grant their prayers. But God, the omnipotent Lord and the absolute Master of this vast universe, Who wields all power and authority, is so close to human beings that they can always approach Him without the intercession of any intermediaries, and can put to Him their prayers and requests.

This announcement of God's closeness to man may open his eyes to the Truth, may turn him to the right way wherein lies his success and well-being.

Abdullah bin 'Umar bin Al-Khattab (May Allah be pleased with them) reported: the Prophet (ﷺ) said:

وعن أبي عبد الرحمن عبد الله بن عمر بن الخطاب رضي الله عنهما عن النبي صلى الله عليه وسلم قال: " إن الله عز وجل يقبل توبة العبد ما لم يغرغر" ((رواه الترمذي وقال: حديث حسن)).

"Allah accepts a slave's repentance as long as the latter is not on his death bed (that is, before the soul of the dying person reaches the throat)". *Source: Al-Tirmidhi narrated it and said: It is a good hadith*

The Grandest Aha Moment for Satan

This is the moment when Satan will step on the stage, in the middle of Hell, and give his speech. He will address the graduates of the Master 1.0 and Master 2.0, praising their excellence in exceeding his level of stupidity and praising himself as the teacher of the masters.

وَقَالَ الشَّيْطٰنُ لَمَّا قُضِيَ الْأَمْرُ إِنَّ اللهَ وَعَدَكُمْ وَعْدَ الْحَقِّ وَوَعَدْتُّكُمْ فَاَخْلَفْتُكُمْ ۖ وَمَا كَانَ لِيَ عَلَيْكُمْ مِّنْ سُلْطٰنٍ إِلَّآ اَنْ دَعَوْتُكُمْ فَاسْتَجَبْتُمْ لِيْ ۚ فَلَا تَلُوْمُوْنِيْ وَلُوْمُوْا اَنْفُسَكُمْ ۖ مَآ اَنَا بِمُصْرِخِكُمْ وَمَآ اَنْتُمْ بِمُصْرِخِيَّ ۗ اِنِّيْ كَفَرْتُ بِمَآ اَشْرَكْتُمُوْنِ مِنْ قَبْلُ ۗ اِنَّ الظّٰلِمِيْنَ لَهُمْ عَذَابٌ اَلِيْمٌ

(14:22) After the matter has been finally decided Satan will say: "Surely whatever Allah promised you was true; as for me, I went back on the promise I made to you. I had no power over you except that I called you to my way and you responded to me. So, do not blame me but blame yourselves. Here, neither I can come to your rescue, nor can you come to mine. I disavow your former act of associating me in the past with Allah. A grievous chastisement inevitably lies ahead for such wrong-doers."[120]

The Masterpiece of Hate Speech

Satan spoke twice from his heart telling the truth. Both times were about the same topic, but with a different feel. The first time was in front of Adam while his heart was exploding from envy and hatred for Adam.

In his second and final speech, he also speaks to some of the sons and daughters of Adam in Hell, but with a calm heart having fulfilled his dream, and happy with the accomplishment of the long-life mission. If you want to know what hate speech really is, this is a masterpiece.

إِنَّ الشَّيْطَنَ لَكُمْ عَدُوٌّ فَاتَّخِذُوهُ عَدُوًّا ۚ إِنَّمَا يَدْعُوا حِزْبَهُ لِيَكُونُوا مِنْ اَصْحَٰبِ السَّعِيْرِ

(35:6) Surely Satan is an enemy to you. Therefore, do take him as an enemy. He calls his followers to his way so that they may be among the inmates of the Fire.

Why is Satan Useful?

Nothing in God's kingdom happens without His knowledge or permission (this is the meaning for *InshaaAllah* that you may have heard from Muslim friends). Nothing harms us and does not benefit us except with His permission. If you understand God well, He will let you understand this concept.

قُلْ لَّنْ يُصِيْبَنَا إِلَّا مَا كَتَبَ اللهُ لَنَا ۚ هُوَ مَوْلٰنَا ۚ وَعَلَى اللهِ فَلْيَتَوَكَّلِ الْمُؤْمِنُوْنَ

(9:51) Say: "Nothing will befall us except what Allah has decreed for us; He is our Protector." Let the believers, then, put all their trust in Allah.[121]

This includes even Satan. He works hard to achieve his purpose but

[120] When the confused ones will charge Satan with leading them astray, he will plead guilty, as if to say: You yourselves see now that all the promises and warnings made by Allah have come out true and all the promises which I made have proved to be false. I also confess that it was all deception that I gave you false assurances of prosperity, beguiled you by greed and enticed you in the snare of great expectations. I assured you that in the first instance there will be no life in the Hereafter, and that, if there be any, you will be freed by the intercession of such and such a saint. The only thing you have to do is to make offerings before him: then you may do whatever you please, for he will deliver you from all the consequences. I repeat that I said all these things and asked my agents to say the same.

That is, you cannot say and prove that it was I who forced you to follow the wrong way, whereas you wanted to follow the right way. You will yourselves admit that it is not so. I did no more than this that I invited you to falsehood in opposition to the invitation to the truth and tempted you to vice instead of virtue. But I had no power to force you to the wrong way, if you desired to follow the right way, when you had the power and the option to follow either of the ways. Now I am ready to bear the burden of the wicked invitation I extended to you, but you are not justified in any way to throw on me the burden of accepting my invitation for you did it on your own responsibility. You should, therefore, yourselves bear all its consequences.

This is a clear proof of shirk in practice, as apart from shirk in creed. As Satan will charge his followers with making him a partner with God, it is obvious that as far as creed is concerned there is no one who makes Satan a partner with God in His Godhead or His worship: nay, every one curses him for his evil ways. Nevertheless, people obey and submit to him and follow him blindly, as if he were their god and that is what has been termed shirk.

Let us now consider this thesis from the opposite point of view. Someone might say that this does not hold good, for this is based on a mere saying of Satan which has been cited here. First, this objection is not sound because Allah Himself would have refuted it, had it been baseless.

Secondly, this is not the only instance of shirk in practice in the Quran. Here are a few more instances of this.
(a) It charges the Jews and Christians with shirk because they set up their priests and monks as their Lords besides Allah. (Surah At-Tauba, Ayat 31).
(b) Those who follow the superstitious customs have been called mushriks. (Surah Al-Anaam, Ayats 136-139).
(c) Those who follow their lusts have been charged with making their selves as their god. (Al-Furqan, Ayat 43).
(d) Those who are disobedient to Allah have been accused of worshiping Satan. (Surah Saba, Ayat 60).
(e) Those who follow man made laws without Allah's sanction have been reproved for setting up the makers of the laws without Allah's sanction as partners with God. (Surah Ham-Sajdah, Ayat 21).

still serves harmony.

إِلَّا عِبَادَكَ مِنْهُمُ الْمُخْلَصِينَ

(15:40) except those of Your servants whom You have singled out for

---

All the above instances are clear proofs of the fact that shirk is not confined to this creed alone that one might set up a partner with Allah in His Godhead as an article of faith. But it is also shirk that one should follow and surrender to someone other than Allah without any divine sanction or in spite of a divine prohibition. Such a one shall be guilty of shirk even though the follower might be at the same time cursing him whom he follows and obeys. The only difference between the two kinds of shirk may be the extent of the crime and not its nature.

[121] In this passage a demarcation has been made between the attitudes of a man of the world and of a man of God. Whatever the man of the world does, he does it to please his own self. He exults if he attains some worldly ends but feels utterly dejected if he fails to attain them. Besides, he depends entirely on his material resources for his success and feels encouraged if these are favorable, but loses heart if these are unfavorable.

In contrast to the man of the world, whatever the man of God does, he does it to please Him and trusts in Him and not in his own powers nor in material resources. Therefore he is neither exultant over his success in the cause of Allah, nor loses heart by failure, for he believes that it is the will of God that is working in both the cases. Therefore he is neither disheartened by disasters nor is filled with conceit by successes. This is because he believes that both prosperity and adversity are from Allah and are nothing but a trial from Him. Therefore his only worry is to do his best to come out successful in His test. Besides, as there are no worldly ends before him, he does not measure his success or failure by the achievement or failure of his ends. On the other hand, the only object before him is to sacrifice his life and wealth in the Way of Allah, and he measures the success or failure of his efforts by the standard he achieves in the performance of this duty.

Therefore if he is satisfied that he has done his best to perform this duty, he believes that he has come out successful by the grace of God, though he might not have been able to accomplish anything from the worldly point of view; for he believes that his Allah in whose cause he has expended his life and wealth will not let go waste the reward of his efforts. As he does not depend on the material resources only, he is neither grieved if they are unfavorable, nor feels exultant when these are favorable.

His entire trust is in God who is the controller of all the resources; therefore he goes on doing his duty even under the most unfavorable circumstances with the same courage and perseverance that is shown by the worldly people in favorable circumstances alone. That is why Allah asked the Prophet (peace be upon him) to say to the hypocrites, "There is a basic difference between you and us in regard to the conduct of affairs. We believe that both the good and the bad are from Allah: therefore the apparent result does not make us happy or sad. Moreover, we depend on Allah in our affairs and you depend on material resources: so we are content and happy in all circumstances."

Yourself."

قَالَ هَٰذَا صِرَاطٌ عَلَيَّ مُسْتَقِيمٌ

(15:41) Allah said: "Here is the path that leads straight to Me.

إِنَّ عِبَادِي لَيْسَ لَكَ عَلَيْهِمْ سُلْطَانٌ إِلَّا مَنِ اتَّبَعَكَ مِنَ الْغَاوِينَ

(15:42) Over My true servants you will be able to exercise no power, your power will be confined to the erring ones, those who choose to follow you.[122]

وَإِنَّ جَهَنَّمَ لَمَوْعِدُهُمْ أَجْمَعِينَ

(15:43) Surely Hell is the promised place for all of them.[123]

Satan brings contrast for good: shows darkness next to light, displays hate next to love, exhibits the wicked choices over the good, distinguishes the hypocrites from the honest. He is helping in sorting out selfish people like him from the loyal people.

---

[122] You will have no power over My servants (common people) to force them to disobey Me. However, We will give freedom of action to those who will willingly or deliberately follow you, and we will not forcibly prevent them from your way, if they intended to follow you. According to the first rendering, these verses will mean this: The way followed by My sincere servants is the only straight way to reach Me. Satan will have no power over those people who follow it, for I will choose them to be My own servants. Satan himself admitted that he will not be able to entice them. On the contrary, he will succeed in beguiling those people who themselves will deviate from the way of obedience. They will then wander farther and farther away following his temptations and allurements.

According to the second meaning, the passage will mean this: When Satan challenged that he would beguile people from the way of Allah by making this worldly life very tempting to them, Allah accepted his challenge but made it clear to him that he was being allowed only to beguile people with temptation, but was not being given any power to force them to deviate from the right way. At this, Satan clarified that his challenge did not apply to those people whom Allah will choose for Himself. As this exception might have led to a misunderstanding that Allah may choose any people for Himself to keep them safe and secure from the reach of Satan, Allah clarified it, saying: Only that person will follow you, who himself will deviate from the right way. As a corollary to this, that person, who will not deviate from the right way will not follow you, and will, thus become Our servant, whom We will choose for Ourself.

[123] You yourselves are responsible for your wrong deeds and not Satan; for, the most he can do is to beguile you from the obedience of Allah and hold temptations before you. It is, therefore, your own concern and responsibility to be beguiled or not to be beguiled by Satan.

God fulfills our dreams. He connects us with the right company for us. It all depends on which team we want to belong to!

The Short Cut

You can go to the gym with all the books on fitness. You may spend hours watching exercise videos, visit the gym every day, and go through all the machines, but it could take years to get fit, or you could end up hurting yourself and maybe others.

Nothing is better than getting a good master. There is no Islam without the prophet Muhammad, peace and blessings be upon him. He is the grand master of Rumi and all Muslims. Some have to read the Qur'an on their own. They won't understand it properly, or might end up with catastrophes completely the opposite of what it is meant to offer.

The key to understanding Islam is to read the Prophet's (ﷺ) biography, learn his teachings, and how he applied Islam step by step over the course of 23 years. The most important decisions you need to make are choosing the right gym and companions as well as some certified masters, and there are plenty of them out there.

You need to get more familiar with the Prophets in general and then we will dive deeper in the topic of love.

CHAPTER 14

Islamophilia 5

The Prophet of Harmony

Concept of Teaching Humanity by Sending Messengers

The ultimate goal of a teacher is to provide assistance with a comprehensive set of knowledge and skills that will help the student perform their lifelong mission during their lifetime.

The relationship between different teachers complements each other. They do not conflict or cooperate rather they build on each other's efforts. This includes the parents at the beginning in the home, then kindergarten, preschool, primary, secondary, and so on.

This is what the Prophets have been doing since Adam, peace be upon him. Up until college courses came! Theoretical foundation courses by Moses and Jesus, and finally graduation with practical courses by Muhammad, peace be upon them all.

قُوْلُوٓا اٰمَنَّا بِاللهِ وَمَآ اُنْزِلَ اِلَيْنَا وَمَآ اُنْزِلَ اِلٰٓى اِبْرٰهٖمَ وَاِسْمٰعِيْلَ وَاِسْحٰقَ
وَيَعْقُوْبَ وَ الْاَسْبَاطِ وَمَآ اُوْتِىَ مُوْسٰى وَعِيْسٰى وَمَآ اُوْتِىَ النَّبِيُّوْنَ مِنْ رَّبِّهِمْ ۚ
لَا نُفَرِّقُ بَيْنَ اَحَدٍ مِّنْهُمْ وَنَحْنُ لَهٗ مُسْلِمُوْنَ

(2:136) Say: "We believe in Allah, and in what has been revealed to us and to Abraham, Ishmael, Isaac, Jacob and the descendants (of Jacob) and in what was given to Moses and Jesus and in what the other Prophets received from their Lord. We make no distinction between any of them, and we are those who submit to Allah."[124]

---

[124] To make no distinction between the Prophets means not to hold some of them to be right and the others to be wrong, not to recognize some to have been the recipients of Divine revelation and the others not. All the Prophets sent by God invited men to the same Truth and to the same way. Hence for anyone who is really a lover of Truth it is necessary that he should recognize all of them to be its bearers. Those who believe in one particular Prophet and disbelieve in others do not in fact believe even in that particular Prophet in whom they, claim to believe, for they have not grasped the nature of that universal 'Straight Way' (al-sirat al-mustaqim) which was enunciated by Moses, Jesus and the other Prophets. When such people claim to follow a Prophet they really mean that they do so out of deference to their forefathers. Their religion in fact consists of bigoted ancestor-worship and blind imitation of inherited customs rather than sincere adherence to the directives of any Prophet of God.

What Do Teachers Teach?

The main task of mankind is to be able to use both halves of the brain (logical and intuitive) to solve the puzzle on their own. Man needs to believe in God without seeing Him, and build a relationship with Him by following His instructions that bring him closer to getting to know Him even more.

This task came at the opening of the Qur'an after Al-Fatihah in Surat Al-Baqarah.

الَّذِينَ يُؤْمِنُونَ بِالْغَيْبِ وَ يُقِيمُونَ الصَّلوةَ وَمِمَّا رَزَقْنٰهُمْ يُنْفِقُونَ

(2:3) for those who believe in the existence of that which is beyond the reach of perception, who establish Prayer and spend out of what We have provided them[125]

Are You Funny?

The essential essence of the challenge is that there is no embodiment of God Himself. We know Him through His Messengers and creation.

We are all students who have to pass this challenge in our lives. If you're complaining about not being able to see God, this may sound funny. It's like someone in the middle of an exam shouting where are my results!

وَلَوْ شَاءَ رَبُّكَ لَجَعَلَ النَّاسَ أُمَّةً وَّاحِدَةً وَّلَا يَزَالُونَ مُخْتَلِفِينَ

(11:118) Had your Lord so willed, He would surely have made mankind one community. But as things stand, now they will not cease

---

[125] This is the second prerequisite for deriving benefit from the Qur'an. Ghayb signifies the verities which are hidden from man's senses and which are beyond the scope of man's ordinary observation and experience, for example the existence and attributes of God, the angels, the process of revelation, Paradise, Hell and so on. 'Belief in the ghaib' means having faith in such matters, based on an absolute confidence in the Messengers of God and despite the fact that it is impossible to experience them.

to differ among themselves and to follow erroneous ways

This entire challenge is highly dependent on the harmony between the right side of the brain, and the left.

Left Hemisphere People

With a dominant left side, you follow the path of reasoning. You take any physical object or event, and begin to question the cause, which leads to another cause, which proceeds still to another cause. When the material reasons are over, then the right side comes, leading you to God, to the One behind all the reasons. He doesn't need reason, we only do.

إِنَّ فِى خَلْقِ السَّمٰوٰتِ وَالْأَرْضِ وَاخْتِلَافِ الَّيْلِ وَالنَّهَارِ لَأْيٰتٍ لِّأُولِى الْأَلْبَابِ ۞

(3:190) Surely in the creation of the heavens and the earth, and in the alternation of night and day, there are signs for men of understanding.

"The lefties" need to get out of their comfort zone and learn more about the topic of emotional intelligence. At first, they will deal with it, through logic, by rationalizing feelings and following rules. This will take them further but slowly. They will advance step by step but steadily towards love.

At this point they will be the strongest believers in God and will admire His reasoning (wisdom) in His creation. They will understand that He taught them to love, in the way they prefer: a love based on reason, justice, free choice, work, and fidelity. It is not easy. They will feel that they have won love and that they are free to make a decision about it without pressure. Just like that this brings them the ability to see and talk with God.

Right Hemisphere People

The people dominated by their right side need to see God Almighty in beauty. They will be interested in admiring the reality of the weakness and vulnerability of humanity.

Ever since they have been babies, they have needed compassion, someone to care for them, until they get older. They know that there should be someone to care for them, until they rest in peace. They have been spending their life believing in this idea. There is always someone caring, or a possibility for themselves to care for others. They die with the belief that there is God to care for us. They believe in Mercy as the most important.

That is why God chose from all of His names these two names: the Merciful, the Compassionate, to be placed next to His name God, in the first verse of the first Surah and throughout the entire Qur'an.

بِسْمِ اللهِ الرَّحْمٰنِ الرَّحِيْمِ

(1:1) In the name of Allah, the Merciful, the Compassionate[126]

Two in One, One for All

The last three religions (university courses) have three different

---

[126] One of the many practices taught by Islam is that its followers should begin their activities in the name of God. This principle, if consciously and earnestly followed, will necessarily yield three beneficial results. First, one will be able to restrain oneself from many misdeeds, since the habit of pronouncing the name of God is bound to make one wonder when about to commit some offence how such an act can be reconciled with the saying of God's holy name. Second, if a man pronounces the name of God before starting good and legitimate tasks, this act will ensure that both his starting point and his mental orientation are sound. Third - and this is the most important benefit - when a man begins something by pronouncing God's name, he will enjoy God's support and succour; God will bless his efforts and protect him from the machinations and temptation of Satan. For whenever man turns to God, God turns to him as well.

cognitive approaches to creating harmony. Moses, peace be upon him, was taking people from left to right: the elements in himself, the miracle and the message were set work on a material basis. On the other hand, Jesus, peace upon him, had a message that worked from right to left bringing balance, with strong spiritual elements. Both had the same goal, to achieve harmony.

Muhammad's, may God's blessings and peace be upon him, message has a combined approach of balance. It delivers to both sides at the same time, it is balanced from the start.

وَكَذَٰلِكَ جَعَلْنَٰكُمْ أُمَّةً وَسَطًا لِّتَكُونُوا شُهَدَاءَ عَلَى النَّاسِ وَيَكُونَ الرَّسُولُ عَلَيْكُمْ شَهِيدًا ۚ وَمَا جَعَلْنَا الْقِبْلَةَ الَّتِي كُنتَ عَلَيْهَا إِلَّا لِنَعْلَمَ مَن يَتَّبِعُ الرَّسُولَ مِمَّن يَنقَلِبُ عَلَىٰ عَقِبَيْهِ ۚ وَإِن كَانَتْ لَكَبِيرَةً إِلَّا عَلَى الَّذِينَ هَدَى اللهُ ۗ وَمَا كَانَ اللهُ لِيُضِيعَ إِيمَانَكُمْ ۚ إِنَّ اللهَ بِالنَّاسِ لَرَءُوفٌ رَّحِيمٌ

(2:143) And it is thus that We appointed you to be the community of the middle way so that you might be witnesses to all mankind and the Messenger might be a witness to you. We appointed the direction which you formerly observed so that We might distinguish those who follow the Messenger from those who turn on their heels. For it was indeed burdensome except for those whom Allah guided. And Allah will never leave your faith to waste. Allah is full of gentleness and mercy to mankind.

Teaching Love and Compassion

Those attached substantially more to one side of the brain lack optimal harmony, and their corpus callosum needs a kick.

Both types of people came, they were sent to give this kick and fulfill their requirements. They came to give people help to understand love and trust as examples manifesting genuine care and showing empathy. In the end all the messengers have been teaching humanity only love and compassion.

وَمَآ اَرْسَلْنٰكَ اِلَّا رَحْمَةً لِّلْعٰلَمِيْنَ

(21:107) We have sent you forth as nothing but mercy to people of the whole world.[127]

Education is Optional

In case the message has been the same all around, the students' (humanity's) response to the teaching has been and is highly variable. Some prefer not to have it at all (learning from the street), others will drop out at a certain point or stop at a certain level or course, and a part will graduate successfully. Some will later join adult education and others will change their career etc. If God wanted to make the education compulsory, He could have made everyone complete the education, but He gave you freedom to make your decision.

عَمَّ يَتَسَآءَلُوْنَ ۚ

(78:1) About what are they asking one another?

عَنِ النَّبَاِ الْعَظِيْمِ

(78:2) Is it about the awesome tiding

الَّذِيْ هُمْ فِيْهِ مُخْتَلِفُوْنَ ؕ

---

[127] This verse can also be translated as: We have sent you only as a blessing for the people of the world. In both cases it will mean that the appointment of the Prophet (peace be upon him) is indeed a blessing and mercy of Allah to the whole world. This is because he aroused the neglectful world from its heedlessness and gave it the knowledge of the criterion between truth and falsehood, and warned it very clearly of both the ways of salvation and ruin. This fact has been stated here to tell the disbelievers of Makkah that they were quite wrong in their estimate of the Prophet (peace be upon him) that he was an affliction and distress for them because they said: This man has sown seeds of discard among our clans and separated near relatives from each other. They have been told here: O people, you are wrong to presume that he is an affliction for you; but he is in reality a blessing and mercy of Allah for you.

(78:3) that they are in utter disagreement?[128]

Latest Messenger and The Latest Teaching Scope

Former teaching was meant to last for a certain period and focus on certain people in certain nations. The last message is supposed to cover three main dimensions of life: time, place and people. In order to meet the needs of the next generations, during all times and of all the nations in the different places at the same time, it is necessary to conclude the previous education and to build on top of it. Now if you want to learn how to deal with your daily life and remain self-confident in different situations, what is the most suitable option for you? Is it just learning from the book or getting a demo from someone, who has mastered the book, to guide you what to do step by step?

This was exactly the scope of Prophet Muhammad's (ﷺ) teaching mission! Book and practical application (Sunnah).

وَأَطِيعُوا اللَّهَ وَالرَّسُولَ لَعَلَّكُمْ تُرْحَمُونَ

(3:132) And obey Allah and the Messenger, that you may be shown

---

[128] Another meaning of fi-hi mukhtalifun also can be: As these people themselves have not agreed on any one view about the end of the world, they hold varying views about it. Some one has been influenced by the Christian belief and believes in the life after death but thinks that the second life would not be a physical but only a spiritual life. Another does not deny the Hereafter absolutely but doubts whether it was possible or not.

The Quran relates the view of these very people when it says: We do only guess: we are not certain. And another plainly said: There is no other life than this present life, and we shall never be raised back to life after our death. Then, there were some atheists, who said: Life is only this worldly life of ours. Here we shall die and live and nothing but the change of time destroys us. There were some others who were not atheistic but they regarded the second life as impossible. According to them it was beyond the power of God to raise the dead back to life. They said: Who will give life to these bones when they are rotten. Their different views by themselves were a proof that they had no knowledge in this regard; they were only conjecturing and guessing. Had they any knowledge, they would have agreed on one view.

mercy.

The Miracle of The Prophet is Not to Be a Supernatural Force

The Messenger is an integral part of the last message as well as the miracle, and he is containing the entire humanity!

With the miracle of the Qur'an, it took you some time to grasp it because it's a book. The same happens with the Prophet, may God bless him and grant him peace. What he did is a miracle, but you can't grasp it easily, because he is a human being like you and me.

He is not a God himself nor a son of God, an angel or any supernatural power.

لَقَدْ جَآءَكُمْ رَسُولٌ مِّنْ اَنْفُسِكُمْ عَزِيزٌ عَلَيْهِ مَا عَنِتُّمْ حَرِيصٌ عَلَيْكُمْ بِالْمُؤْمِنِينَ رَءُوفٌ رَّحِيمٌ

(9:128) There has come to you a Messenger of Allah from among yourselves, who is distressed by the losses you sustain, who is ardently desirous of your welfare and is tender and merciful to those that believe.

This was the way it unfolded for the obvious reason that humans need a role model, with whom anyone can relate. The miracle should be up to our standards, and it should help us perform, not to make us feel overwhelmed and helpless!

قُلْ لَّوْ كَانَ فِى الْاَرْضِ مَلَئِكَةٌ يَّمْشُونَ مُطْمَئِنِّينَ لَنَزَّلْنَا عَلَيْهِمْ مِّنَ السَّمَآءِ مَلَكًا رَّسُوْلًا

(17:95) Say: "Had angels been walking about in peace on the earth, We would surely have sent to them an angel from the heavens as Messenger."

The Miracle is Himself

Himself being the miracle made the identification as the Messenger of God (ﷺ) more difficult than with any other prophet. The others could prove to people their miracles immediately. Muhammad's, may God bless him and grant him peace, miracle was a book, and the Qur'an was still revealing verses after verses.

He had to be patient and deal with the expected and unexpected resistance from people as well as exaggerated reactions. They tried him from every angle and accused him of being a liar, a madman. They blamed him for having something to do with the jinns or for being a part of witchcraft!

They put him under every kind of manipulation trying to cause many kinds of confusion and stress on his nerves. Some times were tough, up to amounting to physical violence, while others were soft, including offers of wealth, power or prestige. The testing is not over yet! There are still some people around the world who are trying their best to put more pressure, and calling it freedom of expression. None of the earlier ways worked at all, and none will!

The only way he did this was by remaining confident all the time under every circumstance, never surprised by a question or situation and never yielding to any pressure, distraction or panic. He himself was the Miracle, the role model of a confident self, of a confident loving self!

إِنَّا كَفَيْنَاكَ الْمُسْتَهْزِئِينَ

(15:95) Surely We suffice to deal with those who scoff at you,

الَّذِينَ يَجْعَلُونَ مَعَ اللهِ إِلَٰهًا اٰخَرَ ۚ فَسَوْفَ يَعْلَمُونَ

(15:96) those who set up another deity alongside Allah. They shall soon come to know.

وَلَقَدْ نَعْلَمُ أَنَّكَ يَضِيقُ صَدْرُكَ بِمَا يَقُولُونَ

(15:97) We certainly know that their statements sorely grieve you.

وَلَقَدْ نَعْلَمُ أَنَّكَ يَضِيقُ صَدْرُكَ بِمَا يَقُولُونَ

281

(15:98) When (you feel so) glorify your Lord with His praise and prostrate yourself before Him,

$$\text{وَاعْبُدْ رَبَّكَ حَتَّى يَأْتِيَكَ الْيَقِينُ}$$

(15:99) and worship your Lord until the last moment (of your life) that will most certainly come.[129]

The Perfect Confident Self

This is why you're reading this book! I can guess it's because you want to know more about how to be confident and in tune with your world. Your wishes include having a peace of mind and to be loving towards your surroundings. You desire to be happy, to be alive and to stay that way forever.

360 Degree Mission

The way in which the Prophet Muhammad (ﷺ) completed his mission was a miracle, and his education covered all aspects of professional life and every range of social relationships. He had to remain confident, balanced, logical and emotionally harmonious, in showing a balance between professional and social life. His teachings covered the full range of activities of the human intellect including what we should imagine, dream, feel, think, and how to put it all into practice in our own way.

---

[129] That is Salat and worship of your Lord are the only means which can generate in you that power of sustenance which is required to stand resolutely against the troubles and afflictions you will inevitably encounter in the propagation of the message of the truth and reform of humanity. This will comfort you, fill you with courage and enable you to perform that divine mission for which you have been sent in the face of abuse, derision and obstacles.

Teaching by Doing

He had the capacity to wear all the hats at a certain point in his life and to remain transparent even in the smallest details, up to personal hygiene. This was necessary, in order to create a 360-degree panorama of human relationship and activities. He had no assistant, smart agencies nor ministers to help. He has no one but God.

You're Covered

What kind of hats do you know of? There's the orphan, difficult childhood, single, married, father, and grandfather. What is your profession? Is it in teaching, engineering, social work, finance, military, politics, medicine or is it creative? Are you an intern, CEO, chairman or a president?

Do you think that no one can understand your responsibilities or your feelings? Don't worry, he (ﷺ) has understanding for you, and you'll be surprised that you're covered.

Are You a Lady?

If you're a man, for sure you're covered! But what if you are a woman? Are you covered?

What are you doing: young lady, wife, mother, or grandmother? Secular, atheist, Jew or Christian? Are you a businesswoman, scientist, fighter or an artist? Again, are you a trainee, CEO, chairman or a president? Do you think that no one can understand your responsibilities or your feelings? Don't worry, he (ﷺ) has understanding for you, and you'll be surprised that you're covered.

All these women were a big part of the 360 panorama in one way or another. For this reason, it was necessary to have a different number of wives and daughters. Now you're not left out of his education. You can find yourself in one of them in a way that you can relate to. They all admired him (ﷺ), finding him to be the man who understands, respects, loves and cares, in both happy and difficult times, whatever the mood swings of others may be.

The Super Grand Master of Rumi

Let's leave it to Hind bin Abi Hala (stepson from the Prophet's (ﷺ) first marriage), a fair witness, to describe to us the Messenger of God, the super grand master of Rumi, may God bless him and grant him peace.

His physical appearance and body language

"The Messenger of Allah (saw) was imposing and majestic. His face shone like the full moon. He was somewhat taller than medium height and a little shorter than what could be described as tall. His head was large, and he had hair that was neither curly nor straight. If his hair parted, he would leave it parted and it did not go beyond the lobes of his ears if he allowed it to go long. He was very fair skinned with a wide brow and had thick eyebrows with a narrow space between them. He had a vein there which throbbed when he was angry. He had a long nose (aquiline) with a line of light over it which someone might unthinkingly take to be his nose. His beard was thick and full. He had black eyes, firm and high cheeks, a wide mouth and white teeth with slight gaps (between his front teeth). The hair of his chest formed a fine line. His neck was like that of a statue made of pure silver. His physique was finely balanced (in perfect harmony and proportion). His body was firm and full. His belly and chest were equal in size. His chest was broad and the space between his shoulders wide. He had full calves. He was luminous (the parts of his body that could be seen while he was clothed shone a brilliant white). Between his neck and his navel there was a line of hair, but the rest of his torso was free of it. He had hair on his forearms and shoulders and the upper part of his chest. He had thick wrists, wide palms, thick hands and feet. His fingers were long. He was fine sinewed. He had high insteps and his feet were so smooth that water ran off them.

When he walked, he walked as though he were going down a hill. He walked in a dignified manner and walked easily. He walked swiftly. When he walked, it was as though he were heading down a slope. When he turned to address somebody, he turned his whole body completely (giving full attention). He lowered his glance, glancing downwards more than upwards. He restrained his glance. He would lead his Companions by walking behind them and was the first to greet any person he met".

His speech and communication

"The Messenger of Allah (saw) was always subject to grief and was always reflective. He had no rest and he only spoke when it was necessary. He spent long periods in silence. He began and ended what he said correctly (with full expression). His words were comprehensive without being either superfluous or wordy or inadequate. He had a mild temperament, being neither harsh nor cruel. He valued a gift / blessing, even if it was small.

He did not censure anything nor criticize or praise the taste of food. He did not get angry because of it. He did not attend to securing his own due nor did he get angry for himself nor would he seek to avenge himself. When he pointed, he did so with his whole hand. When he was surprised about something, he turned his palm upside down, (i.e., facing upwards). When he talked, he held/struck his right thumb in his left palm. When he was angry, he turned away and averted his face. When he was happy, he looked downwards. Generally, his laughter consisted of a smile and he showed his teeth which were as white as hailstones".

His time management at home and concern for others

"It was allowed him to enter his house for his own comfort. When he retired to his house, he divided his time into three parts – one part for Allah, one for his family and one for himself. Then he divided his part between his people and himself.

He used the time for the people more for the common people than for the elite. He did not reserve anything for himself to their exclusion. Of his conduct in the part reserved for himself was that he would show preference to the people of merit and would divide the time according to their excellence in the religion.

Some people needed one thing, some needed two, and some had many needs. He concerned himself with them and kept them busy doing things that were good for them and the community. He always asked about them and what was happening to them. He used to say, "Those who are present should convey things to those who are absent, and you should let me know about what is needed by people who cannot convey their needs to me. On the Day of Rising, Allah will firm the feet of a person who conveys to a ruler the need of someone who cannot convey it himself." This was all that was mentioned in his presence and he would only accept this from people".

His behavior outside

"The Messenger of Allah (saw) held his tongue except regarding what concerned people. He brought people together and did not split them. He honored the nobles of every group of people and appointed them over their people. He was cautious about people and on his guard against them, but he did that without averting his face from them or being discourteous. He asked about his Companions (ra) and he asked people how other people were.

He praised what was good and encouraged it and disliked what was ugly and foul and discouraged it. He took a balanced course, without making changes. He was not negligent, fearing that people would become negligent or weary. He was prepared for any eventuality. He did not neglect a right nor did he let his debts reach the point where

286

others had to help him. The best and most preferred people in his eyes were those who had good counsel for all. Those he most esteemed were those who supported / served and helped (people)".

His meetings and assemblies

'The Messenger of Allah did not sit down or stand up without mentioning Allah. He did not reserve a special place for himself and forbade other people to do so. When he came to people, he sat down at the edge of the assembly and told other people to do the same. He gave everyone who sat with him his share so that no one who sat with him thought that anyone was honored more than he was. If anyone sat with him or stood near him to ask something, he put up with that person until the person turned away. When someone asked him for something he needed, he either departed with it or with some consoling words. He had the kindest and best behavior of all people, being like a father to them. They were all equal in respect of their rights with him.

His assembly was one of clemency, modesty, patience and trust. Voices were not raised in it nor were shortcomings made public or lapses exposed. Its members were attached to each other by fear of Allah and were humble. They respected the old and showed mercy to the young. They helped those with needs and showed mercy to strangers'.

His behavior with the Companions and his moments of silence

'The Messenger of Allah (saw) was always cheerful, easy-tempered and mild. He was neither rough nor coarse. He did not shout (even in the marketplaces) nor utter obscenities. He did not find fault with nor over-praise people. He ignored what was superfluous and left it. He abandoned three things in himself: ostentation, storing things up and what did not concern him. He also abandoned three things in respect of other people: he did not censure anyone, he did not scold them, nor try to find out their faults.

He only spoke about things for which he expected a reward from Allah. When he spoke, the people sitting with him were as still as if there were birds on their heads. When he was silent, they talked, but did not quarrel in his presence. When someone talked in front of him, they kept quiet until he had finished. Their conversation was about the first topic broached (until they had finished with it). He laughed at what they laughed at and was surprised at what surprised them. He was patient with a stranger who had coarse language.

He said, "When you find someone asking for something he needs, then give it to him". He did not look for praise except to counterbalance something. He did not interrupt anyone speaking until that person had himself come to an end by either speaking or getting up from where he was sitting'.

What Was His Motive?

He (ﷺ) had no motive in life except completing his mission. He didn't leave behind wealth, a statue, or a street named after him, but the Qur'an, his teaching (Sunnah) and a mosque.

Michael H. Hart has ranked him on the top in his book *The 100: A Ranking of the Most Influential Persons in History*. God praises him:

$$وَإِنَّكَ لَعَلَى خُلُقٍ عَظِيمٍ$$

(68:4) and you are certainly on the most exalted standard of moral excellence.[130]

---

[130] That you stand exalted to a high and noble character; that is why you are enduring all these hardships in your mission of guiding the people to the right way, otherwise a man of weak character could not have done so.

By the Way, Did I Tell You That Love is Something We Learn to Earn?

If I didn't, let's speak clearly. Yes, yes, yes! Love needs to be first learned, then practiced and after that one needs to work hard to keep it. This is what Rumi was saying all the time in his poems. This is what the Prophet (ﷺ) did: living, teaching and coaching love.

What is Love? And Where is It?

You have been very patient, you have put in a lot of effort, thank you very much. Now it's time to be satisfied, rewarded for your curiosity. Especially if you have been looking for Love-No-Stress, this has been a 300-page ad, right? An ad that's adding on you!

Initially when we talked about love, you may have been expecting to read about some breathing techniques or meditation for self-love. Those surely have their place but that has nothing to do with love! You may have reached a point of frustration or even desperation while looking for love. And you are not alone, lack of love is one of the most critical challenges of humanity right now and one of the definite root causes of psychological struggles even among the professionals. You must have encountered endless propositions trying to teach you about love. Now you know where the problem lies! You have been misled by fake love based on pampering, even though love is in the exact opposite direction. (Guess who switched the labels!!!)

From the first page on I was talking about love. Didn't you see it? Or maybe you know it? The most important thing you should learn about true love is that it's not something you expect and that's why it's love. It will always surprise you! It is in the last place you would think about. It has been all the time everywhere, but you never saw it. That's what the story is all about!

Tell Me More About Love!

Good fitness in love means that you will be able to move smoothly and smartly from one task to another, from one person to another, and from one moment to the next. You'll be elegant, good-looking, wearing a humble smile, and thinking without thinking. You'll do the right thing in the right way at the right time with the proper extent, just perfect! This includes all, and does not exclude any second nor breath in your life. If you can see what's behind you, you will not experience selfishness, nor disruptive self!!

Are We All Getting the Same Love?

Do we go to the gym, do the same exercises and get the same results? Of course not. There are a lot of programs and fitness machines. There is a lot of difference in our genetics. We also have different levels of motivation and passion to go to the gym. Despite all these factors, the mechanism and basics of muscle growth are the same. All these factors combined will make something special of you. There is something very unique about you, there is no other version of you. The gym is open to all of us, do your best! Do!

Islam also includes endless programs; it is able to satisfy all of our needs and passions for love. The mechanism and the basics are the same. All will fit into the hardware of our psyche, and in the know-how of the X-Harmony Factor. Everything must work together. In the end you will get your very own version of love!

Islamophiles In Action

Now, if you wanted to put everything you've read so far together, turn it on, and put it into action, what would it look like? What will these actions be?

Part III

Islam Like You Never Knew It Before

CHAPTER 15

The Deal

Trap or Ad

We are all seduced by different things, and everyone is seduced by certain things more than others. Some will be attracted to the opposite sex, but others will prefer the same sex. Some don't care about sex at all but prefer fortune, self-admiration, nature's beauty, power, fame. The list is endless! But we don't every time rush to do so, when we feel tempted. There is a level of self-control in order to find the right balance to satisfy our temptation, and never to overstep our boundaries.

Do ads help you find that limit or do they manipulate your temptations? Do the advertisers have your good in mind? Is it a win-win story? In fact, manipulating temptations is one of the greatest conquest techniques that Satan can perform, and he may be the only one! Once you see something promoted so strongly and showed to you in a view of extreme goodness, take a moment! This is not an ad; this is a trap!

قَالَ رَبِّ بِمَا أَغْوَيْتَنِى لَأُزَيِّنَنَّ لَهُمْ فِى الْأَرْضِ وَلَأُغْوِيَنَّهُمْ أَجْمَعِينَ

(15:39) Iblis said: "My Lord! In the manner You led me to error, I will make things on earth seem attractive to them and lead all of them to error

Advertising That is Not a Trap, But Not for Everyone

A good ad is one that tells you the truth, the truth that you wouldn't like to hear! It is not always the good things that we like to hear. I told you earlier that you might like my question: "What's the difference between stupid and smart?" My answer would not be for everyone, but is it better to hear it from me now or later from Satan?

This is the way we are from birth. We are those kids who cry to get what they love although it is not necessarily good for us. This is the reality of human beings, that is why we can't be treated only with justice. Our life will be hard, we will lose, and we will not bear for long. God knows, that is why He created compassion.

Who Is Smart?

The smart ones are the humble, who affirm their humanness and stop playing the intelligent. They submit to God and ask for His mercy. This is real smartness. Knowing that you will be one of the most brilliant people by getting to know one of the most obvious but not so easy facts to comprehend, is this then the exact definition of genius?

You may wonder, what is the difference between being intelligent and being smart? I can tell you that you may be smart, but you don't need to be intelligent and vice versa. You may be born intelligent but die stupid. Intelligence is related to our IQs, and it usually shows up in brilliant scientists or innovators. But if they do not know the above-mentioned fact, then that IQ is worthless.

On the other hand, our IQ may be very limited but if we have been able to see and process the truth (that is a sign of intelligence and genius) we have made our future. Smartness is directly related to the ability to process the truth, the ability to be honest, and the ability to choose the right advertisement, not the ones that manipulate you.

The Beauty and The Beast

Now let's lay down the groundwork so that we can talk further. If you want to create a category for Islam in your head, it should be different from all sugar-coated ads.

Islam will tell you the truth and you will fear it at first when you see it!

It feels like you're facing a beast, but when you get used to it, you'll love it! You won't be able to live without it, and you will understand the truth behind all, even the scary part of it. After a certain point you will be surprised that the beauty (of Islam) is not only beautiful, but also sweet and merciful, and that the beast never existed. It was an illusion.

What is The Message Behind the Pain of The Soul?

Why does God make us feel the pain inside our psyche, stress, insecurity and all these psychological problems? Does this have anything to do with love?

Let me ask you, do you know why cancer is such an evil disease? Because it is painless, it secretly grows until it is too late and cannot be cured. Only then it starts to show its face and becomes very painful (similar to the behavior of Satan). On the contrary benign disease is painful from the start and early pain is a good sign to seek treatment!

Satan would like to promote for you anything that will shut your pain or brain. He intends to mask your psyche's pain. If his intentions don't affect you, this is a very good sign! God wished for you a full recovery! He made you feel a little anxious, buy this book, and read so far. He is giving you a chance to find true love. If you want!

Is It Genius?

What we're talking about here is your psyche. The most valuable thing in your life! What have you all in all been investing in it? You are losing from it every moment! Is there a way to stop it? Can it be fixed, replaced or slowed down? No. Will you lose it in any case?

مَثَلُ مَا يُنْفِقُونَ فِى هٰذِهِ الْحَيٰوةِ الدُّنْيَا كَمَثَلِ رِيحٍ فِيهَا صِرٌّ أَصَابَتْ حَرْثَ قَوْمٍ ظَلَمُوٓا أَنْفُسَهُمْ فَأَهْلَكَتْهُ ۚ وَمَا ظَلَمَهُمُ اللهُ وَلٰكِنْ أَنْفُسَهُمْ يَظْلِمُوْنَ

(3:117) The example of what they spend in the life of this world is like that of a wind accompanied with frost which smites the harvest of a people who wronged themselves, and lays it to waste. It is not Allah who wronged them; rather it is they who wrong themselves.[131]

This is the challenge we all face. Have you found a solution to this problem? Have you thought that it is your right to think about this problem, find your own solution and make your own choice? What is the best investment for your psyche? Have you ever thought about it yourself? Or have you been told not to try? Was it said to you that you just have to accept it as it is, don't even try to think, go ahead, live it, and don't waste your time! Is this what you learned or thought about?

Could this situation be the reason you feel stressed, insecure or uncomfortable? It makes you feel like you are in a corner and facing an impossible problem without a solution!

Did you know it's for sale? Yes, it is! Seriously speaking, you can sell it! In fact, this is the coolest and most genius surprise proposal on earth, even if it's the only one! Is this strange? Didn't you know this before? You didn't know that Islam is a business offer, a deal to buy your

---

[131] The term 'harvest' in this parable refers to this life which resembles a field of cultivation the harvest of which one will reap in the World to Come. The 'wind' refers to the superficial appearance of righteousness, for the sake of which unbelievers spend their wealth on philanthropic and charitable causes. The expression 'frost' indicates their lack of true faith and their failure to follow the Divine Laws, as a result of which their entire life has gone astray.

By means of this parable God seeks to bring home to them that while wind is useful for the growth of cultivation if that wind turns into frost it destroys it. So it is with man's acts of charity: they can prove helpful to the growth of the harvest one will reap in the Hereafter but are liable to be destructive if mixed with unbelief. God is the Lord and Master of man as well as of all that man owns, and the world in which he lives. If a man either does not recognize the sovereignty of his Lord and unlawfully serves others or disobeys God's Laws then his actions become crimes for which he deserves to be tried; his acts of 'charity' are but the acts of a servant who unlawfully helps himself to his master's treasure and then spends it as he likes.

psyche!

يَا أَيُّهَا الَّذِينَ آمَنُوا هَلْ أَدُلُّكُمْ عَلَى تِجَارَةٍ تُنْجِيكُمْ مِّنْ عَذَابٍ أَلِيمٍ

(61:10) Believers, shall I direct you to a commerce that will deliver you from a grievous chastisement?[132]

تُؤْمِنُونَ بِاللهِ وَرَسُولِهِ وَتُجَاهِدُونَ فِى سَبِيلِ اللهِ بِأَمْوَالِكُمْ وَأَنْفُسِكُمْ ذَٰلِكُمْ خَيْرٌ لَّكُمْ إِنْ كُنْتُمْ تَعْلَمُونَ

(61:11) Have faith in Allah and His Messenger and strive in the Way of Allah with your possessions and your lives. That is better for you if you only knew.[133]

Here's the Deal

Those moments that are anyway depreciating from our lives (aging), God will buy them and pay you the highest possible value!

فَلَا تَعْلَمُ نَفْسٌ مَّا أُخْفِيَ لَهُمْ مِّنْ قُرَّةِ أَعْيُنٍ جَزَاءً بِمَا كَانُوا يَعْمَلُونَ

(32:17) No one knows what delights of the eyes are kept hidden for them as a reward for their deeds.[134]

This means that whatever your dreaming strategy is and whatever you expect to achieve it is possible to carry them with you after your death.

---

[132] A bargain is something in which a person employs his wealth, time, labor and talent in order to earn a profit. In the same sense the faith and jihad in the cause of Allah have been called a bargain, as if to say: If you exert all your powers and spend all your resources in the way of Allah, you will get the profits that are being mentioned in the following verses.

[133] When the believers are asked to believe, it automatically gives the meaning that they should become sincere Muslims: they should not rest content with oral profession of the faith but should be ready and willing to make every sacrifice in the cause of their faith. That is, this bargain is far superior for them to every worldly bargain.

[134] On the authority of Abu Hurairah said that the Prophet (peace be upon him) said: "Allah says: I have made ready for My righteous servants that which has neither been seen by the eye, nor heard by the ear, nor ever conceived by any man."

This makes it a fact that this stage of life is dreaming during sleep. During this nap we actively dream until we die. Whatever time will pass after death, we will wake up and have a chance to discuss our dream. According to this discussion we will all fulfill these dreams.

كَأَنَّهُمْ يَوْمَ يَرَوْنَهَا لَمْ يَلْبَثُوا إِلَّا عَشِيَّةً أَوْ ضُحٰىهَا

(79:46) On the Day they see it, they will feel as though they had stayed (in the grave) no more than one evening or one morning.

وَإِذَا الْأَرْضُ مُدَّتْ

(84:3) and when the earth is stretched out[135]

وَأَلْقَتْ مَا فِيهَا وَتَخَلَّتْ

(84:4) and casts out what is within it and is emptied,[136]

وَأَذِنَتْ لِرَبِّهَا وَحُقَّتْ

(84:5) and hearkens to the command of its Lord, doing what it should.[137]

يَٰأَيُّهَا الْإِنسَانُ إِنَّكَ كَادِحٌ إِلَىٰ رَبِّكَ كَدْحًا فَمُلَاقِيهِ

(84:6) O man, you are striving unto your Lord and you will meet Him.[138]

فَأَمَّا مَنْ أُوتِيَ كِتَٰبَهُ بِيَمِينِهْ

---

[135] When the earth is stretched out: when the oceans and rivers are filled up, the mountains are crushed to pieces and scattered away, and the earth is leveled and turned into a smooth plain.

[136] That is, it will throw out all dead bodies of men and also the traces and evidences of their deeds lying within it, so that nothing remains hidden and buried in it.

[137] Here, it has not been expressly told what will happen when such and such an event takes place, for the subsequent theme by itself explains this, as if to say: O man, you are moving towards your Lord and are about to meet Him; you will be given your conduct book; and rewarded or punished according to your deeds."

[138] That is, "You may if you so like think that all your efforts and endeavors in the world are confined to worldly life and motivated by worldly desires, yet the truth is that you are moving, consciously or unconsciously, towards your Lord and you have ultimately to appear before Him in any case.

(84:7) Whoever is given the Record in his right hand

فَسَوْفَ يُحَاسَبُ حِسَابًا يَّسِيْرًا ۟

(84:8) shall be called to an easy accounting,[139]

وَّيَنْقَلِبُ اِلٰى اَهْلِهٖ مَسْرُوْرًا ۟

(84:9) and shall return to his people joyfully.[140]

This discussion is based on a signed contract that we must make now.

A Dream That Was Not on The List!

Since birth it was agreed that you will be part of a deal you didn't choose. It was decided that you have to spend your life on something. No matter what it is, you have to waste you.

You are programmed to dream within certain choices (pre-set dreaming strategy). You have grown up, gotten an education, eaten and worked nonstop. You have run after a carrot of your choice, which

---

[139] That is, his reckoning will be less severe. He will not be asked why he had done such and such a thing and what excuses he had to offer for it. Though his evil deeds will also be there along with his good deeds in his records, his errors will be overlooked and pardoned in view of his outweighing good deeds. In the Quran, for the severe reckoning of the wicked people the words su-al-hisab (heavy reckoning) have been used, and concerning the righteous it has been said: From such people, We accept the best of their deeds and overlook their evils. The explanation of it given by the Prophet (peace be upon him). According to one of the traditions the Prophet (peace be upon him) said: Doomed will be he who is called to account for his deeds. Aishah said: O Messenger of Allah, has not Allah said: He whose record is given in his right hand shall have an easy reckoning? The Prophet (peace be upon him) replied: That is only about the presentation of the deeds, but the one who is questioned would be doomed. In another tradition Aishah has related: I once heard the Prophet (peace be upon him) supplicate during the prayer, thus: O God, call me to a light reckoning. When he brought his Prayer to conclusion, I asked what he meant by that supplication. He replied: Light reckoning means that one's conduct book will be seen and one's errors will be overlooked. O Aishah, the one who is called to account for his deeds on that Day, would be doomed.

[140] His kinsfolk: his family and relatives and companions who will have been pardoned even like himself.

will all the time stay as a carrot, until you die and leave it. We are talking about very basic things: food, house, car, spouse, children, wealth, power, values, rights; you name it. They are all trivial!

You have earned something, but you have to pay for it something: tax, insurance, pension fund, etc. Of course, you have tried to be clever. But however clever you would consider the measures taken, the fact is that you could be paying for far more valuable things and even totally get them! You missed the possibility to dream to be the true you, the everlasting version of you.

This was the forbidden dream that you were not supposed to realize, dream or even think about. You shouldn't know that it already exists and that it's a choice. You were not meant to take any of the signs seriously, better to stay distracted all the way. How shady is that?

قُلْ هَلْ نُنَبِّئُكُم بِالْأَخْسَرِينَ أَعْمَالًا

(18:103) Say, (O Muhammad): "Shall We tell you who will be the greatest losers in respect of their works?

اَلَّذِينَ ضَلَّ سَعْيُهُمْ فِى الْحَيٰوةِ الدُّنْيَا وَهُمْ يَحْسَبُونَ أَنَّهُمْ يُحْسِنُونَ صُنْعًا

(18:104) It will be those whose effort went astray in the life of the world and who believe nevertheless that they are doing good.[141]

أُولٰٓئِكَ الَّذِينَ كَفَرُوا بِاٰيٰتِ رَبِّهِمْ وَلِقَآئِهِ فَحَبِطَتْ أَعْمَالُهُمْ فَلَا نُقِيمُ لَهُمْ يَوْمَ الْقِيٰمَةِ وَزْنًا

(18:105) Those are the ones who refused to believe in the revelations of their Lord and that they are bound to meet Him. Hence, all their

---

[141] This verse has two meanings. The one is the same that we have adopted in the translation. The other meaning is this: Those who confined all their endeavors to the worldly life. That is, whatever they did, they did for this world without paying any regard to God and the Hereafter. As they considered the worldly life to be the real life, they made the success and prosperity in this world their sole aim and object. Even if they professed the existence of Allah, they never paid any heed to the two implications of this profession: to lead their lives in a way to please Allah and to come out successful on the Day they shall have to render an account of what they did in this world. This was because they considered themselves to be mere rational animals who were absolutely independent and free from every kind of responsibility and had nothing else to do but to enjoy the good things of the world like animals in a meadow.

deeds have come to naught, and We shall assign no weight to them on the Day of Resurrection.[142]

ذٰلِكَ جَزَآؤُهُمْ جَهَنَّمُ بِمَا كَفَرُوْا وَاتَّخَذُوْۤا اٰيٰتِيْ وَرُسُلِيْ هُزُوًا

(18:106) Hell is their recompense for disbelieving and their taking My revelations and My Messengers as objects of jest.

اِنَّ الَّذِيْنَ اٰمَنُوْا وَعَمِلُوا الصّٰلِحٰتِ كَانَتْ لَهُمْ جَنّٰتُ الْفِرْدَوْسِ نُزُلًا

(18:107) As for those who believe and do good works, the Gardens of Paradise shall be there to welcome them;

خٰلِدِيْنَ فِيْهَا لَا يَبْغُوْنَ عَنْهَا حِوَلًا

(8:108) there they will abide for ever, with no desire to be removed from there."[143]

Your Life Insurance Needs Insurance

The life insurance you have right now is the biggest lie you have ever

---

[142] "So worthless will be their deeds" in the sense that they will be of no avail to them in the life after death, even though they might have considered them as their great achievements but the fact is that they will lose all their value as soon as the world shall come to an end. When they will go before their Lord, and all their deeds shall be placed in the scales, they will have no weight at all whether they had built great palaces, established great universities and libraries, set up great factories and laboratories, constructed highways and railways, in short, all their inventions, industries, sciences and arts and other things of which they were very proud in this world, will lose their weights in the scales.

The only thing which will have weight there will be that which had been done in accordance with the divine instructions and with the intention to please Allah. It is, therefore, obvious that if all of one's endeavors were confined to the worldly things and the achievement of worldly desires whose results one would see in this world, one should not reasonably expect to see their results in the Hereafter, for they would have gone waste with the end of this world. It is equally obvious, that only the deeds of the one, who performed them strictly in accordance with His instructions to win His approval with a view to avail of their results in the Hereafter, will find that his deeds had weight in the scales.

[143] "No desire will they have to be removed there from" because they will find no place and no condition better than those in Paradise.

faced. This is the one deal you will never take advantage of, sometimes you could lose your life because of it, and at best, someone will be glad you lost yours. In fact, your insurance system is a good example of how New Trinity affects you.

Insurance has a conflict of interest with your psychological safety. Insurance is insurance only by its name. Having one makes you feel forever more anxious and insecure, so you keep paying! And these companies insure themselves with tons of lawyers and experts to make sure all account balances are positive, and they get millions of times more than what they pay.

You know it all too well, but you have no other options. You pay all of your insurance on a regular basis and you are careful not to miss any payment. You keep paying but if and when you count your balance, you'll cry like a rat in a maze.

By the way, are you wondering why Muslims pray five times a day from their puberty until their death? Because they discovered this New Trinity trap and signed another insurance contract to secure the insurance!

You Are Property

Our psyche (the interaction between the body and the soul) is not ours, we are responsible for managing it until we get it back to God (i.e., fulfill the trust given to us by God).

الَّذِيْنَ اِذَآ اَصَابَتْهُمْ مُّصِيْبَةٌ ۙ قَالُوْٓا اِنَّا لِلّٰهِ وَاِنَّآ اِلَيْهِ رٰجِعُوْنَ

(2:156) those who when any affliction smites them, they say: "Verily, we belong to Allah, and it is to Him that we are destined to return."

Is this trust not obvious? Your soul demanded to bear it and accepted the task of the guardian.

اِنَّا عَرَضْنَا الْاَمَانَةَ عَلَى السَّمٰوٰتِ وَالْاَرْضِ وَالْجِبَالِ فَاَبَيْنَ اَنْ يَّحْمِلْنَهَا

305

وَأَشْفَقْنَ مِنْهَا وَ حَمَلَهَا الْإِنْسَانُ إِنَّهُ كَانَ ظَلُومًا جَهُولًا ۚ

(33:72) We offered the trust to the heavens and the earth and the mountains, but they refused to carry it and were afraid of doing so; but man carried it. Surely he is wrong-doing, ignorant.

This is why you feel like something is wrong all the time, that something is missing, and you feel uncomfortable. This is the reason why you will feel a sudden relief from the burden when you submit it back (the rebirth by Islam).

God knows that we will forget this promise and even deny it.

وَ إِذْ أَخَذَ رَبُّكَ مِنْ بَنِيَ آدَمَ مِنْ ظُهُورِهِمْ ذُرِّيَّتَهُمْ وَ أَشْهَدَهُمْ عَلَى أَنْفُسِهِمْ ۚ
أَلَسْتُ بِرَبِّكُمْ قَالُوا بَلَى ۛ شَهِدْنَا ۛ أَنْ تَقُولُوا يَوْمَ الْقِيَٰمَةِ إِنَّا كُنَّا عَنْ هَٰذَا غَٰفِلِينَ ۚ

(7:172) And recall (O Prophet) when your Lord brought forth descendants from the loins of the sons of Adam, and made them witnesses against their ownselves. asking them: 'Am I not your Lord?' They said: 'Yes, we do testify.' We did so lest you claim on the Day of

Resurrection: 'We were unaware of this.'[144]

This is why God sent commissioners (Prophets) on behalf of Him to ask us to hand over His possessions while we are alive.

The Creator has proven His ownership and creation. He has told the whole story of your body and your soul, giving signals that only He knows. We only find out later and there is more to come. This means that we do not have the right to use it as we like but according to the instructions of the owner and creator. (Do you really need me to mention this here again?)

---

[144] God gathered all human beings, divided them into different groups, granted them human form and the faculty of speech, made them enter into a covenant, and then making them witnesses against themselves. He asked them: 'Am I not your Lord?' They replied: 'Assuredly you are Our Lord.' Then God told them: 'I call upon the sky and the earth and your own progenitor, Adam, to be witness against you lest you should say on the Day of Judgement that you were ignorant of this. Know well that no one other than Me deserves to be worshipped and no one other than Me is your Lord. So do not ascribe any partner to Me. I shall send to you My Messengers who will remind you of this covenant which you made with Me. I shall send down to you My Books.' In reply all said: 'We witness that You are Our Lord and our Deity. We have no lord or deity other than You.'

So God caused all human beings whom He intended to create until the Last Day to come into existence. He endowed upon them life, consciousness and the faculty of speech, and brought home to them that there is no god or lord besides Him, and that Islam alone is the right way to serve Him.

If someone considers calling all human beings together in one assembly impossible, that shows, more than anything else the woeful paucity of his imagination. For if someone accepts that God has the power to create countless human beings in succession, there is no reason to suppose that He did not have the power to create them all at some given moment prior to the creation of the universe, or that He will be unable to resurrect them all at some given moment in the future. Again, it stands to reason that at a time when God wanted to designate man as His vicegerent on earth after endowing him with reason and understanding, He took from him an oath of allegiance. All this is so reasonable that the actual occurrence of the covenant should not cause any wonder. On the contrary, one should wonder if the event did not take place.

Freedom to Shout or Whisper

Freedom does not mean that you get lost as you like or to run away confidently thinking that you will not be caught. Death, a signed official order is there to stop you and bring you back.

وَمَا كَانَ لِنَفْسٍ أَنْ تَمُوتَ إِلَّا بِإِذْنِ اللهِ كِتَابًا مُؤَجَّلًا ۗ وَ مَنْ يُرِدْ ثَوَابَ الدُّنْيَا نُؤْتِهِ مِنْهَا ۗ وَمَنْ يُرِدْ ثَوَابَ الْآخِرَةِ نُؤْتِهِ مِنْهَا ۗ وَسَنَجْزِى الشَّاكِرِينَ

(3:145) It is not given to any soul to die except with the leave of Allah, and at an appointed time. And he who desires his reward in this world, We shall grant him the reward of this world; and he who desires the reward of the Other World, We shall grant him the reward of the Other

World. And soon shall We reward the ones who are grateful.[145]

It's your right to be free, if you understand the consequences. You may agree with this or not, this is your opinion. He has given you the full options to make good or bad decisions.

يَٰٓأَيُّهَا النَّاسُ اتَّقُوا رَبَّكُمْ وَاخْشَوْا يَوْمًا لَّا يَجْزِىٰ وَالِدٌ عَن وَلَدِهِ وَلَا مَوْلُودٌ هُوَ جَازٍ عَن وَالِدِهِ شَيْئًا إِنَّ وَعْدَ اللهِ حَقٌّ فَلَا تَغُرَّنَّكُمُ الْحَيَوٰةُ الدُّنْيَا وَلَا يَغُرَّنَّكُم بِاللهِ الْغَرُورُ

(31:33) O people, fear (the wrath) of your Lord, and dread the Day when no father will stand for his child, nor any child stand for his

---

[145] The purpose of this directive is to bring home to the Muslims that it would be futile for them to try to flee from death. No one can either die before or survive the moment determined for death by God. Hence one should not waste one's time thinking how to escape death. Instead, one should take stock of one's activities and see whether one's efforts have either been directed merely to one's well-being in this world or to well-being in the Hereafter.

The word thawab denotes recompense and reward. The 'reward of this world' signifies the totality of benefits and advantages which a man receives as a consequence of his actions and efforts within the confines of this world. The 'reward of the Other World' denotes the benefits that a man will receive in the lasting World to Come as the fruits of his actions and efforts. From the Islamic point of view, the crucial question bearing upon human morals is whether a man keeps his attention focused on the worldly results of his endeavours or on the results which will acrue to him in the Next World.

The 'ones who are grateful' are those who fully appreciate God's favour in making the true religion available to them, and thereby intimating to them knowledge of a realm that is infinitely vaster than this world. Such people appreciate that God has graciously informed them of the truth so that the consequences of human endeavour are not confined to the brief span of earthly life but cover a vast expanse, embracing both the present life and the much more important life of the Hereafter.

A grateful man is he who, having gained this breadth of outlook and having developed this long-range perception of the ultimate consequences of things, persists in acts of righteousness out of his faith in God and his confidence in God's assurance that they will bear fruit in the Hereafter. He does so even though he may sometimes find that, far from bearing fruit, righteousness leads to privation and suffering in this world. The ungrateful ones are those who persist in a narrow preoccupation with earthly matters. They are those who disregard the evil consequences of unrighteousness in the Hereafter, seizing everything which appears to yield benefits and advantages in this world, and who are not prepared to devote their time and energy to those acts of goodness which promise to bear fruit in the Hereafter and which are either unlikely to yield earthly advantages or are fraught with risks. Such people are ungrateful and lack appreciation of the valuable knowledge vouchsafed to them by God.

father. Surely Allah's promise is true. So let the life of this world not beguile you, nor let the Deluder delude you about Allah.[146]

You are free to shout out loud or whisper, there is no God and stop

---

[146] "Allah's promise": the promise of Resurrection, when the court of Allah will be established and everyone will be called to render an account of his deeds.

The life of the world involves the people, who only see the superficial, in different kinds of misunderstandings. Someone thinks that life and death only belong to this world, and there is no life after this; therefore, whatever one has to do, one should do it here and now. Another one who is lost in his wealth and power and prosperity, forgets his death and gets involved in the foolish idea that his grandees and his power are everlasting. Another one overlooking the moral and spiritual objectives regards the material gains and pleasures in themselves as the only objectives and does not give anything any importance but the standard of living, no matter whether his standard of humanity goes on falling lower and lower as a result thereof. Someone thinks that worldly prosperity is the real criterion of truth and falsehood: every way of life that ensures this is the truth and everything contradictory to it is falsehood. Someone regards this very prosperity as a sign of being Allah's favorite and assumes the law that whoever is leading a prosperous life here is Allah's beloved no matter by what means he might have achieved this prosperity, and whoever is leading a miserable life in the world, even if it be so due to his love of the truth and his uprightness, will live a miserable life in the Hereafter, too. These and other such misunderstandings have been called deceptions of the worldly life by Allah.

Al-gharur (the deceiver) may be Satan or a man or a group of them, or even man's own self, or something else. The reason for using this comprehensive and meaningful word in its absolute form without identifying a particular person or thing is that for different people there are different means that cause them deception. Any particular means or cause that deceived a person to be misled and misguided from the right way to the wrong way, will be al-gharur in his particular case.

"To deceive about Allah" are also comprehensive words, which include countless kinds of deceptions. The deceiver deceives one man with the idea that there is no God at all, and another man with the idea that God after making the world has handed over its control and administration to the men and is no more concerned with it; he misleads another one, saying, "There are some favorite ones of God: if you attain nearness to them, you will surely win your forgiveness whatever you may do, or may have done, in the world;" he deceives another one, saying, "God is All- Forgiving and All-Merciful: you may go on committing sins freely, and He will go on forgiving each sin of yours." He gives another person the idea of determinism and misguides him, saying, "Everything that you do is pre-ordained: if you commit evil, it is God Who makes you commit it: if you avoid goodness, it is God Who makes you avoid it." Thus, there are countless types of such deceptions with which man is being deceived concerning God. When analyzed, it comes to light that the basic cause of all errors and sins and crimes is that man has been deceived concerning God in one way or the other, and that is how he has been misled to some ideological deviation or moral error.

310

there or continue: there is no God but Allah! Nobody can force you.

Prophet could not persuade his child

وَنَادَىٰ نُوحٌ رَّبَّهُ فَقَالَ رَبِّ إِنَّ ابْنِي مِنْ أَهْلِي وَإِنَّ وَعْدَكَ الْحَقُّ وَأَنْتَ أَحْكَمُ الْحَاكِمِينَ

(11:45) And Noah called out to his Lord, saying: 'My Lord! My son is of my family. Surely Your promise is true, and You are the greatest of those who judge.[147]

قَالَ يَا نُوحُ إِنَّهُ لَيْسَ مِنْ أَهْلِكَ إِنَّهُ عَمَلٌ غَيْرُ صَالِحٍ فَلَا تَسْأَلْنِ مَا لَيْسَ لَكَ بِهِ عِلْمٌ إِنِّي أَعِظُكَ أَنْ تَكُونَ مِنَ الْجَاهِلِينَ

(11:46) In response Noah was told: 'Most certainly he is not of your family; verily he is of unrighteous conduct. So do not ask of Me for that concerning which you have no knowledge. I admonish you never

---

[147] That is, You promised that You will save the members of my family from this calamity; so save my son for he is also a member of my family.

That is, You are the greatest of all rulers: therefore Your decision is final and there can be no appeal against it. And You are the best of all rulers: therefore all Your decisions are based on perfect knowledge and absolute justice.

to act like the ignorant ones.[148]

Child cannot guide his parents

وَإِذْ قَالَ اِبْرَهِيْمُ لِاَبِيْهِ اٰزَرَ اَتَتَّخِذُ اَصْنَامًا اٰلِهَةً ۚ اِنِّىْ اَرٰىكَ وَقَوْمَكَ فِىْ ضَلٰلٍ مُّبِيْنٍ

(6:74) And recall when Abraham said to his father, Azar: 'Do you take idols for gods? I see you and your people in obvious error.'

Wife could not convince her husband

وَضَرَبَ اللّٰهُ مَثَلًا لِّلَّذِيْنَ اٰمَنُوا امْرَاَتَ فِرْعَوْنَ ۘ اِذْ قَالَتْ رَبِّ ابْنِ لِيْ عِنْدَكَ بَيْتًا فِى الْجَنَّةِ وَنَجِّنِيْ مِنْ فِرْعَوْنَ وَعَمَلِهٖ وَنَجِّنِيْ مِنَ الْقَوْمِ الظّٰلِمِيْنَ

(66:11) Allah has set forth for the believers the parable of Pharaoh's wife. She prayed: "My Lord, build for me a house with You in Paradise and deliver me from Pharaoh and his misdeeds; and deliver me from the iniquitous people."

Prophets could not impose on their wives

ضَرَبَ اللّٰهُ مَثَلًا لِّلَّذِيْنَ كَفَرُوا امْرَاَتَ نُوحٍ وَّ امْرَاَتَ لُوطٍ ۗ كَانَتَا تَحْتَ عَبْدَيْنِ مِنْ عِبَادِنَا صَالِحَيْنِ فَخَانَتٰهُمَا فَلَمْ يُغْنِيَا عَنْهُمَا مِنَ اللّٰهِ شَيْئًا وَّقِيْلَ ادْخُلَا النَّارَ مَعَ الدّٰخِلِيْنَ

(66:10) Allah has set forth for the unbelievers the parable of the wives of Noah and Lot. They were wedded to two of Our righteous servants, but each acted treacherously with her husband, and their husbands could be of no avail to them against Allah. The two of them were told: "Enter the Fire with all the others who enter it."[149]

You Are Your Own Property Manager

Those who have agreed to this submission (Islam), have entered into an agreement with the Owner (Creator), that they are responsible for managing His belongings (only their own psyche) according to His instructions.

وَإِذْ قَالَ رَبُّكَ لِلْمَلٰئِكَةِ اِنِّىْ جَاعِلٌ فِى الْاَرْضِ خَلِيْفَةً ۗ

(2:30) Just think when your Lord said to the angels: "Lo! I am about

[148] Allah has called the wicked son of Prophet Noah (peace be upon him), as "His conduct was other than righteous", for children are entrusted by the Creator to the care of parents so that they may bring them up and train them to become good persons, and fulfill the purpose for which He created man. If a father does his very best to process and turn the child into a righteous person, but fails in his efforts, the child, who was a sort of raw material in his hands, would be likened to a worthless act. It is obvious that the wicked son was a worthless act, for he was not the sort of good work which his father had desired him to be. So in this sense he did not belong to the family of Prophet Noah (peace be upon him), whom the Creator had sent to mold all his people into good acts, especially those who were of his own flesh and blood. Thus that unrighteous son had forfeited all the rights of blood he had with the Prophet as far as the torment of the deluge was concerned.

Now let us consider the other question: Why was not the request of the Prophet regarding his own flesh and blood granted? The answer is this: If any part of the body of a man becomes so rotten that the surgeon is of the definite opinion that that part must be cut off for the sake of the safety of the rest of the body, the surgeon will not comply with the request of the man not to cut that part of his body, but will say: It is not a part of your body because it is rotten. This will not, however, mean that it was never actually a part of the body but will imply only this: As it has ceased to function rightly as a part of the body, it is no more a part of the body in the sense and for the purpose the healthy parts of the body are its parts. Likewise, when it was said to Prophet Noah (peace be upon him): He is not of your family, it did not negate the fact that he was from his loins but implied: He does not deserve to be treated as a member of your righteous family because of his spoiled morals and conduct. As the torment of the deluge has been brought about to punish those who had sided with the unbelievers in the conflict of kufr and faith, your son does not deserve to be rescued from it along with the believers. Had it been a conflict between your descendants and those of the unbelievers, the result would have been different, but this being a conflict between the righteous and the unrighteous, the former alone will be delivered from it.

The epithet, a worthless act, has been purposely applied to the son of Noah, for it is very meaningful. It points to the two different objects that the parents have in view in bringing up their children. Those parents who look merely at the surface of things, bring up and love their children because they are from their loins or their wombs, irrespective of the fact whether they are righteous or unrighteous. But this epithet requires the believers to look upon their children as pieces of work entrusted to them in a natural way by their Creator, so that they should prepare and mold them so as to fulfill the object for which Allah has created man. Therefore, if a certain parent fails in his efforts to mold his child in a way to fulfill the very object for which the child was entrusted to him and the latter becomes a servant of Satan instead of his Lord, the parent should regard all his efforts for the child to have gone utterly waste. In that case there is no reason why that parent should have any consideration for that worthless act.

to place a vicegerent on earth," [150]

The main article of the agreement is that we fully understand that God

As a corollary to the above, the same rule will apply to the other relationships of a believer. As a believer is one who believes in certain creeds and behaviors, all his relationships with the other people will be determined by those creeds and behaviors. If his blood relations have the qualities of a believer, their relationship with him becomes doubly stronger. But if they are void of the qualities of a believer; the believer will confine his relationship with them only to the extent of blood relationships and will have no spiritual relationship with them. Consequently, if such a relative comes face to face with the believer in the conflict between kufr and the faith, the believer should fight with him just as he would with any other unbeliever.

This warning from his Lord does not mean that Prophet Noah (peace be upon him) was suffering from the lack of faith or that his faith had any tinge of weakness or that he had beliefs like those of the ignorant people. His response to this is rather a proof of his high moral character. As Noah was like the other Prophets, a human being, he also suffered from the common human weakness, that is, natural parental love for children. So he begged his Lord to deliver his son from the deluge. Allah admonished him because the high character of a Prophet demanded that he ought not to have made such a request even for his own flesh and blood. That is why no sooner was the warning administered to him than he realized that he had come down from the high position of a Prophet to the level of a mere father because of the critical psychological human weakness. Therefore immediately after the warning, he repented of his weakness, and behaved as if his own son had not been drowned in the deluge a moment before this. This character shown by him is a clear proof that he was a true Prophet. He returned to the same height and meekly asked his Lord's forgiveness for showing any concern for his own son who had forsaken the truth and sided with falsehood.

[149] This betrayal was not in the sense that they had committed an indecency but in the sense that they did not follow the Prophets Noah and Lot (peace be upon them) on the way of faith but sided with their enemies against them. Ibn Abbas said: No Prophet's wife has ever been wicked and immoral. The betrayal of these two women in fact was in the matter of faith and religion. They did not acknowledge the religion of the Prophets Noah and Lot (peace be upon them). The Prophet Noah's wife used to convey news about the believers to the wicked of her people, and the Prophet Lot's wife used to inform the immoral people about those who visited him in his house.

[150] 'Khalifah' or vicegerent is one who exercises the authority delegated to him by his principal, and does so in the capacity of his deputy and agent. Hence, whatever authority he possesses is not inherently his own, but is derived from, and circumscribed by, the limits set by his principal. A vicegerent is not entitled to do what he pleases, but is obliged to carry out the will of his master. If the vicegerent were either to begin thinking himself as the real owner and to use the authority delegated to him in whatever manner he pleased, or if he were to acknowledge someone other than the real owner as his lord and master and to follow his directions, these would be deemed acts of infidelity and rebellion.

is the sole owner of our psyche and we are responsible not to submit ourselves to someone or something else, partially or fully, directly or indirectly in any circumstances.

قُلْ يَـاَهْلَ الْكِتٰبِ تَعَالَوْا اِلٰى كَلِمَةٍ سَوَآءٍ بَيْنَـنَا وَبَيْنَكُمْ اَلَّا نَـعْبُدَ اِلَّا اللّٰهَ وَلَا نُشْرِكَ بِهٖ شَيْـئًا وَّلَا يَتَّخِذَ بَعْضُنَا بَعْضًا اَرْبَابًا مِّنْ دُوْنِ اللّٰهِؕ فَاِنْ تَوَلَّوْا فَقُوْلُوا اشْهَدُوْا بِاَنَّا مُسْلِمُوْنَ

(3:64) Say: 'People of the Book! Come to a word common between us and you: that we shall serve none but Allah and shall associate none with Him in His divinity and that some of us will not take others as lords besides Allah.' And if they turn their backs (from accepting this call), tell them: 'Bear witness that we are the ones who have submitted ourselves exclusively to Allah.'

In the second main article we hold ourselves responsible for our safety, and freedom of submission. We also recognize here the rights and safety of other psyches. Putting this article at risk renders our contract void as if it did not exist.

يَـاَيُّهَا الَّذِيْنَ اٰمَنُوْا لَا تَاْكُلُوْٓا اَمْوَالَكُمْ بَيْنَكُمْ بِالْبَاطِلِ اِلَّآ اَنْ تَكُوْنَ تِجَارَةً عَنْ تَرَاضٍ مِّنْكُمْ وَلَا تَقْتُلُوْٓا اَنْفُسَكُمْؕ اِنَّ اللّٰهَ كَانَ بِكُمْ رَحِيْمًا

(4:29) Believers! Do not devour one another's possessions wrongfully; rather than that, let there be trading by mutual consent. You shall not kill yourselves. Surely Allah is ever Compassionate to you.[151]

The Property

The property is defined as the psyche including all of its possessions and its propagation from within to outside during its lifetime. The psyche is defined as the outcome of the interaction between soul and body. Each psyche has been given the same total value with different types of assets (livelihood) for each individual's life. Livelihood includes all the various gifts to the body and soul e.g. a fixed number of breaths, features of the body, health, fitness, skills, talent, family, and wealth.

---

[151] The expression 'wrongfully' embraces all transactions which are opposed to righteousness and which are either legally or morally reprehensible. By contrast, 'trade' signifies the mutual transfer of benefits between the parties concerned, such as that underlying those transactions in which one person provides whatever satisfies the needs of another person and is paid in return. 'Mutual consent' means that the exchange should be free of undue pressure, fraud and deception. Although bribery and interest apparently represent transactions based on mutual consent, closer examination reveals that such consent takes place by constraint and under pressure. In games of chance, too, the participants seem to consent freely to the outcome. This kind of consent, however, is due to the expectation entertained by the participants that they will win. No one takes part anticipating loss. Fraudulent transactions also seem to be based on the mutual consent of the parties concerned. That kind of consent, however, is based on the false assumption that no fraud is involved in the transaction. Nobody who knew that he would be subjected to fraud would consent to be a party to that transaction.

This can be considered either as complementary to the preceding sentence or as an independent statement. If it is complementary, it means that to consume the property of others by wrongful means is tantamount to courting one's own destruction; for such practices corrupt society on such a scale that even the most cunning are not spared their destructive consequences. This is in addition to the severe punishment that is bound to be meted out to such people in the Next Life. Taken as an independent statement, it can mean either that one should not kill others or that one should not kill oneself. Both the words used and the sequence in which they have been placed by God in this verse make each of these three meanings feasible.

God wishes His creatures well; their well-being and salvation please Him, and it is out of benevolence that He has forbidden things harmful to human beings.

Abdullah ibn Masud reported: the Messenger of Allah, peace and blessings be upon him, said:

إِنَّ أَحَدَكُمْ يُجْمَعُ خَلْقُهُ فِي بَطْنِ أُمِّهِ أَرْبَعِينَ يَوْمًا ثُمَّ يَكُونُ فِي ذَلِكَ عَلَقَةً
مِثْلَ ذَلِكَ ثُمَّ يَكُونُ فِي ذَلِكَ مُضْغَةً مِثْلَ ذَلِكَ ثُمَّ يُرْسَلُ الْمَلَكُ فَيَنْفُخُ فِيهِ
الرُّوحَ وَيُؤْمَرُ بِأَرْبَعِ كَلِمَاتٍ بِكَتْبِ رِزْقِهِ وَأَجَلِهِ وَعَمَلِهِ وَشَقِيٌّ أَوْ سَعِيدٌ
فَوَالَّذِي لَا إِلَهَ غَيْرُهُ إِنَّ أَحَدَكُمْ لَيَعْمَلُ بِعَمَلِ أَهْلِ الْجَنَّةِ حَتَّى مَا يَكُونُ بَيْنَهُ
وَبَيْنَهَا إِلَّا ذِرَاعٌ فَيَسْبِقُ عَلَيْهِ الْكِتَابُ فَيَعْمَلُ بِعَمَلِ أَهْلِ النَّارِ فَيَدْخُلُهَا وَإِنَّ
أَحَدَكُمْ لَيَعْمَلُ بِعَمَلِ أَهْلِ النَّارِ حَتَّى مَا يَكُونُ بَيْنَهُ وَبَيْنَهَا إِلَّا ذِرَاعٌ فَيَسْبِقُ
عَلَيْهِ الْكِتَابُ فَيَعْمَلُ بِعَمَلِ أَهْلِ الْجَنَّةِ فَيَدْخُلُهَا

Verily, the creation of each one of you is brought together in his mother's womb for forty days as a drop, then he is a clot for a similar period, then a morsel for a similar period, then there is sent to him the angel who blows the spirit into him and he is commanded regarding four matters: to write down his provision, his life span, his deeds, and whether he is blessed or damned. By Allah, other than whom there is no God, one of you acts like the people of Paradise until he is but an arm's length from it, and what is written overtakes him so he acts like the people of Hellfire and he enters it. Verily, one of you acts like the people of Hellfire until he is but an arm's length from it, and what is written overtakes him so he acts like the people of Paradise and he enters it. *Source: Ṣaḥīḥ al-Bukhārī*

And also considering certain sets of challenges in health, wealth, fortune, and so on.

وَلَنَبْلُوَنَّكُمْ بِشَيْءٍ مِّنَ الْخَوْفِ وَالْجُوعِ وَنَقْصٍ مِّنَ الْأَمْوَالِ وَالْأَنْفُسِ
وَالثَّمَرَاتِ ۗ وَبَشِّرِ الصَّابِرِينَ

(2:155) We shall certainly test you by afflicting you with fear, hunger, loss of properties and lives and fruits. Give glad tidings, then, to those who remain patient;

الَّذِينَ إِذَا أَصَابَتْهُم مُّصِيبَةٌ قَالُوا إِنَّا لِلَّهِ وَإِنَّا إِلَيْهِ رَاجِعُونَ

(2:156) those who when any affliction smites them, they say: "Verily, we belong to Allah, and it is to Him that we are destined to return."

Some life events we can intervene in and make decisions about and others are an inevitable course of events.

The termination of the contract is not known for the psyche. This creates conditions that allow the highest possible efficiency in work with constant dedication and the highest motivation possible during the assignment.

إِنَّ اللهَ عِندَهُ عِلْمُ السَّاعَةِ وَيُنَزِّلُ الْغَيْثَ وَيَعْلَمُ مَا فِى الْأَرْحَامِ وَمَا تَدْرِى نَفْسٌ مَّاذَا تَكْسِبُ غَدًا وَمَا تَدْرِى نَفْسٌ بِأَيِّ أَرْضٍ تَمُوتُ إِنَّ اللهَ عَلِيمٌ خَبِيرٌ

(31:34) Surely Allah alone has the knowledge of the Hour. It is He Who sends down the rain and knows what is in the wombs, although no person knows what he will earn tomorrow, nor does he know in which land he will die. Indeed, Allah is All-Knowing, All-Aware.

All of the above features are collectively called the "Property" also known as the "Trust".

The Mission Statement

This mission statement is more serious than any other mission of any company or organization on earth. For this reason, it is obligatory to practice the mission itself by repeating the statement during the lifetime. It is done while meeting the owner (Creator) 17 times during the five mandatory daily meetings (obligatory prayers) or during any additional meeting (voluntary prayers). The statement is Surat Al-Fatihah, which is the first Surah of the entire Qur'an, and it has 7 verses that must be read in every rak'ah (unit) during prayer.

The purpose of repetition has endless benefits. It brings along supernatural drive and elevation on the level of psychic energy and logic. Some repetitions are there to help our brains to focus, and to see that the only and the very specific purpose of the entire creation, is to love the kindness and mercy of the Creator (the Merciful, the Compassionate). The realization can then be expressed by simple words (Praise be to Allah) while experiencing true gratitude for the Creator's mercy. This simple wording in itself deserves the praise.

We often ask for more of that special kind of compassion in the moment of truth. Like in the moment when we will stand in front of Him, and there is no way out, and He will ask for His rights and trust (The Master of the Day of Recompense). We feel completely happy, from the bottom of our hearts, to be His slaves, only His, and in no way do we feel weak while asking for help from God (You alone do we worship, and You alone do we turn for help).

Up to this point, we keep asking God for help (guidance) to stay on the right track of the mission, (Direct us on to the Straight Way) and to receive complete and accurate guidance toward the goal. So that we would not get lost or turn to the side of Satan (The way of those whom You have favoured, who did not incur Your wrath, who are not astray).

بِسْمِ اللهِ الرَّحْمٰنِ الرَّحِيْمِ

(1:1) In the name of Allah, the Merciful, the Compassionate[152]

اَلْحَمْدُ لِلهِ رَبِّ الْعٰلَمِيْنُ

---

[152] One of the many practices taught by Islam is that its followers should begin their activities in the name of God. This principle, if consciously and earnestly followed, will necessarily yield three beneficial results. First, one will be able to restrain oneself from many misdeed, since the habit of pronouncing the name of God is bound to make one wonder when about to commit some offence how such an act can be reconciled with the saying of God's holy name. Second, if a man pronounces the name of God before starting good and legitimate tasks, this act will ensue that both his starting point and his mental orientation are sound. Third - and this is the most important benefit - when a man begins something by pronouncing God's name, he will enjoy God's support and succour; God will bless his efforts and protect him from the machinations and temptation of Satan. For whenever man turns to God, God turns to him as well.

(1:2) Praise be to Allah, the Lord of the entire universe.[153]

الرَّحْمٰنِ الرَّحِيْمِ

(1:3) The Merciful, the Compassionate[154]

مٰلِكِ يَوْمِ الدِّيْنِ

---

[153] As we have already explained, the character of this surah is that of a prayer. The prayer begins with praise of the One to whom our prayer is addressed. This indicates that whenever one prays one ought to pray in a dignified manner. It does not become a cultivated person to blurt out his petition. Refinement demands that our requests should be preceded by a wholehearted acknowledgement of the unique position, infinite benevolence and unmatched excellence of the One to Whom we pray. Whenever we praise someone, we do so for two reasons.

First, because excellence calls for praise, irrespective of whether that excellence has any direct relevance to us or not. Second, we praise one who, we consider to be our benefactor; when this is the case our praise arises from a deep feeling of gratitude. God is worthy of praise on both counts. It is incumbent on us to praise Him not only in recognition of His infinite excellence but also because of our feeling of gratitude to Him, arising from our awareness of the blessings He has lavished upon us. It is important to note that what is said here is not merely that praise be to God, but that all praise be to God alone. Whenever there is any beauty, any excellence, any perfection-in whatever thing or in whatever shape it may manifest itself-its ultimate source is none other than God Himself. No human beings, angels, Demigods, heavenly bodies-in short, no created beings-are possessed of an innate excellence; where excellence exists, it is a gift from God. Thus, if there is anyone at all whom we ought to adore and worship, to whom we ought to feel indebted and grateful, towards whom we should remain humble and obedient, it is the creator of excellence, rather than its possessor.

In Arabic the word Rabb has three meanings: (i) Lord and Master; (ii) Sustainer, Provider, Supporter, Nourisher and Guardian, and (iii) Sovereign, Ruler, He Who controls and directs. God is the Rabb of the universe in all three meanings of the term.

[154] Whenever we are deeply impressed by the greatness of something we try to express our feelings by using superlatives. If the use of one superlative does not do full justice to our feelings, we tend to re-emphasize the extraordinary excellence of the object of our admiration by adding a second superlative of nearly equivalent meaning. This would seem to explain the use of the word Rahim following Rahman. The form of the word Rahman connotes intensity. Yet God's mercy and beneficence towards His creatures is so great, so extensive and of such an infinite nature that no one word, however strong its connotation, can do it full justice. The epithet Rahim was therefore added to that of Rahman.

(1:4) The Master of the Day of Recompense.[155]

اِيَّاكَ نَعْبُدُ وَاِيَّاكَ نَسْتَعِينُ

(1:5) You alone do we worship, and You alone do we turn for help[156]

اِهْدِنَا الصِّرَاطَ الْمُسْتَقِيمَ

(1:6) Direct us on to the Straight Way,[157]

صِرَاطَ الَّذِينَ اَنْعَمْتَ عَلَيْهِمْ غَيْرِ الْمَغْضُوبِ عَلَيْهِمْ وَلَا الضَّاَلِّينَ

---

[155] God will be the Lord of the Day when all generations of mankind gather together in order to render an account of their conduct, and when each person will be finally rewarded or punished for his deeds. The description of God as Lord of the Day of Judgement following the mention of his benevolence and compassion indicates that we ought to remember another aspect of God as well-namely, that He will judge us all, that He is so absolutely powerful, that on the Day of Judgement no one will have the power either to resist the enforcement of punishments that He decrees or to prevent anyone from receiving the rewards that He decides to confer. Hence, we ought not only to love Him for nourishing and sustaining us and for His compassion and mercy towards us, but should also hold Him in awe because of His justice, and should not forget that our ultimate happiness or misery rests completely with Him.

[156] The term ibadah is used in three sense: (i) worship and adoration; (ii) obedience and submission; and (iii) service and subjection. In this particular context the term carries all these meanings simultaneously. In other words, we say to God that we worship and adore Him, that we are obedient to Him and follow His will, and also that we are His servants. Moreover man is so bound to none save God, that none but He, may be the subject of man's worship and total devotion, of man's unreserved obedience, of man's absolute subjection and servitude.

Not only do we worship God, but our relationship with Him is such that we turn to Him alone for help and succour. We know that He is the Lord of the whole universe and that He alone is the Master of all blessings and benefactions. Hence, in seeking the fulfilment of our needs we turn to Him alone. It is towards Him alone that we stretch forth our hands when we pray and supplicate. It is in Him that we repose our trust. It is therefore to Him alone that we address our request for true guidance.

[157] We beseech God to guide us in all walks of life to a way which is absolutely true, which provides us with a properly based outlook and sound principles of behaviour, a way which will prevent our succumbing to false doctrines and adopting unsound principles of conduct, a way that will lead us to our true salvation and happiness. This is man's prayer to God as he begins the study of the Qur'an. It is, in short, to illuminate the truth which he often tends to lose in a labyrinth of philosophical speculation; to enlighten him as to which of the numerous ethical doctrines ensures a sound course of conduct; to show which of the myriad ways and by-ways is the clear, straight, open road of sound belief and right behaviour.

(1:7) The way of those whom You have favoured, who did not incur Your wrath, who are not astray.[158]

The Responsibility

By signing the Submission Agreement, you are agreeing with God that you will use His **Trust** on behalf of Him in profitable actions as much as possible. Profit is measured by the amount of benefit to yourself, your surroundings, other people, and the environment. This use is defined as the **Responsible Actions** associated with the **Intention**. Responsible Actions are marked from the moment of your arrival to biological puberty and from thereon to death.

Irresponsible Actions caused by an ongoing physical or psychological problem that affects your judgment and ability to perform conscious decisions makes you ineligible to restore the trust. Then God exempts you from responsibility. These people serve other particular purposes in this life, they will have special evaluation in the afterlife.

Temporary Irresponsible Actions including forgetting, falling

---

[158] This defines the 'straight way' which we ask God to open to us. It is the way which has always been followed by those who have enjoyed God's favours and blessings. This is the way which has been trodden from the beginning of time by all those individuals and communities that have unfailingly enjoyed God's favours and blessings.

This makes it clear that the recipients of God's favour are not those who appear, briefly, to enjoy worldly prosperity and success; all too often, these people are among those whom God has condemned because they have lost sight of the true path of salvation and happiness. This negative explanation makes it quite clear that in'am (favour) denotes all those real and abiding favours and blessings which one receives in reward for righteous conduct through God's approval and pleasure, rather than those apparent and fleeting favours which the Pharaohs, Nimrods and Korahs (Qaruns) used to receive in the past, and which are enjoyed even today by people notorious for oppression, evil and corruption.

asleep, having an accident or the action you do against your own will, God will not hold you responsible.

Intention is defined by the deep reasoning behind your actions. The reasoning for your actions can be related to several reasons that are related to each other (semantic relationship) or are scattered. These reasons may be obvious or hidden, located deep in your consciousness. This location is called the **Heart**. It is the core of your spiritual state.

Umar ibn al-Khattab reported: The Messenger of Allah, peace and blessings be upon him, said:

إِنَّمَا الْأَعْمَالُ بِالنِّيَّاتِ وَإِنَّمَا لِكُلِّ امْرِئٍ مَا نَوَى فَمَنْ كَانَتْ هِجْرَتُهُ إِلَى اللَّهِ
وَرَسُولِهِ فَهِجْرَتُهُ إِلَى اللَّهِ وَرَسُولِهِ وَمَنْ كَانَتْ هِجْرَتُهُ لِدُنْيَا يُصِيبُهَا أَوِ
امْرَأَةٍ يَنْكِحُهَا فَهِجْرَتُهُ إِلَى مَا هَاجَرَ إِلَيْهِ

"Verily, deeds are only with intentions. Verily, every person will have only what they intended. Whoever emigrated to Allah and his messenger, his emigration is for Allah and his messenger. Whoever emigrated to get something in the world or to marry a woman, his emigration is for that to which he emigrated." *Source: Ṣaḥīḥ al-Bukhārī 54, Grade: Muttafaqun Alayhi*

The deepest place in your heart should be reserved exclusively for the Creator. An act with the right intention that reaches that depth in the heart is called sincerity **for the sake of God**. The weight of actions depends on the intention, not the action itself.

Some actions may not be completed or even initiated but were based on sincerity. Those actions will be deemed valid with full results.

The result of an action depends on whether it is good (Halal) or bad (Haram). Both halal and haram together are called the framework to the process of Islam, the OS. The exact rewards or consequences depend on how much there is good or bad.

The use of trust in this life (Dunya) is called investing. Your actions will determine your future and success: will you reach the rank of human and gain the honor to receive service in Heaven or will your rank be less than that of an animal and be treated as fuel of Hell.

323

اَمْ تَحْسَبُ اَنَّ اَكْثَرَهُمْ يَسْمَعُوْنَ اَوْ يَعْقِلُوْنَ ۚ اِنْ هُمْ اِلَّا كَالْاَنْعَامِ بَلْ هُمْ اَضَلُّ سَبِيْلًا

(25:44) Do you think that most of them hear or understand? For they are merely like cattle; nay, even worse than them.[159]

اِنَّ الَّذِيْنَ كَفَرُوْا لَنْ تُغْنِيَ عَنْهُمْ اَمْوَالُهُمْ وَلَا اَوْلَادُهُمْ مِّنَ اللهِ شَيْئًا ۚ وَاُولٰئِكَ هُمْ وَقُوْدُ النَّارِ

(3:10) Those who disbelieve, neither their wealth nor their offspring will avail them at all against Allah, and it is they who will be the fuel of the Fire.

The Operation

The operation of lifetime is defined by the religion of Islam (OS framework). The framework of Islam is devided into two main categories called halal and haram. The halal is the most common one including innumerable acts available for life. The haram consists of forbidden, limited acts or things that have harmful consequences.

Most of the actions can be logically placed in the groups. Majority are very clear and others are on the border, and require some thought to see if they are more halal or haram. The results can sow on the spiritual component or the physical component.

Al-Nu'man ibn Bashir reported: The Messenger of Allah, peace and blessings be upon him, said:

الْحَلَالُ بَيِّنٌ وَالْحَرَامُ بَيِّنٌ وَبَيْنَهُمَا مُشَبَّهَاتٌ لَا يَعْلَمُهَا كَثِيرٌ مِنَ النَّاسِ فَمَنْ

---

[159] They are only like the cattle because they follow their lusts blindly. Just as the sheep and cattle do not know where their driver is taking them, to the meadow or to the slaughter house, so are these people also following their leaders blindly without knowing or judging where they are being led, to success or to destruction. The only difference between the two is that the cattle have no intelligence and will not be accountable as to the place where they are being taken by the driver. But it is a pity that human beings who are endowed with reason, should behave like cattle; therefore their condition is worse than that of cattle.

اتَّقَى الْمُشْتَبَّهَاتِ اسْتَبْرَأ لِدِينِهِ وَعِرْضِهِ وَمَنْ وَقَعَ فِي الشُّبُهَاتِ كَرَاعٍ يَرْعَى حَوْلَ الْحِمَى يُوشِكُ أَنْ يُوَاقِعَهُ أَلَا وَإِنَّ لِكُلِّ مَلِكٍ حِمًى أَلَا إِنَّ حِمَى اللَّهِ فِي أَرْضِهِ مَحَارِمُهُ أَلَا وَإِنَّ فِي الْجَسَدِ مُضْغَةً إِذَا صَلَحَتْ صَلَحَ الْجَسَدُ كُلُّهُ وَإِذَا فَسَدَتْ فَسَدَ الْجَسَدُ كُلُّهُ أَلَا وَهِيَ الْقَلْبُ

"Verily, the lawful is clear and the unlawful is clear, and between the two of them are doubtful matters about which many people do not know. Thus, he who avoids doubtful matters clears himself in regard to his religion and his honor, and he who falls into doubtful matters will fall into the unlawful as the shepherd who pastures near a sanctuary, all but grazing therein. Verily, every king has a sanctum and the sanctum of Allah is His prohibitions. Verily, in the body is a piece of flesh which, if sound, the entire body is sound, and if corrupt, the entire body is corrupt. Truly, it is the heart." *Source: Bukhari and Muslim*

Halal is anything you do that does not harm yourself or others in the short or long term. The logic behind this framework is prevention of the harms before they happen. The rationale behind this logic is the fact that we can't have all the universe's knowledge and control of the X-Harmony Factor in ourselves. This is known as the butterfly effect in chaos theory. *In chaos theory, the butterfly effect is a sensitive dependence on initial conditions in which a small change in one state of a deterministic nonlinear system can lead to large differences in a later state. The term is closely related to the work of mathematician and meteorologist Edward Lorenz.*

To avoid this limitation we need to get back to the Creator who has the know-how and follow the instructions (this is called Faith). Faith means obedience to the Creator and trust that He cares for His kingdom and ourselves, more than we do. With time God will give more knowledge. This will happen when we are ready to understand His wisdom from His instructions.

On the other hand, Satan is the enemy who promotes the path of self-destruction. A good part of his efforts goes in creating states of confusion. He wants you to be lost between what is permissible and what is harmful.

The Theoretical Foundation of The Halal and Haram Framework

The theoretical level of the framework is understood by two main categories of knowledge and decision-making process, one matching the left brain nature, and is known as shariah, and the other having a right brain nature, called adab. Similarly, at the level of execution and actions, one has the nature of material life (transactions) and the other has the nature of spiritual life (acts of worship).

Any item in the framework must have at least one clear reference from the Qur'an or the Sunnah to support its classification as halal or haram. The items on the borderline that need more consultations and deep knowledge, are dealt by a specialized field in Islam (Jurisprudence). There are established doctrines of practicing fatwa, which were founded by four scholars earlier in time. These are called The Four Madhabs: Hanafi, Maliki, Shafi'i, and Hanbali.

Anyone can choose to follow any of them for lifelong practice or temporary practice. They vary in offering different solutions to the same borderline situations. These differences give a different level of flexibility to deal with situations.

A fatwa (formal ruling) is considered a highly intellectual scientific exercise for solving problems in Islam. Nowadays every Muslim country has its own specialized and organized institutional body called Dar Al-Fatwa for more up-to-date situations that need fatwa. These Dar Al-Fatwas have cooperation between each other to make common fatwa more generalized for all the Muslims in the world.

Most of these borderline situations are a result of advances in the human way of living and in new innovations developed over time. For example, in the case of withdrawal of life support from a patient in the intensive care unit, is this halal or haram? Is this like killing the patient or this act of kindness?

Framework And X-Harmony Factor Compatibility

This is about taking the theoretical knowledge of the framework to the practical level. We can do this by following the X-harmony Factor's know-how of creating harmony and the path to reach peace as mentioned throughout the book.

You may remember reading in a previous chapter the story of the soup and long spoon dinner. This soup is dunya (where we are living now), and the long spoon is our ego. We are not supposed to use our egos directly to feed ourselves. That would be a mess. It would be like feeding a beast! That's exactly the wrong technique, 100% selfish. This is the direction of Satan, his choice, complete hatred of others and destroying himself.

يَـٰٓأَيُّهَا الَّذِينَ ءَامَنُوا لَا تَتَّبِعُوا خُطُوَٰتِ الشَّيْطَـٰنِ ۚ وَمَن يَتَّبِعْ خُطُوَٰتِ الشَّيْطَـٰنِ
فَإِنَّهُ يَأْمُرُ بِالْفَحْشَاءِ وَالْمُنكَرِ ۚ وَلَوْلَا فَضْلُ اللهِ عَلَيْكُمْ وَرَحْمَتُهُ مَا زَكَىٰ
مِنكُم مِّنْ أَحَدٍ أَبَدًا وَّلَـٰكِنَّ اللهَ يُزَكِّى مَن يَشَاءُ ۗ وَاللهُ سَمِيعٌ عَلِيمٌ

(24:21) Believers! Do not follow in Satan's footsteps. Let him who follows in Satan's footsteps (remember that) Satan bids people to indecency and evil. Were it not for Allah's Bounty and His Mercy unto you, not one of you would have ever attained purity. But Allah enables whomsoever He wills to attain purity. Allah is All- Hearing, All-Knowing.[160]

God asks us to do just the opposite, to activate the X-Harmony Factor

---

[160] Satan is bent upon involving you in all kinds of pollutions and indecencies. Had it not been for the mercy and kindness of Allah Who enables you to differentiate between good and evil and helps you to educate and reform yourselves, you would not have been able to lead a pure and virtuous life on the strength of your own faculties and initiative alone.

It is Allah's will alone which decides whom to make pious and virtuous. His decisions are not arbitrary but based on knowledge. He alone knows who is anxious to live a life of virtue and who is attracted towards a life of sin. Allah hears a person's most secret talk, and is aware of everything that passes in his mind. It is on the basis of this direct knowledge that Allah decides whom to bless with piety and virtue and whom to ignore.

to the fullest. He prepared the entire psyche (body and soul), the relationships and the entire universe to be compatible with His instructions (Islam OS) to facilitate our mission and operation. He is asking us to go in the completely opposite direction than the devil - towards the light- to understand the true meaning of love: giving without hesitation, worrying or conditions.

How to be completely confident and to give without expecting something in return? Imagine being only satisfied with the fact of being able to give. This is the whole story of experiencing something of the qualities of God's love. As we develop this experience of love with His creations, it will help us develop our loving relationship with Him in parallel.

The Main and Extra Halal Practices

All practices must be simple and resonate in all dimensions of knowledge or action. These practices are known as the Five Pillars of Islam. There are four duties: Shahadah (testimony of faith), 5 prayers, fasting and zakat (charity). The last three come with a flexible system of how to perform them or compensate. Conditional Hajj depends on financial, health and security conditions.

الْإِسْلَامُ أَنْ تَشْهَدَ أَنْ لَا إِلَهَ إِلَّا اللَّهُ وَأَنَّ مُحَمَّدًا رَسُولُ اللَّهِ صَلَّى اللَّهُ عَلَيْهِ وَسَلَّمَ وَتُقِيمَ الصَّلَاةَ وَتُؤْتِيَ الزَّكَاةَ وَتَصُومَ رَمَضَانَ وَتَحُجَّ الْبَيْتَ إِنِ اسْتَطَعْتَ إِلَيْهِ سَبِيلًا

Islam is to testify there is no God but Allah and Muhammad is the Messenger of Allah, to establish prayer, to give charity, to fast the month of Ramadan, and to perform pilgrimage to the House if a way is possible.

Any other work in Islam is considered additional work, and it is either strongly recommended or voluntary but not necessary. These actions are called excellence (ihsan). One needs to direct these actions purely to Allah and for this there needs to be a strong connection from the core of one's heart.

أَنْ تَعْبُدَ اللَّهَ كَأَنَّكَ تَرَاهُ فَإِنْ لَمْ تَكُنْ تَرَاهُ فَإِنَّهُ يَرَاكَ

Excellence is to worship Allah as if you see Him, for if you do not see Him, He surely sees you.

Among these additional actions are progress in the abilities of self-discipline e.g., anger and time management as well as working under pressure.

الَّذِينَ يُنْفِقُونَ فِى السَّرَّآءِ وَالضَّرَّآءِ وَالْكَظِمِينَ الْغَيْظَ وَالْعَافِينَ عَنِ النَّاسِ وَاللَّهُ يُحِبُّ الْمُحْسِنِينَ

(3:134) who spend in the way of Allah both in plenty and hardship, who restrain their anger, and forgive others. Allah loves such good-doers." [161]

Extent and Scope of Halal Actions

The scope of actions covers day to day, week to week, month to month, year to year, and once-in-a-lifetime events. The scope of actions has levels, at the top is self-preservation (own and others), and preservation of property as well as relationships. At the core is the relationship with the mother, then the father, the spouse, the kids, the neighbors, the extended family members, and etc.

All of the halal practices will have a powerful and sustainable impact that resonates in multiple dimensions: humanity, society and international level now and in the future. We are not now talking about the EU or the UN ethics manual but much more simple, comprehensive and reliable material, made by the Creator, who created

---

[161] The existence of interest in a society generates two kinds of moral disease. It breeds greed and avarice, meanness and selfishness among those who receive interest. At the same time, those who have to pay interest develop strong feelings of hatred, resentment, spite and jealousy. God intimates to the believers that the attributes bred by the spread of interest are the exact opposite of those which develop as a result of spending in the way of God, and that it is through the latter rather than the former that man can achieve God's forgiveness and Paradise.

this sophisticated universe.

بَدِيعُ السَّمَوَاتِ وَالْأَرْضِ ۖ أَنَّى يَكُونُ لَهُ وَلَدٌ وَلَمْ تَكُن لَّهُ صَاحِبَةٌ ۖ وَخَلَقَ كُلَّ شَيْءٍ ۖ وَهُوَ بِكُلِّ شَيْءٍ عَلِيمٌ

(6:101) He is the Originator of the heavens and the earth. How can He have a son when He has had no mate? And He has created everything and He has full knowledge of all things.

The actions of smiling, greeting, shaking hands, offering any kind of help, removing any obstacle from the way (even only a stone) as well as taking care of plants, water, nature and animals are all explained simply in the teachings of the Messenger, may God bless him and grant him peace. He was granted the ability to give genius speeches.

The Mother of the Believers, Aisha, may God be pleased with her, described it by saying:

ووصفته أم المؤمنين عائشة ـ رضي الله عنها ـ بقولها (ما كان رسول الله ـ صلى الله عليه وسلم ـ يسرد سردكم هذا، ولكن كان يتكلم بكلام بيّن فصل، يحفظه من جلس إليه) (الترمذي.)

"The Messenger of God, may God's prayers and peace be upon him, did not narrate this narration of yours, but he was speaking in clear words, a chapter, which he memorized by those who sat with him."
Source: Tirmidhi

Sustainable Halal Actions

These are very interesting actions. They are distinguished by their possible ceaseless nature, to the persons themselves even after death. They will continue to get a great reward provided that the action is still good for humanity.

Abu Hurairah (May Allah be pleased with him) reported: the Messenger of Allah (ﷺ) said:

وعنه قال: قال رسول الله صلى الله عليه وسلم : "إذا مات ابن آدم انقطع

330

عمله إلا من ثلاث: صدقة جارية ،أو علم ينتفع به، أو ولد صالح يدعو
له" ((رواه مسلم)).

"When a man dies, his deeds come to an end except for three things: Sadaqah Jariyah (ceaseless charity); a knowledge which is beneficial, or a virtuous descendant who prays for him (for the deceased)." *Source: Muslim.*

The Neuroscience Behind the Actions

Islam's OS gives the possibility for the most conscious, aware, organized and focused psyche. The end result depends on the uptake and practice of each individual. This is called the Person ID, a customized version of Islam's operating system.

The outline is maximum perception for time and space, in three dimensions, before, during, and after life. At the core of the psyche (heart) is God. We direct our face and work, from birth until death, towards a clear goal, which is the mission of life.

During the course of life, the personality (the psyche) grows in a systematic, harmonious and balanced way. This is due to the systemic use of the right and left brain following the halal and haram framework. This harmony will improve the ratios between the different brain waves.

The five types of brain waves and their associated frequencies are:

Delta waves, which range between 0.5 and 4 hertz (Hz), occur during states of deep, dreamless sleep.

Theta waves, which range between 4 and 8 Hz, occur during light sleep or deep relaxation.

Alpha waves, which measure between 8 and 12 Hz, occur when people are feeling relaxed and when the brain is idle without focusing on anything.

<u>Beta waves</u>, which measure between 12 and 30 Hz, are the waves that occur during most states of wakefulness and consciousness. It is a quick activity that indicates attention and alertness.

<u>Gamma waves,</u> measuring between 25 and 100 Hz, are the fastest brain waves with wavelengths associated with activities such as learning, problem solving and information processing.

The sum total of these waves is the psyche's three stations of light. The first one is *al-Nafs al-Muthmainnah*: a clear and bright soul with the remembrance of Allah and eradication of the influence of lust and despicable qualities; second is *al-Nafs al-Lawamah:* the soul that regrets itself; and the third is *al-Nafs al-Amarah*, which is the soul that always commands evil.

يَوْمَ تَرَى الْمُؤْمِنِيْنَ وَالْمُؤْمِنٰتِ يَسْعٰى نُوْرُهُمْ بَيْنَ اَيْدِيْهِمْ وَبِاَيْمَانِهِمْ بُشْرٰىكُمُ الْيَوْمَ جَنّٰتٌ تَجْرِىْ مِنْ تَحْتِهَا الْاَنْهٰرُ خٰلِدِيْنَ فِيْهَا ۚ ذٰلِكَ هُوَ الْفَوْزُ الْعَظِيْمُ ۚ

(57:12) On that Day you will see believing men and women that their light will be running before them and on their right hands. (They will be told): "A good tiding to you today." There shall be Gardens beneath which rivers flow; therein they shall abide. That indeed is the great triumph.[162]

The more advanced and sustained your actions are, the more this soul will move from one station to another towards diving into love.

Abu Hurairah (May Allah be pleased with him) reported: the Messenger of Allah (ﷺ) said:

عن أبي هريرة رضي الله عنه قال: قال رسول الله صلى الله عليه وسلم: "إن الله تعالى قال: من عادى لي وليا فقد آذنته بالحرب. وما تقرب إلي عبدي بشيء أحب إلي مما افترضت عليه، وما يزال عبدي يتقرب إلي بالنوافل حتى أحبه، فإذا أحببته كنت سمعه الذي يسمع به، وبصره الذي يبصر به، ويده التي يبطش بها، ورجله التي يمشي بها، وإن سألني أعطيته؛ ولئن استعاذني لأعيذنه" ((رواه البخاري)).

"Allah the Exalted has said: 'I will declare war against him who shows hostility to a pious worshipper of Mine. And the most beloved thing with which My slave comes nearer to Me is what I have enjoined upon

---

[162] This and the following verses show that the light on the Day of Judgment will be specifically meant for the righteous believers only. As for the disbelievers and the hypocrites and the wicked people, they will be wandering about in the darkness as they had been in the world. The light there will be the light of righteous deeds. The sincerity of the faith and the piety of the character and conduct will turn into light that will lend brightness to the personality of the virtuous. The brighter the deed the more luminous will be his person, and when he will walk towards Paradise, his light will be running forward before him.

The Prophet (peace be upon him) said: The light of some one will be so strong and sharp that it will be running on before him equal to the distance between Al-Madinah and Aden, of another equal to the distance between Madinah and Sana, and of another even less than that; so much so that there will be a believer whose light will just extend beyond his steps. In other words, the intensity of the light of a person will be proportionate to the extent of the good done and spread by him in the world, and the beams of his light will be running on before him in the Hereafter extending as far as his good will have extended in the world.

Here, a question may arise in the mind of the reader: One can understand the meaning of their light running on before the believers but what does their light running on only on their right hand mean? Will there be darkness on their left side? The answer is: When a man is walking with a light on his right hand, his left side also will be bright, though the fact of the matter is that the light will be on his right hand. This has been explained by the Hadith, which Abu Dharr and Abu Darda have reported, saying that the Prophet (peace be upon him) said: I shall recognize the righteous people of my ummah by their light which will be running on before them and on their right and on their left.

him; and My slave keeps on coming closer to Me through performing Nawafil (prayer or doing extra deeds besides what is obligatory) till I love him. When I love him I become his hearing with which he hears, his seeing with which he sees, his hand with which he strikes, and his leg with which he walks; and if he asks (something) from Me, I give him, and if he asks My Protection (refuge), I protect him". *Source: Al-Bukhari.*

Monitoring the Actions

The person's activities are fully documented by two angels: the one on the right documents the halal actions, and the other, on the left, documents the haram ones.

إِذْ يَتَلَقَّى الْمُتَلَقِّيَانِ عَنِ الْيَمِينِ وَعَنِ الشِّمَالِ قَعِيدٌ

(50:17) Moreover, there are two scribes, one each sitting on the right and the left, recording everything.

مَا يَلْفِظُ مِن قَوْلٍ إِلَّا لَدَيْهِ رَقِيبٌ عَتِيدٌ

(50:18) He utters not a word, but there is a vigilant watcher at hand.

This documentation will be the main topic of the discussion on the Day of Judgment. The discussion will be followed by the calculation (weighing) of the balance. The final weights of the items depend on their value, not only their amounts. In the end, the balance will determine the final destination and rank either in Heaven or Hell.

Immediate Compensation

Islam will create a clear self-identity, a goal for your psyche, an ability to add value to your surroundings according to your passion and vision, and a competence to participate in the shared dream of the community around you. During the course of life, you will be provided with a complete operating system with options. It will include a comprehensive solution to the anxiety of fear and loss, meaning that you live under New Trinity but not in a maze.

This feeling will make you able to have more energy to contribute positively to your surroundings, either by investing in your God-given capital or spending it in helping others (practicing unconditional love). It will shift your energy and your motivation system to a higher level and provide you with a continuation and progression of satisfaction.

اَلَآ اِنَّ اَوْلِيَآءَ اللهِ لَا خَوْفٌ عَلَيْهِمْ وَلَا هُمْ يَحْزَنُوْنَ

(10:62) Oh, surely the friends of Allah have nothing to fear, nor shall they grieve -

الَّذِيْنَ اٰمَنُوْا وَكَانُوْا يَتَّقُوْنَ

(10:63) the ones who believe and are God-fearing.

لَهُمُ الْبُشْرٰى فِى الْحَيٰوةِ الدُّنْيَا وَفِى الْاٰخِرَةِ لَا تَبْدِيْلَ لِكَلِمٰتِ اللهِ ذٰلِكَ هُوَ الْفَوْزُ الْعَظِيْمُ

(10:64) For them are glad tidings in this world and in the Hereafter. The words of Allah shall not change. That is the supreme triumph.

وَلَا يَحْزُنْكَ قَوْلُهُمْ اِنَّ الْعِزَّةَ لِلّٰهِ جَمِيْعًا هُوَ السَّمِيْعُ الْعَلِيْمُ

(10:65) (O Prophet!) Let not the utterances of the opponents distress you. Indeed all honour is Allah's. He is All-Hearing, All-Knowing.

اَلَآ اِنَّ لِلّٰهِ مَنْ فِى السَّمٰوٰتِ وَمَنْ فِى الْاَرْضِ وَمَا يَتَّبِعُ الَّذِيْنَ يَدْعُوْنَ مِنْ دُوْنِ اللهِ شُرَكَآءَ اِنْ يَتَّبِعُوْنَ اِلَّا الظَّنَّ وَاِنْ هُمْ اِلَّا يَخْرُصُوْنَ

(10:66) Verily whoever dwells in the heavens or the earth belongs to Allah. Those who invoke others beside Allah, associating them with Him in His divinity, only follow conjectures and are merely guessing.

Later Compensation: A New Psyche with New Features

Later compensation is for the ones who have succeeded in their mission and in their efforts to create harmony and activate the X-Harmony Factor. They have overcome hatred as it is essential in creating harmony outside the self. They have also overcome the internal difficulty of establishing balance (pairing/marriage) between their souls and their bodies as well as the right and the left sides of their brains and it has been evident in their actions.

$$يَٰٓأَيَّتُهَا النَّفْسُ الْمُطْمَئِنَّةُ$$

(89:27) (On the other hand it will be said): "O serene soul![163]

$$ارْجِعِىٓ إِلَىٰ رَبِّكِ رَاضِيَةً مَّرْضِيَّةً$$

(89:28) Return to your Lord well-pleased (with your blissful destination), well-pleasing (to your Lord).[164]

$$فَادْخُلِىٓ فِىٓ عِبَٰدِىٓ$$

(89:29) So enter among My (righteous) servants

$$وَادْخُلِىٓ جَنَّتِى$$

(89:30) and enter My Paradise."

A new psyche will be introduced with new features to those who have successfully completed this task. These features will allow the psyche

---

[163] Peaceful and fully satisfied soul: The man who believed in Allah, the One, as his Lord and Sustainer, and adopted the way of life brought by the Prophets as his way of life, with full satisfaction of the heart, and without the least doubt about it, who acknowledged as absolute truth whatever creed and command he received from Allah and His Messenger, who withheld himself from whatever he was forbidden by Allah's religion, not unwillingly but with perfect conviction that it was really an evil thing, who offered without sacrifice whatever sacrifice was required to be offered for the sake of the truth, who endured with full peace of mind whatever difficulties, troubles and hardships he met on this way and who felt no remorse on being deprived of the gains and benefits and pleasures in the world which seemed to accrue to those who followed other ways but remained fully satisfied that adherence to true faith had safeguarded him against those errors. This very state has been described at another place in the Quran as sharh sadr.

[164] This he will be told at the time of his death as well as on the Day of Resurrection when he will rise from the dead and move towards the Plain of Assembly and also on the occasion when he will be presented in the divine court. At every stage he will be assured that he is moving towards the Mercy of Allah Almighty.

to be peaceful but effortless.

God will remove bitterness (rancour) from the psyche.

وَنَزَعْنَا مَا فِىْ صُدُوْرِهِمْ مِّنْ غِلٍّ اِخْوَانًا عَلٰى سُرُرٍ مُّتَقٰبِلِيْنَ

(15:47) And We shall purge their breasts of all traces of rancour; and they shall be seated on couches facing one another as brothers.[165]

God will complete the pairing permanently, there will be no need to think or make an effort to create harmony.

وَاِذَا النُّفُوْسُ زُوِّجَتْ

(81:7) when the souls shall be rejoined (with their bodies), [166]

When entering Heaven, the psyche will not continue in eternal love without stress but instead in a mood of true lasting peace, receiving a venerable salutation.

دَعْوٰىهُمْ فِيْهَا سُبْحٰنَكَ اللّٰهُمَّ وَ تَحِيَّتُهُمْ فِيْهَا سَلٰمٌ وَاٰخِرُ دَعْوٰىهُمْ اَنِ الْحَمْدُ لِلّٰهِ رَبِّ الْعٰلَمِيْنَ

(10:10) Their cry in it will be: 'Glory be to You, Our Lord!', and their greeting: 'Peace!'; and their cry will always end with: 'All praise be to

---

[165] That is, if any spite might have been caused in their hearts in this world because of misunderstandings between the pious people, it shall be removed at the time of their entry into Paradise and they will bear no ill feelings there against each other.

[166] From here begins mention of the second stage of Resurrection. That is, men will be resurrected precisely in the state as they lived in the world before death with body and soul together.

Allah, the Lord of the universe.[167]

Peace to you (*Assalamu alaikum*) is the greeting that a Muslim should use and express in everyday actions (Halal) during one's life.

The Sustainable Welfare State

The peaceful psyche will then get permanent residency in a sustainable welfare state called Heaven. God will give this psyche the right to own land and properties in this state, with various services and facilities either in line with our desires or offered in a wide variety of options we would have never even thought about.

This includes, but is not limited to, all the desires that have been sources of temptation to our psyche in this life. The major categories for both men and women can be defined broadly as nature, wealth, family, company, fortune, drink, food, and intimate pleasure.

More specifically by gender, for women there will be offered unlimited possibilities of being the most attractive, influential and admirable in Heaven. She will have the possibility to feel admired and that everything that appears in the eyes of others is under her control. Every time the others look at her, they are dazzled as if they had never seen

---

[167] These facts about the life in Paradise have been stated in order to make conspicuous the high thinking and the noble qualities of the believers. When they enter Paradise after coming out successful in this worldly test, they will manifest the same high qualities of character that they had in this world. Instead of making urgent and immediate demands for beautiful articles of luxury, musical instruments, wine and women, they will sing hymns of praise to their Lord. This also belies that picture of the life in Paradise that some crooked people have formed of it. The fact is that the noble personalities which the believers build in this world and the high ways of thinking and the excellent moral characters they form in this world and the great and rigid training they give to their feelings, emotions and desires, will become all the more prominent in the pure surroundings and environments of Paradise. That is why they will love it most to sing hymns of praise to Allah and glorify His name just as they did in this world. Besides this, their greatest wish and desire in Paradise will be peace for one another, as it was in their collective life in this world.

her before. The women have the possibility to choose or modify their partner according to their liking.

Since men don't concern themselves with admiration as much as women, God has prepared for them a possibility to admire other's beauty. They will have the right to try all the varieties of beauty in one way or another, as convenient as possible.

Everyone will therefore have a new kind of experience while feeling rejuvenated through a sense of progressive satisfaction, harmony, and peace. This is all together also known as the ecstasy of love. The highest and most luxurious moments are the direct encounters from time to time with the Creator at private ceremonies.

The exact specification of each individual's rights in this welfare depends on our performance in the life we are leading now. Are we able to accomplish our mission in accordance with the agreed contract?

Who Has No Deal with God Yet?

They are the ones who have not yet thought of returning back the trust (psyche) either because they did not know enough about the deal or they received the message but they ignored it or refused to return the trust. This group has the right to think about it until their last breath in this life. Others (Muslims, non-Muslims, secularists, atheists, agnostics, media, etc) should give them space and time for uninterrupted reflection. In fact, God allowed the differences to happen to help everyone reach the truth of their own good. The purpose of this wisdom is to create sufficient curiosity to exchange information and learn from each other.

يَـٰٓأَيُّهَا ٱلنَّاسُ إِنَّا خَلَقْنَٰكُم مِّن ذَكَرٍ وَأُنثَىٰ وَجَعَلْنَٰكُمْ شُعُوبًا وَقَبَآئِلَ لِتَعَارَفُوٓا۟ إِنَّ أَكْرَمَكُمْ عِندَ ٱللَّهِ أَتْقَىٰكُمْ إِنَّ ٱللَّهَ عَلِيمٌ خَبِيرٌ

(49:13) Human beings, We created you all from a male and a female, and made you into nations and tribes so that you may know one

339

another. Verily the noblest of you in the sight of Allah is the most

God-fearing of you. Surely Allah is All-Knowing, All-Aware.[168]

We Are Free but Responsible, And God is Patient

God has the right to collect His trust as He pleases, but He is patient no matter what you shout at Him now or what you think! Some respond poorly to His trust or even deny His existence. God is very patient, more than the word itself reveals, for He is the one who created patience. The most patient (*Al-Sabur*) is one of His names.

وَلَوْ يُؤَاخِذُ اللهُ النَّاسَ بِمَا كَسَبُوْا مَا تَرَكَ عَلٰى ظَهْرِهَا مِنْ دَاۤبَّةٍ وَّلٰكِنْ يُّؤَخِّرُهُمْ اِلٰۤى اَجَلٍ مُّسَمًّى ۚ فَاِذَا جَاۤءَ اَجَلُهُمْ فَاِنَّ اللهَ كَانَ بِعِبَادِهٖ بَصِيْرًا

(35:45) If Allah were to take people to task for their deeds, He would not leave any living creature on earth, but He grants them respite to an appointed time. When their appointed time comes to an end, surely Allah fully observes His servants.

The only requirement is to be polite! Everyone has the right to express himself and know the pros and cons of his choices. This is called freedom of speech and freedom of choice, but every choice comes with responsibility, and understanding this is called maturity.

Why Is God Patient?

Maturity requires time, we need to be able to understand our minds. What is on our minds? Who put those things there? Why? Are they there whether we like it or not? Understanding all this takes a bit of time. When we are fully aware about this then we are mature.

وَاللهُ اَخْرَجَكُمْ مِّنْۢ بُطُوْنِ اُمَّهٰتِكُمْ لَا تَعْلَمُوْنَ شَيْـًٔا ۙ وَّ جَعَلَ لَكُمُ السَّمْعَ وَالْاَبْصَارَ وَالْاَفْـِٔدَةَ ۙ لَعَلَّكُمْ تَشْكُرُوْنَ

(16:78) Allah has brought you forth from your mothers' wombs when you knew nothing, and then gave you hearing, and sight and thinking

341

[168] In this verse the whole of mankind has been addressed to reform it of the great evil that has always been causing universal disruption in the world, that is, the prejudices due to race, color, language, country, and nationality. On account of these prejudices man in every age has generally been discarding humanity and drawing around himself some small circles and regarding those born within those circles as his own people and those outside them as others. These circles have been drawn on the basis of accidental birth and not on rational and moral grounds. In some cases their basis is the accident of being born in a particular family, tribe, or race, and in some particular geographical region, or in a nation having a particular color or speaking a particular language. Then the discrimination between one's own people and others is not only confined to this that those who are looked upon as one's own people are shown greater love and cooperation than others, but this discrimination has assumed the worst forms of hatred, enmity, contempt and tyranny. New philosophies have been propounded for it, new religions invented, new codes of law made and new moral principles framed; so much so that nations and empires have made this distinction a permanent way of life with them and practiced it for centuries.

On this very basis no religion should consider its believers the chosen people of God or in the practice of their religious rites look upon the other as inferior to them in rights and rank, as some do. This very discrimination gave birth to class distinctions (varnashrama) among the Hindus according to which superiority of the Brahmins was established, all other human beings came to be regarded as inferior and unclean and the shudras cast into the depths of disgrace and degradation. Every person can see for himself even in this 20th century what atrocities have been committed against the colored people in Africa and America on account of the distinction between the white and the black. The treatment that the Europeans meted out to the Red Indian race in America and to the weak nations of Asia and Africa had the same concept underlying it. They thought that the rights and property and honor of all those who had been born outside the frontiers of their own land and nation were lawful for them and they had the right to plunder and take them as their slaves and exterminate them if need be. The worst examples of how the nationalism of the western nations has turned one nation against the others and made it their bloodthirsty enemy have been seen in the wars of the recent past and are being seen even in the present time. In particular, if what was manifested by the racism of the Nazi Germany and the concept of the superiority of the Nordic race in the last World War is kept in view. One can easily judge how stupendous and devastating is the error for whose reform this verse of the Quran was revealed.

In this brief verse, Allah has drawn the attention of all mankind to three cardinal truths:

(1) The origin of all of you is one and the same. Your whole species has sprung up from one man and one woman. All your races that are found in the world today are, in fact, the branches of one initial race that started with one mother and one father. In this process of creation there is no basis whatsoever for the divisions and distinctions in which you have involved yourselves because of your false notions. One God alone is your Creator. Different men have not been created by different gods. You have been made from one and the same substance. It is not so that some men have been made from some pure and superior substance and some other men from some impure and inferior substance. You have been created in one and the same way; it is not also so that different men have been created in different ways. And you are the offspring of the same parents; it is not so that in the beginning there were many human couples which gave birth to different populations in the different regions of the world.

(2) In spite of being one in origin, it was natural that you should be divided into nations and tribes. Obviously, all the men on the earth could not belong to one and the same family. With the spread of the race it was inevitable that countless families should arise, and then tribes and nations should emerge from the families. Similarly, it was inevitable that after settling in different regions of the earth, there should be differences of colors, features, languages and ways of living among the people, and it was also natural that those living in the same region should be closer in affinity and those living in remote regions not so close. But this natural difference never demanded that distinctions of inequality, of high and low, of noble and mean, should be established on its basis, that one race should claim superiority over the other, the people of one color should look down upon the people of other colors, and that one nation should take preference over the other without any reason. The Creator had divided the human communities into nations and tribes for that was a natural way of cooperation and distinction between them. In this way alone could a fraternity, a brotherhood, a tribe and a nation combine to give birth to a common way of life and to cooperate with each other in the affairs of the world. But it was all due to satanic ignorance that the differences among mankind created by Allah to be a means of recognition, were turned into a means of mutual boasting and hatred, which led mankind to every kind of injustice and tyranny.

(3) The only basis of superiority and excellence that there is, or can be, between man and man is that of moral excellence. As regards birth, all men are equal, for their Creator is One, their substance of creation is one, and their way of creation is one, and they are descended from the same parents. Moreover, a person's being born in a particular country, nation, or clan is just accidental. Therefore, there is no rational ground on account of which one person may be regarded as superior to the other. The real thing that makes one person superior to others is that one should be more God-conscious, a greater avoider of evils, and a follower of the way of piety and righteousness. Such a man, whether he belongs to any race, any nation and any country, is valuable and worthy on account of his personal merit. And the one who is reverse of him in character is in any case an inferior person whether he is black or white, born in the east or the west.

These same truths that have been stated in this brief verse of the Quran have been explained in greater detail by the Prophet (peace be upon him) in his addresses and traditions. In the speech that he made on the conquest of Makkah, after going round the Kabah, he said:

343

Thank God Who has removed from you the blemish of ignorance and its arrogance. O people, men are divided into classes: the pious and righteous, who are honorable in the sight of Allah, and the sinful and vicious, who are contemptible in the sight of Allah, whereas all men are the children of Adam and Adam had been created by Allah from clay.

On the occasion of the Farewell Pilgrimage, in the midst of the Tashriq days, he addressed the people, and said: O people, be aware: your God is One. No Arab has any superiority over a non-Arab, and no non-Arab any superiority over an Arab, and no white one has any superiority over a black one, and no black one any superiority over a white one, except on the basis of taqwa (piety). The most honorable among you in the sight of Allah is he who is the most pious and righteous of you. Say if I have conveyed the Message to you? And the great congregation of the people responded, saying: Yes, you have, O Messenger of Allah. Thereupon the Prophet (peace be upon him) said: Then let the one who is present convey it to those who are absent.

In a Hadith he has said: You are all the children of Adam, and Adam was created from the dust. Let the people give up boasting of their ancestors, otherwise they will stand more degraded than a mean insect in the sight of Allah.

In another Hadith the Prophet (peace be upon him) said: Allah will not inquire about your lineage on the Day of Resurrection. The most honorable in the sight of Allah is he who is most pious. In still another Hadith he said: Allah does not see your outward appearances and your possessions but He sees your hearts and your deeds.

These teachings have not remained confined to words only but Islam has practically established a universal brotherhood of the believers on the basis, which does not allow any distinction on account of color, race, language, country and nationality which is free from every concept of high and low, clean and unclean, mean and respectable, which admits all human beings with equal rights, whether they belong to any race and nation, any land or region. Even the opponents of Islam have to admit that no precedent is found in any religion and any system of the success with which the principle of human equality and unity has been given practical shape in the Muslim society, nor has it ever been found. Islam is the only religion which has welded and combined innumerable races and communities scattered in all corners of the earth into one universal ummah.

344

hearts so that you may give thanks.[169]

God who created knowledge and brains and gave man the power to ask questions, discuss, think, feel, visualize, plan, try, compare, understand and decide, gave also the people the right to use all of these, to help us to be mature! We are not in a power game, but we are in a maturity challenge!

In this connection, a misunderstanding also needs to be removed. In the case of marriage, the importance that Islamic law gives to kufv (likeness of status) has been taken by some people in the sense that some brotherhoods are noble and some mean, and matrimonial relations between them are objectionable. But this, in fact, is a wrong idea. According to the Islamic law, every Muslim man can marry every Muslim woman, but the success of the matrimonial life depends on maximum harmony and conformity between the spouses as regards habits, characteristics and ways of life, family traditions and economic and social status, so that they may get on well with each other. This is the real object of being equal and alike. Where there is unusual difference and disparity between the man and the woman in this regard, lifelong companionship will be difficult. That is why the Islamic law disapproves of such intermarriages, and not for the reason that one of the spouses is noble and the other mean, but for the reason that in case there is a clear and apparent difference and distinction in status, there would be a greater possibility of the failure of the matrimonial life if the marriage relationship was established.

That is, this is only known to Allah as to who is really a man of high rank and who is inferior in respect of qualities and characteristics. The standards of high and low that the people have set up of their own accord, are not acceptable to and approved by Allah. May be that the one who has been regarded as a man of high rank in the world is declared as the lowest of the low in the final judgment of Allah, and maybe that the one who has been looked upon as a very low person here, attains to a very high rank there. The real importance is not of the honor and dishonor of the world but of the honor and dishonor that one will receive from Allah. Therefore, what man should be most concerned about is that he should create in himself those real qualities and characteristics which make him worthy of honor in the sight of Allah.

[169] This is to remind them that when they were born they were more helpless and ignorant than the young one of an animal, but Allah gave them ears to hear, eyes to see and minds to think and reflect. These have enabled them to acquire every kind of information and knowledge to carry on their worldly affairs efficiently. So much so that these sensory faculties are the only means which help man attain so much progress as to rule over everything on the earth.

That is, you should be grateful to that Allah Who has bestowed upon you such blessings as these. It will be ingratitude on your part if you hear everything with your ears except the word of God, and see everything with your eyes except the signs of Allah and consider seriously about all the matters except your Benefactor Who has blessed you with these favors

345

We are not in a position to object or fight with God, He has the absolute power. The only way is to talk to Him. Our being polite is the only way that He will reply.

وَمَا قَدَرُوا اللهَ حَقَّ قَدْرِهٖ ۚ وَالْأَرْضُ جَمِيعًا قَبْضَتُهٗ يَوْمَ الْقِيٰمَةِ وَالسَّمٰوٰتُ مَطْوِيّٰتٌۢ بِيَمِينِهٖ ۚ سُبْحٰنَهٗ وَتَعٰلٰى عَمَّا يُشْرِكُونَ

(39:67) They did not recognise the true worth of Allah. (Such is Allah's power that) on the Day of Resurrection the whole earth will be in His grasp, and the heavens shall be folded up in His Right Hand. Glory be to Him! Exalted be He from all that they associate with Him.[170]

Whatever we would like to ask, He offered to listen to us and reply.

وَإِذَا سَأَلَكَ عِبَادِيْ عَنِّيْ فَإِنِّيْ قَرِيْبٌ ۚ أُجِيْبُ دَعْوَةَ الدَّاعِ إِذَا دَعَانِ فَلْيَسْتَجِيْبُوا لِيْ وَلْيُؤْمِنُوا بِيْ لَعَلَّهُمْ يَرْشُدُوْنَ

(2:186) (O Muhammad), when My servants ask you about Me, tell them I am quite near; I hear and answer the call of the caller whenever he calls Me. Let them listen to My call and believe in Me; perhaps they

---

[170] That is, they have no conception of the greatness and glory of Allah; they have never tried to understand how high is the position of the Lord of the Universe and how insignificant are the beings whom these foolish people have made associates in Godhead and worthy of their worship.

This is a figurative way of describing the complete control and authority of Allah over the earth and heavens. Just as a man encloses a small ball in the hollow of his hand with perfect ease, or a person rolls up an handkerchief in his hand without any difficulty, so will all men (who fail to conceive the greatness and glory of Allah) see with their own eyes, on the Day of Resurrection, that the earth and the heavens are like an ordinary ball and a small scroll in the hand of Allah. On the authority of Abdullah bin Umar and Abu Hurairah, that once during a sermon the Prophet (peace be upon him) recited this verse and then said: Allah will hold the heavens and the earths (i.e. the planets) in His grasp and will roll them about in such a way as a child rolls a ball, and will say: I am God, the One: I am the King: I am the All-Mighty, Owner of glory: Where are the kings of the world? Where are the tyrants? Where are the arrogant? Saying these words he started so shaking that we feared that he might topple over along with the pulpit.

That is, there is no comparison whatever between Allah's greatness and glory and the insignificance of those who are associated with Him in Godhead.

will be guided aright.[171]

During the last breath, this opportunity and patience ends. Then the story of justice begins. It's time to restore the rights of each one, and when necessary pay the price!

وَرَبُّكَ الْغَفُورُ ذُو الرَّحْمَةِ ۖ لَوْ يُؤَاخِذُهُم بِمَا كَسَبُوا لَعَجَّلَ لَهُمُ الْعَذَابَ ۚ بَل لَّهُم مَّوْعِدٌ لَّن يَجِدُوا مِن دُونِهِ مَوْئِلًا

(18:58) Your Lord is All-Forgiving, full of mercy. Had He wished to take them to task for their doings, He would have hastened in sending His scourge upon them. But He has set for them a time-limit which they cannot evade.[172]

Live Without A Lie

God forgives everything except the concealment of truth, and the lies. If the story of life is about the right to find the truth in peace, nothing ruins this opportunity and peace but lies. The biggest lie of all is

---

[171] Even though people can neither see God nor subject Him to any other form of sense perception this should not make them feel that God is remote from them. On the contrary, He is so close to each and every person that whenever any person so wishes he can communicate with his Lord. So much so that God hears and responds even to the prayers which remain within the innermost recesses of the heart.

People exhaust themselves by approaching false and powerless beings whom they foolishly fancy to be their deities but who have neither the power to hear nor to grant their prayers. But God, the omnipotent Lord and the absolute Master of this vast universe, Who wields all power and authority, is so close to human beings that they can always approach Him without the intercession of any intermediaries, and can put to Him their prayers and requests.

This announcement of God's closeness to man may open his eyes to the Truth, may turn him to the right way wherein lies his success and well-being.

[172] This is to warn the immature people that they should not be deluded by the respite that is given to them and presume that they will never be taken to task whatever they may go on doing. They forget that Allah gives them respite because He is Forgiving and Forbearing and does not punish the evil doers on the spot, for His Mercy demands that the evil doers should be given respite so that they may mend their ways.

denying His message or His uniqueness as one God.

إِنَّ اللَّهَ لَا يَغْفِرُ أَن يُشْرَكَ بِهِ وَيَغْفِرُ مَا دُونَ ذَٰلِكَ لِمَن يَشَاءُ ۚ وَمَن يُشْرِكْ بِاللَّهِ فَقَدِ افْتَرَىٰ إِثْمًا عَظِيمًا

(4:48) Surely Allah does not forgive that a partner be ascribed to Him, although He forgives any other sins for whomever He wills. He who associates anyone with Allah in His divinity has indeed forged a mighty lie and committed an awesome sin.[173]

God asks us to be honest and to not to lie even in jokes. It's important to understand that any fact-finding, news, given statements, and talk behind someone's back are strictly categorized under halal and haram. Spreading false accusations, rumors or misbehaving with knowledge can have long-term and long-running consequences. Therefore truthfulness goes without saying in Islam. It is the first and most important task that you must be aware of if you accept to submit, return the trust and become a Muslim. Get used to living without even a single lie until you return to God.

وَلَا تَقْفُ مَا لَيْسَ لَكَ بِهِ عِلْمٌ ۚ إِنَّ السَّمْعَ وَالْبَصَرَ وَالْفُؤَادَ كُلُّ أُولَٰئِكَ كَانَ عَنْهُ مَسْئُولًا

(17:36) Do not follow that of which you have no knowledge. Surely the hearing, the sight, the heart - each of these shall be called to

---

[173] Although the People of the Book claimed to follow the Prophets and the Divine Books they had, in fact, fallen prey to polytheism.

The purpose of this verse is not to tell man that he may commit any sin as long as he does not associate others with God in His divinity. The object is rather to impress upon those who had begun to regard polytheism as a trivial matter that it constitutes the most serious offence in God's sight, an offence so serious that while other sins may be pardoned this will not.

account.[174]

وَالَّذِينَ لَا يَشْهَدُونَ الزُّورَ وَ إِذَا مَرُّوا بِاللَّغْوِ مَرُّوا كِرَامًا

(25:72) (The true servants of the Merciful One) are those who do not bear witness to any falsehood and who, when they pass by frivolity, pass by it with dignity;[175]

يَأَيُّهَا الَّذِينَ أَمَنُوا إِنْ جَاءَكُمْ فَاسِقٌ بِنَبَأٍ فَتَبَيَّنُوا أَنْ تُصِيبُوا قَوْمًا بِجَهَالَةٍ فَتُصْبِحُوا عَلَى مَا فَعَلْتُمْ نَدِمِينَ

(49:6) Believers, when an ungodly person brings to you a piece of news, carefully ascertain its truth, lest you should hurt a people unwittingly

---

[174] The meanings of "Do not follow that of which you have no knowledge" are very comprehensive. It demands that both in individual and collective life, one should not follow mere guess work and presumption instead of knowledge. This instruction covers all aspects of Islamic life, moral, legal, political, administrative and applies to science, arts and education. It has thus saved the society from numerous evils which are produced in human life by following guesswork instead of knowledge. The Islamic moral code demands: Guard against suspicion and do not accuse any individual or group without proper investigation. In law, it has been made a permanent principle that no action should be taken against anyone without proper investigation. It has been made unlawful to arrest, beat or imprison anyone on mere suspicion during investigation. In regards to foreign relations, the definite policy has been laid down that no action should be taken without investigation, nor should rumors be set afloat. Likewise in education the so called sciences based on mere guess work, presumptions and irrational theories have been disapproved. Above all, it cuts at the very root of superstitions, for this instruction teaches the believers to accept only that which is based on the knowledge imparted by Allah and His Messenger.

[175] This also has two meanings: (1) They do not give evidence (in the court of law etc.) in regard to a false thing in order to prove it right, when in fact it is a falsehood, or at best a doubtful thing. (2) They have no intention to witness anything which is false, evil or wicked as spectators. In this sense, every sin and every indecency, every sham and counterfeit act is a falsehood. A true servant of Allah recognizes it as false and shuns it even if it is presented in the seemingly beautiful forms of art.

The Arabic word laghv implies all that is vain, useless and meaningless and it also covers falsehood. The true servants pass by in a dignified manner if they ever come across what is vain, as if it were a heap of filth. They do not stay there to enjoy the filth of moral impurity, obscenity or foul language, nor do they intentionally go anywhere to hear or see or take part in any sort of filth.

349

and thereafter repent at what you did.[176]

---

[176] When the tribe of the Bani al-Mustaliq embraced Islam, the Prophet (peace be upon him) sent Walid bin Uqbah to collect the Zakat from them. When he arrived in their territory, he became fearful due to some reason and without visiting the people of the tribe returned to Al-Madinah and complained to the Prophet (peace be upon him) that they had refused to pay the Zakat and had even wanted to kill him. On hearing this, the Prophet (peace be upon him) became very angry and he made up his mind to dispatch a contingent to punish those people. According to some traditions he had dispatched the contingent, and according to others, he was about to dispatch it. In any case, all agree that in the meantime the chief of the Bani al-Mustaliq, Harith bin Dirar, father of Juwairiyah, wife of the Prophet (peace be upon him), arrived at the head of a deputation, and submitted: By God, we did not at all see Walid; therefore, there could be no question of refusing to pay the Zakat and wanting to kill him. We are steadfast to the faith and have no intention to withhold the Zakat. At this, this verse was sent down.

On this critical occasion when on account of believing in a baseless report a grave blunder was about to be committed, Allah gave the Muslims this guiding principle to be followed on receipt of news: Whenever you receive important news bearing upon a vital matter, you should not accept it immediately but should first examine the man who has brought it. If he is an evil man whose report is not authentic normally, you should inquire into it carefully to ascertain the truth instead of accepting it and acting on it immediately. From this divine command an important legal principle is deduced, the sphere of application of which is very vast. According to it, it is not permissible for a Muslim government to take any action against a person or a group or a nation on the basis of the reports provided by the secret agents whose character might be doubtful.

On the basis of this very principle the traditionalists introduced the art of critical appraisal in the science of Hadith in order to determine the value and worth of the people through whom traditions of the Prophet (peace be upon him) reached the later generations. And the jurists established this principle in the law of evidence that in a matter from which a Shariah value can be deduced, or a duty imposed on a person; the evidence of an evil man would be unacceptable. However, all scholars agree that as far as the common worldly matters are concerned it is not necessary to ascertain the truth of every news and the reliability of every informer.

For the word used in the verse is naba, which does not apply to every news but only to the news of consequence. That is why the jurists say that this principle does not apply in the case of ordinary matters. For example, if a person goes to visit somebody and seeks permission to enter the house, and a person comes out and conveys the permission, he can enter the house accordingly no matter whether the one conveying the permission from the master of the house was good or bad. Likewise, the scholars also agree that the evidence, as well as the report, of the people whose evil does not relate to lying and immorality, but they are regarded as unrighteous only on account of false beliefs, will also be acceptable. Only the falsehood of their creed cannot be a hindrance to accepting their evidence or reports.

350

يَـٰٓأَيُّهَا الَّذِينَ ءَامَنُوا لَا يَسْخَرْ قَوْمٌ مِّن قَوْمٍ عَسَىٰٓ أَن يَكُونُوا خَيْرًا مِّنْهُمْ وَلَا نِسَآءٌ مِّن نِّسَآءٍ عَسَىٰٓ أَن يَكُنَّ خَيْرًا مِّنْهُنَّ ۖ وَلَا تَلْمِزُوٓا أَنفُسَكُمْ وَلَا تَنَابَزُوا بِٱلْأَلْقَـٰبِ ۖ بِئْسَ ٱلِٱسْمُ ٱلْفُسُوقُ بَعْدَ ٱلْإِيمَـٰنِ ۚ وَمَن لَّمْ يَتُبْ فَأُو۟لَـٰٓئِكَ هُمُ ٱلظَّـٰلِمُونَ

(49:11) Believers, let not a group (of men) scoff at another group, it may well be that the latter (at whom they scoff) are better than they; nor let a group of women scoff at another group, it may well be that the latter are better than they. And do not taunt one another, nor revile one another by nicknames. It is an evil thing to gain notoriety for ungodliness after belief. Those who do not repent are indeed the wrong-doers.[177]

يَـٰٓأَيُّهَا الَّذِينَ آمَنُوا اجْتَنِبُوا كَثِيرًا مِّنَ الظَّنِّ إِنَّ بَعْضَ الظَّنِّ إِثْمٌ وَّلَا تَجَسَّسُوا وَلَا يَغْتَبْ بَّعْضُكُم بَعْضًا ۚ أَيُحِبُّ أَحَدُكُمْ أَن يَّأْكُلَ لَحْمَ أَخِيهِ مَيْتًا فَكَرِهْتُمُوهُ ۚ وَاتَّقُوا اللَّهَ ۚ إِنَّ اللَّهَ تَوَّابٌ رَّحِيمٌ

(49:12) Believers, avoid being excessively suspicious, for some suspicion is a sin. Do not spy, nor backbite one another. Would any of you like to eat the flesh of his dead brother? You would surely detest it. Have fear of Allah. Surely Allah is much prone to accept repentance, is Most Compassionate.[178]

It was narrated that 'Ali, may Allah be pleased with him, said: the Messenger of Allah (ﷺ) said:

حَدَّثَنَا مُحَمَّدُ بْنُ فُضَيْلٍ، عَنِ الْأَعْمَشِ، عَنْ حَبِيبٍ، عَنْ ثَعْلَبَةَ، عَنْ عَلِيٍّ، رَضِيَ اللَّهُ عَنْهُ قَالَ قَالَ رَسُولُ اللَّهِ صَلَّى اللَّهُ عَلَيْهِ وَسَلَّمَ مَنْ كَذَبَ عَلَيَّ مُتَعَمِّدًا فَلْيَتَبَوَّأْ مَقْعَدَهُ مِنَ النَّارِ.

"Whoever tells a lie about me deliberately, let him take his place in Hell." *Source: Sahih (Darussalam)*

The Line Between Believers and Unbelievers

If you see some people sitting with their backs towards a fire, the expected reaction of the people around them is to make sure that they are aware that something is going on. Then if they really don't see what you see and they don't ask you for more help, that means you can't cross. Things should stop at this point but while leaving open doors for any further cooperation and discussions in peace.

قُلْ يَـٰٓأَيُّهَا الْكَافِرُونَ

(109:1) Say: "O unbelievers!"

لَآ أَعْبُدُ مَا تَعْبُدُونَ

(109:2) I do not worship those that you worship

[177] In the preceding two verses after giving necessary instructions about the Muslim people's mutual fighting, the believers were made to realize that by virtue of the most sacred relationship of the faith they were brothers to one another, and they should fear God and try to keep their mutual relations right. Now, in the following two verses, they are being enjoined to avoid and shun those major evils which generally spoil the mutual relationships of the people in a society. Slandering and taunting the people and harboring suspicions and spying on others are, in fact, the evils that cause mutual enmities and then lead to grave mischief. In this connection, from the commandments that are being given in the following verses and the explanations of these found in the Hadith a detailed law of libel can be compiled. The western law pertaining to libel in this regard is so defective that a person who sues another under this law may well cause some loss to his own honor. The Islamic law, on the contrary recognizes a basic honor for every person and gives nobody the right to attack it, no matter whether the attack is based on reality or not, and whether the person who has been attacked has a reputation of his own or not. Only the fact that a person has debased and humiliated the other person is enough to declare him a criminal unless, of course, it is proved that the humiliation caused had a legal ground for it.

Mocking does not only imply mocking with the tongue but it also includes mimicking somebody, making pointed references to him, laughing at his words, or his works, or his appearance, or his dress, or calling the people's attention to some defect or blemish in him so that others also may laugh at him. All this is included in mocking. What is actually forbidden is that one should make fun of and ridicule another, for under such ridiculing there always lie feelings of one's own superiority and the other's abasement and contempt, which are morally unworthy of a gentleman. Moreover, it hurts the other person, which causes mischief to spread in society. That is why it has been forbidden.

To make mention of the men and the women separately does not mean that it is lawful for the men to mock the women or the women to mock the men. The actual reason for making a separate mention of the two sexes is that Islam does not at all believe in mixed society. Therefore, in a Muslim society it is inconceivable that the men would mock a woman, or the women would mock a man in an assembly.

The word lamz as used in the original is very comprehensive and applies to ridiculing, reviling, deriding, jeering, charging somebody or finding fault with him, and making him the target of reproach and blame by open or tacit references. As all such things also spoil mutual relationships and create bad blood in society, they have been forbidden. Instead of saying: Do not taunt one another, it has been said: Do not taunt yourselves, which by itself shows that the one who uses taunting words for others, in fact, taunts his own self. Obviously, a person does not use invectives against others unless he himself is filled with evil feelings and is almost in a state of bursting like a volcano. Thus, the one who nourishes such feelings has made his own self a nest of evils before he makes others a target. Then, when he taunts others, it means that he is inviting others to taunt him. It is a different matter that the other person may evade his attacks because of a gentle nature, but he himself has opened the door to mischief so that the other may treat him likewise.

This command requires that a person should not be called by a name or a title which may cause him humiliation, e.g. calling somebody a sinner or a hypocrite, or calling someone a lame or blind one, or one-eyed, or giving him a nickname containing a reference to some defect or blemish in him, or in his parents, or in his family, or calling a person a Jew or a Christian even after his conversion to Islam, or giving such a nickname to a person, or a family, or a community, or a group, which may bring condemnation or disgrace on it. Only those nicknames have been made an exception from this command, which though apparently offensive, are not intended to condemn the persons concerned, but they rather serve as a mark of recognition for them. That is why the traditionists have allowed as permissible names like Suleman al-Amash (the weak-eyed Suleman) and Wasil al-Ahdab (the hunchbacked Wasil) among the reporters of the Hadith. If there are several men of the same name and a particular man among them may be recognized only by a particular title or nickname of his, the title or nickname can be used, even though the title by itself may be offensive. For instance, if there are several men called Abdullah, and one of them is blind, he may be called Abdullah the blind, for his recognition. Likewise, those titles also are excluded from this command, which though apparently offensive, are in fact, given out of love and the people who are called by those titles themselves approve them, like Abu Hurairah (father of the kitten) and Abu Turab (father of the dust).

That is, it is very shameful for a believer that in spite of being a believer he should earn a name for using abusive language and for immodest behavior. If a disbeliever earns reputation for himself for mocking the people, or taunting them, or for proposing evil and offensive titles for others, it may not be a good reputation from the point of view of humanity, but it at least goes well with his disbelief. But if a person after affirming the faith in Allah and His Messenger and the Hereafter earns reputation on account of these base qualities, it is simply regrettable.

What is forbidden is not conjecture as such but excessive conjecture and following every kind of conjecture, and the reason given is that some conjectures are sins. In order to understand this command, we should analyze and see what are the kinds of conjecture and what is the moral position of each.

One kind of conjecture is that which is morally approved and laudable, and desirable and praiseworthy from religious point of view, e.g. a good conjecture in respect of Allah and His Messenger and the believers and those people with whom one comes in common contact daily and concerning whom there may be no rational ground for having an evil conjecture.

The second kind of conjecture is that which one cannot do without in practical life, e.g. in a law court a judge has to consider the evidence placed before him and give his decision on the basis of the most probable conjecture, for he cannot have direct knowledge of the facts of the matter, and the opinion that is based on evidence is mostly based on the most probable conjecture and not on certainty. Likewise, in most cases when one or the other decision has to be taken, and the knowledge of the reality cannot possibly be attained, there is no way out for men but to form an opinion on the basis of a conjecture.

354

The third kind of conjecture, which is although a suspicion, is permissible in nature, and it cannot be regarded as a sin. For instance, if there are clear signs and pointers in the character of a person (or persons), or in his dealings and conduct, on the basis of which he may not deserve to enjoy one's good conjecture, and there are rational grounds for having suspicions against him, the Shariah does not demand that one should behave like a simpleton and continue to have a good conjecture about him. The last limit of this lawful conjecture, however, is that one should conduct himself cautiously in order to ward off any possible mischief from him; it is not right to take an action against him only on the basis of a conjecture.

The fourth kind of conjecture which is, in fact, a sin is that one should entertain a suspicion in respect of a person without any ground, or should start with suspicion in forming an opinion about others, or should entertain a suspicion about the people whose apparent conditions show that they are good and noble. Likewise, this also is a sin that when there is an equal chance of the evil and goodness in the word or deed of a person, one should regard it as only evil out of suspicion. For instance, if a gentleman while leaving a place of assembly picks up another one's shoes, instead of his own, and we form the opinion that he has done so with the intention of stealing the shoes, whereas this could be possible because of oversight as well, there is no reason for adopting the evil opinion instead of the good opinion except the suspicion.

This analysis makes it plain that conjecture by itself is not anything forbidden; rather in some cases and situations it is commendable, in some situations inevitable, in some permissible up to a certain extent and un-permissible beyond it, and in some cases absolutely unlawful. That is why it has not been enjoined that one should refrain from conjecture or suspicion altogether but what is enjoined is that one should refrain from much suspicion. Then, to make the intention of the command explicit, it has been said that some conjectures are sinful. From this warning it follows automatically that whenever a person is forming an opinion on the basis of conjecture, or is about to take an action, he should examine the case and see whether the conjecture he is entertaining is not a sin, whether the conjecture is really necessary, whether there are sound reasons for the conjecture, and whether the conduct one is adopting on the basis of the conjecture is permissible. Everyone who fears God will certainly take these precautions. To make his conjecture free and independent of every such care and consideration is the pastime of only those people who are fearless of God and thoughtless of the accountability of the Hereafter.

355

[178] "Do not spy": Do not grope after the secrets of the people: do not search for their defects and weaknesses: do not pry into their conditions and affairs. Whether this is done because of suspicion, or for causing harm to somebody with an evil intention, or for satisfying one's own curiosity, it is forbidden by the Shariah in every case. It does not behoove a believer that he should spy on the hidden affairs of other people, and should try to peep at them from behind curtains to find out their defects and their weaknesses. This also includes reading other people's private letters, listening secretly to private conversation, peeping into the neighbor's house, and trying to get information in different ways about the domestic life or private affairs of others. This is grave immorality which causes serious mischief in society. That is why the Prophet (peace be upon him) once said in an address about those who pry into other people's affairs:

O people, who have professed belief verbally, but faith has not yet entered your hearts: Do not pry into the affairs of the Muslims, for he who will pry into the affairs of the Muslims, Allah will pry into his affairs, and he whom Allah follows inquisitively, is disgraced by Him in his own house. (Abu Daud).

Muawiyah says that he himself heard the Prophet (peace be upon him) say: If you start prying into the secret affairs of the people, you will pervert them, or at least drive them very near perversion. In another he said: When you happen to form an evil opinion about somebody, do not pry about it.

According to still another Hadith, the Prophet (peace be upon him) said: The one who saw a secret affair of somebody and then concealed it is as though he saved a girl who had been buried alive.

This prohibition of spying is not only applicable to the individuals but also to the Islamic government. The duty of forbidding the people to do evil that the Shariah has entrusted to the government does not require that it should establish a system of spying to inquire too curiously into the people's secret evils and then punish them, but it should use force only against those evils which are manifested openly. As for the hidden evils, spying is not the way to reform them but it is education, preaching and counseling, collective training of the people and trying to create a pure social environment. In this connection, an incident concerning Umar is very instructive. Once at night he heard the voice of a person who was singing in his house. He became curious and climbed the wall. There he saw wine as well as a woman present. He shouted at the man, saying: O enemy of God, do you think you will disobey Allah, and Allah will not expose your secret? The man replied: Do not make haste, O commander of the faithful: if I have committed one sin, you have committed three sins: Allah has forbidden spying, and you have spied; Allah has commanded that one should enter the houses by the doors, and you have entered it by climbing over the wall; Allah has commanded that one should avoid entering the other people's houses without permission, and you have entered my house without my permission. Hearing this reply Umar confessed his error, and did not take any action against the man, but made him to promise that he would follow the right way in future. This shows that it is not only forbidden for the individuals but also for the Islamic government itself to pry into the secrets of the people and discover their sins and errors and then seize them for punishment. The same thing has been said in a Hadith in which the Prophet (peace be upon him) has said: When the ruler starts searching for the causes of suspicions among the people he perverts them.

The only exception from this command are the special cases and situations in which spying is actually needed. For instance, if in the conduct of a person (or persons) some signs of corruption are visible and there is the apprehension that he is about to commit a crime, the government can inquire into his affairs; or, for instance, if somebody sends a proposal of marriage in the house of a person, or wants to enter into business with him, the other person can, inquire and investigate into his affairs for his own satisfaction.

Ghibat (back-biting) has been defined thus: It is saying on the back of a person something which would hurt him if he came to know of it. This definition has been reported from the Prophet (peace be upon him) himself. On the authority of Abu Hurairah, the Prophet (peace be upon him) defined ghibat as follows: It is talking of your brother in a way irksome to him. It was asked: What, if the defect being talked of is present in my brother? The Prophet (peace be upon him) replied: If it is present in him, it would be ghibat; if it is not there, it would be slandering him.

These traditions make it plain that uttering a false accusation against a person in his absence is calumny and describing a real defect in him ghibat; whether this is done in express words or by reference and allusion, in every case it is forbidden. Likewise, whether this is done in the lifetime of a person, or after his death, it is forbidden in both cases.

357

The only exceptions to this prohibition are the cases in which there may be a genuine need of speaking in of a person on his back, or after his death, and this may not be fulfilled without resort to backbiting, and if it was not resorted to, a greater evil might result than backbiting itself. The Prophet (peace be upon him) has described this exception as a principle, thus: The worst excess is to attack the honor of a Muslim unjustly. In this saying the condition of unjustly points out that doing so with justice is permissible. Then, in the practice of the Prophet (peace be upon him) himself we find some precedents which show what is implied by justice and in what conditions and cases backbiting may be lawful to the extent as necessary.

Two of the companions, Muawiyah and Abu Jahm, sent the proposal of marriage to a lady, Fatimah bint Qais. She came to the Prophet (peace be upon him) and asked for his advice. He said: Muawiyah is a poor man and Abu Jahm beats his wives much. In this case, as there was the question of the lady's future and she had consulted the Prophet (peace be upon him) for his advice, he deemed it necessary to inform her of the two men's weaknesses.

One day when the Prophet (peace be upon him) was present in the apartment of Aishah, a man came and sought permission to see him. The Prophet (peace be upon him) remarked that he was a very bad man of his tribe. Then he went out and talked to him politely. When he came back into the house, Aishah asked: You have talked to him politely, whereas when you went out you said something different about him. The Prophet (peace be upon him) said, On the day of Resurrection the worst abode in the sight of Allah will be of the person whom the people start avoiding because of his abusive language. A study of this incident will show that the Prophet (peace be upon him) in spite of having a bad opinion about the person talked to him politely because that was the demand of his morals; but he had the apprehension lest the people of his house should consider the person to be his friend when they would see him treating him kindly, and then the person might use this impression to his own advantage later. Therefore, the Prophet (peace be upon him) warned Aishah telling her that he was a bad man of his tribe. Once Hind bint Utbah, wife of Abu Sufyan, came to the Prophet (peace be upon him) and said: Abu Sufyan is a miserly person: he does not provide enough for me and my children's needs. Although this complaint from the wife in the absence of the husband was backbiting, the Prophet (peace be upon him) permitted it, for the oppressed one has a right that he or she may take the complaint of injustice to a person who has the power to get it removed.

From these precedents of the Sunnah of the Prophet (peace be upon him), the jurists and traditionalists have deduced this principle: Ghibat (backbiting) is permissible only in case it is needed for a real and genuine (genuine from the Shariah point of view) necessity, and the necessity may not be satisfied without having resort to it. Then on the basis of the same principle the scholars have declared that ghibat is permissible in the following cases:

(1) Complaining by an oppressed person against the oppressor before every such person who he thinks can do something to save him from the injustice.

(2) To make mention of the evils of a person (or persons) with the intention of reform before those who can be expected to help remove the evils.

358

(3) To state the facts of a case before a legal expert for the purpose of seeking a religious or legal ruling regarding an unlawful act committed by a person.

(4) To warn the people of the mischief of a person (or persons) so that they may ward off the evil, e.g. it is not only permissible but obligatory to mention the weaknesses of the reporters, witnesses and writers, for without it, it is not possible to safeguard the Shariah against the propagation of false reports, the courts against injustices and the common people or the students against errors and misunderstandings. Or, for instance, if a person wants to have the relationship of marriage with somebody, or wishes to rent a house in the neighborhood of somebody, or wants to give something into the custody of somebody, and consults another person, it is obligatory for him to apprise him of all aspects so that he is not deceived because of ignorance.

(5) To raise voice against and criticize the evils of the people who may be spreading sin and immorality and error or corrupting the people's faith and persecuting them.

(6) To use nicknames for the people who may have become well known by those names, but this should be done for the purpose of their recognition and not with a view to condemn them.

Apart from these exceptions it is absolutely forbidden to speak ill of a person behind his back. If what is spoken is true, it is ghibat; if it is false, it is calumny. And if it is meant to make two persons quarrel, it is malicious. The Shariah has declared all these as forbidden. In the Islamic society it is incumbent on every Muslim to refute a false charge made against a person in his presence and not to listen to it quietly, and to tell those who are speaking ill of somebody, without a genuine religious need, to fear God and desist from the sin. The Prophet (peace be upon him) has said: If a person does not support and help a Muslim when he is being disgraced and his honor being attacked, Allah also does not support and help him when he stands in need of His help; and if a person helps and supports a Muslim when his honor is being attacked and he is being disgraced, Allah Almighty also helps him when he wants that Allah should help him.

As for the backbiter, as soon as he realizes that he is committing this sin, or has committed it, his first duty is to offer repentance before Allah and restrain himself from this forbidden act. His second duty is that he should compensate for it as far as possible. If he has backbitten a dead person, he should ask Allah's forgiveness for the person as often as he can. If he has backbitten a living person, and what he said was also false, he should refute it before the people before whom he had made the calumny. And if what he said was true, he should never speak ill of him in future, and should ask pardon of the person whom he had backbitten. A section of the scholars has expressed the opinion that pardon should be asked only in case the other person has come to know of it; otherwise one should only offer repentance, for if the person concerned is unaware and the backbiter in order to ask pardon goes and tells him that he had backbitten him, he would certainly feel hurt.

وَلَا أَنْتُمْ عَٰبِدُوْنَ مَآ أَعْبُدُ ۚ

(109:3) neither do you worship Him Whom I worship;

وَلَا أَنَا عَابِدٌ مَّا عَبَدْتُّمْ

(109:4) nor will I worship those whom you have worshipped;

وَ لَا أَنْتُمْ عَٰبِدُوْنَ مَآ أَعْبُدُ ۗ

(109:5) nor are you going to worship Him Whom I worship.

لَكُمْ دِيْنُكُمْ وَلِىَ دِيْنِ

(109:6) To you is your religion, and to me, my religion.

God is The Absolute Just

God is the only one, who has the right to question people. When we turn to God, He alone has the right to ask us about His trust and our dealings.

In general, in civil law, a person who uses the property of others without permission for his own benefit is liable for the aggravated

---

In this sentence Allah by likening backbiting to eating the dead brother's flesh has given the idea of its being an abomination. Eating the dead flesh is by itself abhorrent; and when the flesh is not of an animal, but of a man, and that too of one's own dead brother, abomination would be added to abomination. Then, by presenting the simile in the interrogative tone it has been made all the more impressive, so that every person may ask his own conscience and decide whether he would like to eat the flesh of his dead brother. If he would not, and he abhors it by nature, how would he like that he should attack the honor of his brother-in-faith in his absence, when he cannot defend himself and when he is fully unaware that he is being disgraced. This shows that the basic reason of forbidding backbiting is not that the person being backbitten is being hurt but speaking ill of a person in his absence is by itself unlawful and forbidden whether he is aware of it, or not, and whether he feels hurt by it or not. Obviously, eating the flesh of a dead man is not forbidden because it hurts the dead man; the dead person is wholly unaware that somebody is eating of his body, but because this act by itself is an abomination. Likewise, if the person who is backbitten also does not come to know of it through any means, he will remain unaware throughout his life that somebody had attacked his honor at a particular time before some particular people and on that account he had stood disgraced in the eyes of those people. Because of this unawareness he will not feel at all hurt by this backbiting, but his honor would in any case be sullied. Therefore, this act in its nature is not any different from eating the flesh of a dead brother.

crime of appropriation and misuse of other people's property for a private purpose. What about the law of Heaven?

After the time has elapsed, and resurrection happens after death, people will realize that their whole lives have been only like an hour (time is relative). How did you treat God's property? Also God calls the ones who didn't submit, from this point on, criminals.

وَيَوْمَ تَقُومُ السَّاعَةُ يُقْسِمُ الْمُجْرِمُونَ ۙ مَا لَبِثُوا غَيْرَ سَاعَةٍ ۚ كَذَٰلِكَ كَانُوا يُؤْفَكُونَ

(30:55) On that Day when the Hour will come to pass the wicked shall swear that they had stayed (in the world) no more than an hour. Thus they used to be deceived in the life of the world.[179]

Their deeds and words will have left a trace, according to the recording in the book from both of the angels.

وَوُضِعَ الْكِتَابُ فَتَرَى الْمُجْرِمِينَ مُشْفِقِينَ مِمَّا فِيهِ وَ يَقُولُونَ يَا وَيْلَتَنَا مَالِ هَٰذَا الْكِتَابِ لَا يُغَادِرُ صَغِيرَةً وَّلَا كَبِيرَةً إِلَّا أَحْصَاهَا ۚ وَوَجَدُوا مَا عَمِلُوا حَاضِرًا ۗ وَ لَا يَظْلِمُ رَبُّكَ أَحَدًا

(18:49) And then the Record of their deeds shall be placed before them and you will see the guilty full of fear for what it contains, and will say: "Woe to us! What a Record this is! It leaves nothing, big or small, but encompasses it." They will find their deeds confronting them. Your Lord wrongs no one. "And your Lord does not do injustice to anyone"[180]

---

[179] That is, Resurrection, which is being foretold here. That is, from the time of death till Resurrection. Even if thousands of years might have elapsed since their death they will feel that they had gone to sleep a few hours earlier and then a sudden calamity had roused them from sleep.

That is, "They used to make similar wrong estimates in the world. There also they lacked the realization of reality, and therefore, used to assert that there was going to be no Resurrection, no life-after-death, and no accountability before God."

[180] Neither will an evil deed, not committed by someone, have been recorded in his conduct register, nor shall anyone be punished more than one deserved for his crime, nor shall an innocent person be punished at all.

There will be a discussion with them, and hearing of witnesses. They are the most trusted witnesses, parts of our bodies: tongue, hands, and legs.

يَوْمَ تَشْهَدُ عَلَيْهِمْ أَلْسِنَتُهُمْ وَأَيْدِيهِمْ وَأَرْجُلُهُمْ بِمَا كَانُوا يَعْمَلُونَ

(24:24) (Let them not be heedless of) the Day when their own tongues, their hands, and their feet shall all bear witness against them as to what they have been doing.

Also the skin, ears, and eyes will tell their truth, witnessing how you were using the property of God.

حَتَّى إِذَا مَا جَاءُوهَا شَهِدَ عَلَيْهِمْ سَمْعُهُمْ وَأَبْصَارُهُمْ وَجُلُودُهُمْ بِمَا كَانُوا يَعْمَلُونَ

(41:20) and when all have arrived, their ears, their eyes, and their skins shall bear witness against them, stating all that they had done in the life of the world.[181]

وَقَالُوا لِجُلُودِهِمْ لِمَ شَهِدْتُمْ عَلَيْنَا قَالُوا أَنْطَقَنَا اللهُ الَّذِى أَنْطَقَ كُلَّ شَىْءٍ وَهُوَ خَلَقَكُمْ أَوَّلَ مَرَّةٍ وَّإِلَيْهِ تُرْجَعُونَ

(41:21) They will ask their skins: "Why did you bear witness against us?" The skins will reply: "Allah gave us speech, as He gave speech to all others. He it is Who created you for the first time and it is to Him

---

[181] The explanation of this given in the Hadith is that when a stubborn culprit will go on denying his crimes, and will even belie all the witnesses, then the limbs of his body will bear the witness, one after the other, by the command of Allah, and will tell what offenses he had committed through them.

This verse is one of those many verses which prove that the Hereafter will not only be a spiritual world but human beings will be resurrected with the body and soul as they are now in this world. Not only this: they will be given the same body in which they live now. The same particles and atoms which composed their bodies in the world will be collected on the Day of Resurrection, and they will be resurrected with the same previous bodies in which they had lived and worked in the world. Evidently, the limbs of man can bear the witness in the Hereafter only in case they are the same limbs with which he committed a crime in his previous life.

that you will be sent back.[182]

وَمَا كُنْتُمْ تَسْتَتِرُونَ أَن يَّشْهَدَ عَلَيْكُمْ سَمْعُكُمْ وَلَا أَبْصَارُكُمْ وَلَا جُلُودُكُمْ
وَلَكِنْ ظَنَنْتُمْ أَنَّ اللّٰهَ لَا يَعْلَمُ كَثِيرًا مِّمَّا تَعْمَلُونَ

(41:22) When you used to conceal yourselves (while committing misdeeds) you never thought that your ears or your eyes or your skins would ever bear witness against you; you rather fancied that Allah does not know a great deal of what you do.

وَذٰلِكُمْ ظَنُّكُمُ الَّذِى ظَنَنْتُمْ بِرَبِّكُمْ أَرْدٰكُمْ فَأَصْبَحْتُمْ مِّنَ الْخٰسِرِينَ

(41:23) This thought of yours about your Lord has led to your perdition and you have become among the losers."[183]

Any false statements that attempt to justify the actions of the body will not be accepted since the most central decision-making system of the psyche (including the frontal lobe and the intentions) will be available to give full details to answer the question of why you committed each act. You may be surprised to hear your deep inner voice, which you have never shared with anyone before, speaking out loud the details about the intentions behind every action, recorded in the core of your consciousness, the heart.

يُنَبَّؤُا الْإِنْسَانُ يَوْمَئِذٍ بِمَا قَدَّمَ وَأَخَّرَ

(75:13) On that Day will man be apprised of his deeds, both the earlier

---

[182] This shows that not only man's own limbs will bear witness on the Day of Resurrection, but every such thing before which man would have committed any crime will also speak out. The same thing has been said in Surah Al- Zilzal, thus: The earth will cast out all the burdens, which lie within it, and man will say: what has befallen it? On that Day shall it relate whatever had happened (on it), because your Lord will have commanded it (to do so).

[183] Hasan Basri has explained this verse thus: Every man's attitude and conduct is determined by the thought and conjecture that he has about his God. The conduct of a righteous believer is right because his thought and conjecture about his Lord is right, and the conduct of a disbeliever and a hypocrite and a sinful person is wrong because his thought and conjecture about his Lord is wrong. This same theme has the Prophet (peace be upon him) expressed in a comprehensive and brief Hadith, thus: Your Lord says: I am with the thought and conjecture that My servant holds about Me.

and the later.[184]

بَلِ الْإِنسَانُ عَلَىٰ نَفْسِهِ بَصِيرَةٌ ۝

(75:14) But lo, man is well aware of himself,

وَلَوْ أَلْقَىٰ مَعَاذِيرَهُۥ

(75:15) even though he might make up excuses.[185]

---

[184] Bima qaddama wa akhkhara is a very comprehensive sentence, which can have several meanings and probably all are implied:

(1) That man on that Day will be told what good or evil he had earned in his worldly life before death and sent forward for his hereafter, and also informed what effects of his good or evil acts he had left behind in the world, which continued to work and to influence the coming generations for ages after him.

(2) That he will be told everything he ought to have done but which he did not do, and did what he ought not to have done.

(3) That the full date wise account of what he did before and what he did afterwards will be placed before him.

(4) That he will be told whatever good or evil he had done as well as informed of the good or the evil that he had left undone.

[185] That is, the object of placing man's record before him will not be to inform the culprit of his crimes, but this will be done because the demands of justice are not fulfilled unless the proof of the crime is produced before the court; otherwise everyman fully knows what he actually is. For the sake of self-knowledge he does not need that another one should tell him what he is. A liar can deceive the whole world but he himself knows that he lies. A thief can devise a thousand devices to conceal his crime but he himself is aware that he is a thief. A person involved in error can present a thousand arguments to assure the people that he is honestly convinced of the disbelief, atheism or polytheism, which he professes and follows, but his own conscience is never unaware of why he persists in that creed and what, in fact, prevents him from understanding and admitting its error and falsity.

An unjust, wicked, dishonest, unmoral and corrupt person can even suppress the voice of his own conscience by inventing one or another excuse so that it may stop reproaching him and should be satisfied that he is doing whatever he is doing only because of certain compulsions, expediencies and genuine needs, but despite this he has in any case the knowledge of what wrong he has committed against a certain person, how he has deprived another of his rights, how he deceived still another and that unlawful methods he used to gain what he has gained. Therefore, at the time when one appears in the court of the Hereafter, every disbeliever, every hypocrite, every wicked person and culprit will himself be knowing what he has done in the world and for what crime he stands before his God.

The Sentence

According to God's instructions, all humans are potential human beings who are supposed to serve one purpose and one mission. Thus whether or not they are human and worthy of peace will be confirmed. If not, then this creation will be directed to the purpose they have chosen for themselves. There is no longer a place in the kingdom of God for criminals except in the prison of Hell.

The sentence they encounter is the long life in Hell. It will be of the same quality they are used to in this life but in the standard of Hell. The exact standard depends on the amount of abuse of the property that depends on each one's actions.

وَلَنُذِيقَنَّهُمْ مِّنَ الْعَذَابِ الْأَدْنَى دُونَ الْعَذَابِ الْأَكْبَرِ لَعَلَّهُمْ يَرْجِعُونَ

(32:21) We shall certainly have them taste some chastisement in this world in addition to the greater chastisement (of the Hereafter);

perhaps they will retract (from their transgression).[186]

Without the possibility of even dying again, God will provide them with means to survive such as eating, drinking, blaming, fighting, having conflicts, and regretting.

God will leave them the same kind of soul that they used to have regarding religion, hate, and inner strife, but He will give them a more sustainable physical quality that can handle the physical reality of Hell. The current skin cannot resist the heat and after the third degree burn there is no pain anymore, God (the Creator) will constantly replace this skin with another that keeps the pain sensation intact.

إِنَّ الَّذِينَ كَفَرُوا بِآيَاتِنَا سَوْفَ نُصْلِيهِمْ نَارًا كُلَّمَا نَضِجَتْ جُلُودُهُم بَدَّلْنَاهُمْ جُلُودًا غَيْرَهَا لِيَذُوقُوا الْعَذَابَ إِنَّ اللَّهَ كَانَ عَزِيزًا حَكِيمًا

(4:56) Surely We shall cast those who reject Our signs into the Fire; and as often as their skins are burnt out, We shall give them other skins

---

[186] "The greater punishment" is the torment of the Hereafter, which will be imposed on the guilty ones in consequence of disbelief and disobedience. "Nearer punishment", in contrast, implies those calamities which afflict man even in this world, e.g., diseases in the life of individuals, deaths of the near and dear ones, serious accidents, losses, failures, etc. and storms, earthquakes, floods, epidemics, famines, riots, wars and many other disasters, in collective life, which affect hundreds of thousands of the people simultaneously. The reason given for sending these calamities is that the people should take heed even before they are involved in the "greater torment" and give up the attitude and way of life in consequence of which they will have to suffer the greater torment ultimately.

In other words, it means this: Allah has not kept man in perfect security in the world so that he may live in full peace, and become involved in the misunderstanding that there is no power above him, which can cause him harm. But Allah has so arranged things that He sends disasters and calamities on individuals as well as on nations and countries from time to time, which give man the feeling that he is helpless and that there is about him an All- Powerful Sovereign Who is ruling His universal kingdom. These calamities remind each individual and groups and nation that there is another Power above them Who is controlling their destinies. Everything has not been placed at man's disposal. The real Power is in the hand of the Sovereign. When a calamity from Him descends on man, you can neither avert it by any artifice, nor can escape from it by invoking a jinn, or a spirit, or a god or goddess, or a prophet or saint. Considered in this light, these calamities are not mere calamities but warnings of God, which are sent to make man conscious of the reality and to remove his misunderstandings. If man learns a lesson from these and corrects his belief and conduct here in the world, he will not have to face the greater torment of God in the Hereafter.

in exchange that they may fully taste the chastisement. Surely Allah is All-Mighty, All-Wise.

Universal Argument 1

We are addressing here some universal arguments just in case you haven't read any page of the book yet and accidentally opened this section to read. Then you began to wonder why, if God is merciful, he would punish people in Hell. This question is exactly similar to the question: isn't this inhumane, that is coming from someone, who has started to feel uncomfortable with the fact that the authorities have put people behind bars like dangerous animals.

God is patient and truthful and this is how He is doing it. What about mercy? You can ask for mercy, but that request must be polite and timely before it's too late. Too late means just before the last breath.

On the authority of Anas bin Malik: the Messenger of God, may God's prayers and peace be upon him said:

عن أنس بن مالك ـ رضي الله عنه ـ قال: قال رسول الله ـ صلى الله عليه وسلم» :ـ ـللَّهُ أَشَدُّ فَرَحًا بِتَوْبَةِ عَبْدِهِ حِين يَتُوبُ إِلَيْهِ، مِنْ أَحَدِكُمْ كَانَ عَلَى رَاحِلَتِهِ بِأَرْض فَلَاةٍ، فَانْفَلَتَتْ مِنْهُ وَعَلَيْهَا طَعَامُهُ وَشَرَابُهُ، فَأَيِسَ مِنْهَا، فَأَتَى شَجَرَةً، فَاضْطَجَعَ فِي ظِلِّهَا، وقَدْ أَيِسَ مِنْ رَاحِلَتِهِ، فَبَيْنَا هُوَ كَذَلِكَ إِذَا هُوَ بِهَا، قَائِمَةً عِنْدَهُ، فَأَخَذَ بِخِطَامِهَا، ثُمَّ قَالَ مِنْ شِدَّةِ الْفَرَحِ: اللهُمَّ أَنْتَ عَبْدِي وَأَنَا رَبُّكَ! أَخْطَأَ مِنْ شِدَّةِ الْفَرَح

"Verily, Allah is more pleased with the repentance of His slave than a person who has his camel in a waterless desert carrying his provision of food and drink and it is lost. He, having lost all hopes (to get that back), lies down in shade and is disappointed about his camel; when all of a sudden he finds that camel standing before him. He takes hold of its reins and then out of boundless joy blurts out: 'O Allah, You are my slave and I am Your Rubb'. He commits this mistake out of extreme joy." *Source: Al-Bukhari and Muslim*

Is the story of Hell too big to be true? It is true. Why? Because God knows that some will say that, and God replied: It is true!

وَيَسْتَنْبِؤُونَكَ أَحَقٌّ هُوَ ۖ قُلْ إِى وَرَبِّى إِنَّهُ لَحَقٌّ ۖ وَمَا أَنْتُمْ بِمُعْجِزِينَ

(10:53) They ask you if what you say is true? Tell them: 'Yes, by my Lord, this is altogether true, and you have no power to prevent the chastisement from befalling.'

And He knows that some will laugh at the believer.

إِنَّ الَّذِينَ أَجْرَمُوا كَانُوا مِنَ الَّذِينَ آمَنُوا يَضْحَكُونَ

(83:29) Behold, the wicked were wont to laugh at the believers:

وَإِذَا مَرُّوا بِهِمْ يَتَغَامَزُونَ

(83:30) when they passed by them they winked,

وَإِذَا انْقَلَبُوا إِلَى أَهْلِهِمُ انْقَلَبُوا فَكِهِينَ

(83:31) and when they went back to their families, they went back jesting,[187]

وَإِذَا رَأَوْهُمْ قَالُوا إِنَّ هَؤُلَاءِ لَضَالُّونَ

(83:32) and when they saw the believers, they said: "Lo! These are the erring ones";

Universal Argument 2

Do some Muslims go to Hell also? Why do the non-submissive ones stay in Hell forever? What about the believers who have submitted to another kind of god?

Muslims, submissive by definition, realize it is acting on it that counts, not the name alone. According to God, people are either agreeable (submissive) or disagreeable. They are disagreeable because they didn't

---

[187] That is, they returned home rejoicing, thinking that they had made fun of such and such a Muslim, had passed evil remarks against him and subjected him to ridicule among the people.

submit to Him but invented another god to submit for. And some in this group didn't submit to any god but chose to submit to their egos. All the disagreeable have been misled by Satan and are considered to have responded to his call.

The others, who submitted, are considered sincere. They kept their promise to God, kept his trust and worked hard to return it back peacefully.

All those, from Adam until the end of life, who agreed to surrender their trust to the only God are called Muslims. The instructions on how to bring this into action have kept updating since Adam until the last Messenger. Over time these instructions have had different names under the category of religion.

إِنَّ الدِّينَ عِنْدَ اللهِ الْإِسْلَامُ وَمَا اخْتَلَفَ الَّذِينَ أُوتُوا الْكِتَبَ إِلَّا مِنْ بَعْدِ مَا جَاءَهُمُ الْعِلْمُ بَغْيًا ۢ بَيْنَهُمْ ۗ وَمَنْ يَكْفُرْ بِآيَتِ اللهِ فَإِنَّ اللهَ سَرِيعُ الْحِسَابِ

(3:19) The true religion with Allah is Islam. The People of the Book adopted many different ways rather than follow the true way of Islam even after the knowledge of truth had reached them, and this merely to commit excesses against one another. Let him who refuses to follow the ordinances and directives of Allah know that Allah is swift in His reckoning.[188]

Let me ask you a question. What do you call God now? Do you call Him only a God? Or my God? Or perhaps you don't call Him at all.

If you call him "my God" this means that you belong to the category of Muslims and if you disobey Him, you will bear the consequences. You will serve your sentence and then by His mercy receive a place in Heaven.

مَنْ عَمِلَ صَالِحًا فَلِنَفْسِهِ وَمَنْ أَسَاءَ فَعَلَيْهَا ۗ وَمَا رَبُّكَ بِظَلَّامٍ لِّلْعَبِيدِ

(41:46) Whoever does good, does so to his own benefit; and whoever does evil, will suffer its evil consequence. Your Lord does no wrong to His servants.[189]

If you only call Him God but have chosen another God for yourself, you will have the right in Hell to call your God and ask for help to get you out. But the true God told you that you will be surprised that your answer will come from Satan.

---

[188] In the sight of God there is only one system of life and way of conduct which is both in accord with reality and morally right. This consists of man's acknowledging God as his Lord and the sole object of his worship and devotion; of surrendering himself unreservedly to God in obedience and service. In doing so he should follow in to the guidance communicated by God through His Messengers rather than try to devise ways of serving God according to his own plights. This mode of thought and action is known as Islam, and it is only reasonable that the Lord and Creator of the universe should accept nothing less from His creatures and servants. In his folly man thinks that he has the right to believe in and follow every doctrine that comes his way whether it be atheism or idolatry. In the sight of the Sovereign of the universe, however, all such attitudes amount to nothing short of rebellion against God.

This shows that the religion of every Messenger of God, in every age and clime, was none other than Islam (submission to God). Likewise, every Divine book, in whichever language it was revealed, and to whichever people it was addressed, contained the teachings of Islam. The various religions which have spread among mankind are distortions of this true, original religion, and are the result of tampering. Coveting privileges over and above those to which they were entitled, people altered the beliefs, principles and injunctions of the true religion in a manner conducive to their own interests.

[189] That is, your Lord can never be so unjust as to let go to waste the good deeds of a good man and fail to punish the evil-doers for their evil.

وَمِنَ النَّاسِ مَنْ يَتَّخِذُ مِنْ دُونِ اللهِ أَنْدَادًا يُحِبُّونَهُمْ كَحُبِّ اللهِ ۖ وَالَّذِينَ آمَنُوا أَشَدُّ حُبًّا لِلَّهِ ۖ وَلَوْ يَرَى الَّذِينَ ظَلَمُوا إِذْ يَرَوْنَ الْعَذَابَ أَنَّ الْقُوَّةَ لِلَّهِ جَمِيعًا وَأَنَّ اللهَ شَدِيدُ الْعَذَابِ

(2:165) Yet there are some who take others as equals to Allah and love them as Allah alone should be loved; but those who (truly) believe, they love Allah more than all else. If only the wrong-doers were to perceive now – as they will perceive when they will see the chastisement – that all power belongs to Allah alone, and that Allah is severe in chastisement![190]

إِذْ تَبَرَّأَ الَّذِينَ اتُّبِعُوا مِنَ الَّذِينَ اتَّبَعُوا وَرَأَوُا الْعَذَابَ وَ تَقَطَّعَتْ بِهِمُ الْأَسْبَابُ

(2:166) At that moment those who have been followed will disown their followers, and they will see the chastisement, and their resources will be cut asunder.

وَقَالَ الَّذِينَ اتَّبَعُوا لَوْ أَنَّ لَنَا كَرَّةً فَنَتَبَرَّأَ مِنْهُمْ كَمَا تَبَرَّءُوا مِنَّا ۗ كَذٰلِكَ يُرِيهِمُ اللهُ أَعْمَالَهُمْ حَسَرَاتٍ عَلَيْهِمْ وَمَا هُمْ بِخَارِجِينَ مِنَ النَّارِ

(2:167) And the followers will then say: "Oh if only we might return

---

[190] There are certain attributes which belong exclusively to God. Moreover, there are certain duties that man owes to God by virtue of His being his Lord. The indictment of the Qur'an is that the people in question ascribe to others than God the attributes which are exclusively His and likewise consider others to be the rightful claimants of certain rights over man which belong only to God. To be Lord of the entire complex of causal relationships found in the universe, to dispense the needs and requirements of people, to deliver them from distress and affliction, to heed complaints and respond to lamentations and prayers, and having full knowledge of all that is apparent as well as all that is hidden, are the exclusive attributes of God.

Furthermore, there are certain rights which God alone may claim: that His creatures should recognize Him alone as their Sovereign, prostrate themselves before Him alone in recognition of their bondage to Him, turn to Him alone for the fulfilment of their prayers, call Him alone for help and succour, place their trust is none save Him, centre their hopes and expectations only in His Munificence, and fear Him alone both in public and in private.

In the same way, being the only Absolute Sovereign of the universe, it befits none save God to lay down what is permitted and what is prohibited for His subjects, to prescribe their rights and duties, to command them what to do and what not to do, to direct them as to how the energy and resources bestowed on them, by God, should be expended.

Again, it is God alone Who can ask His subjects to acknowledge His sovereignty, to accept His commands as the source of law, to consider Him alone to be the Lord entitled to command men, to consider His commands supreme, and to turn to Him alone for correct guidance. Whoever either ascribes to any being other than God any of the aforementioned attributes or recognizes the claim of anyone save God to be entitled to any of the above-mentioned rights over His creatures is in fact setting up that being as a rival to God, and placing him on the same place as God. By the same token, any individual or institution claiming to possess any of the exclusive attributes and rights of God (as mentioned above), is in fact claiming a position parallel and equal to that of God even though the claim to godhead may not have been categorically spelled out.

True faith requires that a man should give absolute priority to seeking God's good pleasure and should hold nothing too dear to sacrifice for the sake of God.

again, we would disown them as they have disowned us?" Thus Allah will show them their works in a manner causing them bitter regrets. Never will they come out of the Fire.

وَقَالَ الشَّيْطٰنُ لَمَّا قُضِيَ الْأَمْرُ إِنَّ اللهَ وَعَدَكُمْ وَعْدَ الْحَقِّ وَوَعَدْتُّكُمْ فَأَخْلَفْتُكُمْ ۖ وَمَا كَانَ لِيَ عَلَيْكُمْ مِّنْ سُلْطٰنٍ إِلَّا أَنْ دَعَوْتُكُمْ فَاسْتَجَبْتُمْ لِيَ ۖ فَلَا تَلُومُونِيْ وَلُومُوْا أَنْفُسَكُمْ ۖ مَا أَنَا بِمُصْرِخِكُمْ وَمَا أَنْتُمْ بِمُصْرِخِيَّ ۖ إِنِّيْ كَفَرْتُ بِمَا أَشْرَكْتُمُوْنِ مِنْ قَبْلُ ۖ إِنَّ الظّٰلِمِيْنَ لَهُمْ عَذَابٌ أَلِيْمٌ

(14:22) After the matter has been finally decided Satan will say: "Surely whatever Allah promised you was true; as for me, I went back on the promise I made to you. I had no power over you except that I called you to my way and you responded to me. So, do not blame me but blame yourselves. Here, neither I can come to your rescue, nor can you come to mine. I disavow your former act of associating me in the past with Allah. A grievous chastisement inevitably lies ahead for such wrong-doers."

Universal Argument 3

Who would deny God in the first place and ignore His message? Then it is not correct to talk about God's mercy and justice. We will not discuss something that is not in their perception. This means that for now they do not have to worry about His punishment.

They turned a blind eye to Him, as if they had not seen anything. Later when they face the reality, God will make them blind because they overlooked His written messages and His signature, in their brains, psyches, the universe as well as in science.

قَالَ رَبِّ لِمَ حَشَرْتَنِيَ أَعْمٰى وَقَدْ كُنْتُ بَصِيْرًا

(20:125) where-upon he will say: "Lord! Why have You raised me blind when I had sight in the world?"

قَالَ كَذٰلِكَ أَتَتْكَ اٰيٰتُنَا فَنَسِيْتَهَا ۖ وَكَذٰلِكَ الْيَوْمَ تُنْسٰى

(20:126) He will say: "Even so it is. Our Signs came to you and you

373

ignored them. So shall you be ignored this Day."[191]

At this point this person is considered to have no identity, he can't tell who he is Where did he come from? What does he understand about life? What is its purpose? Doesn't he have a life story? About the life that has already disappeared.

وَمَا قَدَرُوا اللَّهَ حَقَّ قَدْرِهِ ۚ وَالْأَرْضُ جَمِيعًا قَبْضَتُهُ يَوْمَ الْقِيَمَةِ وَالسَّمَوَاتُ مَطْوِيَّاتٌ بِيَمِينِهِ ۚ سُبْحَنَهُ وَتَعَالَى عَمَّا يُشْرِكُونَ

(39:67) They did not recognise the true worth of Allah. (Such is Allah's power that) on the Day of Resurrection the whole earth will be in His grasp, and the heavens shall be folded up in His Right Hand. Glory be to Him! Exalted be He from all that they associate with Him. Also, for the sake of logic., let's ponder the following. What do you do with a broken phone? It was supposed to make smart things happen but suddenly it no longer has any purpose! No connection, no calls, no internet, just the screen working without any apps, that's it! Do you consider it a phone? Or do you treat it as a piece of metal or stone! The denying people will be treated with the same logic!

إِنَّ الَّذِينَ كَفَرُوا لَنْ تُغْنِيَ عَنْهُمْ أَمْوَالُهُمْ وَلَا أَوْلَادُهُمْ مِنَ اللَّهِ شَيْئًا ۚ وَأُولَئِكَ هُمْ وَقُودُ النَّارِ

---

[191] The Quran has described the different conditions and experiences through which the criminals will pass from the Day of Resurrection to the time of their entry into Hell: You were neglectful of this, now We have removed the curtain from before you and your sight has become very sharp. He is only deferring them to the Day when all eyes shall stare with consternation. They will be running in terror with heads uplifted and eyes fixed upwards and hearts void.

We have fastened the augury of every man to his own neck and on the Day of Resurrection We will bring forth a writing which he will find like an open book. It will be said to him: Here is your record: read it. Today you can yourself reckon your account. It appears that in the Hereafter, the criminals shall be enabled to see the horrible sights and to realize the consequences of their evil deeds, but in other respects they will be like the blind man who cannot see his way and is deprived of even a staff to feel his way, nor is there anyone to guide him. So he stumbles and is knocked about and does not know where to go and how to satisfy his needs. This very state has been expressed thus: You forgot Our Revelations when they came to you, so you are being forgotten today, as if, you were blind and had no one to look after you.

(3:10) Those who disbelieve, neither their wealth nor their offspring will avail them at all against Allah, and it is they who will be the fuel of the Fire

Dishonesty and Denial

God promised to forgive any mistakes except betraying the trust, lying and denial. God does not want to punish anyone except these ones.

مَا يَفْعَلُ اللهُ بِعَذَابِكُمْ إِنْ شَكَرْتُمْ وَأَمَنْتُمْ ۚ وَكَانَ اللهُ شَاكِرًا عَلِيمًا

(4:147) Why should Allah deal chastisement to you if you are grateful to Him and believe? Allah is All-Appreciative, All-Knowing.[192]

The entire story is about honesty and truth. This is basically the essential core of Islam. God made the religion based on the honest

---

[192] Shukr denotes an acknowledgement of benefaction and a feeling of gratitude. This verse states if a person does not behave ungratefully towards God then there is no reason why God should punish him.

The attitude of gratefulness to God consists of acknowledging His benefaction in one's heart, in confessing it in one's speech and by manifesting it in one's deeds. It is the sum-total of these which is termed shukr. This attitude requires:

(1) that a person should ascribe the benefaction to its real source, letting no one share in either the gratitude or the acknowledgement of benevolence;

(2) that his heart should be overflowing with love for, and loyalty to, the Benefactor, and that he should have no attachment to His opponents;

(3) that he should obey the Benefactor and should not use His bounties contrary to His directives.

The word used here is shakir which we have translated as 'All-Appreciative'. In the context of the God-man relationship, when the word shukr is used in respect of God, it denotes 'appreciation of services'. When it is used in respect of man, it denotes his acknowledgement of God's benefaction and his sense of gratitude to Him. To say that God 'thanks' His creatures stresses that God is fully appreciative of the services which His servants have rendered and will recompense them liberally. This contrasts sharply with the attitude of human beings, who are generally slow and uncharitable in appreciating the services rendered to them, and quick and severe in censuring people for their omissions. As for God, He is lenient and prone to overlook man's omissions. On the contrary, He rewards man manifold for his good deeds.

truth: there is no god but God.

What does it mean for life or for someone without honesty? What is the value of a person who keeps denying the truth? What kind of harmony, love and peace can be expected from this person? What kind of scientist, doctor, engineer, politician, artist, lawyer, judge can he be? What kind of spouse, parent or teacher is he without sincerity?

How do you convince someone to be reliable and honest, if he keeps playing around and refuses to admit the truth? How to change that person's frontal lobe with which he has gotten used to lying? God has told that they would be dragged from the frontal lobe if they won't stop lying and denying!

أَرَءَيْتَ اِنْ كَذَّبَ وَتَوَلّٰىۙ

(96:13) Did you consider: what if he gives the lie (to the Truth) and turns away (from it)?

اَلَمْ يَعْلَمْ بِاَنَّ اللهَ يَرٰىؕ

(96:14) Does he not know that Allah sees everything?

كَلَّا لَىِٕنْ لَّمْ يَنْتَهِ ۙ لَنَسْفَعًۢا بِالنَّاصِيَةِۙ

(96:15) No indeed; if he does not desist, We shall drag him by the forelock;

نَاصِيَةٍ كَاذِبَةٍ خَاطِئَةٍ

(96:16) by the lying forelock steeped in sin.

That really is the whole story. That's all God wants us to learn: be sincere, admit the truth, then talk to Him openly and ask any question. You will see that He has perfect answers for you and that He gives you exactly what you are looking for, may it be freedom, honor, respect, pleasure, love, peace or something else.

Do you like honesty? This is the honesty!

قَالَ اللهُ هٰذَا يَوْمُ يَنْفَعُ الصّٰدِقِيْنَ صِدْقُهُمْؕ لَهُمْ جَنّٰتٌ تَجْرِىْ مِنْ تَحْتِهَا الْاَنْهٰرُ خٰلِدِيْنَ فِيْهَا اَبَدًاؕ رَضِىَ اللهُ عَنْهُمْ وَرَضُوْا عَنْهُؕ ذٰلِكَ الْفَوْزُ الْعَظِيْمُ

(5:119) Thereupon Allah will say: "This day truthfulness shall profit the truthful. For them are Gardens beneath which rivers flow. There they will abide for ever. Allah is well-pleased with them, and they are well-pleased with Allah. That indeed is the mighty triumph.'

What is Love?

Dear Reader, please note that I will only use the pronoun 'you' just for the sake of explanation, but this has nothing to do with you yourself personally. Thank you.

You may be wondering what love is? But I'm interested why are you asking for it? Why do you need it? If you still believe that life is only what you see and what you eat, then the quality of love which you have now, should be enough for this limited understanding about the purpose of life.

Imagine love being a heavenly quality, a true quality! Anything you might be experiencing now or will later, is anything but love. True Love is permanent everlasting peace without impurities, fear of loss, sadness or anxiety. It's pure sweetness! Does what you think of life fit this definition of love? If not, there is no truth in your life, and this is why there is no love.

Why Can't You Find Love?

If you ask where is the love, I ask again, where is the honesty? Honesty, truth, harmony, peace and love are not separate things, it is all one thing. This can't come from negotiations, deals or synthetic pills you buy at a drugstore. It also doesn't come from oil you steal, knowledge you copy, land you occupy, false values you pretend, a movement you initiate, or an activist you follow.

The truth is a fact that many are not willing to admit. That is, they will keep spinning and turning, wondering where the love is. We will not find it alone, because living is like a coin with two sides, one is love (oxygen) and the other light. You cannot take one side and leave the other. The more time passes, the more people experience stress and phobias due to the feelings of suffocation and tightness. Anything for them can be a cause of phobia: any loss, disease, shout or piece of news. Even Muslims, when they are speaking about islamophilia, can bring on a phobia!

Bravo! Yes, you remembered right. It is Satan and his students who work in this way. Now you are even more familiar with his tricks!

If You Feel No Shame, Then Do Whatever You Like

No one in the last 800 years has been successful to talk about love as much as Mawlānā Jalāl ad-Dīn Muḥammad Rūmī'. Does it mean he was able to teach it? Will anyone who reads all of his poetry reach the same love as him? No. And again we ask why? Why? Because his work is translated from Persian to English without honesty?

The translation in English is fake. The translator is not honest, he took the words out of their context and other words have been changed completely. In the end no one will understand that Rumi was talking about God, sincerity and submitting. And these fake books are the best-selling books in the USA? *https://www.rumiwasmuslim.com/*

On the authority of Abu Masood Uqbah bin 'Amr al-Ansaree al-Badree (may Allah be pleased with him) who said: the Messenger of Allah (peace and blessings of Allah be upon him) said:

عَنْ أَبِي مَسْعُودٍ عُقْبَةَ بْنِ عَمْرِو الْأَنْصَارِيِّ الْبَدْرِيِّ رَضِيَ اللهُ عَنْهُ قَالَ: قَالَ رَسُولُ اللهِ صلى الله عليه و سلم" إِنَّ مِمَّا أَدْرَكَ النَّاسُ مِنْ كَلَامِ النُّبُوَّةِ الْأُولَى :إِذَا لَمْ تَسْتَحِ فَاصْنَعْ مَا شِئْت. "

"Verily, from what was learnt by the people from the speech of the earliest prophecy is: If you feel no shame, then do as you wish." *Source: Al-Bukhari*

Where is The Love?

Our bodies indeed breathe the air and see the light of the sun. For the souls, love is the oxygen of life, and the truth is the sun. If the soul is in life without love and truth, it is trapped like in an underwater dark cave.

It is a matter of time how much phobias you will experience, it's actually an equation! It depends on a few variables: how much love you have had, how much struggle in life you have now, and how long you will survive. Nowadays, we have the biggest alarm ever because of deprivation from love. There is a continuing increase in the number of young people around the world who commit suicide. Youngsters and children go through extreme distress in search of love and care, and this is because adults do not have it themselves, they themselves are almost gasping.

Surprisingly we carry "the coin of life" all the time inside us, but we never check it. We carry love and truth in our hearts all the time, but we never think about it. If you listen to your weeping soul it will tell you the truth. We've all been underwater in the dark cave (in the womb) with one oxygen mask for the body and one for the soul. When we are born the nurse cuts the umbilical cord and you breathe on your own. This is the body that is born. But the soul stays connected, it's not on its own. It has to be connected all the time. Unlike the body, the soul has to breathe voluntarily, of your own will. Love can't be enforced!

وَلَقَدْ خَلَقْنَا الْإِنْسَانَ وَنَعْلَمُ مَا تُوَسْوِسُ بِهِ نَفْسُهُ ۖ وَنَحْنُ أَقْرَبُ إِلَيْهِ مِنْ حَبْلِ الْوَرِيدِ

(50:16) Surely We have created man, and We know the promptings of his heart, and We are nearer to him than even his jugular vein.

Some even deny the soul, which carries them all the time and as soon as it will leave permanently, the body will get buried. The soul is a breath of God that eases our breathing, and its breathing is love of God. The body is from God through your parents to you, but the soul is always and forever directly from God to you. So, who is closest to you? Who is loving you the most? Who should you love the most?

وَإِذْ قَالَ رَبُّكَ لِلْمَلَـٰئِكَةِ إِنِّي خَالِقٌ بَشَرًا مِّن صَلْصَالٍ مِّنْ حَمَإٍ مَّسْنُونٍ

(15:28) Recall when your Lord said to the angels: "I will indeed bring into being a human being out of dry ringing clay wrought from black mud.

فَإِذَا سَوَّيْتُهُ وَنَفَخْتُ فِيهِ مِن رُّوحِي فَقَعُوا لَهُ سَـٰجِدِينَ

(15:29) When I have completed shaping him and have breathed into him of My Spirit, then fall you down before him in prostration."[193]

فَسَجَدَ الْمَلَـٰئِكَةُ كُلُّهُمْ أَجْمَعُونَ

(15:30) So, the angels - all of them - fell down in prostration,

إِلَّا إِبْلِيسَ أَبَىٰ أَن يَكُونَ مَعَ السَّـٰجِدِينَ

(15:31) except Iblis; he refused to join those who prostrated.

قَالَ يَـٰإِبْلِيسُ مَا لَكَ أَلَّا تَكُونَ مَعَ السَّـٰجِدِينَ

---

[193] "And have breathed into him of My Spirit" means when I have cast a reflection of My divine characteristics on him. This shows that the soul of man implies life, knowledge, power, will, discretion and other human characteristics in the aggregate. These are in reality a slight reflection of divine characteristics that have been cast on the human body, which was originally created from dried clay. And it is this divine reflection on the human body which has raised him to the position of the vicegerent of Allah and made him that worthy being before whom angels and every earthly thing should bow down.

As a matter of fact, the source of each characteristic of everything is one divine characteristic or the other, as is borne by a tradition: Allah divided mercy into one hundred parts: then He reserved ninety-nine parts for Himself and sent down the remaining one part to the earth. It is because of that one part that the creatures show mercy to one another. So much so that it is due to this that an animal refrains from placing the hoof on its young ones.

In this connection one has to be on strict guard against the notion that the possession of a part of any divine characteristic amounts to the possession of a part of Godhead. This is because Godhead is absolutely beyond the reach of each and every creation.

(15:32) The Lord inquired: "Iblis! What is the matter with you that you did not join those who prostrated?"

قَالَ لَمْ اَكُنْ لِّاَسْجُدَ لِبَشَرٍ خَلَقْتَهُ مِنْ صَلْصَالٍ مِّنْ حَمَإٍ مَّسْنُونٍ

(15:33) He said: "It does not behove of me to prostrate myself before a human being whom You have created out of dry ringing clay wrought from black mud."

قَالَ فَاخْرُجْ مِنْهَا فَاِنَّكَ رَجِيمٌ

(15:34) The Lord said: "Then get out of here; you are rejected,

وَّاِنَّ عَلَيْكَ اللَّعْنَةَ اِلٰى يَوْمِ الدِّينِ

(15:35) and there shall be a curse upon you till the Day of Recompense."[194]

قَالَ رَبِّ فَاَنْظِرْنِيٓ اِلٰى يَوْمِ يُبْعَثُونَ

(15:36) Iblis said: "My Lord! Grant me respite till the Day when they will be resurrected."

قَالَ فَاِنَّكَ مِنَ الْمُنْظَرِينَ

(15:37) Allah said: "For sure you are granted respite

اِلٰى يَوْمِ الْوَقْتِ الْمَعْلُومِ

(15:38) until the day of a known time."

قَالَ رَبِّ بِمَآ اَغْوَيْتَنِيْ لَاُزَيِّنَنَّ لَهُمْ فِى الْاَرْضِ وَلَاُغْوِيَنَّهُمْ اَجْمَعِينَ

(15:39) Iblis said: "My Lord! In the manner You led me to error, I will make things on earth seem attractive to them and lead all of them to error,

اِلَّا عِبَادَكَ مِنْهُمُ الْمُخْلَصِينَ

(15:40) except those of Your servants whom You have singled out for Yourself."

قَالَ هٰذَا صِرَاطٌ عَلَيَّ مُسْتَقِيمٌ

(15:41) Allah said: "Here is the path that leads straight to Me.

---

[194] That is, you shall remain accursed up to the Resurrection. Then you shall be punished for your disobedience on the Day of Judgment.

اِنَّ عِبَادِىْ لَيْسَ لَكَ عَلَيْهِمْ سُلْطٰنٌ اِلَّا مَنِ اتَّبَعَكَ مِنَ الْغٰوِيْنَ

(15:42) Over My true servants you will be able to exercise no power, your power will be confined to the erring ones, those who choose to follow you.

وَاِنَّ جَهَنَّمَ لَمَوْعِدُهُمْ اَجْمَعِيْنَ

(15:43) Surely Hell is the promised place for all of them."

لَهَا سَبْعَةُ اَبْوَابٍ لِكُلِّ بَابٍ مِّنْهُمْ جُزْءٌ مَّقْسُوْمٌ

(15:44) There are seven gates in it, and to each gate a portion of them has been allotted.[195]

If you keep denying the fact, you make a decision to suffocate your soul. If you are still asking where is love and mercy, let your soul breathe. Be honest! Be loyal! Do you now understand why God will call some, after their last breath in their bodies, criminals?

اَلَّذِيْنَ اٰمَنُوْا وَتَطْمَئِنُّ قُلُوْبُهُمْ بِذِكْرِ اللهِ اَلَا بِذِكْرِ اللهِ تَطْمَئِنُّ الْقُلُوْبُ

(13:28) Such are the ones who believe (in the message of the Prophet) and whose hearts find rest in the remembrance of Allah. Surely in Allah's remembrance do hearts find rest.

اَلَّذِيْنَ اٰمَنُوْا وَعَمِلُوا الصّٰلِحٰتِ طُوْبٰى لَهُمْ وَحُسْنُ مَاٰبٍ

(13:29) So those who believe (in the message of the Truth) and do good are destined for happiness and a blissful end.

What is The Nationality of Islam?

Do you think that Islam is for Muslims or Arabs only? Or that you have to be born as a Muslim to be a Muslim? This is not Islam at all.

---

[195] Sinners will be divided into different groups in accordance with their different sins for their entry into Hell from seven different gates specified for each different sin. For instance, the group of atheists shall enter into Hell by one of the seven gates specified for their group. Likewise, mushriks, hypocrites, self-seekers, sensualists, tyrants, propagandists and leaders of disbelief etc. shall each enter into Hell through the gates specified for their group.

In fact, the last version of the religion, which is known as Islam, began when the people were adults, who did not have a religion before or were of another religion. Islam is a process of thinking and feeling and not a transition of genes. As a matter of fact, Islam does not encourage genetic passage at all, it just totally depends on your free thinking and actions.

Even if you were born as a Muslim, you have to review and filter the Islam you received through your genes and go back only to the original. This is the process of self-purification. This process and the preservation of Islam are guaranteed by God.

إِنَّا نَحْنُ نَزَّلْنَا الذِّكْرَ وَإِنَّا لَهُ لَحَافِظُونَ

(15:9) As for the Admonition, indeed it is We Who have revealed it and it is indeed We Who are its guardians.[196]

Live by The Truth in The Lying World

There are very interesting stories about people who entered, and who left Islam. You should know about these stories. You will see that it is a very dynamic process, hearts are constantly being filtered in order to discover only the loyal. The amount of those, who are lost in a lying life, and who have been defeated by Satan, is greater than you can imagine.

وَلَا تُخْزِنِي يَوْمَ يُبْعَثُونَ

(26:87) and disgrace me not on the Day when people will be raised to

---

[196] That is, you should note it well that it is We Who have sent down this zikr. Thus it is not Our Messenger whom you are calling insane but in fact this abusive remark applies to Us. Moreover, you should know that it is Our Word and We are preserving it. Therefore, you can do no harm to it, nor can you discredit it by your ridicules, taunts and objections, nor can you hamper its progress. Whatever you may do against it, no one will ever be able to change or tamper with it.

life,[197]

يَوْمَ لَا يَنفَعُ مَالٌ وَّلَا بَنُوْنَ

(26:88) the Day when nothing will avail, neither wealth nor offspring,

إِلَّا مَنْ أَتَى اللهَ بِقَلْبٍ سَلِيْمٍ

(26:89) but only he that brings to Allah a sound heart will (attain to success)."[198]

What Does "Ours" Mean?

All this leads us to the fact that Islam is not mine, not yours, not theirs. Islam is ours. But who is included in "ours"? I'm not only talking about us as human beings but also about Jinns. What are Jinns? They are one of the creatures around us but we cannot see them, because they are beyond our senses.

قُلْ أُوْحِيَ إِلَيَّ أَنَّهُ اسْتَمَعَ نَفَرٌ مِّنَ الْجِنِّ فَقَالُوْا إِنَّا سَمِعْنَا قُرْآنًا عَجَبًا

(72:1) Say, (O Prophet), it was revealed to me that a band of jinn attentively listened to (the recitation of the Qur'an) and then (went back to their people) and said:

يَّهْدِيَ إِلَى الرُّشْدِ فَآمَنَّا بِهِ وَلَنْ نُّشْرِكَ بِرَبِّنَا أَحَدًا

(72:2) "We have indeed heard a wonderful Qur'an which guides to the

---

[197] That is, do not put me to disgrace on the Day of Judgment by inflicting punishment on my father in front of all mankind, when I myself shall be witnessing his punishment helplessly.

[198] It cannot be said with certainty whether verses 88, 89 are a part of Prophet Abraham's (peace be upon him) prayer, or they are an addition by Allah. In the first case, they will mean that Prophet Abraham (peace be upon him) while praying for his father had a full realization of these facts. In the second case, they will be a comment by Allah on Abraham's (peace be upon him) prayer, as if to say: On the Day of Judgment, only a sound heart, sound in faith and free from disobedience and sin, will be of any avail to man and not wealth and children, for wealth and children can be useful only if one possesses a sound heart. Wealth will be useful if one would have spent it sincerely and faithfully for the sake of Allah, otherwise even a millionaire will be a poor man there. Children also will be of help only to the extent that a person might have educated them in faith and good conduct to the best of his ability; otherwise even if the son is a Prophet, his father will not escape punishment if he died in the state of unbelief, because such a father will have no share in the goodness of his children.

Right Way; so we have come to believe in it, and we will not associate aught with Our Lord in His Divinity"[199]

Our physical space is observed to have three large spatial dimensions and, along with time, is a boundless 4-dimensional continuum known as spacetime. However, nothing prevents a theory from including more than 4 dimensions. In the case of string theory, consistency requires spacetime to have 10 dimensions (3D regular space + 1 time + 6D hyperspace). *Source: The D = 10 critical dimension was originally discovered by John H. Schwarz in Schwarz, J. H. (1972). "Physical states and pomeron poles in the dual pion model". Nuclear Physics, B46(1), 61–74.*

This theory makes room for assimilating the infinite facts and creations that surround us, but we are not aware of them. One of them is the Jinns. They as well as Satan see us but we can't see them.

يَٰبَنِىٓ ءَادَمَ لَا يَفْتِنَنَّكُمُ الشَّيْطَٰنُ كَمَآ أَخْرَجَ أَبَوَيْكُم مِّنَ الْجَنَّةِ يَنزِعُ عَنْهُمَا لِبَاسَهُمَا لِيُرِيَهُمَا سَوْءَٰتِهِمَآ إِنَّهُۥ يَرَىٰكُمْ هُوَ وَقَبِيلُهُۥ مِنْ حَيْثُ لَا تَرَوْنَهُمْ إِنَّا جَعَلْنَا الشَّيَٰطِينَ أَوْلِيَآءَ لِلَّذِينَ لَا يُؤْمِنُونَ

(7:27) Children of Adam! Let not Satan deceive you in the manner he deceived your parents out of Paradise, pulling off from them their clothing to reveal to them their shame. He and his host surely see you from whence you do not see them. We have made satans the guardians

---

[199] This shows that the jinn at that time were not visible to the Prophet (peace be upon him), nor he knew that they were hearing the Quran being recited, but Allah informed him of the incident afterwards by revelation. Abdullah bin Abbas has also, in connection with this incident, stated: The Messenger (peace be upon him) of Allah had not recited the Quran before the jinn, nor did he see them.

of those who do not believe. [200]

---

[200] These verses bring into focus several important points. First, that the need to cover oneself is not an artificial urge in man; rather it is an important dictate of human nature. Unlike animals, God did not provide man with the protective covering that He provided to animals. God rather endowed man with the natural instincts of modesty and bashfulness. Moreover, the private parts of the body are not only, related to sex, but also constitute 'sawat' that is, something the exposure of which is felt to be shameful. Also, God did not provide man with a natural covering in response to man's modesty and bashfulness, but has inspired in him the urge to cover himself. This is in order that man might use his reason to understand the requirements of his nature, use the resources made available by God, and provide himself a dress.

Second, man instinctively knows that the moral purpose behind the use of dress takes precedence over the physical purpose. Hence the idea that man should resort to dress in order to cover his private parts precedes the mention of dress as a means of providing protection and adornment to the human body. In this connection man is altogether different from animals, With regard to the latter, the natural covering that has been granted serves to protect them from the inclemencies of weather and also to beautify their bodies. However, that natural covering is altogether unrelated to the purpose of concealing their sexual organs. The exposure of those organs is not a matter of shame for them and hence their nature is altogether devoid of the urge to cover them. However, as men fell prey to Satanic influences, they developed a false and unhealthy notion about the function of dress. They were led to believe that the function of dress for human beings is no different from that for animals, viz., to protect them from the inclemencies of weather and to make them look attractive. As for concealing the private parts of the body, the importance of that function has been belittled. For men have been misled into believing that their private parts are, in fact, like other organs of their body. As in the case of animals, there is little need for human beings to conceal their sex organs.

Third, the Qur'an emphasizes that it is not enough for the dress to cover the private parts and to provide protection and adornment to the human body. Man's dress ought to be the dress of piety. This means that a man's dress ought to conceal his private parts. It should also render a man reasonably presentable - the dress being neither too shabby and cheap nor overly expensive and extravagant relative to his financial standing. Nor should dress smack of pride or hauteur, or reflect that pathological mental state in which men prefer characteristically feminine dresses and vice versa: or that the people belonging to one nation mimic people of other nations so as to resemble them, thereby becoming a living emblem of collective humiliation and abasement. The Qur'anic ideal can only be achieved by those who truly believe in the Prophets and sincerely try to follow God's Guidance. For as soon as man decides to reject God's Guidance, Satan assumes his patronage and by one means or another manages to lead him into error after error.

Fourth, the question of dress constitutes one of the numerous signs of God which is visible virtually throughout the world. When the facts mentioned above are carefully considered it will be quite clear as to why dress is an important sign of God.

A Group with The Same Heart Disease

There is a mysterious group of Muslims called the hypocrites. They are, by their own will, stuck somewhere in the gray area between believers and unbelievers. They are trying to be clever. They may have been born as Muslims, but they live and act violently as if they will live on earth forever and there is no other life.

They live according to two standards. They are trying to get as much as possible in this life (Dunya) without following the contract with God. At the same time, they would still like to be compensated in the Hereafter. They were diagnosed by God with the worst heart disease: lying and cheating. God has clearly described their mentality and called them losers.

وَمِنَ النَّاسِ مَن يَقُولُ اٰمَنَّا بِاللهِ وَبِالْيَوْمِ الْاٰخِرِ وَمَا هُم بِمُؤْمِنِينَ ۟

(2:8) There are some who say: "We believe in Allah and in the Last Day," while in fact they do not believe.

يُخَادِعُونَ اللهَ وَالَّذِينَ اٰمَنُوا ۖ وَمَا يَخْدَعُونَ إِلَّا اَنفُسَهُمْ وَمَا يَشْعُرُونَ

(2:9) They are trying to deceive Allah and those who believe, but they do not realize that in truth they are only deceiving themselves.[201]

فِى قُلُوبِهِم مَّرَضٌ فَزَادَهُمُ اللهُ مَرَضًا ۖ وَلَهُمْ عَذَابٌ اَلِيمٌ بِمَا كَانُوا يَكْذِبُونَ

(2:10) There is a disease in their hearts and Allah has intensified this disease. A painful chastisement awaits them for their lying.[202]

وَإِذَا قِيلَ لَهُمْ لَا تُفْسِدُوا فِى الْاَرْضِ قَالُوا إِنَّمَا نَحْنُ مُصْلِحُونَ

---

[201] These people delude themselves that their hypocritical behaviour will profit them when in fact it will prove harmful both in this world and the Next. A hypocrite may be able to fool people for a while, but it does not last long; his hypocrisy is ultimately seen through. As for the Next Life, it is obvious that his claim to be a true believer is contradicted by his own actions and is thus quite worthless.

[202] 'Disease' here refers to the disease of hypocrisy. The statement that 'Allah has intensified this disease' means that He does not punish the hypocrites immediately but allows them to indulge in their hypocrisy and exult in the success of their ruses. This feeling of success intensifies their hypocrisy.

(2:11) Whenever they are told: "Do not spread mischief on earth," they say: "Why! We indeed are the ones who set things right."

اَلَاۤ اِنَّهُمْ هُمُ الْمُفْسِدُوْنَ وَلٰـكِنْ لَّا يَشْعُرُوْنَ

(2:12) They are the mischief makers, but they do not realize it.

وَاِذَا قِيْلَ لَهُمْ اٰمِنُوْا كَمَاۤ اٰمَنَ النَّاسُ قَالُوْۤا اَنُؤْمِنُ كَمَاۤ اٰمَنَ السُّفَهَاۤءُۙ اَلَاۤ اِنَّهُمْ هُمُ السُّفَهَاۤءُ وَلٰـكِنْ لَّا يَعْلَمُوْنَ

(2:13) Whenever they are told: "Believe as others believe," they answer: "Shall we believe as the fools have believed?" Indeed it is they who are the fools, but they are not aware of it.[203]

وَاِذَا لَقُوا الَّذِيْنَ اٰمَنُوْا قَالُوْۤا اٰمَنَّاۖ وَاِذَا خَلَوْا اِلٰى شَيٰطِيْنِهِمْۙ قَالُوْۤا اِنَّا مَعَكُمْۙ اِنَّمَا نَحْنُ مُسْتَهْزِءُوْنَ

(2:14) When they meet the believers, they say: "We believe," but when they meet their evil companions (in privacy), they say: "Surely we are with you; we were merely jesting."[204]

اَللّٰهُ يَسْتَهْزِئُ بِهِمْ وَيَمُدُّهُمْ فِيْ طُغْيَانِهِمْ يَعْمَهُوْنَ

(2:15) Allah jests with them, leaving them to wander blindly on in their rebellion.

اُولٰۤئِكَ الَّذِيْنَ اشْتَرَوُا الضَّلٰلَةَ بِالْهُدٰى فَمَا رَبِحَتْ تِّجَارَتُهُمْ وَمَا كَانُوْا مُهْتَدِيْنَ

(2:16) These are the ones who have purchased error in exchange for guidance. This bargain has brought them no profit and certainly they

---

[203] They are being asked to become Muslims in the same manner as others of their community became Muslims. They think that those people who sincerely embraced Islam and thereby exposed themselves to all kinds of trials and persecutions, and confronted risks and dangers, were merely fools. To them it seems sheer folly to invite the hostility of the entire land merely for the sake of Truth and righteousness. In their view, wisdom consists not in bothering oneself with the distinction between truth and falsehood, but in remaining concerned only with one's own interests.

[204] 'Satan' in Arabic means refractory, rebellious and headstrong, and is used for both human beings and jinn. Although this word is generally used in the Qur'an for the satans amongst the jinn, it is also used occasionally for human beings possessing satanic characteristics. The context generally explains whether the word 'satan' refers to jinn or to human beings. In this particular case the word 'satans' refers to those influential leaders of the time who were in the vanguard of opposition and hostility to Islam.

are not on the Right Way.

God is warning them and asks to consider again this miscalculation or else they will be in a worse situation than unbelievers.

This group consists of Muslims around the world. They can be in key positions, and talk about the behavior of Muslims, and Islam and have nothing to do with Islam. They are the most confusing party to all of humanity and the first helpers of Satan. Their hallmark is that they talk about what they don't do and do what they don't say.

How Do You Feel When You Become a Muslim?

You will have a new version of the moment you were born but this one you will certainly remember for the rest of your life. On this occasion you will be able to celebrate with people the first moment you breathe when your soul is seeing the light for the first time. You will experience a sudden relief of distress, and a sense of survival after a long, dark period of isolation and insecurity.

You will feel the happiness in the hearts around you, they are happy for you more than even you yourself. In this moment you will feel that you belong to a big family. You are likely to cry, perhaps straight away or later when you think about it.

فَمَنْ يُرِدِ اللهُ اَنْ يَّهْدِيَهُ يَشْرَحْ صَدْرَهُ لِلْاِسْلَامِ ۚ وَمَنْ يُّرِدْ اَنْ يُّضِلَّهُ يَجْعَلْ صَدْرَهُ ضَيِّقًا حَرَجًا كَاَنَّمَا يَصَّعَّدُ فِى السَّمَآءِ ۚ كَذٰلِكَ يَجْعَلُ اللهُ الرِّجْسَ عَلَى الَّذِيْنَ لَا يُؤْمِنُوْنَ

(6:125) Thus, (it is a fact that) whomsoever Allah wills to guide, He opens his breast for Islam; and whomsoever He wills to let go astray, He causes his breast to become strait and constricted, as if he were climbing towards the heaven. Thus Allah lays the abomination (of flight from and hatred of Islam) on those who do not believe[205]

The feelings you go through when you become a Muslim give you an intense and distinct perception of your life now in two zones, the difference is like the one of day and night. You will most likely see this line much more clearly than someone born as a Muslim. This will give you a lot of strength to hold on to what you got. You know what it's like to live without it, and you won't be willing to go back into the dark at any cost.

This will make you completely change the way you dream. It will give you the energy to move forward, to appreciate yourself and your life, to feel respected and confident. You'll believe that you can move mountains. From this moment on, you will have a safety rope, you may sail freely and with courage in life. It is a fresh start. There is no need to regret the things you did earlier, they are all deleted. You are a newborn and have the mindset, abilities, and opportunities of an adult.

Does Islam Heal All Your Psychological Pain?

Most newcomers to Islam have made the decision after they have first taken some time read and think about it. This means that they were moved by what they found. They felt something, a certain kind of emotion. They tasted the sweetness, and they would like to have more. At this point most of the feelings and thoughts you have will help you to change your energy, motivation, and appetite for life. Simply because your perception of life will be different.

For example, this stage of life in Islam is called Dunya, not Heaven. We need to wait until the next stage comes (Akhirah). This requires a

---

[205] 'To open someone's breast to Islam' means to make him feel fully convinced of the truth of Islam and to remove all his doubts, hesitations and reluctance.

little practice and living. Islam gives you a good reason to wait and tolerate various life events. Your stamina will increase over time, and your capacity as well as your body will absorb from situations differently than what you are used to. Islam is all about giving you the possibility to contribute more to your surroundings. The more effort you put in, the more comfortable you will feel here and Hereafter. At first you may have some pain but sweet pain!

You might go to the gym and put in some effort to grow your muscles or improve your fitness. That also will bring you some pain but it's satisfying. You asked for it, you wanted it, and you know it's a way to make you better. You will get used to it. You will not be able to live without the gym. You will love it, and find that pain is an illusion, not a beast!

Islam is the different programs that you are supposed to practice in Dunya (the gym) to develop your muscles (the ability to love) and get the result later (Paradise). Is your psyche feeling better now?

How Long Does It Take to Become a Muslim?

Can you guess how long it takes? How long does it take to activate the entirety of harmony's symphony, starting with the simple fusion of your left and right brain for nonstop love, and a journey of 24/7 satisfaction?

The time depends on how much time you have left in this life. If you have one minute, Islam can offer you something to do in this moment and you'll get it! And if you have ahead of you 100 years, you will have something to do in Islam, and you are never bored or getting enough! The range of programs can be counted with the fingers of one hand. Each program has a name of one word, and a description of less than one line. These are the Five Pillars of Islam. They are your way to true love without stress, here and Hereafter! Isn't the X-Harmony Factor genius?

The entire curriculum of Islam and its highest stations were taught in less than a few minutes from Jibril (Gabriel), peace be upon him, to the Prophet, peace be upon him, in front of other Muslims.

والإحسان والإيمان الإسلام

Islam, Faith and Excellence

Umar ibn al-Khattab reported: We were sitting with the Messenger of Allah, peace and blessings be upon him, one day when a man appeared with very white clothes and very black hair. There were no signs of travel on him and we did not recognize him. He sat down in front of the Prophet and rested his knees by his knees and placed his hands on his thighs. The man said, "O Muhammad, tell me about Islam." The Prophet said:

الْإِسْلَامُ أَنْ تَشْهَدَ أَنْ لَا إِلَهَ إِلَّا اللهُ وَأَنَّ مُحَمَّدًا رَسُولُ اللهِ صَلَّى اللهُ عَلَيْهِ وَسَلَّمَ وَتُقِيمَ الصَّلَاةَ وَتُؤْتِيَ الزَّكَاةَ وَتَصُومَ رَمَضَانَ وَتَحُجَّ الْبَيْتَ إِنْ اسْتَطَعْتَ إِلَيْهِ سَبِيلًا

Islam is to testify there is no God but Allah and Muhammad is the Messenger of Allah, to establish prayer, to give charity, to fast the month of Ramadan, and to perform pilgrimage to the House if a way is possible.

The man said, "You have spoken truthfully." We were surprised that he asked him and then said he was truthful. He said, "Tell me about faith." The Prophet said:

أَنْ تُؤْمِنَ بِاللهِ وَمَلَائِكَتِهِ وَكُتُبِهِ وَرُسْلِهِ وَالْيَوْمِ الْآخِرِ وَتُؤْمِنَ بِالْقَدَرِ خَيْرِهِ وَشَرِّهِ

Faith is to believe in Allah, His angels, His books, His messengers, the Last Day, and to believe in providence, its good and its evil.

392

The man said, "You have spoken truthfully. Tell me about excellence."
The Prophet said:

أَنْ تَعْبُدَ اللَّهَ كَأَنَّكَ تَرَاهُ فَإِنْ لَمْ تَكُنْ تَرَاهُ فَإِنَّهُ يَرَاكَ

Excellence is to worship Allah as if you see Him, for if you do not see
Him, He surely sees you.

During this chapter "The Deal" I was explaining the Islamic approach
according to my personal knowledge with references from the Qur'an
and Sunnah.

You will find endless resources in the internet, books and mosques to
learn the five main pillars of Islam step by step. But how about
Excellence? It's not a matter of education. Many can get you there, but
no one knows for sure whether his Excellence will work for you or
not. This is a secret between you and God alone. It's progression
within the heart. It has nothing to do with how you look or how
knowledgeable you are.

Abu Hurairah (May Allah be pleased with him) reported: the
Messenger of Allah (ﷺ) said:

وعنه قال: قال رسول الله صلى الله عليه وسلم: "رب أشعث أغبر
مدفوع بالأبواب لو أقسم على الله لأبره " ((رواه مسلم)).

"Many a person with shaggy and dusty hair, dusty and driven away
from doors (because of their poverty and shabby clothes) were to
swear by Allah (that something would happen), Allah will certainly
make it happen". *Source: Muslim*

Signs of excellence you will surely find in your life day in and day out,
but you should not be too aware or proud of it. This is the opposite of
excellence, not any kind of Islam whatsoever. This, pride, is the
signature of Satan! Very deceptive.

The Prophet, peace and blessings be upon him, is surely the most
perfect and noble, but you will not see pride in any of his actions or
words.

Ibn Mas'ud (May Allah be pleased with him) said: the Prophet (ﷺ) said:

393

وعن ابن مسعود رضي الله عنه عن النبي صلى الله عليه وسلم قال: "لا
يدخل الجنة من كان في قلبه مثقال ذرة من كبر" فقال رجل: إن الرجل
يحب أن يكون ثوبه حسنًا، ونعله حسنة، فقال: "إن الله جميل يحب
الجمال، الكبر بَطَر الحق، وغمط الناس".((رواه مسلم)).

"He who has, in his heart, an ant's weight of arrogance will not enter
Jannah." Someone said: "A man likes to wear beautiful clothes and
shoes?" Messenger of Allah (ﷺ) said, "Allah is Beautiful, He loves
beauty. Arrogance means ridiculing and rejecting the Truth and
despising people." *Source: Muslim*

If you understand that you're never perfect, that's great. The best way
is to carefully follow the answer of the Prophet (ﷺ): by seeing God all
the time. And if you can't, then remember that He sees you.

Imagine that you are dead but still alive! You will see God in the
afterlife, what would you like to feel at this moment? What would you
regret? What would you wish to have done more? Keep this picture in
your mind for as long as you can. While you're doing anything from
now on, this picture might drive you to Excellence.

Back to Breathing, Quickly

By now you should be fully familiar with the story of honesty and the
essence of mental health and well-being. This does not yet mean that
you have bought a new psyche for everlasting love without stress. You
still need to act, take the step, and sign the deal. In the next chapter
you will find out how you can get back on track quickly, start breathing
and help others to breathe.

CHAPTER 16

The Contract

The First Pillar:

أشهد أن لا إله إلا الله وأشهد أن محمدا رسول الله

I bear witness that there is no god to be worshiped but Allah, and that Muhammad is the Messenger of Allah

This is the first and most important pillar of Islam. It is also the only universal truth and your contract to submit the trust back by your heart. This can be accomplished in less than a second, simply by moving your right hand's index finger up. Then you will spend your entire life learning new knowledge and wisdom every day to understand what it includes. However, what it includes is not limited to this life! The only one who can completely fulfill it is God Himself.

شَهِدَ اللهُ أَنَّهُ لَا إِلَهَ إِلَّا هُوَ وَالْمَلَـٰئِكَةُ وَأُولُوا الْعِلْمِ قَائِمًا ۢ بِالْقِسْطِ ۚ لَا إِلَهَ إِلَّا هُوَ الْعَزِيزُ الْحَكِيمُ

(3:18) Allah Himself bears witness that there is no God but He; and likewise do the angels and the men possessed of knowledge bear witness in truth and justice that there is no God but He, the All-Mighty, the All-Wise.[206]

This is the shortest ever contract in your life, but it's the most important and the only significant one here and in the life to come. You have to be careful with the exact specifications below.

---

[206] The testimony in question is from God Himself, Who knows directly all the realities of the universe, Who observes every existing thing without obstruction. It is the testimony of the One from Whose sight nothing is hidden, and who can be a better first-hand witness than He? His testimony is that no one but He is possessed of the attributes of godhead; no one has the power to govern the universe, and no one has the right to claim the rights which belong exclusively to God.

After God, the most trustworthy testimony is that of the angels, for they carry out the administration of the universe. The testimony of the angels, based on their own observations, is that the Will of God alone reigns supreme in the universe, and they turn to Him alone in the governance of the heavens and the earth. Moreover, all creatures possessing knowledge of reality have testified, unanimously, that no one except the One True God reigns and rules over the universe.

Contract Name: Sincere Devotion

<u>Start</u>

أشهد أن لا إله إلا الله وحده لا شريك له وأن محمدا عبده ورسوله

I bear witness that there is no god but Allah alone, who has no partner, and that Muhammad is His servant and Messenger.

<u>End</u>

Form: This contract will not be written anywhere but in your heart.

Signature: This is the signing part of the contract. It is the most important and essential part; any small mistake makes the entire contract void. You will need to use your voice. It cannot be written as a signature by any means. It must be done with the core of your heart; it must come from a place that no one has the power to access except you and God.

Validity: This contract is binding only from the moment you sign it; God will not invalidate it. However, God has the right to check honesty and signature, and any doubt in this matter will jeopardize the validity of the entire contract.

Parties to the agreement:

<u>You:</u> Known as one psyche (interaction between soul and body) and including all your belongings. actions, feelings, thoughts, strength and will. He created you to be unique, with a unique ID, not only your fingerprint, or voice, or DNA, but also your soul and psyche are unique. He made you a miracle in its own, smart and beautiful. You are to be honored by the other creatures including the angels.

<u>God:</u> His name is Allah. He is unlike anything else you can think of or fantasize about. He is as He describes himself in Surah Al-Ikhlas

بِسْمِ اللهِ الرَّحْمٰنِ الرَّحِيْم

قُلْ هُوَ اللهُ أَحَد

399

(112:1) Say: "He is Allah, the One and Unique; [207]

ٱللهُ الصَّمَد

(112:2) Allah, Who is in need of none and of Whom all are in need;[208]

لَمْ يَلِدْ ۬ وَلَمْ يُولَد

(112:3) He neither begot any nor was He begotten,[209]

وَلَمْ يَكُنْ لَّهُ كُفُوًا اَحَد

(112:4) and none is comparable to Him.[210]

Authorized Representatives: They are all of His Prophets and Messengers, peace be upon them all, and the original books of commandments from the Torah and the Bible.

On the behalf of all His Prophets is the seal of His Prophets is Muhammad bin Abdullah, peace be upon him. On the behalf of all His books is the latest and last, known as Qur'an. And on behalf of all the previous instructions, religions, is the latest update known as the religion of Islam.

I hereby affirm that God sent all these Prophets to mankind with the same message and deal.

Agreement: All human beings are subject to Allah with the same deal. This is called unification, and it is the impetus behind the harmony chain to bring the differences together. It is known as the X-Harmony Factor. Harmony leads to a chain of gratitude, peace and love.

Mission Statement:

بِسْمِ اللهِ الرَّحْمٰنِ الرَّحِيْم

(1:1) In the name of Allah, the Merciful, the Compassionate

اَلْحَمْدُ لِلّٰهِ رَبِّ الْعٰلَمِيْن

(1:2) Praise be to Allah, the Lord of the entire universe.

الرَّحْمٰنِ الرَّحِيْم

(1:3) The Merciful, the Compassionate

400

مٰلِكِ يَوْمِ الدِّين

(1:4) The Master of the Day of Recompense.

إِيَّاكَ نَعْبُدُ وَإِيَّاكَ نَسْتَعِين

(1:5) You alone do we worship, and You alone do we turn for help

اِهْدِنَا الصِّرَاطَ الْمُسْتَقِيمَ

(1:6) Direct us on to the Straight Way,

صِرَاطَ الَّذِينَ اَنْعَمْتَ عَلَيْهِمْ غَيْرِ الْمَغْضُوبِ عَلَيْهِمْ وَلَا الضَّاۤلِّينَ

(1:7) The way of those whom You have favoured, who did not incur Your wrath, who are not astray.

Task: I shall do my best to contribute to the well-being of others in this life until my last breath. I will be selfless and remain away from any diabolical road or action.

Rewarding: I will avoid the same fate as Satan (Hell). I will be offered a perpetually peaceful psyche without effort or feelings of hate in a state of sustained celestial well-being (Heaven). This is a unique experience since God will offer whatever I wish. I may ask from Him and He will respond.

The Power of "No"

You may ask why the contract begins with "no", why doesn't it state affirmatively that "there is only one God"?

In fact, the religion and practice of Islam is all about being able to say "no." That is, if we sum up Islam in one word, it will be "no". Satan said "no" to God, and yes to his selfish arrogance. But God requires you to say "no" to Satan and "no" to your selfish ego. All your life Satan will persuade you to follow yourself and to give in to every temptation this Dunya life has to offer. He's wish is that you submit to

401

many things including yourself. All you want to say is "No". Especially the moment before the last breath.

It is the development of the individual's abilities to be able to resist his desires and control himself in order to be free. If a person living in the West sets out with all his might towards liberation and democracy, then this is a very small and marginalized part of the path to true freedom.

The surprise is not that the dictatorship is nothing but the inflation of one's ego until it enslaves those around it. But the fact that this dictatorial ego is present within every human soul, dictating its owner's desires, even if they are against his interests and safety may still be surprising for you. Was it clear to you that the one who enslaves you is you? May it be anger, envy, greed, laziness, hunger, sex, love of power, etc.

Anything that takes you out of control of your feelings by force and overwhelms one aspect of your life or the life of those around you, is the thing you are a slave to. The definition of slavery here is that you are weak-willed in front of something and you cannot control it.

The nature of this thing may be anything, it can be in the beginning something important and necessary for your life, such as food, drink, sex, sleep, money or work. But this necessary thing may sometimes get out of control and you do not have the willpower to control it. At this moment you became a slave to this thing. The slavery you are experiencing will not be limited only to this one thing, but you yourself and all your life is now captured by your inflated ego.

The Second Pillar: The Pray

"And I testify that Muhammad is the Messenger of Allah". You might be asking why the name of the Prophet, may God bless him and grant him peace, is part of the main contract: "I bear witness that there is no God to be worshiped but Allah, and that Muhammad is the Messenger of Allah"

The Prophet, may God bless him and grant him peace, is the vicegerent chosen by God and the representative of the other Prophets, humanity, and the other creations.

وَإِذْ قَالَ رَبُّكَ لِلْمَلَٰئِكَةِ إِنِّى جَاعِلٌ فِى الْأَرْضِ خَلِيفَةً

(2:30) Just think when your Lord said to the angels: "Lo! I am about to place a vicegerent on earth,"

God Almighty is The Truth and the Prophet is The Reality. The Reality is the manifestation of The Truth. The Connection between The Truth and The Reality is a love story. Allah is asking us to pray for Him, as the main mandatory worship.

فَإِذَا قَضَيْتُمُ الصَّلَوٰةَ فَاذْكُرُوا اللهَ قِيَامًا وَّقُعُودًا وَّعَلَىٰ جُنُوبِكُمْ ۚ فَإِذَا اطْمَأْنَنْتُمْ فَأَقِيمُوا الصَّلَوٰةَ ۚ إِنَّ الصَّلَوٰةَ كَانَتْ عَلَى الْمُؤْمِنِينَ كِتَٰبًا مَّوْقُوتًا

(4:103) When you have finished the Prayer, remember Allah -standing, and sitting, and reclining. And when you become secure, perform the regular Prayer. The Prayer is enjoined upon the believers at stated times.

At the same time Allah and His angels pray to the Prophet. How can prayer be in both directions? Thus we need to ask what is the meaning of the prayer.

إِنَّ اللهَ وَمَلَٰئِكَتَهُ يُصَلُّونَ عَلَى النَّبِيِّ ۚ يَٰأَيُّهَا الَّذِينَ أَمَنُوا صَلُّوا عَلَيْهِ وَسَلِّمُوا تَسْلِيمًا

(33:56) Allah and His angels bless the Prophet. Believers, invoke blessings and peace on him.[211]

How Does This Connection Happen?

Prayer is the time when you stop worrying about yourself and completely submit to someone else to take care of you as if you were a newborn. Prayer is the time to let go of admiring yourself and admire someone else as if you are not then in your life.

The purpose of prayer is to stay connected with God, angels, Prophets and each other, as in one harmony (unification). The Arabic word salah, meaning prayer, is communication carried out by saying (asking) or doing (worship). It creates a circuit of connections for everyone to participate depending on their position. God gives infinitely love energy that the creatures receive ceaselessly. If God ceases to give, the creature disappears.

إِنَّ اللّهَ يُمْسِكُ السَّمٰوٰتِ وَالْأَرْضَ أَنْ تَزُوْلَا ۚ وَلَئِنْ زَالَتَآ إِنْ أَمْسَكَهُمَا مِنْ أَحَدٍ مِّنْ بَعْدِهٖ ۗ إِنَّهٗ كَانَ حَلِيْمًا غَفُوْرًا

(35:41) Surely Allah holds the heavens and the earth, lest they should be displaced there, for if they were displaced none would be able to hold them after Him. Surely He is Most Forbearing, Most Forgiving.[212]

Life is Like One Prayer

The first call to prayer that a Muslim hears is immediately after birth: one in the right ear (Adhan), followed by the other (Iqamah) in left ear. This call is completed by the prayer that you will be performed when you are dead, in the coffin just before the grave. It is as if we come to life to do one single prayer. Then we turn back to God, we can't stay away any longer or have something else to do.

وَمَا خَلَقْتُ الْجِنَّ وَالْإِنْسَ إِلَّا لِيَعْبُدُوْنِ

(51:56) I created the jinn and humans for nothing else but that they may serve Me

مَآ أُرِيْدُ مِنْهُمْ مِّنْ رِّزْقٍ وَّمَآ أُرِيْدُ اَنْ يُّطْعِمُوْنِ

(51:57) I desire from them no provision, nor do I want them to feed Me.[213]

اِنَّ اللهَ هُوَ الرَّزَّاقُ ذُو الْقُوَّةِ الْمَتِيْنُ

(51:58) Surely Allah is the Bestower of all provision, the Lord of all power, the Strong.[214]

The Story of The Love Story

Since Adam was sent to earth, all the updated instructions from God to man have been through Gabriel, peace be upon him. Angel Gabriel is the messenger of Heaven to earth, to the Prophets. This applies to all instructions except prayer.

The year before the pray was revealed was the Year of Sorrow (Arabic: عام الحزن, 'Ām al-Huzn, also translated Year of Sadness). That was the

---

[213] That is, I do not stand in need of any kind of help from the jinn and men: that My Godhead would not function if they did not worship Me: that I would be no more God if they turned away from My service. I indeed do not stand in need of their service, but it is the demand of their own nature that they should serve Me. They have been created for this very object, and fighting nature would be to their own detriment. And in saying: I do not ask any sustenance of them nor do I ask them to feed Me, there is a subtle hint to this. Those whom the people, who have turned away from God worship in the world, worship, they indeed stand in need of these their worshipers. If they do not help sustain their godhead, it would not function even for a day. The gods do not provide for the worshipers but the worshipers provide for the gods instead. The gods do not feed them but they feed the gods instead. The gods do not protect them but the worshipers protect the gods instead. The worshipers, in fact, are their army through whom their godhead functions. Wherever the worshipers of the false gods have ceased to exist, or the worshipers have given up their worship, the gods have lost all their pomp and glory and the world has seen how helpless they have become. Of all the deities Allah Almighty is the only real Deity Whose Godhead is functioning by His own power and might, Who does not take anything from His servants, but He alone gives His servants everything.

[214] The word mateen as used in the original means strong and stable whom nobody can shake and move.

Hijri year in which the Prophet's wife Khadijah and his uncle and protector Abu Talib died. The next year approximately coincided with 619 and was the tenth year after the Prophet's first revelation. Allah invited the Prophet, peace be upon him for the journey of Isra and Miraj.

سُبْحٰنَ الَّذِىٓ اَسْرٰى بِعَبْدِهٖ لَيْلًا مِّنَ الْمَسْجِدِ الْحَرَامِ اِلَى الْمَسْجِدِ الْاَقْصَا الَّذِىْ بٰرَكْنَا حَوْلَهٗ لِنُرِيَهٗ مِنْ اٰيٰتِنَاؕ اِنَّهٗ هُوَ السَّمِيْعُ الْبَصِيْرُ

(17:1) Holy is He Who carried His servant by night from the Holy Mosque (in Makkah) to the farther Mosque (in Jerusalem) whose surroundings We have blessed that We might show him some of Our Signs. Indeed He alone is All-Hearing, All-Seeing.[215]

From this moment on the connection manifested and became the five daily prayers. They are available for everyone on earth for the same purpose: to organize the lives of Muslims to be part of the cosmic harmony as well as to calm the soul and recharge it.

Opening His Door 24/7

Perhaps you are wondering what to do, what to say, how to act if you are to meet God Almighty! Is there a special protocol, a ceremony?

---

[215] The event referred to in this verse is known as Miraj and Isra. According to authentic traditions, this took place a year before Hijrah. In this verse, the Quran mentions only a part of the Journey, i.e. from Masjid-i-Haram to the Temple at Jerusalem. The object of this journey as stated here was that Allah willed to show His servant some of His signs. The Quran does not give any details other than this but we find further details in the traditions, which are to this effect:

One night the Angel Jibril took the Prophet (peace be upon him) on al-Buraq from Masjid-i-Haram to Masjid-i-Aqsa (the Temple). There the Prophet (peace be upon him) offered his prayers along with the other Prophets. Then he took him towards the higher spheres, where he met some of the great Prophets in different spheres. At last he reached the Highest Place in the Heavens, and was received in audience by Allah. It was there that, besides other important instructions, five daily Prayers were prescribed. Then he returned to the Temple and from there came back to Masjid-i-Haram.

What could be the agenda? The answer to all these questions is simply the formula of the prayer.

These encounters take place five times a day and follow the 24-hour cycle of the sun. Both men and women start them from the age of reaching puberty and continue them until death. If you miss one, you need to replace it, except for the ladies, who pray in accordance with the changes of their hormonal cycle. You continue to do this even during illness or disability, only with your heart if you cannot move any part of the body. This is lifelong dedication and discipline.

This is the obligatory prayer; any other prayer is either recommended or carried out voluntarily. There are recommended prayers, to confront almost every kind of feelings or cosmic events. For example, there is a prayer in which you consult before you make any decision. There is another one you can resort to when you are afraid, a prayer asking for rain, and prayer that can be said during the solar and lunar eclipses.

Whatever happens in your life, just reach out to God, He will be available! Someone who is reliable, available, and will never turn you down. Not even once, just be patient and polite. Is this the reliability, the quality of love you can expect from anyone around you?

وَاسْتَعِينُوا بِالصَّبْرِ وَالصَّلٰوةِ ۚ وَإِنَّهَا لَكَبِيرَةٌ إِلَّا عَلَى الْخٰشِعِينَ

(2:45) And resort to patience and Prayer for help. Truly Prayer is burdensome for all except the devout,[216]

---

[216] That is, if they feel difficulty in keeping to righteousness, the remedy lies in resorting to Prayer and patience. From these two attributes they will derive the strength needed to follow their chosen course.

The literal meaning of 'sabr' is to exercise restraint, to keep oneself tied down. It denotes the willpower, the firm resolve and the control over animal desires which enables man to advance along the path of his choice - the path that satisfies his heart and conscience - in utter disregard of the temptations within, and of all obstacles and opposition without. The purpose of this directive is to urge man to develop this quality and to reinforce it from the outside by means of Prayer.

Continuous Washing

When you intend to sign the submission contract, and become a Muslim, you will need to take a shower (ghusl) first before signing the contract. Then you would say it from your heart:

أشهد أن لا إله ألا الله و اشهد أن محمد رسول الله

I bear witness that there is no god but God and I bear witness that Muhammad is the Messenger of God.

After that each time you will pray you need ablution (wudu) if you lose your purity.

يَـٰٓأَيُّهَا الَّذِينَ أَمَنُوٓا إِذَا قُمْتُمْ إِلَى الصَّلَوٰةِ فَاغْسِلُوٓا وُجُوهَكُمْ وَاَيْدِيَكُمْ اِلَى الْمَرَافِقِ وَامْسَحُوٓا بِرُءُوسِكُمْ وَاَرْجُلَكُمْ اِلَى الْـكَعْبَيْنِ ۚ وَاِنْ كُنْتُمْ جُنُبًا فَاطَّهَّرُوٓا ۚ وَاِنْ كُنْتُمْ مَّرْضَىٰٓ اَوْ عَلَى سَفَرٍ اَوْ جَاءَ اَحَدٌ مِّنْكُمْ مِّنَ الْغَائِطِ اَوْ لَمَسْتُمُ النِّسَاءَ فَلَمْ تَجِدُوٓا مَاءً فَتَيَمَّمُوٓا صَعِيْدًا طَيِّبًا فَامْسَحُوٓا بِوُجُوْهِكُمْ وَاَيْدِيكُمْ مِنْهُ ۚ مَا يُرِيْدُ اللهُ لِيَجْعَلَ عَلَيْكُمْ مِّنْ حَرَجٍ وَّلٰكِنْ يُّرِيْدُ لِيُطَهِّرَكُمْ وَ لِيُتِمَّ نِعْمَتَهُ عَلَيْكُمْ لَعَلَّكُمْ تَشْكُرُوْنَ

(5:6) Believers! When you stand up for Prayer wash your faces and your hands up to the elbows, and wipe your heads, and wash your feet up to the ankles. And if you are in the state of ritual impurity, purify yourselves (by taking a bath). But if you are either ill, travelling, have satisfied a want of nature or have had contact with women and find no water then have recourse to clean earth and wipe your faces and your hands therewith. Allah does not want to lay any hardship upon you; rather He wants to purify you and complete His favours upon you so

408

that you may give thanks.[217]

Other occasions to perform ghusl are after marriage intercourse (man and woman), and after the woman completes her monthly period. The last one is after your death and before going to the grave.

The regular purification with water is for the body. Prayer is the regular purification of the soul. The end result is to keep purifying the whole psyche (body and mind) until death.

The Whole Framework of The Religion in One Prayer

While praying, turn your face toward the House of God on earth the Kaaba (Hajj), ignore anything in the material life around you, and with your heart and mind recite the mission (Al-Fatihah). You have devoted time and effort (zakah), and you don't eat during the prayer (fasting). You recite the Qur'an, remember and glorify God, give thanks and supplicate.

Usually especially men perform the obligatory prayer in congregation, gently bending with others for harmony. You pray just as the Prophet (ﷺ) did, and before the end of the prayer, you recite the dialogue

---

[217] The explanation of this injunction by the Prophet (peace be on him) indicates that washing of the face includes rinsing one's mouth and inhaling water into the nostrils. Unless this is done the washing of the face is not considered complete. Likewise, since the ears are part of the head, 'wiping the head' includes wiping one's hands over the external and internal parts of the ears as well. Moreover, before starting to wash the other parts one should first wash one's hands so that the instruments of washing are themselves clean.

Janabah (the state of major ritual impurity) - whether caused by the sexual act or merely by seminal discharge - renders it unlawful to perform the ritual Prayer and to touch the Qur'an.

Just as purity of the soul is a blessing, so is cleanliness of the body. God's favour to man can be completed only when he has received comprehensive direction in respect of both spiritual purity and physical cleanliness.

between God and the Prophet, and confirm the contract of submission by saying:

التحيات لله، والصلوات، والطيبات، السلام عليك أيها النبي ورحمة الله وبركاته، السلام علينا وعلى عباد الله الصالحين، أشهد أن لا إله إلا الله، وأشهد أن محمداً عبده ورسوله

"Greetings are for Allah, as well as prayers and good works. May peace be upon the prophet as well as the mercy of Allah and His blessing. Peace be upon us and on the pious servants of Allah. I testify that there is no deity other than Allah, and I testify that Muhammad is His servant and messenger."

Before the conclusion of the prayer, you recite prayers upon the Prophet and upon Prophet Ibrahim, peace be upon them. At the end of the prayer, you pass great peace to your left and right angels.

Doing all this during one prayer you have covered the entire framework of religion, including the Five Pillars and all other practices. Every single action in the prayer can be done on its own as an independent practice.

While Praying, Stop Trying, Stop Thinking!

The dedication to prayer gives you one long-term job. During this job contract you will never be fired, discriminated against nor retire. During any prayer, you just have to be yourself and stop trying to be anything. Just get in without making any effort. Stop thinking, stop the problem-solving loop in your head, and combine your left and right brain as if they were one lobe. Speak from your heart.

Now you may be ready to really understand what it means to be a slave to the Creator. Unlike humans who take slaves to serve them, God does not need work done by someone. There is no need to worry or to think about anything, just calm your head and be at peace. God asks you to submit all your burdens to Him with a wish list that includes the ways you want them to be handled. He'll take care of the rest. Don't be surprised that when you leave from the prayer, you will still work around the clock but He will be the One who takes away the burden. You will be a tireless body and soul. As much as you understand this truth, it will manifest in your life.

Abu Huraira reported: The Messenger of Allah, peace and blessings be upon him, said:

إِنَّ اللَّهَ قَالَ مَنْ عَادَى لِي وَلِيًّا فَقَدْ آذَنْتُهُ بِالْحَرْبِ وَمَا تَقَرَّبَ إِلَيَّ عَبْدِي بِشَيْءٍ أَحَبَّ إِلَيَّ مِمَّا افْتَرَضْتُ عَلَيْهِ وَمَا يَزَالُ عَبْدِي يَتَقَرَّبُ إِلَيَّ بِالنَّوَافِلِ حَتَّى أُحِبَّهُ فَإِذَا أَحْبَبْتُهُ كُنْتُ سَمْعَهُ الَّذِي يَسْمَعُ بِهِ وَبَصَرَهُ الَّذِي يُبْصِرُ بِهِ وَيَدَهُ الَّتِي يَبْطِشُ بِهَا وَرِجْلَهُ الَّتِي يَمْشِي بِهَا وَإِنْ سَأَلَنِي لَأُعْطِيَنَّهُ وَلَئِنْ اسْتَعَاذَنِي لَأُعِيذَنَّهُ وَمَا تَرَدَّدْتُ عَنْ شَيْءٍ أَنَا فَاعِلُهُ تَرَدُّدِي عَنْ نَفْسِ الْمُؤْمِنِ يَكْرَهُ الْمَوْتَ وَأَنَا أَكْرَهُ مَسَاءَتَهُ

Allah said: Whoever shows hostility to a friend of Mine, I have declared war upon him. My servant does not grow closer to Me with anything more beloved to me than the duties I have imposed upon him. My servant continues to grow closer to Me with extra good works until I love him. When I love him, I am his hearing with which he hears, his seeing with which he sees, his hand with which he strikes, and his foot with which he walks. Were he to ask something from Me, I would surely give it to him. Were he to ask Me for refuge, I would surely grant it to him. I do not hesitate to do anything as I hesitate to take the soul of the believer, for he hates death and I hate to displease him. *Source: Bukhari*

What Else?

Does prayer have a benefit for the body? Is it good for stress relief, overcoming depression, obsession or insomnia? Does it help with social anxiety? Does it boost digestion, respiration, blood circulation and immunity? Is it useful for fluid balance, brain and musculoskeletal system function? Does it prevent dementia and Alzheimer's? Does it assist during recovery from a digital addiction or when you need to de-earth from electric charges and electromagnetic waves?

The answer yes contains all of these things and even more. This is something that can be checked anytime online.

Everlasting Love No Stress

If you ask God to pray for Prophet Muhammad (giving love) by saying may God bless him and grant him peace, the Messenger brings love back to you. Then you turn back asking for more love for the Messenger, and so on. This will keep you connected and moving forward in a cycle of love that lasts forever without stress.

At-Tufail bin Ubayy bin Ka'b narrated from his father who said:

حَدَّثَنَا هَنَّادٌ، حَدَّثَنَا قَبِيصَةُ، عَنْ سُفْيَانَ، عَنْ عَبْدِ اللَّهِ بْنِ مُحَمَّدِ بْنِ عَقِيلٍ،
عَنِ الطُّفَيْلِ بْنِ أُبَيِّ بْنِ كَعْبٍ، عَنْ أَبِيهِ، قَالَ كَانَ رَسُولُ اللَّهِ صلى الله عليه
وسلم إِذَا ذَهَبَ ثُلُثَا اللَّيْلِ قَامَ فَقَالَ " يَا أَيُّهَا النَّاسُ اذْكُرُوا اللَّهَ اذْكُرُوا اللَّهَ
جَاءَتِ الرَّاجِفَةُ تَتْبَعُهَا الرَّادِفَةُ جَاءَ الْمَوْتُ بِمَا فِيهِ جَاءَ الْمَوْتُ بِمَا فِيهِ " .
قَالَ أُبَيٌّ قُلْتُ يَا رَسُولَ اللَّهِ إِنِّي أُكْثِرُ الصَّلاَةَ عَلَيْكَ فَكَمْ أَجْعَلُ لَكَ مِنْ
صَلاَتِي فَقَالَ " مَا شِئْتَ " . قَالَ قُلْتُ الرُّبُعَ . قَالَ " مَا شِئْتَ فَإِنْ زِدْتَ فَهُوَ
خَيْرٌ لَكَ " . قُلْتُ النِّصْفَ . قَالَ " مَا شِئْتَ فَإِنْ زِدْتَ فَهُوَ خَيْرٌ لَكَ " . قَالَ
قُلْتُ فَالثُّلُثَيْنِ . قَالَ " مَا شِئْتَ فَإِنْ زِدْتَ فَهُوَ خَيْرٌ لَكَ " . قُلْتُ أَجْعَلُ لَكَ
صَلاَتِي كُلَّهَا . قَالَ " إِذًا تُكْفَى هَمَّكَ وَيُغْفَرُ لَكَ ذَنْبُكَ " . قَالَ أَبُو عِيسَى
هَذَا حَدِيثٌ حَسَنٌ

"When a third of the night had passed, the Messenger of Allah (s.a.w) stood and said: 'O you people! Remember Allah! Remember Allah! The Rajifah is coming, followed by the Radifah, death and what it brings is coming, death and what it brings is coming!'" Ubayy said: "I said: 'O Messenger of Allah! Indeed I say very much Salat for you. How much of my Salat should I make for you?' He said: 'As you wish.'" (He said:) "I said: 'A fourth?' He said: 'As you wish. But if you add more it would be better for you.' I said: 'Then half?' He said: 'As you wish. And if you add more it would be better (for you).'" (He said:) "I said: 'Then two-thirds? 'He said: 'As you wish, but if you add more it would be better for you.' I said: 'Should I make all of my Salat for you?' He said: "Then your problems would be solved and your sins would be forgiven. *Source: Abu Issa said: This is a good, authentic hadith*

Prayer for Prophet Muhammad (Salawat)

Allaahumma salli 'alaa Muhammadin wa 'alaa ali Muhammadin Kamaa sallaita 'alaa Ibraaheema wa 'alaa ali Ibraaheema Innaka hameedun Majeed

Alaahumma baarik 'ala Muhammadin wa 'alaa ali Muhammadin Kamaa baarakta 'alaa Ibraaheema wa 'alaa ali Ibraaheema Innaka hameedun Majeed

O Allah, bless our Muhammad and the people of Muhammad; As you have blessed Abraham and the people of Abraham. Surely you are the Praiseworthy, the Glorious.

O Allah, be gracious unto Muhammad and the people of Muhammad; As you were gracious unto Abraham and the people of Abraham. Surely you are the Praiseworthy, the Glorious.

The Third Pillar: Zakat

Zakat is also a spiritual connection to the Creator - you purify your wealth according to God's will by recognizing that everything we have is His.

It holds the literal meaning of the word "purification". Muslims believe that giving zakat purifies, increases and blesses the part that remains of their wealth.

خُذْ مِنْ أَمْوَالِهِمْ صَدَقَةً تُطَهِّرُهُمْ وَتُزَكِّيهِمْ بِهَا وَصَلِّ عَلَيْهِمْ ۖ إِنَّ صَلَوٰتَكَ
سَكَنٌ لَّهُمْ ۗ وَاللَّهُ سَمِيعٌ عَلِيمٌ

(9:103) (O Prophet)! "Take alms out of their riches and thereby cleanse them and bring about their growth (in righteousness), and pray for them. Indeed your prayer is a source of tranquillity for them." Allah is All-Hearing, All-Knowing.

Zakat is a form of obligatory movement of wealth between individuals. There should not be a commercial reason to circulate it for example, marketing, advertising, gifts, investments, or any commercial or social commitments. The only reason for paying zakat is that it is a form of obligatory worship. This is pure investment to God only. It is as if you are lending this money to God and God is going to pay it back with profit.

وَلَقَدْ أَخَذَ اللَّهُ مِيثَاقَ بَنِىٓ إِسْرَآءِيلَ ۖ وَبَعَثْنَا مِنْهُمُ اثْنَىْ عَشَرَ نَقِيبًا ۖ وَقَالَ اللَّهُ
إِنِّى مَعَكُمْ ۖ لَئِنْ أَقَمْتُمُ الصَّلَوٰةَ وَآتَيْتُمُ الزَّكَوٰةَ وَآمَنتُم بِرُسُلِى وَعَزَّرْتُمُوهُمْ
وَأَقْرَضْتُمُ اللَّهَ قَرْضًا حَسَنًا لَّأُكَفِّرَنَّ عَنكُمْ سَيِّـَٔاتِكُمْ وَلَأُدْخِلَنَّكُمْ جَنَّٰتٍ تَجْرِى
مِن تَحْتِهَا الْأَنْهَٰرُ ۚ فَمَن كَفَرَ بَعْدَ ذَٰلِكَ مِنكُمْ فَقَدْ ضَلَّ سَوَآءَ السَّبِيلِ

(5:12) Surely Allah took a covenant with the Children of Israel, and We raised up from them twelve of their leaders, and Allah said: 'Behold, I am with you; if you establish Prayer and pay Zakah and believe in My Prophets and help them,and lend Allah a good loan, I will certainly efface from you your evil deeds, and will surely cause you to enter the Gardens beneath which rivers flow. Whosoever of you disbelieves thereafter has indeed gone astray from the right way.

Zakat payment can be spent directly to the ones who may need it, or it can be used to provide a non-profit service to the community at large.

لَّيْسَ الْبِرَّ أَن تُوَلُّوا وُجُوهَكُمْ قِبَلَ الْمَشْرِقِ وَ الْمَغْرِبِ وَلَٰكِنَّ الْبِرَّ مَنْ آمَنَ
بِاللَّهِ وَالْيَوْمِ الْآخِرِ وَالْمَلَٰئِكَةِ وَالْكِتَٰبِ وَالنَّبِيِّنَ ۖ وَآتَى الْمَالَ عَلَىٰ حُبِّهِ ذَوِى
الْقُرْبَىٰ وَالْيَتَٰمَىٰ وَالْمَسَٰكِينَ وَابْنَ السَّبِيلِ وَالسَّآئِلِينَ وَفِى الرِّقَابِ ۖ وَأَقَامَ
الصَّلَوٰةَ وَآتَى الزَّكَوٰةَ ۚ وَالْمُوفُونَ بِعَهْدِهِمْ إِذَا عَٰهَدُوا ۖ وَالصَّٰبِرِينَ فِى
الْبَأْسَآءِ وَالضَّرَّآءِ وَحِينَ الْبَأْسِ ۗ أُولَٰئِكَ الَّذِينَ صَدَقُوا ۖ وَأُولَٰئِكَ هُمُ الْمُتَّقُونَ

(2:177) Righteousness does not consist in turning your faces towards the east or towards the west; true righteousness consists in believing in

Allah and the Last Day, the angels, the Book and the Prophets, and in giving away one's property in love of Him to one's kinsmen, the orphans, the poor and the wayfarer, and to those who ask for help, and in freeing the necks of slaves, and in establishing Prayer and dispensing the Zakah. True righteousness is attained by those who are faithful to their promise once they have made it and by those who remain steadfast in adversity and affliction and at the time of battle (between Truth and falsehood). Such are the truthful ones; such are the God-fearing.

How Much Zakat?

Zakat is 2.5% of the wealth that one has in possession for a duration of a lunar year. If the wealth is less than a threshold number called the nisab, then zakat does not have to be paid.

If the money exceeds the nisab, zakat is required. Nisab is equivalent to 58 grams of gold. Any source of income or property must be considered subject to zakat, with some exceptions in certain cases of non-recurring income or (non-commercial) property.

Zakat is The Antidote of The New Trinity

Zakat is the simple yet powerful solution to help you counter the influence of the New Trinity. New Trinity manipulates your psychology and puts you in constant fear of losing a job or a source of income, or a welfare benefit. Zakat asks you to spend it without hesitation and fear.

The foundation is that you understand that this world, wealth and psyche (trust) all belong to God, and He asks you to spend and He will repay. God is strengthening your psyche by pushing you to face your fears and shifting the power to put you in control. This is a cure for fear, insecurity, hate, jealousy and anger. The effect is felt by both the giving and receiving people.

The Muslims' understanding of the accumulation of wealth doesn't mean saving to their bank accounts, rather it is spending within the framework of the lawful and it accumulates in their books (the right angel should be busy recording these deeds).

إِنْ تُقْرِضُوا اللَّهَ قَرْضًا حَسَنًا يُضَاعِفْهُ لَكُمْ وَيَغْفِرْ لَكُمْ ۚ وَاللَّهُ شَكُورٌ حَلِيمٌ

(64:17) If you give Allah a goodly loan, He will increase it for you several fold and will forgive you. Allah is Most Appreciative, Most Forbearing.

God promised to secure your expenses. If you take this understanding seriously, He will take you seriously, and the more you want to give, the more He will give you.

وَإِذْ تَأَذَّنَ رَبُّكُمْ لَئِنْ شَكَرْتُمْ لَأَزِيدَنَّكُمْ وَلَئِنْ كَفَرْتُمْ إِنَّ عَذَابِي لَشَدِيدٌ

(14:7) Also call to mind when your Lord proclaimed: "If you give thanks, I will certainly grant you more; but if you are ungrateful for My favours, My chastisement is terrible.[218]

---

[218] That is, if you are grateful, you will appreciate Our favors and make right use of them, and will not rebel against Our commandments, but will surrender and submit to Us to show your gratitude to Us.

Deuteronomy (Torah) contains a long and detailed discourse to this effect. According to it, Prophet Moses (peace be upon him), on the eve of his death, reminded the Israelites of all important events from their history, and reiterated all the divine commandments of the Torah which Allah had sent to them through him. Then he told them in a long speech that if they obeyed their Lord, they would be given great rewards. But if they adopted the attitude of disobedience, they would get a terrible punishment.

Zakat is The Safety Net for The Economy

It encourages constant growth of the economy and keeps the money flowing, under any circumstances, which means there is no inflation or stagnation. At the same time, it encourages investment, employment and poverty reduction.

الَّذِينَ يُنْفِقُونَ فِى السَّرَّاءِ وَالضَّرَّاءِ وَالْكَاظِمِينَ الْغَيْظَ وَالْعَافِينَ عَنِ النَّاسِ ۗ وَاللَّهُ يُحِبُّ الْمُحْسِنِينَ ۗ

(3:134) who spend in the way of Allah both in plenty and hardship, who restrain their anger, and forgive others. Allah loves such good-doers." [219]

On the other hand, since Zakat needs to be from halal (permissible) sources and activities this means that there shouldn't be monopoly, fraud or unfair competition going on when providing safe products or reliable human-centric services. This will directly translate into lower overall spending and create more satisfaction with less cost and effort. This will result in more efficiency and fun and reduced stress for the individual and society. This is why an honest business person is rewarded as a prophet or a warrior.

Abu Sa'eed narrated that the Prophet (ﷺ) said:

عَنْ أَبِي سَعِيدٍ، عَنِ النَّبِيِّ صلى الله عليه وسلم قَالَ " التَّاجِرُ الصَّدُوقُ الأَمِينُ مَعَ النَّبِيِّينَ وَالصِّدِّيقِينَ وَالشُّهَدَاءِ "

"The truthful, trustworthy merchant is with the Prophets, the truthful, and the martyrs." *Source: Narrated by al-Tirmidhi*

---

[219] The existence of interest in a society generates two kinds of moral disease. It breeds greed and avarice, meanness and selfishness among those who receive interest. At the same time, those who have to pay interest develop strong feelings of hatred, resentment, spite and jealousy. God intimates to the believers that the attributes bred by the spread of interest are the exact opposite of those which develop as a result of spending in the way of God, and that it is through the latter rather than the former that man can achieve God's forgiveness and Paradise.

Muslim Welfare

Another mechanism, to counteract the manipulation of the New Trinity, is that the concept of Muslim welfare is somewhat different. Muslims are encouraged fully to work here in this life, and to provide service for the welfare of others as much as possible. They recognize that their well-being will be simultaneously created for the next heavenly stage of life.

The future of a Muslim is after death. This life as such is a stage of time called present. You need to continue to focus on the moment, using it as much as possible to create a comfortable future. This in comparison to non-Islamic thinking is much more effective. It is a relaxed approach of having a peaceful life on earth without anxiety, fear nor stress. The distinction creates more clarity and focus: this life is for work and the next life is for having fun.

Some don't have a chance to enjoy giving as much as others. This is why it's not about the quantity rather it's the quality that counts, which is related to the heart (intentions). This means that sharing one cent of a single euro that you have is much greater than sharing 10,000 euros from a million euros, provided that the intention behind sharing the one cent is more sincere.

وَالَّذِينَ تَبَوَّءُو الدَّارَ وَالْإِيمَانَ مِنْ قَبْلِهِمْ يُحِبُّونَ مَنْ هَاجَرَ إِلَيْهِمْ وَلَا يَجِدُونَ فِي صُدُورِهِمْ حَاجَةً مِّمَّا أُوتُوا وَيُؤْثِرُونَ عَلَى أَنْفُسِهِمْ وَلَوْ كَانَ بِهِمْ خَصَاصَةٌ ۚ وَمَنْ يُوقَ شُحَّ نَفْسِهِ فَأُولَٰئِكَ هُمُ الْمُفْلِحُونَ ۞

(59:9) It also belongs to those who were already settled in this abode (of Hijrah) having come to faith before the (arrival of the) Muhajirun (Emigrants). They love those who have migrated to them and do not covet what has been given them; they even prefer them above themselves though poverty be their own lot. And whosoever are preserved from their own greed, such are the ones that will prosper.[220]

What Kind of Welfare the Perfect Muslim Psyche Can Create?

The psychic energy generated by this understanding of welfare is extraordinary. I have in this regard three examples. The first is from the past, over 1400 years ago. It is about the founder of the first welfare state, the second Caliph of the Muslims, *Umar ibn al-Khattab*.

The other two are from the present, both recently passed away, about two years ago. Both of them are Egyptians, one is a businessman *Mahmoud Al-Arabi* and the other Dr. *Mohamed Mashally* or the "doctor of the poor". They lived at the same time, but had no connection, relationship, or coordination between each other.

The only connection was indirect, both were applying the islamophilia X-Harmony Factor to the letter. The end result is that both men, despite the demanding socioeconomic situation in Egypt, created one

---

[220] The word used here means "is saved" and not "was safe", for without Allah's help and succor no one can attain to the wealth of the heart (liberal-mindedness) by his own power and effort. This is a blessing of God, which one can attain only by God's bounty and grace. The word shuhha is used for stinginess and miserliness in Arabic. But when this word is attributed to the self of man, it becomes synonymous with narrow-mindedness, niggardliness, mean spiritedness and small-heartedness, and not mere stinginess: it is rather the root cause of stinginess itself. Because of this very quality man avoids acknowledging even the good qualities of another, not to speak of recognizing his rights and discharging them. He wants that he alone should gather up everything in the world, and no one else should have anything of it. He never feels content with his own right, but usurps the rights of others, or at least wants to have for himself all that is good in the world and should not leave anything for others. On this very basis one's being saved from this evil has been described in the Quran as a guarantee for success. The Prophet (peace be upon him) has counted it among the most evil qualities of man which are the root cause of corruption and mischief. Jabir bin Abdullah has reported that the Prophet (peace be upon him) said: Avoid shuhha for it was shuhha which ruined the people before you. It incited them to shed each other's blood and make the sacred and forbidden things of others lawful for themselves.

comprehensive economic and welfare system of their own. The entrepreneur took an interest in creating a business empire that provided jobs with high-quality benefits for more than 10,000 families. The doctor created from himself (one man show) a comprehensive system of social and health care that covered two major cities 24/7 for more than 50 years.

The Founder

Omar Ibn Al-Khattab, (583/584 – 3 November 644), also known as simply Umar or Omar, was the second Rashidun (in English rightly-guided) caliph. He was the founder of welfare literally. Before this stage in history, there was no social welfare linked to economic prosperity and the state's entity.

This man was guided by his morals and devotion while he was establishing a coherent state system based first on perfect justice and secondly on mercy and compassion.

Founder's Life In a Few Lines

Omar Ibn Al-Khattab (May God be pleased with him) was an educated, middle-class, intelligent, strong and brave gladiator.

He was strict in the religion of his forefathers, strict because of his race, clan, traditions and puritanical sect. He did not like Islam and did not like the idea of changing society into a new flat hierarchy that would grant more rights to slaves and women.

The position of women at that time was deplorable. They were treated as commodities in the markets, means of commercial temptation, add-ons in concluding deals and as entertainment to spectators and those with lusts.

420

Do not be surprised that, before Islam, this man who we are talking about, buried his infant daughter while she was alive. This is because he was afraid that his daughter would live in a time when he would have become an old man, and therefore would not be able to protect her from the lusts of those around her.

With the passage of time, Omar became angry at Islam and the speed that it spread, so he decided to get rid of the whole matter and kill the Messenger of Islam, may God bless him and grant him peace. Indeed, he took his sword and went to the house of the Prophet (ﷺ). On the way he found out that his sister had secretly converted to Islam, so he wanted to kill her first, then Muhammad (ﷺ).

His Entry to Islam

After some troubles, Omar's sister decided, with the same courage as her brother, to confront him with the fact that she had converted to Islam and would stick to it. She hadn't even finished her words when he slapped her once on her face, making her bleed. She looked him straight in the eyes with steadfastness and solidity, but with love and respect despite his cruelty.

The look was enough for him to understand the truth. He knew his sister and her sincerity. That is what made him trust this religion, the same one that made his sister that calm, confident, fearless but still loving in such a frightening situation. She knew very well about her brother that he would not hesitate to kill her, if she was faking.

This was a historic turning point in his life and later in the lives of all Muslims. He asked her to recite to him some of the Qur'an. She ordered him first to perform ablution, which he did, and she recited. No one knows what exactly happened to his heart at this moment when he decided to go to the Prophet's house and announce his conversion to Islam. Then he came out astonishing all the leaders and masters by declaring to the whole world his conversion to Islam and announcing his protection for all Muslims.

His Justice

He was an expert Muslim jurist known for his pious and just nature, which earned him the epithet al-Farooq ("the one who distinguishes between right and wrong").

According to a Jewish tradition, Umar set aside the ban made by Christians on Jews and allowed them into Jerusalem and to worship

A Story:

Fabrics from Yemen came to the Commander of the Faithful Omar Ibn Al-Khattab - may God be pleased with him. So, each Muslim man was given a piece that would suffice for one garment. Then he took his share and the share of his son Abdullah and sewed it and put it on.

When Omar ascended the pulpit to address the people and said: O people, listen and obey, a Muslim man stood up to him and said: Neither listen nor obey.

Omar said: Why is that? He said: Because you took advantage of us. Omar said: With what?

The man said: You have given each of us a piece of cloth, which is sufficient for one garment, and you are a tall man, and this piece is not sufficient for you as a garment, and we see that you have sewed it into a complete shirt, so you must have taken more than you gave us.

Then the Commander of the Faithful turned to his son Abdullah, and said: O Abdullah, answer him about his words. Abdullah said: I gave him my clothing that he completed his shirt with. The man said: As from now, it is to listen and obey. *Source: https://www.al-islam.org/restatement-history-islam-and-muslims-sayyid-ali-asghar-razwy/umar-bin-al-khattab-second-khalifa*

His Compassion

To be close to the poor, Omar lived in a simple mud hut without doors and walked the streets every evening. After consulting with the poor, Omar established the first welfare state, Bayt al-mal. The Bayt al-mal aided the Muslim and non-Muslim poor, needy, elderly, orphans, widows, and the disabled. The Bayt al-mal ran for hundreds of years, from the Rashidun Caliphate in the 7th century through the Umayyad period (661–750) and well into the Abbasid era. Omar also introduced a child benefit and pensions for the children and the elderly.

A Story:

Omar ibn Al Khattab, may God be pleased with him, used to patrol the streets of Medina at night, which at that time was the capital of the Islamic state – sometimes he had his freed slave, Aslam, may God be pleased with him, with him and at other times he took Abdur Rahman ibn Awf, may God be pleased with him. In this way, he helped keep himself up to date with what was happening in the Muslim society and to help guard those he was responsible for – that is, the Muslim citizens. He would perform this task himself so that he could see and hear for himself what his agents might hesitate to tell him.

It is narrated from Aslam that: "Umar went to a place located three miles outside Medina, a place where there were black volcanic rocks. There we saw a fire burning. He, may God be pleased with him, said, 'O Aslam, I see here some travelers who are being held up by the night and the cold; let's go.'

"So we went running and when we came near them, we saw a woman with children. There was a pot set up over fire, and her children were crying.

"Umar, may God be pleased with him, said, "Peace be upon you, O people of the light (he did not want to say, O people of the fire).'

423

"She said, 'And upon you be peace.'

"He said, 'May I come closer?'

"She said, 'Come if you can do some good, otherwise leave us alone.'

"He came closer and said, 'What is the matter with you?'

"She said, 'The night and the cold has held us up.'

"He said, 'What is the matter with these children; why are they crying?'

"She said, 'They are hungry.'

"He said, 'What is in this pot?'

"She said, 'Water, to calm them down until they go to sleep, and Allah will judge between us and Omar.'

"He said, 'May Allah have mercy on you, how could Omar know about you?'

"She said, 'How come he is in charge of our affairs, but he is not aware of our situation?'

"He turned to me (Aslam) and said, 'Let's go.'

"So we set off running until we came to a room where wheat was stored. He took out a sack of wheat and a little fat, and said, 'Hoist it up onto me.'

"I said, 'I will carry it for you.'

"He said, 'Will you carry my burden for me on the Day of Resurrection?'

"So, I hoisted it up onto him and he set out running and I ran with him. When he reached her, he put those things down. He took out some of the wheat and said to her, 'Prepare it for me and I will cook it for you.'

"He started blowing beneath the pot and I saw the smoke coming out through his beard. He cooked it for her, and brought it to her, and said, 'Bring me something.'

"So, she brought him a vessel and he poured it into it, then said, 'Feed them and I will spread it out (to cool down) for them.'

"He stayed until they had eaten their fill, and he left the leftover food with her. He got up, and I got up with him, and she started to say, 'May Allah reward you with good; you are more suited to be the Caliph than Ameer ul Mumineen Umar (Leader of the Muslims).'

"He said, 'Say something good, and if you go to the Ameer ul Mumineen, you will find me there inshAllah – Allah willing.'

"Then he walked some distance away from her, then turned to face them again and waited a while. I said to him, 'Is there anything else?' but he did not answer me, until I saw the boys wrestling/playing with each other and then falling asleep, having calmed down. Then he stood up and said, 'Praise be to Allah, the Exalted, the Almighty.'

"Then he turned to me and said, 'O Aslam, hunger kept them awake and made them cry; I did not want to leave until I saw what I saw.'" *Source:https://www.al-islam.org/restatement-history-islam-and-muslims-sayyid-ali-asghar-razwy/umar-bin-al-khattab-second-khalifa*

The Businessman

"The Secret of Business Tycoon Mahmoud Al-Arabi"
Initially written by: Elham AbolFateh

"I don't know how I became like this; it is our God who did all of this." These are the words of late Egyptian businessman *Mahmoud Al-Arabi*, who started his career at the age of 5 years. He was selling balloons and toys in front of the house of his poor family, at this age, he joined Al kuttab- a type of elementary school in the Muslim world-to memorize the Qur'an, he learned honesty, trustworthiness and the difference between halal and haram (right and wrong), and this principle was the basis of his reputation for which he was famous in his life over 88 years, until he became an industrial and trade pioneer in Egypt, leaving 40,000 employees working in his companies.

In his book "The Secret of My Life", he lays down the most important rules for corporate and business success

He says: "I have never said anyone who works for me, but rather works with me, because the worker is like the sustenance from our God, and any company whose people love each other, God bless them."

Al-Arabi remained an ambassador for the honest merchant and the perfect manufacturer, so his products entered all homes and were requested by millions of people in more than 60 countries. He did not believe that "trade is savvy," but rather honesty and integrity.

He was keen to apply these principles since he was a child trading in toys and when he rented a small shop in Al-Mosky. When he became a business owner has factories and companies, even after retirement, he dedicated a large amount of his money for the needy people.

I remember when late President Mubarak asked him "what do you want Hajj Mahmoud? He told him that he wished to employ one thousand young men every year.

Every year he was opening a door for a thousand young people and the more the number increased the more the revenues increased, even in his home and with his wife and children he applied the same principle. He says about his wife that she instilled in our children the value of contentment, patience, and thanking God for the halal revenues!

As a result, when he died, thousands of people attended his funeral, bidding farewell to him and praying for him, including schoolchildren and students at various universities around the world, widows, orphans and industrialists. Thus, he lived as a person who helped everyone to reap the good, and deserved to be one of the pioneers of trade, industry and humanity.

This is the secret of Mahmoud Al-Arabi "Shahbandar Al-Tijjar" one of the trades and industrial pioneers in Egypt whose business talks about him, may God have mercy upon his soul.

The Doctor

Mashally, Egypt's 'Doctor of the Poor'
Initially written by by Yassmine Elsayed

Dr. Mashally was born in the village of Dhahr Al Temsah, in Beheira Governorate, to a father who worked as a teacher and then moved to Gharbia Governorate where he settled with his family.

The late doctor graduated from Qasr Al-Aini Faculty of Medicine, specializing in internal medicine, pediatrics and fevers.

In 1975 he opened his private clinic in Tanta, and for many years he set the value of his clinic fee at only 5 pounds (less than $0.3) and increased to 10 pounds ($0.6). Often, he refused to receive the fees from poor patients, and even bought them treatment, until he became famous as 'The Doctor of the poor'. He gave treatment, investigations and medications to millions of Egyptians who cannot afford medication expenses.

He worked 12-hour days, even while he was in his late 70s, and served 30-50 patients a day, according to an interview with DW. He provided his services all the days of the week even during the official holidays. Dr. Mashali was also known to provide vaccines free of charge to people who could not afford them.

He was appointed to the rural health sector in Gharbia Governorate, and moved between rural units, and he was promoted to the position of Director of the Endemic Diseases Hospital, then Director of Said

Medical Center until he reached the legal age of the pension in 2004.

Dr. Mashally refused to accept a large shady donation to have a new clinic in the most famous streets of Tanta. He only accepted a medical stethoscope worth 80 pounds as a donation from a young donor from UAE.

In a press interview after, Dr. Mashally said: "I am a doctor who grew up in a humble house and graduated from the Faculty of Medicine of Al-Kasr Al-Aini in 1967", stressing that he devoted his knowledge to help the poor; the patient pays a very symbolic fee.

"Just as my father, on his deathbed, advised good things to the poor, and to the sick of the poor," he noted.

The Doctor of the poor cried when he recalled the fact that he was assigned to a health unit in a poor area, saying: "A young child with diabetes came to me crying in pain and saying to his mother, give me the insulin syringe, but she replied: If I bought the insulin syringe, we will not be able to buy food for the rest of your siblings. And I still remember this difficult situation, which made me donate my knowledge to help the poor.

The Welfare Line

These three examples are clear role models on how sincere people can for sure build a sustainable welfare system, but it is not sure that welfare on its own can build sincere people! If you have the right psychological education, the right contract with the right God, you will be given the ability to create the welfare here for the others and later (in the Hereafter) for yourself.

The Fourth Pillar: Fasting Ramadan

Ramadan in Islam is the ninth month of the Muslim calendar and the holy month of fasting. It begins and ends with the appearance of the crescent moon. Because the Muslim calendar year is shorter than the Gregorian calendar year, Ramadan begins 10–12 days earlier each year, allowing it to fall in every season throughout a 33-year cycle.

During Ramadan, Muslims abstain from eating any food, drinking any liquids, smoking cigarettes, and engaging in any sexual activity, from dawn to sunset. That includes taking medication (even if you swallow a pill dry, without drinking any water). Chewing gum is also prohibited. Doing any of those things "invalidates" your fast for the day, and you start over the next day. To make up for days you didn't fast, you can either fast later in the year (either all at once or a day here and there) or provide a meal to a needy person for each day you missed.

Muslims are also supposed to try to curb negative thoughts and emotions like jealousy and anger, and even lesser things like swearing, complaining, and gossiping, during the month. Some people may also choose to give up or limit activities like listening to music and watching television, often in favor of listening to recitations of the Quran. It is meant to be a time of spiritual discipline - of deep contemplation of one's relationship with God, extra prayer, increased charity and generosity, and intense study of the Quran.

All Muslims are required to take part every year, though there are special dispensations for those who are ill, pregnant or nursing, menstruating, or traveling, and for young children and the elderly.

يَـٰأَيُّهَا الَّذِينَ اٰمَنُوا كُتِبَ عَلَيْكُمُ الصِّيَامُ كَمَا كُتِبَ عَلَى الَّذِينَ مِنْ قَبْلِكُمْ لَعَلَّكُمْ تَتَّقُونَ

(2:183) Believers! Fasting is enjoined upon you, as it was enjoined upon those before you, that you become God-fearing.[221]

اَيَّامًا مَّعْدُوْدٰتٍ ۚ فَمَنْ كَانَ مِنْكُمْ مَّرِيْضًا اَوْ عَلٰى سَفَرٍ فَعِدَّةٌ مِّنْ اَيَّامٍ اُخَرَ ۚ
وَعَلَى الَّذِيْنَ يُطِيْقُوْنَهٗ فِدْيَةٌ طَعَامُ مِسْكِيْنٍ ۚ فَمَنْ تَطَوَّعَ خَيْرًا فَهُوَ خَيْرٌ لَّهٗ ۚ
وَاَنْ تَصُوْمُوْا خَيْرٌ لَّكُمْ اِنْ كُنْتُمْ تَعْلَمُوْنَ

(2:184) Fasting is for a fixed number of days, and if one of you be sick,
or if one of you be on a journey, you will fast the same number of
other days later on. For those who are capable of fasting (but still do
not fast) there is a redemption: feeding a needy man for each day
missed. Whoever voluntarily does more good than is required, will find
it better for him; and that you should fast is better for you, if you only
know.[222]

شَهْرُ رَمَضَانَ الَّذِيْٓ اُنْزِلَ فِيْهِ الْقُرْاٰنُ هُدًى لِّلنَّاسِ وَ بَيِّنٰتٍ مِّنَ الْهُدٰى
وَالْفُرْقَانِ ۚ فَمَنْ شَهِدَ مِنْكُمُ الشَّهْرَ فَلْيَصُمْهُ ۚ وَمَنْ كَانَ مَرِيْضًا اَوْ عَلٰى سَفَرٍ
فَعِدَّةٌ مِّنْ اَيَّامٍ اُخَرَ ۚ يُرِيْدُ اللّٰهُ بِكُمُ الْيُسْرَ وَلَا يُرِيْدُ بِكُمُ الْعُسْرَ وَلِتُكْمِلُوا الْعِدَّةَ
وَلِتُكَبِّرُوا اللّٰهَ عَلٰى مَا هَدٰىكُمْ وَلَعَلَّكُمْ تَشْكُرُوْنَ

(2:185) During the month of Ramadan the Qur'an was sent down as a
guidance to the people with Clear Signs of the true guidance and as the
Criterion (between right and wrong). So those of you who live to see
that month should fast it, and whoever is sick or on a journey should
fast the same number of other days instead. Allah wants ease and not
hardship for you so that you may complete the number of days
required, magnify Allah for what He has guided you to, and give thanks

---

[221] Like most other injunctions of Islam those relating to fasting were revealed gradually. In
the beginning the Prophet (peace be on him) had instructed the Muslims to fast three days in
every month, though this was not obligatory. When the injunction in the present verse was
later revealed in 2 A.H., a degree of relaxation was introduced: it was stipulated that those who
did not fast despite their capacity to endure it were obliged to feed one poor person as an
expiation for each day of obligatory fasting missed. Another injunction was revealed later and
here the relaxation in respect of able-bodied persons was revoked. However, for the sick, the
traveller, the pregnant, the breast-feeding women and the aged who could not endure fasting,
the relaxation was retained.

[222] This act of extra merit could either be feeding more than the one person required or both
fasting and feeding the poor. Here ends the early injunction with regard to fasting which was
revealed in 2 A.H. prior to the Battle of Badr. The verses that follow were revealed about one
year later and are linked with the preceding verses since they deal with the same subject.

to Him.[223]

---

[223] Whether a person should or should not fast while on a journey is left to individual discretion. We find that among the Companions who accompanied the Prophet on journeys some fasted whereas others did not; none objected to the conduct of another. The Prophet himself did not always fast when travelling. On one journey a person was so overwhelmed by hunger that he collapsed; the Prophet disapproved when he learned that the man had been fasting. During wars the Prophet used to prevent people from fasting so that they would not lack energy for the fight. It has been reported by 'Umar that two military expeditions took place in the month of Ramadan. The first was the Battle of Badr and the second the conquest of Makka. On both occasions the Companions abstained from fasting, and, according to Ibn 'Umar, on the occasion of the conquest of Makka the Prophet proclaimed that people should not fast since it was a day of fighting. In other Traditions the Prophet is reported to have said that people should not fast when they had drawn close to the enemy, since abstention from fasting would lead to greater strength.

The duration of a journey for which it becomes permissible for a person to abstain from fasting is not absolutely clear from any statement of the Prophet. In addition the practice of the Companions was not uniform. It would seem that any journey which is commonly regarded as such, and which is attended by the circumstances generally associated with travelling, should be deemed sufficient justification for not fasting.

Jurists agree that one does not have to fast on the day of commencing a journey; one may eat either at the point of departure or after the actual journey has commenced. Either course is sanctioned by the practice of the Companions. Jurists, however, are not agreed as to whether or not the residents of a city under attack may abstain from fasting even though they are not actually travelling. Ibn Taymiyah favours the permissibility of abstention from fasting and supports his view with very forceful arguments.

This indicates that fasting need not be confined, exclusively, to Ramadan. For those who fail to fast during that month owing to some legitimate reason God has kept the door of compensation open during other months of the year so that they need not be deprived of the opportunity to express their gratitude to Him for His great bounty, in revealing the Qur'an.

It should be noted here that fasting in Ramadan has not only been declared an act of worship and devotion and a means to nourish piety but has also been characterized as an act of gratefulness to God for His great bounty of true guidance in the form of the Qur'an. In fact, the best way of expressing gratitude for someone's bounty or benevolence is to prepare oneself, to the best of one's ability, to achieve the purpose for which that bounty has been bestowed. The Qur'an has been revealed so that we may know the way that leads to God's good pleasure, follow that way ourselves and direct the world along it. Fasting is an excellent means by which to prepare ourselves for shouldering this task. Hence fasting during the month of the revelation of the Qur'an is more than an act of worship and more than an excellent course of moral training; it is also an appropriate form for the expression of our thankfulness to God for the bounty of the Qur'an.

وَإِذَا سَأَلَكَ عِبَادِي عَنِّي فَإِنِّي قَرِيبٌ أُجِيبُ دَعْوَةَ الدَّاعِ إِذَا دَعَانِ
فَلْيَسْتَجِيبُوا لِي وَلْيُؤْمِنُوا بِي لَعَلَّهُمْ يَرْشُدُونَ

(2:186) (O Muhammad), when My servants ask you about Me, tell them I am quite near; I hear and answer the call of the caller whenever he calls Me. Let them listen to My call and believe in Me; perhaps they will be guided aright.[224]

أُحِلَّ لَكُمْ لَيْلَةَ الصِّيَامِ الرَّفَثُ إِلَى نِسَائِكُمْ هُنَّ لِبَاسٌ لَكُمْ وَأَنْتُمْ لِبَاسٌ لَهُنَّ
عَلِمَ اللّٰهُ أَنَّكُمْ كُنْتُمْ تَخْتَانُونَ أَنْفُسَكُمْ فَتَابَ عَلَيْكُمْ وَعَفَا عَنْكُمْ فَالْآنَ بَاشِرُوهُنَّ
وَابْتَغُوا مَا كَتَبَ اللّٰهُ لَكُمْ وَكُلُوا وَاشْرَبُوا حَتَّى يَتَبَيَّنَ لَكُمُ الْخَيْطُ الْأَبْيَضُ
مِنَ الْخَيْطِ الْأَسْوَدِ مِنَ الْفَجْرِ ثُمَّ أَتِمُّوا الصِّيَامَ إِلَى اللَّيْلِ وَلَا تُبَاشِرُوهُنَّ
وَأَنْتُمْ عَاكِفُونَ فِي الْمَسَاجِدِ تِلْكَ حُدُودُ اللّٰهِ فَلَا تَقْرَبُوهَا كَذَلِكَ يُبَيِّنُ اللّٰهُ آيَاتِهِ
لِلنَّاسِ لَعَلَّهُمْ يَتَّقُونَ

(2:187) It has been made lawful for you to go in to your wives during the night of the fast. They are your garment, and you are theirs. Allah knows that you used to betray yourselves and He mercifully relented and pardoned you. So you may now associate intimately with your wives and benefit from the enjoyment Allah has made lawful for you, and eat and drink at night until you can discern the white streak of dawn against the blackness of the night; then (give up all that and) complete your fasting until night sets in. But do not associate intimately with your wives during the period when you are on retreat in the mosques. These are the bounds set by Allah; do not, then, even draw near them. Thus does Allah make His Signs clear to mankind that they

---

[224] Even though people can neither see God nor subject Him to any other form of sense perception this should not make them feel that God is remote from them. On the contrary, He is so close to each and every person that whenever any person so wishes he can communicate with his Lord. So much so that God hears and responds even to the prayers which remain within the innermost recesses of the heart.

People exhaust themselves by approaching false and powerless beings whom they foolishly fancy to be their deities but who have neither the power to hear nor to grant their prayers. But God, the omnipotent Lord and the absolute Master of this vast universe, Who wields all power and authority, is so close to human beings that they can always approach Him without the intercession of any intermediaries, and can put to Him their prayers and requests.

This announcement of God's closeness to man may open his eyes to the Truth, may turn him to the right way wherein lies his success and well-being.

may stay away from evil.[225]

Ramadan: The Factory Reset for The Psyche

This is the time when some halal actions are temporarily suspended during fasting times and are considered forbidden. It is intense spirituality for a month. There is no external temptation, Satan is chained, the door of Hell is closed, and the gates of Heaven are opened. The goal is to give the soul an advance over the body and material pressure (The New Trinity).

Abu Hurairah (May Allah be pleased with him) reported: the Messenger of Allah (ﷺ) said:

وعنه رضي الله عنه أن رسول الله صلى الله عليه وسلم قال: "إذا جاء رمضان فتحت أبواب الجنة، وغلقت أبواب النار، وصفدت الشياطين"

"When Ramadan begins, the gates of Jannah are opened, the gates of Hell are closed, and the devils are chained." *Source: Muslim*

For the Soul

Ramadan strengthens the will, restores the freedom of the soul from the strict rules of the body. It trains the soul to overcome the physical limitations of the body. These limitations that we slowly develop day by day, are called habits. This tendency in our psyche for creating habits places our will on automatic drive, and brings boredom to everything in life: clothes, shopping, work, travel, family, money, food and sex.

When Ramadan begins, it suddenly takes you out of your habit system, and as the days go by you will begin to re-appreciate every detail in your life upto the drop of water. After the month of Ramadan, you will return to your life as a completely new person. You will celebrate from your heart, first the success in completing the challenge, then the enjoyment of your soul in overcoming boredom and habits. You will also enjoy reclaiming your life habits with the option to create a whole

433

225 Just as nothing intervenes between a person's body and his clothes, so nothing can intervene between a man and his wife; it is a relationship of inalienable intimacy.

Although there was no categorical ordinance in the early days prohibiting sexual intercourse between husband and wife during the nights of Ramadan, people generally assumed that this was not permissible. Despite the feeling that their action was either not permitted or was at least disapproved of, they did at times approach their wives. Such a betrayal of conscience can encourage a sinful disposition. God, therefore, first reproaches them with their lack of integrity, for this is what was objectionable. As for the act itself, God makes it clear that it is quite permissible. Henceforth they might engage in sexual intercourse as a perfectly lawful act unencumbered by feelings of guilt.

In this connection, too, there was a misapprehension at first. Some thought that eating and drinking were absolutely prohibited after the performance of the 'Isha' (Night) Prayer. Others thought that one could eat and drink so long as one had not fallen asleep, but that if one had it was not permissible to eat on reawakening. These were people's own fancies and often caused great inconvenience. This verse seeks to remove all such misconceptions. It clearly lays down the duration of the fast: from dawn until sunset. Between sunset and dawn it is permissible to eat, to drink, and to indulge in the legitimate gratification of sexual desires. At the same time the Prophet introduced the pre-fasting repast, recommending a good meal just before dawn.

In fixing the time of obligatory rites, Islam has been mindful that these timings should be so clear and simple that people, at all stages of development, should be able to follow them. This is why Islam bases its timing on conspicuous natural phenomena and not on the clock.

Some people object that this principle of timing is untenable in areas close to the poles, where night and day each last for about six months. This objection is based on a very superficial knowledge of geography. In point of fact neither day nor night lasts for six months in those areas - not in the sense in which people living near the Equator conceive of night and day. The signs of morning and evening appear at the poles with unfailing regularity and it is on this basis that people time their sleeping and waking, their professional work, their play and recreation. Even in the days before watches were common, the people of countries like Finland, Norway and Greenland used to fix the hours of the day and night by means of various signs that appeared on the horizon. Just as those signs helped them to determine their schedules in other matters, so they should enable them to time their various Prayers, the pre-fast meal and the breaking of the fast.

'Complete your fasting until night sets in' means that the time of fasting ends with nightfall, i.e. sunset marks the breaking of the fast. The precise time of the end of the pre-dawn repast is when a lean strip of aurora appears at the eastern end of the horizon and begins to grow. The time to break one's fast starts when the darkness of night seems to have begun to appear over the eastern horizon.

434

new set of more halal habits.

For the Body

It creates a new body too. It is an annual maintenance for all body systems, not only the stomach but all, including hormone sensitivity, metabolism, and body mind integrity. It is activating stem cell reserve in the body. This will take care of replacing aging, damaged and potential precancerous cells and provides a fresh batch of completely new cells. *Source: Fasting Activates Fatty Acid Oxidation to Enhance Intestinal Stem Cell Function during Homeostasis and Aging, Mihaylova M.M., Cheng C.-W.,et. al, (2018) Cell Stem Cell, 22 (5), pp. 769-778.e4.*

For the Economy and Society

Again, it is a new impetus for the individual exchange of clean money between people. During the month it is highly recommended to spend on charity, debt repayment, and help afflicted people. It is time for rethinking and planning of everything that has been in operation: in business, social, health, education, transportation, and infrastructure facilities. It is time to start cleaning from inside and out, decorating streets and homes etc. Before the end of the month, every adult must

---

In our own time, some people have adopted an attitude of extreme caution with regard to the time of both the end and start of fasting. The Law has not fixed these schedules with rigid precision. If a person wakes up just at the crack of dawn it is proper for him to eat and drink hastily. According to a Tradition the Prophet said: 'If anyone of you hears the call for (the morning) Prayer while he is eating he should not stop immediately, but should finish eating to the extent of his bare need. Similarly, one need not wait for the light of day to disappear fully before breaking the fast. The Prophet, for instance, used to ask Bilil to bring him something to drink as soon as the sun had set. Bilal expressed his astonishment, pointing out that the light of day could still be observed. To this the Prophet replied that the time of fasting came to an end when the darkness of night began to rise from the east.

'On retreat in the mosque' refers to the religious practice of spending the last ten days of Ramadan in the mosque, consecrating this time to the remembrance of God. In this state, known as i'tikaf, one may go out of the mosque only for the absolutely necessary requirements of life, but one must stay away from gratifying one's sexual desire.

pay a certain amount of zakat for the month of Ramadan called zakat al-fitr. The month ends with a three-day celebration called Eid al-Fitr including family time, visits, gifts, invitations to extended meals, and happiness all around.

The Fifth Pillar: Hajj

Hajj translates to English as 'pilgrimage' and refers to the pilgrimage to Mecca, Saudi Arabia, that all able Muslims should undertake. Hajj takes place during the first 10 days of Dhul Hijjah, the 12th and final month in the Islamic (lunar) calendar.

It is expected that all able Muslims undertake the pilgrimage at least once in their life. However, there are a handful of exceptions including children, those who are physically or mentally impaired, elderly, frail or otherwise sick Muslims, and Muslims who cannot afford the expenses of the trip.

وَإِذْ بَوَّأْنَا لِإِبْرَاهِيمَ مَكَانَ الْبَيْتِ اَنْ لَّا تُشْرِكْ بِيْ شَيْئًا وَّطَهِّرْ بَيْتِيَ لِلطَّائِفِينَ وَالْقَائِمِينَ وَ الرُّكَّعِ السُّجُوْدِ

(22:26) Call to mind when We assigned to Abraham the site of the House (Kabah), directing him: "Do not associate aught with Me" and "Keep My House pure for those who walk around it, and for those who stand and who bow down and who prostrate themselves (in worship),

وَأَذِّنْ فِي النَّاسِ بِالْحَجِّ يَأْتُوكَ رِجَالًا وَّعَلٰى كُلِّ ضَامِرٍ يَّأْتِينَ مِنْ كُلِّ فَجٍّ عَمِيقٍ

(22:27) and publicly proclaim Pilgrimage for all mankind so that they come to you on foot and mounted on lean camels from every distant point

لِّيَشْهَدُوْا مَنَافِعَ لَهُمْ وَيَذْكُرُوا اسْمَ اللهِ فِيْٓ اَيَّامٍ مَّعْلُوْمٰتٍ عَلٰى مَا رَزَقَهُمْ مِّنْ بَهِيْمَةِ الْاَنْعَامِ فَكُلُوْا مِنْهَا وَاَطْعِمُوا الْبَآئِسَ الْفَقِيْرَ

(22:28) to witness the benefits in store for them and pronounce the name of Allah during the appointed days over the cattle that He has provided them. So, eat of it and feed the distressed and the needy.[226]

ثُمَّ لِيَقْضُوا تَفَثَهُمْ وَلْيُوفُوا نُذُورَهُمْ وَلْيَطَّوَّفُوا بِالْبَيْتِ الْعَتِيقِ

(22:29) Thereafter, let them tidy up and fulfil their vows and circumambulate the Ancient House."

What Happens on Hajj?

During the pilgrimage to Mecca, Muslims undertake a series of rituals. Below is an outline of the seven main rituals and what happens on Hajj:

Ihram

Muslims should observe Hajj in a state of purity called ihram. This means there is no arguing or fighting, abstaining from sexual activity and refraining from trimming hair and nails. In addition to this, Muslims should wear appropriate ihram clothes. For men, ihram clothes take the form of two white sheets wrapped around the body. The sheets should be seamless, and sandals are to be worn on the feet. Doing so eliminates any trace of wealth or class status and renders everyone equal. For women, there are no set ihram clothes rules aside from leaving the face and hands uncovered, but many women choose to wear white.

Tawaf

The Kaaba is the most sacred site for Muslims around the world and is located in the Masjid Al-Haram. It was built by Prophet Ibrahim (Peace be upon him) and his son, Ismail (Peace be upon him), and

---

[226] "The benefits" include both religious and worldly benefits. It was due mainly to the Kabah that during the period of 2500 years between the times of Prophet Abraham and the Prophet (peace be upon them), the Arabs, in spite of their tribal life, remained attached to one central place and continued to visit it from all parts of Arabia for performing Hajj year after year. This in turn preserved their language, their culture and their Arab identity. Then during the course of the year they were afforded at least four months of perfect peace when anybody and everybody could safely travel alone or in trade caravans; thus the ritual of Hajj was directly beneficial to economic life of the country as well.

whilst performing salat (daily prayers), Muslims do so in the direction of the Kaaba. During Hajj, Muslims move anticlockwise around the Kaaba seven times which is known as Tawaf.

Al-Safa / Al-Marwah

It is said that Prophet Ibrahim (Peace be upon him) was ordered by God to leave his wife, Hajar, and his newborn son, Ismail, in the desert. Prophet Ibrahim (Peace be upon him) left them with limited resources, and when these expired, Hajar ran seven times between Safa and Marwah (two hills) in an attempt to find water. Angel Jibril appeared and directed her to a water spring in the ground. Hajar built a well around the spring which is now known as the well of Zamzam. To honor Hajar's efforts, Muslims run seven times between the Al-Safa and Al-Marwah hills, both located in the Masjid Al-Haram.

Mount Arafat

Prophet Muhammad (ﷺ) received his first revelation from God and performed his final sermon at Mount Arafat on the edge of Mecca. It is now a highly sacred site and during Hajj, Muslims go to Mount Arafat to pray.

Stoning of the devil

After leaving Mount Arafat, Muslims partake in the ritual of stoning the devil. Prophet Ibrahim (Peace be upon him) is said to have been approached by the devil on three separate occasions as he sought to dissuade Ibrahim from obeying God. In response, Prophet Ibrahim (Peace be upon him) threw stones at him. To mark this, Muslims throw stones at three walls in Mina as part of the Hajj.

Eid ul-Adha

On the 10th day of Dhul Hijjah, Eid ul-Adha begins and is marked by the sacred Eid prayer. Eid ul-Adha is the greater Eid and is a designated period of four days of celebration as marked out by the Prophet Muhammad (ﷺ).

Qurbani

The final part of the Hajj pilgrimage is Qurbani which commences following the Eid ul-Adha prayer. Qurbani is the sacrifice of an animal which is observed by Muslims to honour the sacrifice Prophet Ibrahim (Peace be upon him) was willing to make by giving his son, Ismail (Peace be upon him) as per God's command. At the last moment, God saved Ismail (Peace be upon him) and put a goat in his place. For this reason, all Muslims should make a Qurbani sacrifice or a Qurbani donation.

What Does Hajj Mean?

Hajj is like the rehearsal of the life story and the next life. It is a journey of stripping away from the seat of power, the business, the family, the surrounding environment, the concerns of life and its welfare. It is time to leave everything behind your back and go back to God.

We stay all our life praying in the direction of Mecca (Qiblah) directing our face and heart to one house in Mecca, the Sacred House of God. Hajj is time to feel and touch and come closer. This is a time to give the left side of the brain one big boost of harmony to comprehend the intangible right side of the brain.

During this journey the president and the subordinate, the rich and the poor, the young and the old, the women and the men, and the black and white are all equal. They have all come in simple white clothes. The message is clear: we are all equal, and we are all before the Creator. This is especially evident during one specific day of Hajj, when everyone should be standing on Mount Arafat at the same time.

There is no need for anyone to be arrogant or to enslave anyone. A clear call and message have been given to liberate oneself, from the bondages of oneself and others. The whole world witnesses the Hajj every year as a reminder to all Muslims and non-Muslims about equality and unified humanity. There is no hate, and no difference between persons except in the amount of morals with Allah. There is no morality without acknowledging the truth of our purpose in existence.

Abu Nadrah reported: The Messenger of Allah, peace and blessings be upon him, said during the middle of the day at the end of the pilgrimage:

عَنْ أَبِي نَضْرَةَ قَالَ قَالَ رَسُولُ اللَّهِ صَلَّى اللَّهُ عَلَيْهِ وَسَلَّمَ فِي وَسَطِ أَيَّامِ التَّشْرِيقِ فَقَالَ يَا أَيُّهَا النَّاسُ أَلَا إِنَّ رَبَّكُمْ وَاحِدٌ وَإِنَّ أَبَاكُمْ وَاحِدٌ أَلَا لَا فَضْلَ لِعَرَبِيٍّ عَلَى أَعْجَمِيٍّ وَلَا لِعَجَمِيٍّ عَلَى عَرَبِيٍّ وَلَا لِأَحْمَرَ عَلَى أَسْوَدَ وَلَا أَسْوَدَ عَلَى أَحْمَرَ إِلَّا بِالتَّقْوَى أَبَلَّغْتُ قَالُوا بَلَّغَ رَسُولُ اللَّهِ صَلَّى اللَّهُ عَلَيْهِ وَسَلَّمَ

"O people, your Lord is one and your father Adam is one. There is no favor of an Arab over a foreigner, nor a foreigner over an Arab, and neither white skin over black skin, nor black skin over white skin, except by righteousness. Have I not delivered the message?" They said, "The Messenger of Allah has delivered the message." *Source: Ahmad/22396*

Servants as Vicegerents

God has granted mankind the privilege of being His vicegerents on earth. This means that we will have the possibility to be free to create and decide about our actions during this life provided that we understand this power and who bestowed it upon us. We obey Him and keep our promise according to the contract. This experience will extend to the next life and we will live in Heaven with the privilege of wishing and our wishes will come true.

If you understand this clearly, you will not find it difficult to understand our relationship with God as His vicegerents on earth and His servants at the same time. Isn't that wonderful?

Experience God's experience

Being a god obviously means having 'no problem' and if you know Him, you will also enjoy that option of having the feeling of living with 'no problem'.

Life is a medium designed specifically for the exchange of benefits between different creatures, and during these exchanges bonds will be established between them. The strength of this strong bond is the unifying force called love. Love includes all the different forms of energies, known and hitherto unknown. The first known energy of love is the power of the word "be" from God.

The human race has acquired this power of love and it is an essential element built in a part of the psyche called the soul. It is the source of the dream of eternal peace, "the human dream". Achieving this dream is a matter of choice and requires dedication to work wholeheartedly against the body component of the psyche. Working against it means to create a balance between the soul and the body. To make this happen you need a meticulously prepared educational program during life, which is called religion.

The fulfillment of this dream is the sole purpose of human creation. We are here to taste the power and attributes of God. Creating a bond between us and God is based on the power of love bestowed upon us by Him. Within the framework of the religion there are countless ways to pursue this purpose, bringing us to different ranks and closeness to God, depending on our sincerity.

Marriage is a concentrated (focused) life form of exchanging benefits between spouses within the framework of the religion. The hierarchy of benefits is covering everything starting with the primary desires of the body, going through all other needs in life, and ending with the soul's highest need to experience love.

It is essential that the spouses work together in exchanging mutual benefits according to their condition (supply and demand) all through their lifespan. They work as a team on problem solving activities. Diversity, continuous communication, motivation, and celebration of results are the most common assets for enhancing the results of an innovation team. Selfishness is the main challenge in the family, and brainwashing and stress (The New Trinity) is the main challenge to humanity.

The Takeaway

The contract of Islam is simple and comprehensive. It's the Five Pillars. Any of these pillars has its own voluntary extra doings. For example, Zakat as Sadaqah, Hajj as Umrah, fasting the middle lunar days of each month, as well as Mondays and Thursdays, and prayer as Sunnah prayers.

Each action, having a mixture of benefits, activates the harmony system of your psyche, from inside and out, of yourself and your surroundings. They blend spirituality with material life: sow here and gather in the afterlife.

Islam sets out the story of life amazingly. It's a clear concept with even minor details. OS that shows immediate tangible results on anyone's life, so clear that you cannot miss it.

The Gigantic Takeaway

Little story

Once upon a time I was on my way one day to the mosque for Maghrib prayer. A drunk Finnish man stopped me politely and said: "Sorry I'm drunk, but it's okay. May I ask you a question?" Are you going there?, he asked, directing his head to the mosque. I answered: "Yes, it is prayer time." Then he proceeded: "What do you take home after going there?"

The question was very practical and correct, so I told him the first answer off the top of my head: "Our body needs movement, this requires energy, and this energy needs to be charged." He replied quickly: "Thank you and please go ahead to charge."

The question and my answer kept echoing in my head. I liked the question and was thinking more about my answer. What do I mean by charging? and the answer is found in one part of the call to prayer when it is repeated twice by saying "live on the farmer", and the meaning of this phrase is "hurry to success" or "the rush to success".

You might be wondering success of what. Oh no, are you still asking? No problem!

Success lies in answering the most challenging question for us on earth: How should we spend our lives? Did we waste it? Did we spend it the right way?

This is the feeling when you become a Muslim. Every moment you do something in Islam takes you closer to success. It is more or less the same feeling like when you are going to the bank and making a new deposit. So what do you take home with you? You may feel safe and successful for securing the future!

A Muslim is saving his entire life here for the sake of the future life, the hereafter. This saving is a gigantic take away from this life, God and the mosque are branches of this savings bank account. Every moment in our life can be saved and invested, and this is the best motivation to live this life, and the key to feeling of having no problems! How cool is that!?

Who Took the Way?

It is no secret to anyone that comparing the conditions of the countries in which most Muslims live now and Western countries, there is a material gap. At first glance, this does not indicate that Islam has led to progress in the material aspect as much as in the psychological aspects. But it is clear that the psychological aspects make one able to put up with any material difficulties. On top of this, if you look in the past and compare Andalusia with Western life, you will find a wide gap this time in both the material as well as the psychological aspects. In fact, the production of Andalusia was the basis for the launch of Western civilization.

These gaps tell us the truth. Islam and being a Muslim is an honest individual journey in life one can freely choose as one's destiny. Each person will represent only himself on Judgment Day regardless of his position or history of pressures from outside in this life. This choice is independent of political, cultural and civilizational changes. You can live anywhere as a Muslim at peace with your surroundings if allowed. If not, God asks you, if for example you are a Uyghur, to withstand pressure or oppression until you meet Him and He will take care of justice.

We are all challenged to prove ourselves in this life. We have potential to be honorable human beings. That potential will end the moment we die. Then there will be a fair and accurate assessment of each one of us, and accordingly we will be informed if we have reached the rank of humans and to what extent or if not at all.

بِسْمِ اللهِ الرَّحْمٰنِ الرَّحِيْمِ

In the name of God Almighty Most Merciful Most Gracious

لَا أُقْسِمُ بِيَوْمِ الْقِيٰمَةِ

(75:1) Nay, I swear by the Day of Resurrection;

وَلَا أُقْسِمُ بِالنَّفْسِ اللَّوَّامَةِ

(75:2) and nay, I swear by the self-reproaching soul!

444

اَيَحْسَبُ الْإِنْسَانُ اَلَّنْ نَّجْمَعَ عِظَامَهُ

(75:3) Does man imagine that We will not be able to bring his bones together again?

بَلٰى قٰدِرِيْنَ عَلٰى اَنْ نُّسَوِّيَ بَنَانَهُ

(75:4) Yes indeed; We have the power to remould even his finger-tips.[227]

بَلْ يُرِيْدُ الْإِنْسَانُ لِيَفْجُرَ اَمَامَهٗ

(75:5) But man desires to persist in his evil ways.

يَسْئَلُ اَيَّانَ يَوْمُ الْقِيٰمَةِ

(75:6) He asks: "When will the Day of Resurrection be?"[228]

فَاِذَا بَرِقَ الْبَصَرُ

(75:7) When the sight is dazed,

وَخَسَفَ الْقَمَرُ

(75:8) and the moon is eclipsed,[229]

وَجُمِعَ الشَّمْسُ وَالْقَمَرُ

(75:9) and the sun and the moon are joined together,

يَقُوْلُ الْإِنْسَانُ يَوْمَئِذٍ اَيْنَ الْمَفَرُّ

---

[227] That is, not to speak of building up your skeleton once again by gathering together the major bones? We are able to make the most delicate parts of your body exactly with your identity, even your fingerprints.

[228] This question was not put as a question but derisively and to deny Resurrection, That is, they did not want to ask when Resurrection would take place but asked mockingly: What has happened to the day with which you are threatening us. When will it come.

[229] This is a brief description of the chaotic condition of the system of the universe that will prevail in the first stage of Resurrection. The darkening of the moon and the joining of the moon and the sun together can also mean that not only will the moon lose its light, which is borrowed from the sun, but the sun itself will become dark and both will become devoid of light similarly. Another meaning can be that the earth will suddenly start rotating in the reverse order and on that day both the moon and the sun will rise simultaneously in the west. And a third meaning can be that the moon will suddenly shoot out of the earth's sphere of influence and will fall into the sun. There may possibly be some other meaning also of this which we cannot understand today.

(75:10) on that Day will man say: "Whither the refuge?"

كَلَّا لَا وَزَرَ

(75:11) No, there is no refuge.

إِلَى رَبِّكَ يَوْمَئِذٍ ٱلْمُسْتَقَرُّ

(75:12) With your Lord alone will be the retreat that Day.

يُنَبَّؤُا۟ ٱلْإِنسَانُ يَوْمَئِذٍ بِمَا قَدَّمَ وَأَخَّرَ

(75:13) On that Day will man be apprised of his deeds, both the earlier and the later.

بَلِ ٱلْإِنسَانُ عَلَىٰ نَفْسِهِ بَصِيرَةٌ

(75:14) But lo, man is well aware of himself,

وَلَوْ أَلْقَىٰ مَعَاذِيرَهُ

(75:15) even though he might make up excuses.

لَا تُحَرِّكْ بِهِ لِسَانَكَ لِتَعْجَلَ بِهِ

(75:16) (O Prophet), do not stir your tongue hastily (to commit the Revelation to memory).

إِنَّ عَلَيْنَا جَمْعَهُ وَقُرْآنَهُ

(75:17) Surely it is for Us to have you commit it to memory and to recite it.

فَإِذَا قَرَأْنَٰهُ فَٱتَّبِعْ قُرْآنَهُ

(75:18) And so when We recite it, follow its recitation attentively;

ثُمَّ إِنَّ عَلَيْنَا بَيَانَهُ

(75:19) then it will be for Us to explain it.

كَلَّا بَلْ تُحِبُّونَ ٱلْعَاجِلَةَ

(75:20) Nay; the truth is that you love ardently (the good of this world) that can be obtained hastily,

وَتَذَرُونَ ٱلْآخِرَةَ

446

(75:21) and are oblivious of the Hereafter.[230]

وُجُوْهٌ يَّوْمَئِذٍ نَّاضِرَةٌ ۙ

(75:22) Some faces on that Day will be fresh and resplendent,

إِلَى رَبِّهَا نَاظِرَةٌ ۚ

(75:23) and will be looking towards their Lord;

وَوُجُوْهٌ يَّوْمَئِذٍ بَاسِرَةٌ ۙ

(75:24) and some faces on that Day will be gloomy,

تَظُنُّ اَنْ يُّفْعَلَ بِهَا فَاقِرَةٌ ۗ

(75:25) believing that a crushing calamity is about to strike them.

كَلَّا إِذَا بَلَغَتِ التَّرَاقِىَ ۙ

(75:26) Nay; when a man's soul reaches up to the throat,

وَقِيْلَ مَنْ رَاقٍ ۙ

(75:27) and it is said: "Is there any enchanter who can step forward and

---

[230] This is the another reason for denying the Hereafter, the first being the one mentioned in verse 5 above, saying: Since man wants to avoid the moral restrictions which are inevitably imposed by the belief in the Hereafter, his selfish motives, in fact, urge him to deny the Hereafter, and then he tries to present arguments in order to rationalize his denial. Now, the second reason being presented is that the deniers of the Hereafter are narrow-minded and shortsighted; for them only those results are all important, which appear in this world, and they do not give any importance to those effects which will appear in the Hereafter. They think that they should spend all their labor and effort in attaining whatever benefits, pleasures or joys they can attain here, for if one attained this, one attained everything, no matter what evil end this might lead to in the Hereafter. Likewise, they think that the loss or trouble or grief that can afflict one here is a thing that one must avoid, no matter how great a reward it might earn one in the Hereafter if one endured it here. They are only interested in the cash bargain. For the sake of as remote a thing as the Hereafter they can neither abandon a profit nor suffer a loss today. With this mode of thought when they discuss the question of the Hereafter rationally, it is not true rationalism but a mode of thinking because of which they are resolved not to acknowledge the Hereafter in any case even if their conscience might be crying froth within that the arguments for the possible occurrence and necessity of the Hereafter given in the Quran are highly rational and their own reasoning against it is very weak.

help (by his chanting)?"[231]

وَّظَنَّ اَنَّهُ الْفِرَاقُ

(75:28) and he realises that the hour of parting is come,

وَالْتَفَّتِ السَّاقُ بِالسَّاقِ

(75:29) and calf is inter-twined with calf.

اِلٰى رَبِّكَ يَوْمَئِذِ الْمَسَاقُ

(75:30) On that Day you will be driven to your Lord.

فَلَا صَدَّقَ وَلَا صَلّٰى

(75:31) But he did not verify the Truth, nor did he observe Prayer;

وَلٰكِنْ كَذَّبَ وَتَوَلّٰى

(75:32) on the contrary, he gave the lie to the Truth and turned his back upon it,

ثُمَّ ذَهَبَ اِلٰى اَهْلِهٖ يَتَمَطّٰى

(75:33) then he went back to his kinsfolk, elated with pride.[232]

اَوْلٰى لَكَ فَاَوْلٰى

---

[231] The word raqin in the original may he derived from ruqayyah, which means resort to charming, enchanting and exercising, and also from raqi, which means ascending. In the first case, the meaning would be: At last, when the attendants of the patient are disappointed with every remedy and cure, they will say: Let us at least call in an enchanter, who may save him. In the second case, the meaning would be: At that time the angels will say: which angels are to take his soul: the angels of punishment or the angels of mercy? In other words, at that very time the question will be decided in what capacity the dying one is entering the Hereafter; if he is a righteous person, the angels of mercy will take him, and if he is wicked, the angels of mercy will keep away and the angels of punishment will seize him and take him away.

[232] It means that the one who was not prepared to believe in the Hereafter, heard all that has been described in the above verses; yet he persisted in his denial, and hearing these verses went back to his household, arrogantly. The words, He neither affirmed the truth nor offered the Prayer, are particularly noteworthy. They clearly show that the first and necessary demand of acknowledging the truth about Allah and His Messenger and Book is that one should perform the Prayer, The occasion and time to carry out the other injunctions of the divine Shariah come later but the Prayer time approaches soon after one has affirmed the faith, and then it becomes known whether what one has affirmed with the tongue was really the voice of his heart, or it was only a puff of the wind which one sent out from his mouth in the form of words.

(75:34) This (attitude) is worthy of you, altogether worthy;

ثُمَّ اَوْلٰى لَكَ فَاَوْلٰى ۟

(75:35) again, it is worthy of you, altogether worthy.

اَيَحْسَبُ الْاِنْسَانُ اَنْ يُّتْرَكَ سُدًى ۟

(75:36) Does man think that he will be left alone, unquestioned?[233]

اَلَمْ يَكُ نُطْفَةً مِّنْ مَّنِيٍّ يُّمْنٰى ۟

(75:37) Was he not a drop of ejaculated semen,

---

[233] The word suda when used with regard to a camel implies a camel who is wandering aimlessly, grazing at will, without there being anybody to look after him. Thus, the verse means: Does man think that he has been left to himself to wander at will as if his Creator had laid no responsibility on him, had imposed no duty on him, had forbidden nothing to him, that at no time in future he would be required to account for his deeds. On the Day of Resurrection, Allah will ask the disbelievers: Did you think that We had created you without any purpose, and that you would never be brought back to Us. At both these places the argument for the necessity of the life hereafter has been presented as a question. The question means: Do you really think that you are no more than mere animals? Don't you see the manifest difference between yourself and the animal. The animal has been created without the power of choice and authority, but you have been blessed with the power of choice and authority; there is no question of morality about what the animal does, but your acts are necessarily characterized by good and evil. Then, how did you take it into your head that you had been created irresponsible and unanswerable as the animal has been? Why the animal will not be resurrected, is quite understandable. The animal only fulfilled the fixed demands of its instinct, it did not use its intellect to propound a philosophy; it did not invent a religion; it did not take anyone its god nor became a god for others; it did nothing that could be called good or bad; it did not enforce a good or bad way of life, which would influence others, generation after generation, so that it should deserve a reward or punishment for it. Hence, if it perished to annihilation, it would be understandable, for it could not be held responsible for any of its acts to account for which it might need to be resurrected. But how could you be excused from life-after-death when right till the time of your death you continued to perform moral acts, which your own intellect judged as good or bad and worthy of reward or punishment? Should a man who killed an innocent person, and then fell a victim to a sudden accident immediately after it, go off free and should never be punished for the crime of murder he committed? Do you really feel satisfied that a man, who sowed corruption and iniquity in the world, which entailed evil consequences for mankind for centuries after him, should himself perish like an insect; or a grasshopper, and should never be resurrected to account for his misdeeds, which corrupted the lives of hundreds of thousands of human beings after him? Do you think that the man, who struggled throughout his life for the cause of truth and justice, goodness and peace, and suffered hardships for their sake, was a creation of the kind of an insect, and had no right to be rewarded for his good acts.

ثُمَّ كَانَ عَلَقَةً فَخَلَقَ فَسَوَّىٰ

(75:38) then he became a clot, and then Allah made it into a living body and proportioned its parts,

فَجَعَلَ مِنْهُ الزَّوْجَيْنِ الذَّكَرَ وَالْأُنْثَىٰ

(75:39) and then He made of him a pair, male and female?

أَلَيْسَ ذَٰلِكَ بِقَادِرٍ عَلَىٰ أَنْ يُحْيِيَ الْمَوْتَىٰ

(75:40) Does He, then, not have the power to bring back the dead to life?[234]

The fact that we are here to prove ourselves has been realized by some people around you from everywhere in the world. They have made the decision to keep up with the challenge. For example:

Dr. Jeffrey Lang is a Professor of Mathematics at the University of Kansas.

Professor Armstrong works for NASA. He was amazed by what the Quran says about astronomy and how the ancient writing of the Quran agrees with modern science today.

Alfred Kroner, a Professor of the Department of Geosciences,

---

[234] This is an argument for the possibility of life-afterdeath. As for the people who believe that the whole act of creation, starting from the emission of a sperm-drop till its development into a perfect man, is only a manifestation of the power and wisdom of Allah, they cannot in fact refute this argument in any way, for their intellect however shamelessly and stubbornly they might behave, cannot refuse to admit that the God Who thus brings about man in the world, also has the power to bring the same man into being once again. As for those who regard this expressly wise act only as a result of accident, do not in fact have any explanation to offer, unless they are bent upon stubbornness, how in every part and in every nation of the world, from the beginning of creation till today, the birth of boys and girls has continuously been taking place in such proportion that at no time it has so happened that in some human population only males or only females might have been born and there might be no possibility of the continuation of the human race. Has this also been happening just accidentally. To make such an absurd claim one should at least be so shameless as to come out one day with the claim that London and New York, Moscow and Peking, have come into existence just accidentally.

University of Mainz, Germany. He talked about the origin of the universe and how it would be impossible for a man like Prophet Muhammad (ﷺ) to know about this from his own mind. He said science today proves what the Prophet (ﷺ) said 1400 years ago.

Yushidi Kusan, Director of the Tokyo Observatory, Tokyo, Japan. He talks about astronomy and using telescopes. He said that the Quran has true facts about astronomy.

Joram van Klaveren, Former Dutch MP, a politician who attempted to ban mosques and all Islamic practices from Holland. After working on a book to conclusively 'disprove' Islam, Joram's research (and discussions with Timothy Winter) drastically changed his views. He later converted to Islam.

Lin Nu, Chinese scholar of the Ming dynasty who converted to Islam after visiting Persia. He went on to marry a Persian or Arab woman and brought her back to Quanzhou in Fujian province.

Maryam Jameelah, formerly Margret Marcus; author of many books covering several subjects, including modernism, sociology, history, jihad, theology and technology.

Yusuf Islam, English singer-songwriter, instrumentalist and activist; born Steven Demetre Georgiou; known professionally as Cat Stevens.

Mike Tyson, boxer; performer.

Robert Stanley (mayor), British politician.

Abd al Malik (born Régis Fayette-Mikano), French rapper of Congolese descent.

Johann von Leers, Advisor to Mohamed Naguib and head of the Institute for the Study of Zionism.

Saida Miller Khalifa, British author, originally named Sonya Miller.

Knud Holmboe, Danish journalist, author and explorer.

Yusuf Estes, American preacher and founder of Guide US TV.

Isabelle Eberhardt, Swiss explorer and writer.

Arnoud van Doorn, Dutch politician.

Uri Davis, Middle East academic and activist who works on civil rights in Israel, Palestinian National Authority and the Middle East.

Kérim Chatty, Swedish bodybuilding stuntman.

Mohammed Knut Bernström, Swedish ambassador.

Wojciech Bobowski, Polish musician; Bible translator.

Kristiane Backer, German television presenter.

Moments to Remember Forever

Now, what do you think of this book? Did it bring you the feeling that you should think seriously about your future?

At this point, it means nothing except that you have 100% responsibility and freedom of choice regarding the next moment in your life bearing in mind the fact that you never know for sure how many of them you still have!

The message in this book depends largely on your imagination, your intellect, your gut feeling, and your entire intelligence. Whether it is rich enough with the right set of experiences, thoughts and feelings or not. In this case, I suppose, it all should have made sense for you already some time ago while reading.

But if it hasn't clicked yet, that means it's not ready, and that it's not your time yet! But the question is how much time do you still need? How much time do you already have? And what are you waiting for?

452

Either way, I'm sure that the time you spent reading this book and especially these last words, will remain forever in your memory. But what will your response be when you remember it? I don't know but I hope you smile from your heart.

اِنَّ اللهَ عِنْدَهُ عِلْمُ السَّاعَةِ ۚ وَيُنَزِّلُ الْغَيْثَ ۚ وَيَعْلَمُ مَا فِى الْأَرْحَامِ ۖ وَمَا تَدْرِى نَفْسٌ مَّاذَا تَكْسِبُ غَدًا ۖ وَمَا تَدْرِى نَفْسٌ بِأَيِّ أَرْضٍ تَمُوتُ ۚ اِنَّ اللهَ عَلِيمٌ خَبِيرٌ

(31:34) Surely Allah alone has the knowledge of the Hour. It is He Who sends down the rain and knows what is in the wombs, although no person knows what he will earn tomorrow, nor does he know in which land he will die. Indeed, Allah is All-Knowing, All-Aware.

List for Recommended Readings

Islam: The Basics

By Colin Turner

Colin Turner is Reader in Islamic Thought in the School of Government and International Affairs at the University of Durham, UK

Book Description

Now in its second edition, Islam: The Basics provides an introduction to the Islamic faith, examining the doctrines of the religion, the practises of Muslims and the history and significance of Islam in modern contexts. Key topics covered include:

- The Qur'an and its teachings
- The life of the Prophet Muhammad
- Gender, women and Islam
- Sufism and Shi'ism
- Islam and the western world
- Non-Muslim approaches to Islam.

With updated further reading, illustrative maps and an expanded chronology of turning points in the Islamic world, this book is essential reading for students of religious studies and all those new to the subject of Islam.

Islamic Psychology

By G. Hussein Rassool

Human Behavior and Experience from an Islamic Perspective

Professor Dr. G. Hussein Rassool is Professor of Islamic Psychology & Consultant, Riphah Institute of Clinical and Professional Psychology / Centre for Islamic Psychology. He is also the Director of Studies, Department of Islamic Psychology, Psychotherapy & Counseling, Al Balagh Academy. Chair of Al Balagh Institute of Islamic Psychology Research. He was formerly the Dean for the Faculty of Liberal Arts & Sciences. Head of the Department of Psychology and Professor of Islamic Psychology. He is a Fellow of the International Association of Islamic Psychology. Academic Advisor to the South African Institute of Islmic Psychology and Well-Being.

Book Description

Islamic Psychology or ilm an-nafs (science of the soul) is an important introductory textbook drawing on the latest evidence in the sub-disciplines of psychology to provide a balanced and comprehensive view of human nature, behavior and experience. Its foundation to develop theories about human nature is based upon the writings of the Qur'an, Sunna, Muslim scholars and contemporary research findings.

Synthesizing contemporary empirical psychology and Islamic psychology, this book is holistic in both nature and process and includes the physical, psychological, social and spiritual dimensions of human behavior and experience. Through a broad and comprehensive scope, the book addresses three main areas: Context, perspectives and the clinical applications of applied psychology from an Islamic approach.

This book is a core text on Islamic psychology for undergraduate and postgraduate students and those undertaking continuing professional development in Islamic psychology, psychotherapy and counseling. Beyond this, it is also a good supporting resource for teachers and lecturers in this field.

And Muhammad Is His Messenger: The Veneration of the Prophet in Islamic Piety

By Annemarie Schimmel

She has died aged 80, was an orientalist who enriched Harvard university during the last quarter of the 20th century.

Universally acknowledged as the leading expert on Sufism, classical and folk Islamic poetry, and Indo-Pakistani literature and calligraphy, she wrote and translated 105 works, including numerous scholarly and popular articles. Her own poetry was in the spirit of medieval Muslim mystics such as al-Hallaj, Hfiz and Rumi - on whom she was the foremost western specialist.

Book Description

The important role of the Prophet Muhammad in the everyday lives of Muslims is usually overlooked by Western scholars and has consequently never been understood by the Western world. Using original sources in the various Islamic languages, Annemarie Schimmel explains the central place of Muhammad in Muslim life, mystical thought, and poetry. She sees the veneration of Muhammad as having many parallels in other major religions.

In order to understand Muslim piety it is necessary to take into account the long history of the veneration of Muhammad. Schimmel discusses aspects of his life, birth, marriage, miracles, and heavenly journey, all of which became subjects for religious devotions. By using poetic texts and artistic expressions and by examining daily Muslim religious practices, Schimmel shows us the gentler side of Islamic religious culture, providing a much-needed understanding of religion as it is experienced and practiced in the Islamic world.

This is the first book in English to deal with all aspects of the veneration of the Prophet Muhammad. It is an expanded version of Schimmel's Und Muhammad Ist Sein Prophet, originally published in German in 1981.

Towards Understanding the Quran

With kind permission: Islamic Foundation UK.

Islamicstudies.info

Tafheem.net

Dedication

To Almighty Allah and all of his faithful Prophets and Messengers.

To our father Adam, Moses, Jesus and Muhammad peace be upon them.

Oh God, please bear witness that I conveyed your message as much as I could.

Oh God accept this work and grant us your forgiveness.

Thank you, Allah, the Lord of everything.

About the Author

I am an Egyptian heart surgeon, residing in Finland. The reason for coming to Finland was to work on joint scientific research between my university in Egypt and the Tampere Heart Surgery Center. I completed my PhD in cardiac surgery at the end of 2013.

In 2008, while studying in Finland, I established the Human Information Technology Lab in Tampere. As the name indicates, this Laboratory's mission was to make the best use of IT capabilities in solving chronic human problems.

The most important principle in its methods was to find a way to establish a balanced relationship between the economic and social aspects of well-being. What might spark the readers' curiosity, or perhaps surprises them, is what is the relationship between welfare solutions and heart surgery?

To summarize, the relationship lies in my passion for working as a systems analyst, something that I discovered purely by chance in 1998. For the first time in my life, without study or any previous background, I analyzed and designed an artificial intelligence program, an expert system for management, marketing and multi-unit decision making for global pharmaceutical companies. It was an incredibly rewarding and fulfilling experience in which I discovered my deep love and talent for the system analyst profession.

For those who don't know much about this profession, let me tell you little about it. There is a need to tackle an ongoing problem and dealing with it requires unfamiliar methods. A suitable solution is, in the end, found mainly through the application of digital technologies.

It usually begins by delving into the process of systematic analysis in order to be able to connect to the node of the problem. In most cases it can be summarized in just one word, regardless of its complexity. By reaching this point, the system analyst will be able to identify all the important points that must be included in the solution.

The system analyst must also be able to identify the urgency level of implementing this solution, its steps, and the amount of the human, technical and material resources needed to achieve the highest possible efficiency.

There are system analysts who specialize in some areas based on their past experience and preferences. The field that I personally lean towards is the digital economy and welfare, which is a new field that provides broad solutions in the country to help politicians and decision-makers understand the possibilities of using the best technical solutions to overcome the most diligent problems.

Made in United States
Orlando, FL
16 March 2024

44572390R00257